The Myth of the Oil Crisis

Overcoming the Challenges of Depletion, Geopolitics, and Global Warming

ROBIN M. MILLS

Westport, Connecticut
London

Library of Congress Cataloging-in-Publication Data

Mills, Robin M., 1976–
   The myth of the oil crisis : overcoming the challenges of depletion, geopolitics, and global warming / Robin M. Mills.
     p. cm.
   Includes bibliographical references and index.
   ISBN 978-0-313-35479-3 (alk. paper) — ISBN 978-0-313-36498-3 (pbk. : alk. paper)
   1. Petroleum reserves. 2. Petroleum industry and trade. 3. Energy policy. I. Title.
HD9560.5.M553 2008
333.8′232—dc22   2008009948

British Library Cataloguing in Publication Data is available.

Library of Congress Catalog Card Number: 2008009948
ISBN: 978-0-313-35479-3
    978-0-313-36498-3 (pbk.)

First published in 2008

Praeger Publishers, 88 Post Road West, Westport, CT 06881
An imprint of Greenwood Publishing Group, Inc.
www.praeger.com

Printed in the United States of America

The paper used in this book complies with the
Permanent Paper Standard issued by the National
Information Standards Organization (Z39.48-1984).

10 9 8 7 6 5 4 3 2 1

To Sareh, who helped me appreciate
the people and culture of one of the world's great oil nations.

And my parents, Jean and Richard, authors and teachers, always
ready to challenge conventional thinking.

❧ ❦

I must create my own system, or be enslaved by another man's.
—William Blake

Contents

Figures and Tables

FIGURES

TABLES

Abbreviations

ACG	Azeri-Chirag-Guneshli, a complex of large oil fields in Azerbaijan.
AIM	Alternative Investment Market, a section of the London stock market with lower regulatory requirements and mostly smaller companies, including many oil and gas explorers.
ANWR	Arctic National Wildlife Refuge, an area of Alaska off-limits to oil exploration for environmental reasons.
API	American Petroleum Institute; the API scale is used to measure the density of crude oils (and other petroleum liquids).
bbl	Barrel, a commonly used oil-field unit equal to forty-two U.S. gallons or approximately 159 liters.
BG	British Gas, a large, gas-focused British IOC.
boe	Barrels of oil equivalent, a means of expressing oil and gas in a common unit reflecting their energy content (with 6,000 cubic feet of gas approximately equal to 1 boe).
BP	British Petroleum, one of the largest IOCs.
BtL	Biomass-to-liquids, a method for producing liquid fuels from biomass.
CCS	Carbon Capture and Sequestration, a group of methods for removing carbon dioxide from the atmosphere and trapping it to prevent its contributing to climate change.
CERA	Cambridge Energy Research Associates, a major energy consultancy, now owned by IHS.
CNG	Compressed natural gas; natural gas (largely methane) under pressure, a possible means of transporting large volumes of gas by sea, and a fuel for automobiles in countries such as India and Egypt.
CNOOC	China National Offshore Oil Corporation, a large, state-controlled Chinese oil company.

CNPC	China National Petroleum Corporation. the largest state-controlled Chinese oil company.
CO_2	Carbon dioxide, a major byproduct of burning fossil fuels, and the primary cause of anthropogenic global warming.
CtL	Coal-to-liquids, a method for producing liquid fuels from coal.
DME	Dimethyl ether (CH_3OCH_3), a potential future transport fuel.
EGR	Enhanced Gas Recovery, a set of (mostly commercially unproven) advanced techniques for extracting more gas from fields.
EIA	Energy Information Administration, the statistical agency with the U.S. Department of Energy.
EOR	Enhanced oil recovery, equivalent to tertiary recovery, a set of techniques using advanced technologies to extract more oil from fields.
EROEI	Energy return on energy invested; the energy yielded by a process divided by the energy consumed.
EUR	Estimated ultimate recovery, the total oil or gas estimated to be eventually extracted from a field or region.
FSU	Former Soviet Union, the successor states to the USSR, including, among others, the major hydrocarbon powers Russia, Kazakhstan, Azerbaijan, and Turkmenistan.
F-T	Fischer-Tropsch, a set of chemical reactions for producing liquid hydrocarbons from carbon monoxide and hydrogen (generated from various feedstocks), a key part of many XtL processes.
GDP	Gross Domestic Product, a measure of the size of a country's economy.
GtL	Gas-to-Liquids, a method for producing liquid fuels from natural gas.
H_2S	Hydrogen sulphide, a toxic gas sometimes associated with oil and gas fields.
IEA	International Energy Agency, a grouping of the world's developed energy-using economies.
IGCC	Integrated Gasification Combined Cycle, an advanced type of power plant, capable of running on coal, biomass, or petroleum coke, with high efficiency and potential for CO_2 capture.
IHS	Major oil industry consultancy (formerly "Information Handling Services"), now owners of CERA.
IOC	International Oil Company, the group of (largely Western) multinational oil companies, such as Shell, BP, and ExxonMobil, in contrast to National Oil Companies.
IOR	Improved Oil Recovery, a suite of techniques, equivalent to "secondary oil recovery," and involving the injection of gas and water to maintain reservoir pressure and sweep oil towards wells. Less extreme than EOR.
IPC	Iraq Petroleum Company, the consortium of foreign oil companies operating in Iraq until final nationalization in 1971.

JDZ   Joint Development Zone, a petroleum-bearing area between two or more countries developed jointly to solve a border dispute; specifically, the zone of this type between Nigeria and São Tomé.

LNG   Liquefied Natural Gas, natural gas (mostly methane) chilled to about −163°C, so that it can be transported worldwide by special tankers. The main method of transporting natural gas over long distances.

LPG   Liquefied Petroleum Gas, a mixture of propane and butane under pressure, familiar as the bottled gas cylinders for home cooking and camping. Not to be confused with LNG.

NGL   Natural Gas Liquids, a mix of hydrocarbon liquids extracted from natural gas.

NIOC   National Iranian Oil Company.

NOC   National Oil Company, a largely or wholly state-owned oil company, such as Chinese National Petroleum Corporation or National Iranian Oil Company.

OECD   Organisation for Economic Cooperation and Development, a grouping of major developed economies.

ONGC   Oil and Natural Gas Corporation of India, a major state-owned petroleum company.

OPEC   Organization of Petroleum Exporting Countries, a grouping of major oil producers.

PDO   Petroleum Development Oman, the main oil company in Oman, with majority state ownership and participation by Shell, Total, and Partex.

PdVSA   Petróleos de Venezuela S.A., the national oil company of Venezuela.

R/P ratio   Total reserves divided by annual production, a measure of how many years production could continue at a constant rate. A useful benchmark, but not to be taken literally.

SAGD   Steam-Assisted Gravity Drainage, a technique for recovering heavy oil and oil sands by injecting steam into horizontal wells.

SEC   Securities and Exchange Commission, the U.S. government agency responsible for (among other things) setting standards for petroleum reserves disclosure by publicly listed U.S. companies.

SPE   Society of Petroleum Engineers, a professional organization which, among other activities, promotes a set of standards for reporting petroleum reserves.

Tcf   Trillion cubic feet, a commonly used measure for natural gas volumes.

UAE   United Arab Emirates, a Middle Eastern country containing the major oil-producing Emirate of Abu Dhabi.

USGS   United States Geological Survey, a team that prepared an assessment of global oil and gas volumes yet to be discovered.

XtL   X-to-Liquids, a set of techniques for producing liquid fuels from different feedstocks (gas, coal, or biomass).

YtF   Yet-to-find, an estimate of the volumes of hydrocarbons still to be found in a given area.

_____ *Chapter 1* _____

Introduction

In the opening years of the twenty-first century, oil has been one of the dominant issues in the headlines. How will historians, writing about the "Petroleum Period" from the vantage point of 2100, regard the following stories?

On April 10, 2003, American soldiers, who had just entered Baghdad, were guarding the Oil Ministry, while looters plundered the National Museum of Iraq, containing more than 170,000 artifacts from the dawn of civilization.[1]

On January 9, 2004, Shell, that doyen of Anglo-Dutch conservatism and prudent engineering, shocked the industry and markets by announcing that it was cutting its proven oil and gas reserves by 20 percent. Several other major companies were also struggling to replace reserves, although less publicly.

On August 29, 2005,[2] Hurricane Katrina made landfall in Louisiana, on its way to devastating New Orleans and knocking out a quarter of the Gulf of Mexico's oil production.[3] In the aftermath of the disaster, the increased frequency and intensity of hurricanes was widely blamed on global warming caused by our emissions of carbon dioxide (CO_2).[4]

On February 20, 2008, U.S. crude oil closed for the first time ever above the psychological landmark of $100 per barrel (bbl), in response to a refinery explosion in Texas, disputes between Venezuela and foreign oil companies, and limited Organization of Petroleum Exporting Countries (OPEC) supplies. In the following months, it climbed further.

Will these as yet unborn historians view such items in the same light as we interpret the reoccupation of the Rhineland or the Munich Agreement, as the harbingers of a new era of war, this time over oil, the signs that the foreign policy of major nations was largely dictated by their ambitions to gain control of this resource? Will they come to believe in retrospect that world oil reserves were wildly overstated, the true state of affairs mostly kept quiet by a conspiracy of big oil companies and OPEC nations? Sweltering in the malarial swamps of the Hudson or the Thames, will they point to the time that disastrous climate change, induced by the burning of oil, became irreversible? And will they, writing their books by candlelight, see the oil price peak of 2008 merely as a foothill on the way to unaffordable energy, shortages, and economic ruin?

Now consider another news item: a leading economist, supported by an even more famous colleague, has proposed that the energy supply of the greatest country in the world is in imminent decline. He can see no solution to this problem. He predicts a future of energy deficits, industrial collapse, and national decay. His ideas are taken seriously enough to induce the country's leader to reduce the national budget accordingly.

The date was 1865; the economist was William Jevons and his supporter was political thinker John Stuart Mill, the nation was Britain, the leader was the renowned Prime Minister William Gladstone, and the fuel was coal.

Today, inspired by high oil prices, a disparate group is repeating similar arguments. The "peak oil" camp argues that the point is imminent when the world's extraction of oil (and some contend, gas) will begin a rapid decline. Some conclude from this that an era of "resource wars" is approaching, and a subset of them believes therefore that commercial, political, and military means should be used to secure the remaining limited supplies for their favoured nation. Others welcome the onset of decline, seeing in it a solution to global climate change, caused by emissions of CO_2 from burning coal, oil, and gas. Yet others, some with an element of Schadenfreude, welcome the inevitable collapse of industrial civilization and a return to a more "natural" way of life.

In this book, I will argue that these ideas about petroleum depletion and their consequences are mistaken and often grossly overstated.

1. The supply of oil and, even more, gas, from conventional and unconventional sources, is much larger than that imagined by the pessimists.
2. Seeking political, military, or commercial control of oil supplies is unnecessary, self-defeating, and exorbitantly expensive.
3. Oil is merely one reasonably convenient source of energy. Opportunities exist to decrease radically global consumption of oil while maintaining a healthy economy and bettering standards of living in both rich and poor countries.
4. The environmental impact of fossil fuels, particularly in causing climate change, although the most serious problem the world faces today, can be tackled by a portfolio of solutions, some hydrocarbon based, some not.

From these propositions, I will argue that believing the fallacious arguments about the "end of oil" will, ironically, lead the world into flawed policy decisions, environmental and economic damage, and international conflict.

In the short term, current high prices are stimulating a wave of new investment. In the longer term, although parts of the peak oil theorists' argument have merit, the potential resource base of oil, and even more of gas and coal, is extremely large. "Unconventional" oil and gas resources will make up a large, growing, economically viable part of fossil fuel supply. We will develop new energy sources and more efficient uses of energy long before resource depletion strikes. Peak oil is, therefore, if a story about anything, a story about one specific kind of oil—light, "conventional" crude—rather than about transport fuels or energy in general. Geopolitical and economic factors will ensure that, even if we did approach some fundamental limit of the resource base, we would enter a long, undulating plateau of production, followed by a gradual decline, not the sharp fall-off predicted by some.

Oil supplies cannot be "secured" by military or commercial means alone but only by a balanced mutual understanding between consumers and producers, nor is terrorism more than an irritant in the long-term world energy system. On the other hand, recurrent attempts by petro-states to found their economies primarily on oil and gas will lead, as before, to stagnation. The temporary feeling of power given their leaders by their possession of a scarce resource will turn out to be illusory; it will cause them to dally in making fundamental reforms and thus, ironically, make them weaker than their rivals, not stronger.

At the other end of the pipelines, there are more barrels to be found in cars, power stations, and homes than in the ground. These are the "virtual barrels" of energy efficiency. Enormous savings in energy use are possible with low or even negative costs, the value of the energy saved exceeding the price of the required modifications. Oil, although a convenient energy source, has numerous suitable substitutes in all fields except transport, and even in transport, technologies, some emerging today, some already viable, offer a way out of oil dependency for mobility. Such efficiency gains, however, require the incentives of high prices or carbon limits to take hold in the face of demand growth. Even in a world of flat or declining hydrocarbon supplies, growth in the economy and in living standards would be possible. The economic and environmental winners of the twenty-first century will be those countries, companies, and people who lead the change in our energy systems, not those who try, figuratively and literally, to hold back the waves.

I fully accept the reality of anthropogenic climate change; I believe it to be the most serious problem facing the world today. Although there are a number of skeptics, who either suggest that climate change is a natural phenomenon[5] or a less serious issue than many others,[6] the vast majority of scientific opinion now seems to have concluded that it is a human-induced and very real threat.

Oil depletion has appeared to some pundits to be a (admittedly accidental) solution to global climate change. This view, however, is wishful thinking and ignores the likelihood, without some positive resolution to do differently, that burning less oil and gas would mean burning more coal. Because oil resources are not in imminent danger of depletion, there is a very real concern about the environmental impact of burning such a volume of hydrocarbons. Part of the solution is, as mentioned above, the market-based reduction and reallocation of demand. Another element is a shift to cleaner energy, replacing coal and oil with gas and biofuels and moving away from fossil fuels toward renewables and possibly nuclear power. A third component, which can also help to extract more oil from ageing fields, is the sequestration of CO_2—a solution that can pay for itself—and has received less attention than it deserves.

We have, therefore, no imminent shortage of oil and even less of gas, although we have numerous substitutes that will become increasingly competitive, and, as we begin to use them, we will appreciate their cleanliness and convenience. As former Saudi Oil Minister Sheikh Zaki Yamani wisely observed, "The stone age did not end for a lack of stones, and the oil age will end, but not for a lack of oil."[7] Ultimately, oil will not run out; it will simply become irrelevant.

For all these reasons, it is essential that we make well-informed decisions about the future of hydrocarbons. Quoting three examples will illustrate the dangers.

The first example of misinformed policy is the groups who oppose liquefied natural gas (LNG) imports into the United States, partly because some fear that global gas supplies are going to start running out shortly after oil, but more because of safety worries. There has never been an accident involving importing LNG that has led to loss of life or to release LNG to the environment. These campaigners therefore threaten the United States with reliance on dirty and CO_2-intensive coal (ironically, as many are proclaimed environmentalists), and they increase American energy prices, hence weakening the economy and causing job losses.

The second is the geopolitical adventurers who seek to "secure" oil supplies. At their most harmless, they merely waste their shareholders' or nation's money. At the most dangerous, they condone dictatorial and genocidal regimes and use military forces to occupy strategic points, leading to interminable conflicts and destabilizing entire regions. And these activities are entirely pointless, because, for a globally traded commodity like oil, physical control brings at best marginal economic advantages, far less than the money (not to mention lives) expended to achieve it.

The third is those who dismiss conservation. They come from both ends of the political spectrum. On the one hand, "Conservation may be a sign of personal virtue, but it is not a sufficient basis for a sound, comprehensive energy policy,"[8] the view that energy security can be achieved by using and importing ever more energy. On the other hand, we have the "Neo-Luddite" belief that "it'd be a little short of disastrous for us to discover a source of clean, cheap, abundant energy because of what we would do with it,"[9] that there would be some kind of moral virtue in not making use of this miraculous source of nonpolluting energy.

Numerous others, professionals in various fields and concerned amateurs, have written on this subject. What are my own credentials for the task?

As someone who began as a petroleum geologist and moved into economics, working with major private and national oil companies (NOCs) in Europe, the Middle East, and Russia, I have some insights into the true state of the resource picture and an overview of both halves of the central argument: scarcity against plenty. Born and educated in the United Kingdom but presently living in an Arab country and speaking Farsi and Arabic, I have a keen sense of the dangers of founding domestic and international policy on myths about oil. Finally, as an environmentalist[10] and humanitarian, I am desperate to see a rational plan, free of ideology on either side, to minimize the environmental impact of human energy use while creating a prosperous future for all. If anyone is suspicious that, as a petroleum industry insider, I have a vested interest in the continuance of oil and gas, I can only remark that it is true—and I am always suspicious of those whose arguments are personally convenient—but that I have an even greater stake, as a human being, in a prosperous, clean, and safe world.

What about "peak coal"; how did Jevons' predictions fare? British coal production did eventually peak in 1913, but there was no rapid subsequent decline. Its fall was partly attributable to wars and strikes, so extraction did not plummet but maintained an undulating plateau at a somewhat lower level until about 1960.[11] Substitutes for coal were found, considerably superior to it in economic advantage and environmental impact: total U.K. primary energy production,[12] due mainly to North Sea oil and gas, was at its highest in 1999, while the "pea souper" smogs of Victorian London were forever banished by cleaner-burning fuels, culminating in the 1960s. People learned to do more with less: the energy intensity of the British economy fell consistently from about 1880 onward.[13] Other coal sources were developed: world production was higher in 2006 than ever before, although billions of tons of British coal remain in the ground, overtaken by alternatives. Most relevantly, Britain moved away from basing its economy on the brute force of coal and iron, to relying on the inexhaustible wells of knowledge and creativity.

SUMMARY OF THE BOOK

Chapter 2: Opposing Viewpoints

The subject of oil depletion and the wider question of the future of oil is controversial. Five schools of thought can be recognized. The "Geologists" believe that oil production is constrained by geology and that production is shortly going to peak. "Economists" argue that oil supply and demand respond dynamically to price, and oil shortage is not imminent. "Militarists" advocate the military control of remaining oil supplies (with the subset of "Mercantilists" favoring commercial "securing" of oil). "Environmentalists" want to see fossil fuel use rapidly replaced by renewable energy, although they may or may not believe that oil depletion is nigh. "Neo-Luddites" hold that economic growth is ultimately unsustainable and want to see a transition to a low-energy, low-population society.

Chapter 3: Bust and Boom: How We Got to Where We Are Today

Demand destruction and overcapacity after the oil shocks of the 1970s and early 1980s led to a period of low oil prices from 1986 to 1999. This caused underinvestment in the energy complex. Low reserves replacement and lack of exploration success were a result of this underinvestment and weak demand, not of a scarcity of oil in the ground.

From 1999 onward, prices have risen sharply because of rapid economic growth, geopolitical problems, and the erosion of spare capacity. Constraints of people and capital goods in the industry prevented a rapid supply response, yet the world economy has continued to grow, being less dependent on oil than during the previous shocks and making wiser policy choices.

Chapter 4: Half-Full or Half-Empty? Conventional Oil Supply

Geologists and peak oil supporters believe that conventional oil supply is shortly going to peak and then decline. However, multiple predictions of oil decline since 1885 have all been proved wrong. Peak oil theorists mostly use the "Hubbert curve" to predict future oil production, but this method has theoretical flaws, does not take account of future industry dynamics such as changes in price, geopolitics, investments, and technology, and makes demonstrably false forecasts. Use of different models makes very different predictions of peak date.

Current oil reserve classifications, particularly that of the United States Securities and Exchange Commission (SEC), are excessively conservative. Official figures for world reserves are regarded as overstated by peak oil commentators because of anomalous bookings by OPEC countries. However, field data suggest that, although some countries may be exaggerated, global totals are on the whole too low.

Exploration performance is said by Geologists to be declining and to have failed to replace production since 1980. However, this finding is only partially true and is to a considerable extent an artifact of their practice of "backdating" reserve additions to the date of first discovery. Discoveries have also fallen off since the 1970s as a result of nationalizations, lack of access to promising acreage, low oil prices, and a large backlog of undeveloped fields in OPEC states. Massive reserves additions have been made in existing fields since 1980, and new exploration technologies offer considerable promise. Peak oil writers attack the estimate of the United States Geological Survey (USGS) of future exploration potential as overoptimistic, yet their own estimates are radically too low and disagree with independent assessments.

Geologists discount reserves growth, the process by which more oil than originally estimated is extracted from known fields. But reserves growth, aided by new technologies, is a real and important phenomenon, and systematic application of enhanced oil recovery (EOR) could dramatically increase world reserves. "Easy oil" is a fallacy, because oil has always been difficult to extract; our capabilities have advanced in step with our needs.

Analysis of announced major projects, combined with estimates of decline rates in mature fields, strongly suggests that peak oil is not imminent. The marginal cost of new oil is well below current oil prices. Ultimate recovery estimates have progressively increased with time, and peak oil totals are far too low.

Chapter 5: Dead Dinosaurs? The Major Oil Nations

A country-by-country account of the world's major oil provinces suggests enormous remaining scope for reserves growth, exploration success, unconventional oil, and gas developments. Arguments suggesting the imminent decline of Saudi production are weak and depend on a poor understanding of petroleum engineering. Ideas that the Middle East is "played out" fail to take account of the very low recent exploration effort in the major countries. "Peak oil" estimates badly underestimate the potential of deepwater, frontier regions, and even mature Organization for Economic Cooperation and Development (OECD)[14] countries.

Chapter 6: Scraping the Barrel? Unconventional Oil Supply

Key unconventional oil sources include the following: natural gas liquids (NGLs); low-permeability reservoirs; heavy oil and oil sands; oil shales; gas-to-liquids (GtL), coal-to-liquids (CtL), and biomass-to-liquids (BtL); and biofuels. Peak oil theorists' classification of Arctic and deepwater oil as unconventional is incorrect. Unconventional oil forms a continuum with conventional oil and will replace it relatively seamlessly as and when prices, demand, and resources require. Resources are colossal and are widely dispersed across the globe. Much unconventional oil is already commercial and being developed today. It provides strongly positive net energy, and the environmental consequences, although sometimes serious, are manageable and are decreasing with better practices. Reasonable estimates of the speed of unconventional development suggest that it could mitigate most of the effect of a peak of conventional oil, even in the short term.

Chapter 7: Gas Giants

"Peak gas," even more than peak oil, is a long way off, despite some mistaken predictions by peak oil enthusiasts. Colossal scope remains for commercialization of known gas discoveries, exploration, and unconventional gas. Global gas markets are becoming increasingly robust and interconnected. Gas is important to rebutting peak oil doomsday scenarios, because it can substitute for oil in many applications and has less greenhouse impact than oil and coal.

Chapter 8: A Dangerous Neighborhood? Supply, Investment, and Geopolitics

Lack of investment in new oil supply is partly attributable to rational risk-avoidance by major producers but is also caused by increased taxation and political control. "Resource nationalism" is ultimately a self-defeating phenomenon, and oil exporters risk a major loss of market share in the future if high prices persist. Militarist and Mercantilist attempts to control oil are inevitably ineffective, and terrorism is not a serious threat to long-term world oil supplies. Energy security can only be ensured by interdependence and an understanding of the needs of both producers and consumers; "energy independence" is unachievable at any tolerable cost. Given the lack of unanimity within OPEC and the other options available to energy users on the supply and demand sides, a geopolitically induced peak oil is unlikely.

Chapter 9: Keeping the Lights On: Energy Demand

Contrary to the beliefs of Geologists, energy and oil demand are, in the longer term, strongly responsive to prices. Most uses of oil can be substituted by other energy resources, such as gas, coal, uranium, and renewables, which are vastly abundant. "Energy return on energy invested" (EROEI) is a flawed concept, and the energy consumed in energy extraction is not a serious constraint. There is enormous scope for efficiency improvements in energy use, which will, however, be partly offset by increased demand unless prevented by high prices or environmental controls. The least substitutable use of oil, for transport fuel, can be greatly reduced by alternative fuels and improved vehicle designs. Reasonable projections show that a peak oil event could be almost entirely offset by such measures, in the presence of appropriate policies, without serious economic consequences.

Chapter 10: Green Oil: Saving the Environment

Continued use of fossil fuels is compatible with an acceptable standard of environmental protection and is more practicable and economic than a complete replacement by renewables until well past halfway through the twenty-first century. Local impacts of fossil fuels have greatly fallen and continue to decrease. Climate change can be tackled by a broad portfolio of measures, including the key technology of carbon capture and sequestration. This approach is safe, feasible, and already in action, despite misguided opposition from some environmentalists. Neo-Luddite depictions of the collapse of civilization and the need for a low-energy, low-population society are, if taken seriously, mistaken, appalling, and dangerous.

Chapter 11: Conclusion

Oil can continue to be a major and growing energy source for many years to come. Gloomy predictions do not resemble the real world and take no account of human ingenuity. They encourage misguided and counterproductive policies.

Chapter 2

Opposing Viewpoints

Not surprisingly for a subject of fundamental concern for the world economy and environment, the oil depletion debate provokes controversy. The argument is often, simplistically summed up as one between two camps, the Geologists and Economists. However, studying the argument leads me to believe that we can distinguish at least three other viewpoints, which I label the Militarists, Environmentalists, and Neo-Luddites. Oddly, the Economists, Geologists, and Militarists may be the closest in their underlying philosophy, but the conclusions they reach are radically different. The discussion between the Environmentalists and Neo-Luddites on the one hand and the first three groups on the other is to some extent a normative one, about the values of our society, not about the technical efficiency of a particular policy.

I shall explore the various angles of these groups' arguments in later chapters. However, at this stage, I will do my best to give an uncritical summary of each argument. Most of the discussion concentrates on oil. However, many of the points are applicable also to gas, perhaps becoming relevant a few decades later, and Chapter 7 discusses the gas issue.

Of necessity, I use a number of technical terms in this discussion, which I try to define when first introduced.

THE GEOLOGISTS

This group is often named the Geologists,[1] perhaps because several of their leading members, such as their spiritual ancestor, M. King Hubbert, and three contemporary proponents, Colin Campbell, Jean Laherrère[2] and Ken Deffeyes, had careers as geologists with major oil companies[3] but more profoundly because they focus on below-ground, "subsurface" constraints to oil (and sometimes gas) production. Another possible term for them would be "Malthusians," as they stress the ultimate constraint of a resource base confronted by exponential growth. They are concerned that the ultimate resource base, and the speed with which we can extract it, is too low for oil production to continue growing for more than a few years. The moment of maximum production is referred to as peak oil. After this, they believe that an inevitable, possibly rapid, decline will set in. They generally believe that alternative fuel sources and efficiency measures will not fill the gap, because decline will commence so soon, and possibly this gap cannot be closed by any realistic measures. We will therefore face a future of declining energy use, economic depression, and possibly starvation, catastrophic wars, and the end of modern civilization.

Their argument tends to fall into two halves: the inevitability of decline and a gloomy view of the resource base.

Inevitability of Decline

The starting point is the reasonable assumption that the ultimate resource base, the total of oil and gas in the ground, is finite and therefore that production cannot grow forever. In the extreme case, even production that grows steadily and arithmetically—that is, adding a constant increment with time—will ultimately be outrun by demand that rises exponentially. This is a version of the old Malthusian argument about food supplies, that food production grows linearly while population and hence food demand expands exponentially.

Most of the Geologists point to the work of M. King Hubbert, which I examine in more detail in Chapter 4. His "Hubbert curve" is used by most of the writers on the subject to predict the onset of declining production, although, as I shall discuss, belief in the curve itself is not essential, either way, to the general argument. Perhaps the greater importance of Hubbert is not that he did point out the possibility of oil depletion (because many had done so before him), but that he predicted an actual date and provided a quantitative forecasting method.

The crude version of the idea of inevitable depletion has it that price elasticity of supply and demand is very small (or, even less sophisticated, ignores the issue of price elasticity entirely). If the price elasticities of supply and demand are low, even sharply rising prices will neither call forth very much supply nor depress demand significantly. At some point, actual physical shortage, gasoline lines and so forth, will strike. The conceptual basis for this argument is that people have to travel to work, heat and light their homes and offices, cook, and so on. If energy prices rise, people will reduce every discretionary expenditure to maintain their spending on energy. A point will come at which even this minimum quantity of energy can no longer be afforded, and then only economic collapse, or even starvation, will equalize demand with a greatly reduced supply.

A more sophisticated refinement might concede that demand elasticity, at least in the long run, is considerable, but that ultimately declining supply will overwhelm even a reduced level of demand, or, perhaps, reducing our demand accordingly will be so painful that it will still trigger a crisis. Most Geologists do not allow for any significant degree of supply price elasticity; they do not believe that sharply higher prices will increase supply much, because they hold that we are running up against physical limits. We will examine these arguments in Chapters 4 and 9.

Pessimism on the Resource Base

The second half of the Geologists' case generally holds that the world's ultimate endowment of oil is rather small, radically lower than estimated by official bodies such as OPEC, the International Energy Agency (IEA) or USGS. This leads to their conclusion, mentioned above, that supply is likely to fall imminently regardless of efforts expended to increase it.

They make four key points.

First, they maintain that OPEC reserves are misstated and are probably greatly exaggerated.[4] They point to the increasing age of the main OPEC fields, to a considerable slackening in new discoveries, and to hints of growing technical challenges in some OPEC countries.[5] A key fact for them is the large and suspicious jumps in quoted OPEC reserves during the mid 1980s and their maintenance subsequently despite continuing production.

Second, they believe that little more oil remains to be found in unexplored parts of the world. They point to the declining sizes of finds in known petroleum basins[6] such as the North Sea. They scoff at USGS estimates, which assign, for instance, 50 billion bbl to be discovered in Greenland, more than the stated reserves of Libya or Nigeria. (Despite on-off exploration since the 1970s,[7] no commercial oil has yet been discovered in Greenland.) They point to a move by the international oil companies (IOCs) into progressively more difficult, remote, hostile, and costly environments (the Arctic, deepwater) and trumpet the end of the age of easy oil. (Oddly, this line of reasoning runs counter to the instincts of many oil company geologists, who tend to be intrigued by the prospects of exploring remote frontiers, more from scientific curiosity than from greed.)

Third, the Geologists argue that improved technology will only accelerate the pace of oil depletion rather than unlocking significant new reserves. This is perhaps where their "geological" bias shows most clearly. They believe that the reserves in a field are largely fixed when it is discovered and that technological breakthroughs of the last two decades, notably horizontal drilling and three-dimensional seismic imaging, can only accelerate the depletion of a field and lower its cost but not add significantly to the ultimate amount of oil recovered.

Fourth, they are generally convinced that various unconventional sources (which will be discussed in Chapter 6) will not make a significant contribution to supplies. Such hydrocarbons may be technically too difficult, or too expensive, to extract. An argument made by some, and taken up by the Environmentalists and Neo-Luddites, is that the energy required to produce these unconventional resources will be so great that the net yield of energy will be minimal or even negative. A linked theme is that the exploitation of deposits such as oil sands and oil shale will lead to catastrophic environmental damage. Finally, although there does not seem to be too much argument that the in-place volumes of these hydrocarbons are very large, some suggest that only a small fraction is amenable to development or that the enormous cost of extraction, and the materials and skills required, will delay the arrival at markets of this oil and gas until after the decline in conventional production is well under way.

The Consequences

Combining the two halves of this argument leads to the Geologists' conclusion that oil supply is fundamentally limited and that demand is not. The arrival of peak oil will therefore herald a savage economic dislocation.

Most writers on peak oil cannot resist going beyond that moment to an account of the "day after." This usually features 1970s vignettes such as gasoline lines and the Three Day Week, along with energy shortages, dark and cold cities, economic collapse, and possibly mass starvation, wars (see The Militarists), and dramatic population decline. The more hopeful propose the immediate beginning of "managed decline," either to a world with a dramatically smaller population and lower energy needs (the Neo-Luddites) or via technological changes, to a comparable standard of living to today's but using less energy or different energy sources.

THE ECONOMISTS

The Economists[8] are the usual opponents of the Geologists. They tend to be less prominent in books and societies than the Geologists but more so in the mainstream media (*The Financial Times*, *The Economist*, and so on) because they represent a conventional free-market view. Key supporters of this viewpoint include Peter Odell, Morry Adelman, Duncan Clarke, Michael Lynch, Bjørn Lomborg,[9] the consultancy Cambridge Energy Research Associates (CERA), and an industry figure, Michael Economides.[10] They might also be called Cornucopians,[11] seeing a world in which resources do not decline with time but grow as a result of increases in investment and advances in technology.[12]

The Economist argument is essentially a mirror image of that of the Geologists. They hold that price will bring supply and demand into balance in a way that does not result in intolerable economic damage, and they view the ultimate resource base much more favorably. They may even, like Lynch and Adelman, consider it irrelevant.

Elasticity of Supply and Demand

The foundation for the Economist position is free-market economics. Supply and demand both respond to price. There can never be a physical shortage of oil in a free market, because rising prices will encourage supply and choke off demand until equilibrium is restored. (Of course, many Geologists would accept this in theory, too, but they believe the equilibrium oil price would be intolerably high and will lead to economic collapse.) The only time that an actual physical shortage of oil will occur would be in case the government interferes with the working of the market, for instance by imposing price caps or rationing.

The Economists' position here rests partly on observations as to how the industrialized world responded to the 1970s oil price hikes. If prices rise, demand will drop, partly as a result of "demand destruction" and conservation (economic activity is reduced or other inputs are substituted for energy) and partly because of efficiency. This is not an instantaneous process, and therefore the price elasticity of demand may be rather low in the short term, higher in the long term. In the very long term, the whole structure of the economy, the built environment, and society may change.

Similarly, the Economists consider that supply, especially in the longer term, is rather price elastic. They point to the flood of new oil that broke OPEC's pricing power from 1986 onward. They expect similar "greenfield" areas to open up in response to the current price situation, and this sanguine outlook owes much to their positive view on global resources.

Optimism on the Resource Base

The Economists are generally much more bullish on the total world endowment of oil resources than the Geologists. They arrive at this position in three steps.

First, they usually begin by pretty uncritically accepting standard statistics on world oil reserves, with all their pitfalls. If they are concerned about the sharp increases in OPEC quoted reserves in the late 1980s, they argue that reserves before that date were understated.

Second, they often then add a healthy allowance for improved recovery from existing fields and new discoveries. This is partly a technical judgement (sometimes from nontechnical people) that new technology can recover much more oil from known fields, whereas, as noted, the Geologists mostly posit that this technology just accelerates the pace of extraction of an essentially finite amount. The Economists believe, often following USGS estimates, that large new reserves remain to be found, in both existing basins and new areas that have seen little or no exploration.

Third, they are bullish on the outlook for unconventional resources. Probably most Geologists would not disagree with them that the potential volume in place of such resources is almost unimaginably large, but the Economists believe that these resources are practically as well as theoretically available. They point out that the distinction between conventional and unconventional is a moving target, dependent on technology and price. Offshore drilling was unconventional in the 1940s; deepwater was unconventional in the 1980s; "shale gas" was almost an oxymoron until recently. Rises in prices either make existing techniques economic to use or stimulate research into new technologies. Once the breakthrough has been made, costs tend to fall as methods are refined and applied on a large scale. Other nonrenewable resources, such as uranium or coal, can also help to prop up supply and substitute for oil and gas in some applications, mainly power generation.

The Economists, though, have generally not addressed well the issue of how fast these new provinces and unconventional resources can be brought on line (leaving that to the market's invisible hand), to what extent national policies put some resources off-limits or at least slow down investment, or of whether the associated environmental impacts are tolerable. Sometimes, they consider global climate change but are often either skeptical of its link to human pollution or think (like Lomborg) that the consequences will be relatively benign.

THE MILITARISTS

The term Militarist, which I use here, is rather a sweeping one. They are a rather less well-defined group, possibly because, unlike the others, many of them focus only tangentially on petroleum. Perhaps it would be fairer to call the group the Three Ms, because it covers "Militarists," "Media," and "Mercantilists." The Militarists *sensu stricto* include some genuine warmongers, amateur or practical geostrategists, and conspiracy theorists. The Media encompasses some commentators who, though often decrying violence and the use of power to secure energy supplies, and who, like Michael Klare and Lutz Kleveman, may only be observers, nevertheless see this struggle as reality, possibly inevitable. The Mercantilists are embodied by many commentators, politicians, and corporate heads—some, although by no means all, from China and India—who believe that commercial control of oil, gas, and the related infrastructure is a good way to securing reasonably priced energy.

Perhaps contrary to popular stereotypes, there are not, in my experience, many oil industry insiders among the true Militarists. For a start, most petroleum professionals do not believe that petroleum is imminently running out. Also, many have had international careers that gave them some sympathy for the people and cultures of oil-exporting countries or at least trained them in flexibility and taught them the limits of hard power. Even military professionals tend to be wary of the Militarist viewpoint, having some idea of the human costs to both sides and the great difficulty of achieving economic means by force. Instead, the Militarists tend to be amateur generals, theoretical strategists, and politicians.

Militarists may follow the Geologists in believing that we are imminently running out of oil. However, probably more of them incline ideologically to the position of the Economists: that oil in the ground is not in itself an immediate constraint. They do believe, however, that the short-term availability of oil is limited. They also believe that, as an essential supply for the economic and military machine of their country, the physical facilities for its production and transport, wells, facilities, and pipelines have to be secured or, alternatively, denied to the "enemy." The Japanese invasion of the Dutch East Indies, Hitler's offensive toward Baku in 1942, and the Allied bombing of synthetic oil plants in 1944–1945 were all born of this school of thought. They were, in their strategic (although not moral) context, understandable reactions. In wartime, following this line of thought may lead to attacks aimed at physical control or destruction of oil supplies. In peacetime or Cold Wars, this approach manifests itself in the political domination of nations or areas, the establishment of military alliances and bases, the rerouting of pipelines, and the control of real or supposed "chokepoints" for oil transport.

The Militarist viewpoint in the Media is also a staple of myriad diverse groups, including conspiracy theorists, bloggers, peace activists,[13] and so on. It has become a commonplace of discussion about oil that virtually all political and military activities, particularly those in the Middle East or by the United States, have as their aim the control of oil. This school of thought sees the contest between the United States and Russia for influence in the Caucasus and Caspian as a means to control pipeline routes,[14] the occupation of Afghanistan as a way to route oil and gas from Central Asia to export, bypassing Russia, and, of course, the Iraq War as an attempt to secure the vast Iraqi oil reserves. An obvious step made by many of those who are concerned about oil depletion is to predict a future of recurrent wars over diminishing oil supplies.[15]

The Mercantilists sometimes resemble Militarists without armies. Churchill was perhaps an early oil Mercantilist, with his dictum that "Safety and security in oil lie in variety and variety alone" (1915) and his purchase of a controlling government stake in Anglo-Persian, later British Petroleum (BP).[16] Churchill, of course, had the world's leading navy to enforce control of oil, "Military Mercantilism," perhaps. The modern breed of Mercantilists seek to secure oil supplies for their countries by buying oil assets. Examples of this include the persistent Japanese attempts since at least the 1970s to build up a major oil company, the Russian moves to secure state ownership and control of the domestic petroleum industry and its foreign offshoots, the purchase of various oil fields around the world by state-controlled Chinese and Indian corporations, and the American counter-reaction to the attempt by the Chinese National Offshore Oil Company (CNOOC) to buy the American firm Unocal, ensuring that it ended up in the hands of California-headquartered Chevron. Mercantilists come in two different breeds: those from consuming countries (e.g., United States, India, and China) and those from exporters (e.g., Russia and Venezuela) or, as they are often termed, the Resource Nationalists.

THE ENVIRONMENTALISTS

We are all environmentalists now, most of us, at any rate, and in varying ways. We are nearly all concerned about the general issue of human impact on the environment and the specific problem of climate change induced by emissions of CO_2 and other greenhouse gases. We may, however, have different ideas about how to solve environmental challenges. Environmentalists in the context of oil and gas depletion are therefore a broad group, because this perspective informs all our thinking.

However, I am concerned most here with a smaller group of people, Greenpeace and the Sierra Club[17] being examples. A typical viewpoint here tends to incline to the Geologists' position that oil will imminently deplete. Environmentalists tend to consider, however, that even burning just the oil we have already discovered will be enough to cause irreversible and catastrophic climate change. This is not to mention the other negative impacts of oil production and use: nongreenhouse pollution (e.g., particulates and acid rain), spillages, damage to fragile ecosystems, the disruption of native peoples' way of life, and so on. They are also opposed to extending oil exploration into new areas, particularly the Arctic, and they campaign against many unconventional resources, particularly heavy oil[18] and oil shales[19] because of their environmental impact.

It is probably fair to say that many self-confessed Environmentalists are broadly anticapitalist. They observe, with justification, that the current world capitalist system does not produce many of the desired outcomes (not just in protecting the environment but also with reducing poverty, for example). They may proceed from this to propose changes within the free-market framework, for example, Kyoto and its related emissions trading schemes, they may fight against those broad trends within modern capitalism that are grouped under the heading of globalization, or they may reject the capitalist system entirely, a group that shades into the Neo-Luddites. The latter two tendencies advocate nonmarket solutions to oil depletion and climate change, primarily a large reduction in energy demand (and possibly in population), a lower-tech lifestyle, and a move to renewable energy.

Of course, there is an immense diversity of views within the Environmentalist camp. For example, a minority band of heretics within the Environmentalist movement have swallowed their dislike of nuclear power, because they see it as the only realistic solution to climate change. (Strangely, mainstream Environmentalists pay less attention to coal, despite its high carbon intensity and polluting nature.) Some are opposed to particular renewable technologies, such as wind, wave, and tidal power, either because they have impacts on the landscape, kill migrating birds, and so on, or because they believe that the energy input to these technologies is almost as high as what they produce. Similarly, they are often against biofuels, because these may be genetically modified, may require more energy input than they produce, may actually increase rather than reduce greenhouse gas emissions, and take up land that could be growing food for the poor or that could be a natural habitat. There is also a general suspicion of CO_2 sequestration technologies, perhaps because these are linked to the oil companies and may seem like an easy way out.

Many Environmentalists have a touch of the Militarist paradigm. There is a tendency to see oil as the root of numerous conflicts and oil depletion as the inevitable harbinger of an era of conflict. This concern may be bound up with other environmental worries, such as water wars. Of course, they are resolutely opposed to such wars, which is where they depart from the Militarist viewpoint.

THE NEO-LUDDITES

The Neo-Luddites might almost be considered as the extreme wing of the Environmentalists. They include writers such as Richard Heinberg[20] and Julian Darley.[21] I apologize for the possibly insulting term I apply to them, but perhaps they would be proud of the comparison because their spiritual ancestors, the Luddites or machine breakers, were fighting against early industrialism and capitalism. The argument between, say, a Neo-Luddite and a mainstream economist is a normative one: about values and principles, not facts.

Like the Environmentalists, Heinberg, Darley, and other Neo-Luddites maintain that oil and gas are running out. For this part of their argument, they follow the Geologists. They borrow the resource wars part of the Militarist worldview and argue that, without a radical change in society, oil depletion will lead to systems collapse (e.g., Jared Diamond[22]). They are generally skeptical of conservation and efficiency measures, because they argue that being more efficient lowers the cost of energy and hence just encourages us to use even more. In their view, it actually does not matter whether oil and gas are running out or not; we should behave as if they are. Heinberg goes so far as to say that, even if we discovered a limitless, nonpolluting source of free energy, it would still not solve the basic problem.

Rising energy use, and the concomitant economic and population growth, puts an increasingly unsustainable stress on ecosystems. And it does not deliver happiness, because we measure our success against others and half of us are poorer than average. They blame the ills of modern society on consumerism and materialism, on an economic system that demands perpetual exponential growth.

The only solution to the capitalist treadmill and the endless quest for economic growth is to abandon the race. Following Schopenhauer,[23] the sole way to happiness is the renunciation of desire. The Neo-Luddites advocate a world of small, relatively isolated communities, living low-tech, low-intensity, low-energy lives, perhaps, in the words of Michael Palin, in "an anarcho-syndicalist commune."[24]

_____ *Chapter 3* _____

Bust and Boom: How We Got to Where We Are Today

A year after I started work in the oil industry, on June 18, 1998, the oil price reached $10.11/bbl, almost the lowest, adjusted for inflation, in the entire twentieth century. Many in the major companies lost their jobs, fresh graduates and veterans alike. *The Economist* published an article titled "Drowning in Oil." Oil industry executives talked gloomily about the need to survive in a "ten dollar world." Just ten years later, in February 2008, prices for U.S. oil reached record highs when they for the first time ever breached the $100 mark.

This rollercoaster indicates that today's headlines tell us almost nothing about the future. News items are seized on by those who believe oil is running out or those who believe we have an abundance of it. To clear the ground for the debate to come, this chapter will tackle some of the current issues in the oil market. Why is the current price shock so different from previous ones? And what might it tell us about the future of oil?

THE DOLDRUMS, 1986–1998

When J. P. Morgan was asked by a reporter what he thought stock prices would do, he replied, "They'll fluctuate."[1] I venture to forecast that the same is true of oil prices. In the late 1990s, $16/bbl was considered a very attractive price by the oil companies, scarred by a brief flirtation with $10/bbl. In early 2007, people were talking about a crash in the oil market because prices had fallen to $50/bbl! It was, after all, just a little earlier in 2006 that Goldman Sachs had forecast a possible rise to $105, which became reality in early 2008.

The current situation is unique, and yet "plus ça change, plus c'est la même chose": we have seen it all before. It develops out of a similarly unique situation from 1986 onward. The oil price shocks of 1973 and 1979–1980 led to a widespread mentality, similar to today's, that oil was running out. Price forecasts trended to $100/bbl by the year 2000. A grizzled petroleum engineer, a veteran of those days, once told me that Fridays were strictly for golf; it was boom times for the industry. The Middle Eastern countries, indeed most oil exporters, predicated their economic policies on ever-increasing revenues and embarked on crash programs of modernization, industrial development, social subsidy, and armament.

However, the high prices provoked an extremely effective response from the industrialized world. The OECD brought on-stream vast new oil supplies outside OPEC, in Alaska, the North Sea, and Mexico, at the same time as they drastically reduced oil use. OPEC countered with a desperate defense of the price by cutting production. Saudi Arabia, which had ramped up output in the early 1980s to replace volumes from Iran and Iraq lost as a result of the revolution and the subsequent war, bore the bulk of the subsequent cuts. Eventually, the Kingdom tired of its swing producer role, getting little support from the rest of OPEC and facing the prospect of virtually halting output in a fruitless attempt to prop up prices. In 1986, the Saudis raised production once more, triggering a price collapse and the end of the boom.

The loss, voluntary and involuntary, of OPEC capacity between 1978 and 1985 had provided a protective shield for a renaissance in non-OPEC production. Once unleashed, this wave was unstoppable. With the first phase of North Sea development complete, new supplies could be brought on-stream relatively easily. Similarly, a generation of energy-efficient infrastructure had been brought into service. From 1986 to 1998, oil prices fell, on average, at almost $1 per year in real terms. The global industry had developed an enormous shut-in capacity, concentrated in the main OPEC countries. Investment in the underlying productive base, especially people and rigs, dried up. Only three new offshore rigs were delivered worldwide between 1994 and 1997 (compared with one hundred planned for 2007–2010), whereas from the early 1980s to 1999, the U.S. industry shed 520,000 jobs, an astonishing 64 percent of the workforce.

Not only the upstream[2] oil industry suffered. Refining margins (the operating profit made by a refinery on each barrel of oil processed) remained low throughout the later 1980s and 1990s: the margin for an advanced refinery on the U.S. Gulf Coast averaged $2/bbl between 1992 and 1999, with a low of a mere 62¢ in January 1995, and the return on capital in refining between 1976 and 2000 was a dreadful 5 percent.[3] The building of new refineries ceased entirely, and many were shut.

This period of low prices reached its nadir (or apogee, depending on your point of view) in 1998, when, triggered by the Asian economic crisis, Iraq's resumption of exports, and a poorly timed increase in OPEC production, prices went briefly below $10/bbl. *The Economist*[4] predicted that oil would be at $5/bbl for a decade if Iraq really opened the taps.

Every reaction has its counter-reaction, and the oil industry's response was to institute mass layoffs, merge to reduce costs, and slash capital spending and exploration. This was particularly acute in areas such as the North Sea, which had broken OPEC's pricing power during the 1980s. The great advantage of these regions was that new fields could be developed there relatively quickly, in contrast to mega projects in deepwater or the Caspian, so meeting sudden increases in demand, but with prices at $10/bbl, the North Sea was dying. Some forty-six exploration wells were drilled in the United Kingdom sector in 1998; in 1999, this fell to a mere 15.[5] Russia could also ramp up production easily through drilling simple onshore wells, but Russian production, inefficient and high cost, was decimated by a combination of low prices and the collapse of central planning, the end of the Soviet Union itself being speeded by the 1986 crash. Russian oil output had reached an all-time high in 1987 of 11.5 million bbl/day[6] (plus additional increments from the other Soviet republics), the most that any single country has ever produced. By 1996, this had fallen to 6.1 million bbl/day, barely half of its peak.

The drying up of investment inevitably stored up problems for the future, because every action brings its overreaction. Of these, the most dramatic was the Shell reserves downgrade.[7] Although it occurred in the midst of the "oil price hurricane," this event was a product of the doldrums. Many articles on peak oil begin with this debacle, a godsend to depletion theorists, who seized on it as confirmation of their prophecies: that world oil reserves in general were overstated and that it was becoming increasingly hard to find new fields.

Yet this is a simplistic and incorrect interpretation. The Shell debacle resulted from the low prices and underinvestment of the 1986–1999 period. Shell was the only one of the major IOCs to miss out on the merger wave of the turn of the century, when Exxon bought Mobil, British Petroleum (BP) took over Amoco and Arco, Total gained control of Petrofina and Elf, Conoco merged with Phillips, and Chevron merged with Texaco. Shell was, at a stroke, relegated from first to third among the new "super-majors" and did not have the suite of opportunities or the cost-cutting synergies of its rivals. The company came under increasing pressure from investors to match its competitors' growth and returns. Some senior managers chose, unwisely, to make very aggressive reserves bookings that did not conform to the SEC rules.

Yet the vast majority of these reserves bookings were not incorrect because the oil and gas was not in the ground, or was not technically recoverable. Most related to gas fields that had no customers (and hence were, at least temporarily, noncommercial), and to oil, particularly in Nigeria, that could not be produced because of OPEC quotas or that would be extracted after the expiry of the company's production licences in Nigeria, Abu Dhabi, Brunei, and Oman. The lack of customers for gas was primarily attributable to the Asian economic crisis of 1997; Asian buyers would have been the main consumers of gas, exported in liquefied form (LNG), from the giant Gorgon Field offshore Western Australia. Similarly, the OPEC quotas were limiting production in an attempt to shore up weak prices. Additional cuts related to underinvestment, another response to low prices, in places such as Oman. In any case, the debookings were more in gas than oil, and, as we shall see, we are in no imminent danger of peak gas.

The Shell reserves recategorization[8] was a disaster for the company, but it tells us almost nothing about world reserves. Its only global significance is to highlight that oil and gas demand growth was subdued during the late 1990s and that supply was abundant, a fact that is clear from the low prices during this period. The end of oil was being proclaimed to a world drowning in oil, because there was too much, not because there was not enough.

THE HURRICANE, 1999–2007

Demand Bites Back

However, another oil shock was about to bite. Unlike the 1973–1974 and 1978–1980 crises, this was triggered by demand rather than supply. During the 1986–1998 era of underinvestment, the world's cushion of spare capacity had become dangerously low. The maintenance of large volumes of spare capacity had never been a policy objective of producers, because spare capacity is extremely expensive. For Saudi Arabia to build the approximately 7 million bbl/day of spare capacity that it accidentally acquired during the 1980s would cost between $20 and $40 billion,[9] some 6–12 percent of its annual gross domestic product (GDP), equivalent to the United States investing $1.5 trillion. The loss of spare capacity is not, as Geologists see it, attributable to declining oil supplies. It is due to the reversal of an economically irrational and unsustainable situation that had arisen by accident.

In March 1999, realizing the consequences of their ill-timed decision to raise production just before the Asian Contagion, OPEC managed to reach agreement on output cuts and roped in Norway, Mexico, and Russia to help (although Russia's compliance was weak, the symbolism was important). OPEC production was 1.3 million bbl/day lower in 1999 compared with 1998, and prices recovered modestly. OPEC had regained its discipline. They settled on a band of $22–28 as "fair for both producers and consumers." This band of fairness was to be raised repeatedly in the following years. OPEC did not cut production in September 2001, seeing that this would be highly unpopular around the world after the 9/11 attacks and not wanting to tip the world into a recession, which would hit demand for their products. However, they did enforce additional cutbacks in November 2001 as prices fell again below \$20/bbl. OPEC adopted a policy of targeting stocks: whenever stockpiles of crude oil in consuming countries rose above a certain limit, they cut back production. This policy was highly successful in sustaining prices, because consumers were never able to build up a substantial buffer against shocks.

Despite this success, the markets were slow to perceive OPEC's renewed market power and consistently expected their coherence to disintegrate again into pricing wars. In all of the late 1990s, talk about a "ten dollar world," there was no appreciation of OPEC's own internal position. Heavily burdened by debt, unproductive economies, and high unemployment, and in the cases of Iran, Iraq, and Kuwait, the repair of war damage, several of these countries, particularly Saudi Arabia, faced collapse if prices stayed low. They prioritized debt repayment and economic reform over investment in additional capacity, which would only drive prices back down, and the almost universal nationalization of the petroleum industry throughout OPEC had removed a powerful constituency, the IOCs, who would have pushed for higher output.

However, the world still did not realize how narrow the safety margin had become. Spare capacity of around 5 million bbl/day in 1999 and 2002 dropped to less than 1 million bbl/day in 2005, barely 1 percent of global production, and virtually all concentrated in Saudi Arabia. The oil price rose as spare capacity fell.

Rapid demand growth, usually blamed on China and India, but also significant in the United States, ate up the remaining surplus. In the United States, low energy prices encouraged unrestrained consumption and undid the hard work of energy efficiency in the decades after 1973. In China, India, and other rapidly industrializing nations, a significant percentage of the population for the first time reached income levels sufficient to afford personal automobiles, car ownership in China rising by 80 percent in 2003, 15 percent in 2004, and 12 percent in 2005.[10] Demand for consumer goods made from plastics led to a boom in petrochemicals. Bottlenecks in gas supply forced the burning of fuel oil to meet electricity demand from legions of new televisions and air conditioners.

These three countries accounted for a stunning 137 percent of world demand growth (in absolute terms) in 1998 (greater than 100 percent because the rest of the world's consumption fell), 68 percent in 1999, 86 percent in 2000, and more than 60 percent in 2002, 2003, and 2004, the only break in the sequence coming as a result of depressed U.S. consumption in 2001. In 2005, under the burden of high prices, all three countries ran out of steam but rebounded in 2006 despite even higher prices, with Chinese growth at 7 percent. Percentage growth was, obviously, very high in China, but the absolute growth (in terms of barrels) was greater in the United States because the starting point was much higher.

The demand growth was so rapid that the oil industry, psychologically unready for higher prices and renewed expansion, could not react in time. The usual metaphor is a super-tanker turning around. A whole generation of industry managers had grown up believing in cost cutting to beat perpetually low prices. The majors' internal bureaucracy was painfully slow to respond to the new reality: investment approval committees continued to focus on metrics at sub-$20/bbl and to concentrate on eliminating any risk, even as the price remorselessly rose past $30 (March 2000), $40 (July 2004), and $50 (October 2004). The move into new frontier exploration areas was similarly slow and was primarily led by smaller, more adventurous companies, such as Cairn (India), Hardman (Mauritania), and Tullow (Uganda), not by majors with the skills and financial resources to develop discoveries rapidly.

Oil industry projects have long lead times. An exploration campaign may take three or four years to make a discovery; an additional four years or more may then elapse before it enters production. For example, of major discoveries before the price slump, Azeri-Chirag-Guneshli (ACG) (Azerbaijan; "Contract of the Century" signed in 1994) came online in 2006 and Girassol (Angola; discovered in 1996) entered production in 2002, Bonga (Nigeria; 1995) in 2005 and Ormen Lange (Norway; 1997) in 2007. I mentioned already the fall in exploration drilling in the U.K. North Sea in 1999; even by 2005, activity had not recovered to the 1998 level, because decimated exploration departments took time to gear up to renewed drilling. There was therefore a "ripple effect" from the 1998 price crash, a shortage of new prospects, and discoveries entering the development funnel. Those big projects that did come on-stream in this period had mostly been planned years before.

High prices brought in a bonanza to the oil companies. At first, they were wary, choosing to rebuild their balance sheets by cutting debt, to raise dividends modestly and to reward shareholders who had stuck with them through the difficult times with share buybacks. Wary of repeating the mistakes of the last boom, they did not expect high prices to persist, and they made only minor increases in their budgets. The $70 billion that ExxonMobil, Shell, BP, Total, and Chevron handed back to their shareholders could have financed some 5 million bbl/day of oil production capacity.[11] The companies, of course, would complain that there were no projects. There is some truth in this: I and many other executives spent interminable, fruitless stretches during these years trying to pull off big deals in Abu Dhabi, Baghdad, Caracas, Dhahran, Kuwait City, Moscow, Tehran, or wherever. However, a contributory problem was a caution, somewhat understandable given the trauma of $10/bbl, to push ahead with perfectly viable projects in the North Sea, Gulf of Mexico, Nigeria, Australia, Russia, and elsewhere.

When the boom had gone on longer than they expected, many companies did begin to increase capital spending, but they quickly came up against other constraints. The turn-of-the-century redundancies had left them short of skilled geoscientists and engineers; in fact, this had been obvious to most people at the working level even as the layoffs were happening. Now project managers in the Middle East were offered million dollar signing bonuses, and truck drivers in Alberta earned $150,000 a year.

Similarly, there was a shortage of drilling rigs, engineering contractors, and compressors. The day rate to hire a North Sea drilling rig increased by about 50 percent from February 2004 to July 2005 and then exploded, doubling in the next six months. From August 2004 to the present, the utilization rate of these rigs has been almost continuously at 100 percent, an almost unheard of situation.[12] Even where there was oil to be produced, there were no rigs to do it, at any price. Later, ships for shooting seismic surveys became a constraint. China's voracious demand for raw materials drove up steel prices, which rose from about $150/ton in June 2002 to $400/ton in December 2003, raising the costs of wells, pipelines, and platforms; the costs of cement and copper also rose sharply, as did, of course, the price of energy itself, for example, the diesel used to power rigs and the natural gas used to extract heavy oil.

In this way, much of the increased capital spending was eaten up by rising costs. A typical offshore oil project today is 70 percent more expensive than four or five years ago.[13]

The story was the same in refining. In general, global refining capacity is overstretched. For example, a new refinery has not been built in the United States since 1976.[14] At the same time, refineries have come, rightly, under stricter environmental legislation, the required output slate has become lighter (i.e., less fuel oil, more gasoline, diesel, and jet fuel), and different U.S. states have introduced widely varying specifications for "boutique fuels." Therefore, refineries, squeezed for two decades on one hand by poor margins and on the other by market requirements, were for many years reluctant to invest in increased capacity, particularly in facilities to process inconvenient, heavy, sulphurous crudes. With rising demand, those refineries that had invested in higher complexity[15] at last saw some returns: margins have averaged nearly $6/bbl so far during the twenty-first century and hit $17/bbl in July 2005.

When the price runup got out of control, OPEC began to release oil on to the market to cool it off. By September 19, 2005, OPEC had agreed to make all of its spare capacity available, but this theoretical spare capacity was primarily in heavy, sour (high sulphur) crudes, which the world refining industry was not equipped to handle.

Geopolitical disturbances and other loss of production capacity also played a part in the price run up from 1999 to 2007, of course, but the role of this can easily be overstated. Several major oil-producing countries were operating at below capacity during this period. The most headline-grabbing outages involve Iraq, with repeated closure of the main export pipeline from Kirkuk in the north to Ceyhan in Turkey, trouble between Kurdish fighters and Turkey in the north, conflict with militias in the south, and a general prevalence of violence and instability that has prevented badly needed investment. The politically motivated dismantling of Mikhail Khodorkovsky's Yukos company, among the most progressive and successful of the Russian firms, and further cooling of the investment climate for, among others, Shell and BP, has brought an end to a spectacular run of Russian production growth. Unrest in Nigeria, strikes at the Venezuelan NOC Petróleos de Venezuela S.A. (PdVSA), aimed at unseating President Chávez, hurricanes in the Gulf of Mexico, and pipeline leaks in the United States (symptomatic of the aging of much of the world's energy infrastructure) have further harmed global output.

In addition to these major disruptions, there were a host of smaller interruptions in oil supply, often of minor producers or over trivial causes: strikes in Norway and the United Kingdom, fires in heavy oil upgraders in Canada, safety-related shutdowns in the United Kingdom, a tax dispute in Chad, an explosion on a platform in India, bans on gas flaring in Kazakhstan, lifeboat flaws in Norway again, rusting pipelines in Alaska, and an oil-field fire in California. Oil executives of the past century would have found it inconceivable that any event in Chad could possibly influence world oil prices, but, under the very tight supply–demand balance and the nervous markets of the past five years, even minor outages sharply shift the supply-demand balance. The highest level of disruption over this period was somewhat more than 2 million bbl/day (excluding the hypothetical loss from the slowing of Russian growth). This is less than 3 percent of total world production, yet it had a disproportionate effect on price. There was no world spare capacity to call on; Saudi Arabia's theoretical reserve was composed of heavy, sour crudes for which there was no refining capacity. Everyone else was producing flat out.

Compare this with 1990–1991, when Iraq's invasion of Kuwait knocked out 6.5 percent (4.3 million bbl/day) of world supply. Every OPEC member except Qatar and the two embattled countries increased production: Saudi Arabia and the United Arab Emirates (UAE) filled half the gap between them. The oil price rose briefly to $41/bbl during the crisis, but even the destruction of most of Kuwait's infrastructure and the embargoing of Iraq did not stop it falling back below $18 once Desert Storm had clearly succeeded.

Disappearance of the capacity cushion added a "fear premium" to the oil price. Traders were anxious about being caught short of oil in the case of another supply disruption. In this climate, rumors and threats rather than actual disruptions drove the price. There were persistent worries over Iran because of the ongoing dispute over its nuclear program, but neither this dispute nor Turkish operations against Iraqi Kurdish opponents directly affected oil output. There were also concerns about terrorist attacks on oil infrastructure in Saudi Arabia and Yemen, although, again, no loss of production resulted. Israel's attack on Lebanon, a war involving two nonoil producers, led to a particularly sharp price increase because of fears of escalation into a wider Middle East conflict. Similarly North Korea's bellicose rhetoric and nuclear test stirred the oil markets, although the country is not an oil producer, not near any major exporters, and is more likely to reduce demand by affecting the Japanese and South Korean economies.

Speculation has also been widely blamed for high prices. Ali Al Naimi, the Saudi Oil Minister, said, "There is absolutely no relationship between price and supply and demand,"[16] indicating that he believed the price was determined by the market of oil companies, traders, investment, vehicles, and hedge funds. Speculation and, more generally, investment activities, do certainly play a role in determining the short-term oil price and probably exaggerate fluctuations. Hedge funds have grown in importance in recent years, and commodities as an asset class have become fashionable because of their lack of correlation with, and outperformance relative to, the anaemic stock markets of the early 2000s. Funds invested in commodity indices grew from $8 billion in 2000 to $70 billion in 2005.[17] However, despite frequent suggestions otherwise, the markets do ultimately rely on fundamentals, and speculation can drive prices down just as much as up. In principle, the various energy derivatives are risk management tools, which should increase rather than reduce economic efficiency.

Far from rising oil prices over the past few years because of oil depletion, we can see that they are a response to robust demand growth and the inevitable bottlenecks. Prices for iron, copper, aluminium, uranium, corn, coffee, and most other commodities have all risen sharply in recent years. It is improbable that we are suddenly running out of all these resources simultaneously; far more plausible is that the global economic boom pushed up prices of all inputs. The industry's response to high demand and prices and their counter to claims of peak oil is demonstrated by the following: from 1991 to 2002, production rose annually on average by 0.75 million bbl/day; from 2003 to 2006, the increase was more than twice that, 1.8 million bbl/day.

The Dog That Didn't Bark

Possibly the biggest difference between previous price shocks and this one is that there has been no price shock! Of course, prices have risen sharply, but, at least until 2008, the global economy sailed on almost untroubled. This points out the fallacy of claims by peak oil theorists and Neo-Luddites of the inevitability of economic collapse.

Why have high prices failed to repeat the chaos for which they were blamed in 1973–1974 and 1978–1980? There are a number of theories about contributory factors related to the nature of the price shock itself and the change in the global energy economy over the past twenty to thirty years.

In my opinion, the key differences are as follows.

- The price run-up has been rather slow compared with previous shocks. Prices increased more in percentage terms during 1998–2000 than in 1973–1974, but they took four times longer to do so. This gave the economy time to adjust. Increases in price have been attributable to the cumulative effect of underinvestment, supply outages in several regions, and strong demand rather than to a sudden geopolitical event. Thus, the oil price increase has not led, in the main, to a feeling of crisis and ill-advised panic measures.

- Energy, and particularly oil, forms a much smaller part of global GDP than it did at the time of the first two oil shocks. At the height of the Iranian Revolution and Iran–Iraq War in 1980–1981, 4.5 percent of U.S. GDP and 7.2 percent of U.S. consumer expenditure went for gasoline. Even in the middle of Hurricane Katrina, these figures were just 2.6 and 3.7 percent, barely half as much. It takes less than half as much oil to generate $1 of U.S. GDP today as it did in 1973.

- For many uses, particularly power generation, oil has been substituted by other energy sources, notably natural gas and nuclear power. Oil made up 48 percent of global primary energy consumption in 1973 but only 36 percent by 2006, whereas gas has risen from 19 to 24 percent and nuclear from approximately 0 to 6 percent. Gas has acted as a release valve, taking some of the burden off oil, substituting in power generation and petrochemicals.

- The global economy of the early twenty-first century has been robust. The growth in Chinese and Indian productivity led to a world of low inflation and low interest rates. In such a situation, inflationary shocks can be absorbed much more easily than in the 1970s. For instance, in 1973, the U.K. short-term interest rates stood at 11.5 percent compared with 5 percent in 2001.[18] Monetary and fiscal policies have balanced controlling inflation with promoting growth, avoiding 1970s-style stagflation.

- Europe and Japan, in particular, have devised a series of coping mechanisms for high oil prices, notably high fuel taxes, which may make up 60 percent of the pump price in the United Kingdom.[19] The input price of crude oil is relatively a much smaller part of the final price than was the case in 1973, and so the consumer feels less effect from oil price hikes. Government policies have also been better advised this time round. In 1973, the response of several consuming countries was to impose price caps, which led to "gas lines," queues of vehicles waiting for nonexistent gasoline. These price caps prevented allocation of reduced supplies in a rational way, reduced domestic oil production, and delayed consumers' adoption of efficiency measures, as well as fostering a feeling of panic. In the 2000s, OECD politicians have resisted occasional calls for price curbs.

- Unlike 1973, the OECD especially has developed a system of emergency stocks that can meet temporary shortfalls, partly offsetting the impact of low global spare production capacity. The United States has 727 million bbl of capacity in its strategic petroleum reserve, enough for thirty-seven days of normal consumption, a facility developed and filled at a cost of $21 billion. In the aftermath of Katrina, the release of up to 30 million bbl was authorized.[20] All twenty-six members of the IEA must hold ninety days worth of oil imports in reserve.

- U.S. dollar weakness has reduced the impact of high oil prices on many other countries. As mentioned previously, for many consumers, oil prices have not risen nearly as much in their local currency as for dollar-denominated buyers. Between November 2000 and November 2007, the oil price, if expressed in euros, rose by some 70 percent, but, if in dollars, the increase was 200 percent.

- Although prices have been hitting nominal highs, they were, for most of the period, still much lower than historic peaks. In constant year 2006 dollars, the oil price reached $65.14/bbl in 2006, but this was significantly lower than the $90.46 recorded in 1980. Only in early 2008 did the oil price break historic inflation-adjusted highs.

- Also as mentioned previously, the price run-up has been much more in light, sweet crudes than in heavy, sour grades. Heavy oil refiners (such as the U.S. company Valero), fuel-oil burning power stations and ships, and so on have benefited from this price disparity. The situation is thus entirely different from the oil price shocks of 1973 and 1978–1980, when there was plenty of refining capacity but not enough crude.

- The oil windfall has been spent much more wisely than in the past. I think this point has received less attention than it deserves. The enormous sums of money accruing to OPEC members and the Soviet Union during the 1970s and 1980s represented a transfer of wealth from relatively efficient economies (the United States, Europe, and Japan) to less efficient ones. The value of OPEC oil exports was $37 billion in 1973, jumped to $121 billion in 1974, and then jumped to $265 billion in 1981.[21] Seventy-seven percent of the export earnings went to a mere 18 percent of OPEC's population, 54 million people, representing nearly $4,000 per person. Inevitably, the absorptive capacity of these economies, some of which, like the UAE, Saudi Arabia, Qatar, and Libya, had only recently emerged from tribal or feudal conditions, or, like Iraq, Nigeria, or Indonesia, were attempting to build national states on colonial foundations, was low. Much money was spent on "white elephant" projects, weaponry and social subsidies. In the words of legendary soccer player George Best, the rest was just squandered.[22]

Compare this with the situation in the 2000s. With a few exceptions, notably in Venezuela and to some extent Iran, the increased revenues have primarily been spent wisely: repayment of debt; investment in domestic development, particularly in diversifying away from oil; and on overseas assets as a store of wealth for future generations. Such foreign spending has helped to fund the rise of Asia, particularly the Subcontinent. Thus, the Middle East is becoming much more connected to the rest of the world economy and is establishing a reputation in fields other than oil such as aviation, leisure, and tourism.

So now we have highlighted the reasons for the price increases of 2000–2008. The primary drivers are, on the supply side, more than a decade of underinvestment, and, on the demand side, robust global growth. In this regard, the current high prices are completely different, in their causes and economic impact, from the shocks of 1973 and 1978–1981. They are primarily driven by neither geopolitical upsets nor resource depletion. But what about the future? Are the Geologists correct, that fundamental constraints on oil production are beginning to bite?

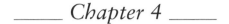

Chapter 4

Half-Full or Half-Empty?
Conventional Oil Supply

Our ignorance is not so vast as our failure to use what we know.
Dr. M. King Hubbert[1]

The argument that we are about to enter a phase of declining conventional oil supplies, as usually told by Geologists and peak oil believers in general, consists of the following assertions.

1. When the world has produced about 50 percent of its endowment of recoverable oil, production will begin to decline. Hubbert's curve, first used by the distinguished American geologist M. King Hubbert, is usually adduced as a method to predict the timing of this peak and the rate of the subsequent decline.
2. The amount of new oil found by exploration is declining sharply and is not replacing production. The world's ultimate endowment is about 2 trillion bbl[2] (2,000 billion), with about 1,100 billion bbl produced to date.[3] Therefore, the world is very close to having produced 50 percent of its oil.
3. Estimates of world potential much higher than 2 trillion bbl are wrong because OPEC reserves are heavily overreported and exploration estimates overoptimistic.
4. Oil decline is primarily determined by geology and hardly at all by oil price or technology. The world's "easy oil" has all been found and developed, and future supplies will be much more difficult and costly to obtain. Conventional oil determines the peak date, because oil from other sources (heavy oil, tar sands, oil shale, and possibly Arctic or deepwater oil) will, for various reasons, not be a major source or will come too late to offset decline.
5. Once we pass the peak, decline will be swift and irreversible.

These points are often accepted as gospel. The idea that oil will one day run out seems self-evident to many. Current high prices confirm a general belief in an imminent day of reckoning, yet these propositions contain some half-truths and numerous falsities.

Peak Oil

Forecasts of the imminent depletion of oil have been made ever since the beginning of the industry. As the State Geologist of Pennsylvania observed in 1885, "The amazing exhibition of oil [is] a temporary and vanishing phenomenon—one which young men will see to come to its natural end."[4] Most of those young men lived to hear David White of the USGS predict in 1919 that world oil production would peak by 1928 and the Federal Trade Commission warn in 1923 that "The supply of crude petroleum in this country is being rapidly depleted."[5] Their children probably read Wallace Pratt, a Standard Oil geologist and M. King Hubbert manqué, who in 1943 predicted ultimate world recovery at 600 billion bbl (production to date currently stands at more than 1 trillion bbl).

The children of those young Pennsylvanians would have been growing old when the Shah of Iran warned the western countries about their dependence on oil in the 1970s, so it was probably their grandchildren who read Colin Campbell's 1989 article[6] stating that oil production had already peaked. If they stayed in touch with Campbell's work, then seven years later, they would have heard his words, "At the time of writing in late 1996, there are still three more years to go until the end of the transition."[7] When this frightening transition began, as it turned out, a transition to almost unprecedentedly low prices, Mike Bowlin, CEO of the large U.S. oil company Arco, said, "We've embarked on the beginning of the last days of the Age of Oil,"[8] and showed his confidence in his own words in a strange way, by promptly selling his corporation to BP for a knockdown price. Six years into Bowlin's "last days," Kenneth Deffeyes put the peak, rather precisely, at December 16, 2005, thus defying the advice of a senior British civil servant: "By all means give a number—or a date—but never both together,"[9] while in 2004, Ali Samsam Bakhtiari, a former National Iranian Oil Company (NIOC) employee, suggested, from his WOCAP[10] model, a peak in 2006–2007 at about 81 million bbl/day.[11] Global supply was 86 million bbl/day in July 2007, up from 84.8 million bbl/day in December 2005.

Like prophets of the end of the world, these doom mongers always maintain that, yes, last time the world did not end, but this time it will. If nothing else, one has to admire their dogged persistence and their courage in making predictions despite repeatedly being proved wrong. As with most prophets of doom, their audiences are surprisingly forgiving of their repeated failures. The scientific method relies on the principle that numerous "corroborations" of a theory, i.e. tests that fit its predictions, do not prove it but that a single failure is sufficient to discredit it.[12]

Given this principle, the peak oil predictions have been repeatedly proved false. Repeated upward revisions have had to be made in estimated ultimate recovery (EUR), a view on the total global endowment of petroleum, produced to date and to be produced in the future. Hubbert increased his estimate from 1,350 million bbl in 1969 to 2,000 million bbl in 1973. A leading modern peak oil proponent, Campbell, has upped his numbers from 1,650 million bbl in 1995 to 1,850 million bbl in 2005. The peak oil writers defend themselves by saying that they are "refining" their estimates, but, in fact, they are consistently wrong, and always in the same direction. If I were a stock analyst and my predictions for Google profits were sometimes too high, sometimes too low, I might be forgiven if the average were correct; however, if I were always too low, investors would conclude that I did not understand the company, the industry, economics, or all three. Yet many investors are now taking peak oil arguments at face value when making decisions about oil companies.

It is usually forgotten that even the revered Hubbert's seminal paper was focused on promoting nuclear power. Although right about the date of the onshore U.S. lower forty-eight states production peak, several of his other predictions were wrong, enough to invalidate his theory, as we will see later. After this long history of repeatedly false predictions, if world oil production finally peaks in 2050 at an EUR of 4 trillion bbl, peak oilers will probably smile and say, "I told you so."

Hubbert's Curve

Nevertheless, M. King Hubbert is the patron saint of the peak oil theorists. His importance was not that he predicted the end of oil; as we have seen, plenty of forecasters have acquired posthumous reputations for foolishness from doing that. He is significant because he derived a quantitative method for predicting the date of peak oil production that, in the case of the United States, turned out to be more or less correct, giving him a retrospective halo of approval. Hubbert's genius (or luck) is that he is the only person to have made a correct quantitative prediction of oil depletion using his method; all else who have applied it, to the United Kingdom, the world, or wherever, have been egregiously wrong.

Hubbert was a Shell geophysicist and therefore the original member of the Geologist camp on oil depletion. In 1956, he predicted that oil production from the U.S. lower forty-eight states would peak in about 1970 and decline thereafter. Although largely disregarded when he wrote, his prediction did, in fact, come true and was seized on by observers during the 1970s. It is instructive, however, to consider why specialists were so keen to promote his ideas at this time. In the atmosphere of the first oil shock, it was convenient for the U.S. government to be pessimistic about the future of oil (to promote conservation) and also for the oil companies (to limit calls for windfall taxation and legitimize their heavy investment requirements and unrelated diversification).

The impact of the U.S. production peak was felt just three years later. As Daniel Yergin recounts in *The Prize*, his masterly history of the world oil business, the Texas Railroad Commission in March 1971 announced a 100 percent allowable[13]—that is, Texan oil fields were, for the first time outside of emergencies, allowed to pump flat out. No longer did the West have an easily accessible buffer to oil supply disruptions. Previous crises, such as Suez (1956) and the Six-Day War between Israel and its Arab neighbors (1967), had led to no significant increases in oil price, because Texas was always available to offer spare capacity. In contrast, the October War of 1973 and the subsequent Arab embargo on oil shipments were followed by a dramatic run-up in prices, on the order of 350 percent.

Despite this sharp price increase, U.S. oil production from the lower forty-eight states has continued to decline ever since. Peak oil aficionados point to this as evidence that Hubbert was right: that once 50 percent of the resource base has been produced, decline is inevitable and irreversible and that, contrary to the Economists, higher prices cannot call forth significant volumes of new production.

Hubbert's quantitative method relied on a mathematical curve that is now forever referred to in the peak oil literature as Hubbert's curve (Figure 4.1)[14] and its peak as "Hubbert's peak." This is sometimes mistakenly referred to

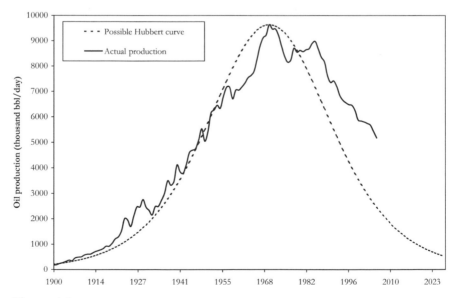

Figure 4.1
Possible Hubbert's curve for the United States.

as a normal, bell, or Gaussian curve, but one of Hubbert's innovations was to use a superficially similar-looking function, the logistic curve. After initially proposing that oil production in a country would follow a curve that he schematically drew as a bell curve, he later proposed that a logistic curve was an appropriate fit. Either way, his theory was that once 50 percent of the oil reserves in a region or country had been produced, that production would begin to decline. He shifted the debate from "oil running out," i.e. when 100 percent of the reserves would have been produced, to the peak of production. After this date, he pointed out that substitutes would have to be found if energy consumption were to continue to grow.

Most subsequent forecasters have used Hubbert's method to predict the peak of world oil production, despite several flaws. They do not have to do so; there are more detailed ways of modeling the future of oil production. Nevertheless, it is an intuitive and easy method, possibly accounting for its popularity: intuitive, in that it "feels right" that oil production should decline once the glass is half-empty. I will come to the weaknesses in Hubbert's method shortly, but let us first examine the line of argument of the Geologists.

Hubbert's work is often misinterpreted to mean that production from an individual oil field follows a Hubbert curve. As one peak oil website states, "The production lifecycle of an oil field follows a 'Hubbert Curve,' conceived by the late Dr. M. King Hubbert of the Colorado School of Mines. After discovery, production rises to a peak and then falls off."[15] It does Dr. Hubbert a disservice to credit him with the surprising discovery that production from an oil field rises and then falls. Another site is more explicit: "oil production reaches a peak when half of its oil has been extracted and then declines. When it is clear that the decline is occurring, you can simply take the amount extracted up to the peak and double it to find the approximate total oil that initially existed in that field."[16] This is utterly incorrect. Even ignoring the confusion between how much oil is below the ground in a given field and how much of this can be extracted, estimating an oil field's ultimate recovery is a complicated business involving intensive data gathering and computer modeling. I wonder why, early in my career, I wasted so many months determining the reserves of various fields if I could just have doubled the historic production before peak.[17]

Many fields enter decline before, or more often well after, producing half their ultimate reserves, for example Ekofisk in Norway, and that is assuming we know the ultimate recovery, which we do not, until the last barrel of oil is extracted and the field is abandoned.[18] Ultimate recovery is an elastic number: it depends very heavily not only on geology but also on how a field is developed. Many fields, such as Al Shaheen in Qatar, have appeared to be entering decline, only for additional investment, perhaps using new technologies, to lead to even higher levels of production and increased ultimate recovery.

Trying to fit Hubbert curves to these fields is just drawing lines on a graph; it tells us nothing about the future, because a field's production is a complex function of its geology, fluid content, and development activities, not a simple function like the logistic curve. However, we must not blame Hubbert for this, because he never claimed that individual fields fitted his curve, only that a whole basin or country did. It is his overenthusiastic supporters, mostly those without a knowledge of the industry, who have overapplied his theory.

To meet these objections, the believers in imminent depletion have developed another method, the "Hubbert linearization," that always reminds me of Isaac Asimov's fictional "psychohistorian" Hari Seldon, asking a sweating student, "Surely you can perform a field-differentiation,"[19] in the context of an empire about to fall. Peak oilers no doubt ask their acolytes, "Surely you can perform a Hubbert linearization." However, rather than give the impression that this is a meaningless piece of mumbo jumbo, I should describe the procedure.

Peak oil supporters believe that field reserves are understated in the early years, so, lacking good engineering and geological data to predict the actual reserves, they need a way to estimate the ultimate recovery from a field based on almost no information, just the reported production, in fact. The method is to plot cumulative production against annual production and to extrapolate a straight line wherever production appears to be in decline to predict the ultimate recovery. This is relying on the property of a logistic curve that, in the decline phase, a constant proportion of cumulative production should be extracted each year. Figure 4.2 shows this for the Forties Field, the largest in the United Kingdom.

A solid line has been drawn to show the Hubbert linearization for the decline phase. This suggests an ultimate recovery of about 2,600 million bbl (where the black line crosses the horizontal axis). Notice the deviation from the straight line circled around 1,750 million bbl produced; this represents the application of gas lift, a procedure involving adding gas to the oil to lift it from the bottom of the well to the surface more efficiently (this is entirely different from gas injection to maintain reservoir pressure). Laherrère points to this as proof that technology does not increase reserves, because the resumption of the linear trend after this excursion leads to the same ultimate recovery.

However, look at the points enclosed in the lower circle around 2,500 million bbl recovered, representing the 2004–2006 period (after Laherrère examined the subject in his 2003 paper[20]). At this time, the long-standing operator BP sold the field to a more aggressive competitor, Apache, who immediately reversed years of underinvestment and succeeded in increasing production again. It is clear that, even if production declines cataclysmically from now on, that the new ultimate recovery will be higher than the Hubbert linearization predicts, possibly by as much as 10

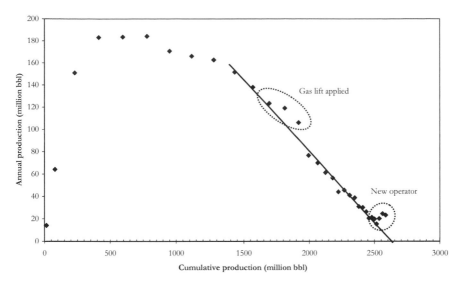

Figure 4.2
Hubbert linearization for Forties Field.

percent. Apache have also announced (November 2005) that they have found another 800 million bbl of oil in place in the field, which should add 400 million bbl or so of additional reserves.[21] This confirms the prediction of Lynch, a leading Economist: "What assurances are there that Forties will not plateau, as N. Cormorant did?"[22]

Another example provided by Laherrère is the super-giant Samotlor in West Siberia, whose ultimate recovery he puts at 20 billion bbl from his linearization procedure,[23] noting a fall in output to about 400,000 bbl/day by 1999. However, the field has already produced 20 billion bbl, output is actually rising again, toward 700,000 bbl/day by 2010,[24] and the operator, BP-TNK estimates ultimate recovery at 24 billion bbl.[25] Its 55 billion bbl of oil initially in place might suggest that the final figure could be even higher, perhaps as much as 33 billion, if a benchmark North Sea recovery factor[26] can be achieved. Neglecting such occurrences and simplistically applying the Hubbert linearization to fields or basins to predict a country's ultimate recovery will badly underestimate the final total.

To apply Hubbert's method correctly, therefore, to a basin, country, or the world (or, indeed, to predict the course of world oil production by any other method), we need an estimate of the total oil reserves, discovered and undiscovered. This assumes that the total reserves base is fixed and does not grow through opening up new areas, improvements in technology, or increases in price. It also, crucially—and we shall return to this point later—assumes that the rate of extraction does not change after passing the depletion midpoint, due to, for instance, new technologies.

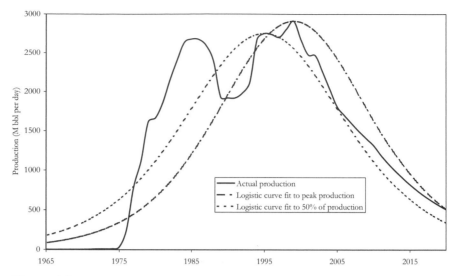

Figure 4.3
Hubbert's curve fitted to total U.K. production.

Figure 4.3 depicts two possibilities for fitting Hubbert's curve to the production of the U.K. (declined, for illustrative purposes only, at a constant rate after 2007), both using the same conservative estimate for U.K. ultimate recovery. One (dashed-dotted line) has peak production in 1999 and the other (dotted) on the point at which 50 percent of EUR was produced (in 1995). Because of the double peak, the fit is poor in both cases. If we instead attempted to model the early buildup more accurately (if we were doing this exercise in, say, 1990), we would miss the mid-1990s recovery entirely, and the United Kingdom is a country that, unlike many others, has had a fairly smooth oil production history, a single basin with rather uniform geographical conditions, developed continuously, with no revolutions, wars, or nationalizations. Peak oil theorists might maintain that the U.K. picture is distorted by the 1988 Piper Alpha disaster, which forced a shutdown of facilities for safety upgrades,[27] but actually this premature, misleading decline had already begun after 1985, induced by the oil price crash. Even if the down slope from 2005 looks comparable in both cases, consider that the annual difference is of the order of 0.5 million bbl/day, a lot in a world with barely 1 million bbl/day of spare capacity. EUR for both Hubbert's curves is the same at about 28 billion bbl, but, between 2006 and 2020, the 1999 peak delivers more than two billion bbl extra, 50 percent more than the 1995 peak. A difference of 50 percent in some major countries will mean the difference between two entirely different scenarios of future oil supplies.

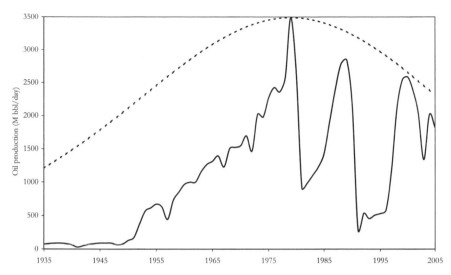

Figure 4.4
Hubbert's curve fitted to total Iraq production.

Let us consider how Hubbert's curve suits a country with an unusual or turbulent productive history. In fact, let's take the most turbulent of all: Iraq (Figure 4.4), with Campbell's EUR of 100 billion bbl (which appears to be a gross underestimate). It is impossible to get a reasonable fit, even ignoring the unfortunate and nongeologically induced troughs in 1980, 1991, and 2003. In fact, if we take the historic production to 2005 and Hubbert's curve from 2006 onward, we would predict an ultimate recovery for Iraq out to 2100 (at which point, a significant amount of oil would still be being produced) of only 50 billion bbl.

I might be accused of setting up "straw men" by attempting to fit a Hubbert curve to Iraq, because I would imagine not even peak oil supporters would say that its production history has been primarily determined by geology. But what is the use of a method for predicting oil depletion that cannot account for the world's third largest proven reserves? We have seen that, even for a "classic" Hubbert curve country like the United Kingdom, the fit is poor, especially for predicting output after the peak.

So, despite its near-universal use by the Geologists, the Hubbert method has severe weaknesses, some of which are common to most estimates of the date of peak oil.

First, it is just a model. Some followers of Hubbert have investigated other curves, but Hubbert's logistic curve remains the overwhelming choice of peak oilers, most of whom use it without mathematical sophistication. Furthermore, there have not been any scientifically rigorous attempts to assess the goodness of fit of various models or give them any theoretical underpinning. Despite what some ill-informed journalists have written ("Hubbert … showed mathematically that exploitation of any oil-field follows a predictable 'bell curve' trend"[28]), there is no physical reason why the logistic curve should apply to oil other than its use in superficially similar problems in population dynamics (in which, again, its conclusions have been challenged and have broken down). In many cases, the Hubbert curve does not match reality let alone predict the future reasonably. As we have seen, production from real fields and many real countries does not even approximate the Hubbert curve. Of fifty-one non-OPEC countries presented by Campbell, only eight have even vaguely Hubbert-shaped curves, whereas fit for OPEC countries is even worse, as should be expected given the interference of politics and quotas. Production can peak well after 50 percent of the EUR has been produced (Pakistan at 62 percent, United Kingdom at 65 percent, and Australia at 67 percent) or well before (Papua New Guinea at 25 percent).[29] Most strikingly, production in one major basin, the San Joaquin Valley of California, peaked at approximately 72 percent of EUR.[30]

Second, Hubbert's followers have leapt to the dangerous and unscientific conclusion that one correct prediction proves a theory, whereas they should know that, on the contrary, one incorrect prediction disproves a theory; successful predictions merely show that a theory has not been disproved yet.[31] We cannot know whether it was right because it is correct or merely by chance. We have already seen that Hubbert's one (debatably) correct forecast was accompanied by several false ones.

- He actually proposed 1965 as his most likely peak date; 1970 was a fallback if secondary recovery[32] proved to be more successful than he expected (as it did).
- Although arguably correct on the date of the peak, he was wrong about its height: total annual U.S. production in 1970 was 20 percent higher than he expected. So it was only more rapid production growth than his model predicted that made his prediction right. If production had grown more slowly, the peak would have been several years later.
- He forecast that world oil production would peak between 1995 and 2000 at 33 million bbl/day.[33] The true figure was 75 million bbl/day in 2000, and it has continued to rise subsequently.
- He suggested that annual U.S. natural gas production would be about 8 trillion cubic feet (Tcf)[34] in 2000 (the actual figure was 19.2 Tcf).

Furthermore, the U.S. production peak was not purely geologically determined. It came partly as a result of geological maturity, but also in the context of record low oil prices, wellhead price controls (that reduced the price to the producer even further), poor returns that caused domestic producers to employ their capital in the downstream[35] or to spend it abroad, and underinvestment (in 1971, the number of U.S. drilling rigs was only one-third the level of the mid-1950s[36]). One stock analyst recounts a telling story:

In 1971, the world's most famous contrarian investor, Jim Rogers, went to visit a Tulsa drilling-rig company. Jim was bullish on oil and he was looking for a safe way to buy into the industry. A drilling-rig manufacturer seemed like the perfect play.

"Oh lord, Jim," said the chairman. "I know I shouldn't say this, since we need all the support we can get, but you seem like a nice young fellow, even if you are from New York. Don't buy our stock. It would be a big mistake. If only I weren't 55 years old but 28, I'd get out of this business in a minute. I'd start over in anything rather than oil. Drilling is a dying business."[37]

Such a lack of activity suggests economic factors for the shortfall in investment, not depleting reservoirs,[38] which, combined with high prices, encourage frantic drilling, as was seen in Texas in the early 1980s or in the North American natural gas business in 2003–2006. This story is much more reminiscent of the underinvestment of the late 1990s. As a final insult, when the peak came, a complex system of price controls and windfall taxation of the oil industry prevented a full production response. It has been estimated that U.S. domestic production could have been 0.3–1.4 million bbl/day higher if it had not been for these restrictions,[39] an amount that, at the high end, could have kept U.S. production above the 1970 peak until 1987. Geology was only one, and perhaps not even the most important, factor in the U.S. production peak.

Third, Hubbert's curve is not a forecasting tool, no matter how often it is used that way. To make forecasts from Hubbert's method, one has also to estimate the total reserves in some other way, typically by trying to extrapolate production decline or by looking at historical discovery rates. It has no crystal ball that can predict events such as the opening up of Alaska or deepwater. The Hubbertians (Hubbertistas?) observe that peak production follows peak discovery, with a lag, but they have no way of predicting how large this lag will be, and it varies greatly between basins and countries, between five and forty years. A five- or ten-year lag might represent the time taken to bring discovered fields into production, but what interpretation can we put on a forty-year lag? It takes nothing like forty years to turn discoveries into producing fields, so using such long lags clearly does not have any value as a forecasting tool. If, say, Kazakhstan's discovery curve peaked five years ago (Kashagan, its largest field), then what lag is appropriate? Ten years (about the time Kashagan will take to come into production)? Twenty years (about the time to Kashagan's peak)? What if (like the Netherlands gas industry and many OPEC countries) government policy constrained the maximum production rate from the large, early fields? What about countries like Nigeria or Brazil, with an early phase of large onshore finds followed much later by similarly big or even bigger deepwater fields? By superimposing many Hubbert curves and shifting them with different lags, as Laherrère does, we can indeed model many (probably any) country's production profile, but this has no predictive value. Mining large sets of data usually gives rise to curious but meaningless statistics.

Fourth, the Hubbert's curve is a "black box." The curve gives no information about the underlying factors driving production. We have only a single variable: total reserves. We cannot experiment with oil price, costs of development, advances in technology, national or corporate strategies, discovery rates, or any other variables that might influence the production profile. Geologists would counter that the production profile is, in a kind of Marxist way, almost entirely determined by the geology (reserves) and only to a very limited extent by other factors. A true believer in the curve would argue that it models geological depletion and cannot allow for wars, revolutions, and so on (indeed, it is hardly fair to expect that it could).

Unfortunately, most of the world's major oil producers have been affected by such happenings. Iran's production was upset by the 1951–1954 nationalization,[40] by the 1979 Revolution, and the 1980–1988 Iran–Iraq War. Russia's was heavily impacted by the collapse of the Soviet Union, before rebounding. Being developed under communism, Russia should perhaps, ironically, be the best example of a pure Hubbert system, in which production is determined primarily by geology, not by oil price, demand, or technology. Saudi Arabia, Kuwait, Qatar, and the UAE have been affected by attempts to adhere to OPEC quotas (and Kuwait, additionally, has been hit by war), while Nigeria's and Venezuela's production has been disrupted by civil unrest. Finally, investment conditions in the rest of the former Soviet Union (FSU), Iraq, Indonesia, Mexico, Libya, and Algeria have hardly been of the kind that would permit these countries to realize their full geological potential. Even the United States has been affected by price caps and environmental moratoria.

Fifth, Hubbert's curve depends on selling into an infinite market or at least that supply is not restricted by demand. The contrary situation has pertained to most of oil's history, with a series of semi-cartels (the "Seven Sisters," the Texas Railroad Commission, and OPEC) restraining the production of their members to support prices. In this case, not all oil that is found can be sold immediately. Oil on the rising limb of Hubbert's curve will be produced more slowly, relative to reserves, than that on the falling limb. Presumably, the quota restrictions will be lifted when production is falling, because the market will then take all the oil that is available. The same will happen if technology advances with time, not increasing reserves (that sacred cow of the peak oil theorists) but increasing the rate at which a fixed quantum of reserves can be produced. Everyone in the peak oil camp, at least those whose arguments with which I am familiar, agrees that modern petroleum technologies, "super-straws" as they are often derisively dismissed,[41] such as horizontal or "maximum reservoir contact" wells and water floods, produce the same reserves but more quickly.

So, if either or both of these conditions applies, the inevitable corollary—which, to my knowledge, no peak oil supporter has grasped or at least discussed[42]—is that production can continue rising well after 50 percent of the oil has been produced. In a way, this possibility should be obvious. If fields are developed in a conservative way, at low annual depletion rates, the peak will come much later and well after half the reserves have been produced. Most of the major OPEC countries have followed such a cautious strategy (indeed, partly imposed on them by deliberate restraint of output to protect prices). The production policy followed heavily influences when the peak comes and how high it is. The restriction on production does not need to be OPEC or a national depletion policy; it could be that a major new play[43] is only developed rather late, perhaps as a consequence of technological or infrastructural limits (e.g., Alaska and the subsalt fields of the North Caspian) or that a previously closed area is opened to exploration (e.g., the Iraqi border region of Iran and the Norwegian Barents Sea). Hubbert's model imposes equally swift (or slow) depletion in the decline phase as in the buildup. In contrast, the USGS model, mentioned below, does allow for more rapid depletion in the later period.

Campbell has said, "oil is ultimately controlled by events in the Jurassic which are immune to politics."[44] However, the Hubbert curve implies something more than this. It suggests that future oil production is controlled by events in the past century, because it requires a peak when 50 percent of the resource has been produced. Because we have produced the first half of our reserves rather slowly (global R/P ratio[45] [total reserves divided by annual production] currently being 35 even under conservative ultimate recovery estimates), this model proposes that we are doomed to produce the second half slowly too and to be unable to ramp up to a higher depletion rate.

Sixth, the model assumes that the total reserves are fixed. They cannot be increased by improvements in technology or higher oil prices. This is disproved by many instances, of which we can cite one: the previously mentioned peak in California's San Joaquin Valley production when more than 72 percent of the EUR had been produced. This was achieved by the extensive implementation of thermal recovery methods under the stimulus of high oil prices, which led to a real and very considerable growth in reserves and production. This reserves growth leads to persistent and large underestimates of ultimate recovery using the Hubbert method: EUR in the San Joaquin Valley increased by some 50 percent from 1964 to 1982 and an additional 30 percent from 1982 to 2000, with scope for an additional 12 percent increase by 2020, even in an extremely mature and well-understood region. Ultimate recovery may be somewhat more than 18 billion bbl compared with the naive Hubbertian estimate of about 8 billion.

Compare the model assumptions of fixed reserves and zero price response to the real United States in 1970, from which peak oil theorists draw confirmation of their opinions. The United States was approximately an infinite market, at least in 1970 when it was a net oil importer. Any oil found could be sold without markedly affecting the price. However, it had not been in this situation before 1970, because production was restrained by pro-rationing and the Texas Railroad Commission.

What happened when U.S. production peaked? First, prices rose noticeably between 1970 and 1973, from $9.38 (in real terms, 2006 dollars) to $14.99 in 1973. Then, with the Arab embargo and OPEC's realization of its newfound pricing power, the oil price shot up sharply. The response was pretty much as classical economics would predict (excluding some market distortions imposed by ill-conceived responses to the crisis). Demand fell, partly as a result of economic recession ("demand destruction"), in part (particularly in the longer term) because of substitution away from oil as an energy source, and to increased efficiency. And supply rose. Decline in the U.S. onshore lower forty-eight states slowed markedly, largely because of EOR efforts, and high prices spurred greater development of the offshore and the construction of the Trans-Alaska Pipeline.

It is no defense of Hubbert's method to say that he did not foresee the importance of Alaskan or offshore oil. When he published his 1956 paper, Alaska had been producing oil since 1902; the first offshore well came near Creole, Louisiana in 1938; the first well drilled out of sight of land had been sunk, in the Gulf of Mexico, nine years before he wrote; the 1956 article specifically makes an estimate of offshore reserves[46]; and in 1971, he refers to Prudhoe Bay, Alaska, the United States' largest ever field, found in 1967.[47] In any case, a major criticism of the curve-fitting method is its inability to allow for new production that does not fit the pattern of the old. The contribution from EOR, Alaska, and the offshore was such that, instead of declining sharply and smoothly after 1970 as Hubbert followers would predict, total U.S. production maintained an undulating plateau at about 10 million bbl/day, some 1 million bbl/day below the peak, for sixteen years (1970–1986). This plateau was only disrupted by a more rapid decline in the onshore because of the 1986 price crash (again proving, contrary to Hubbertians, that price does matter). The United States, being an open economy, could suck in imports in response to declining supply, undercutting the highest-cost domestic output. If oil had stayed at its 1980 peak of some $100/bbl (in 2008 real terms), there would have been intense political pressure to open up offshore areas for exploration, deepwater and Alaskan exploration and development would have proceeded apace, and industry interest in EOR schemes and oil shales would have been maintained.

Other methods for predicting future production have been used. One is to sum all future known developments and then possibly to add an allowance for future exploration assuming a pace of discovery. Adding up future developments works well in the short term and is the method I use later in this chapter to examine production out to about 2010. In the longer term, it becomes increasingly pessimistic because projects are announced only four or five years ahead of start-up and the portfolio becomes very thin farther out in time. Modeling the exploration success also requires a number of assumptions about how much oil will be found and how fast it will be developed. Another hard-to-estimate factor is how quickly, if at all, existing fields will decline.

Another alternative model, used by the USGS, relies on the R/P ratio. They assume that the world's R/P ratio will trend to 11, that being a reasonable number in mature producing basins, i.e., one-eleventh of the total reserves will be produced annually. Production will increase, and reserves will be added (albeit at a declining rate), until the R/P ratio reaches 11. Then production will decline so as to maintain this ratio constant. This approach mimics the greater effort that is put into mature regions. Figure 4.5 shows Hubbert's curve (dotted line) compared with the USGS method (dashed line), with annual demand growth of 1.5 percent until peak is reached.

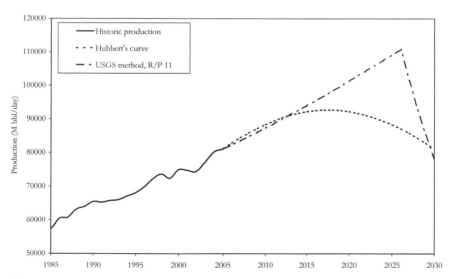

Figure 4.5
Comparison of Hubbert's curve and USGS method for future oil production.

The USGS curve is obviously less aesthetically pleasing than the Hubbert one, and its sharp peak and decline looks unrealistic. However, I think the underlying concept is sound: as we start approaching the limits of the resource, we try harder (for instance, drill more wells) to increase production, until it becomes physically impossible. This chart shows that, even with the same resource volumes, the date of peak oil is sensitive to the model used—2017 with Hubbert's curve, 2026 with the USGS model. Therefore, when and if resource depletion starts becoming apparent, we can buy ourselves considerable time, perhaps a decade, to put solutions in place, by devoting greater effort to maximizing production from a shrinking reserves base. This, furthermore, assumes growing demand, whereas the high prices needed to justify such expanded effort would probably hold back demand growth, leading to the "undulating plateau" concept.

Whether we adopt the Hubbert model or a different one, it is true that many significant oil-producing nations have passed a peak. Note that I say "a peak" and not "the peak," because some of these countries, such as Russia, Iran, the United Kingdom, and others have had or may still have a second peak that as in the case of Saudi Arabia, may be even higher than the first. Some of these, such as Syria, manage geological rebounds, that is, a successful new exploration campaign reverses the decline in older producing basins. Syria's first production phase, centered on the heavy oil fields of the northeast, peaked at 200,000 bbl/day in 1976, before decline began, to only 155,000 bbl/day in 1982, but exploration in the Euphrates Graben,[48] primarily by Shell, was then so successful that a new, much higher peak was reached in 1995 at almost 600,000 bbl/day. Figure 4.6 shows a selection of countries who have entered or passed a plateau phase. Note that, contrary to the Hubbert model, the plateau phase can be enormously extended, as in the case of the United States, Canada, or Brunei. Countries with short plateaux, such as Colombia, tend to be those with heavy reliance on one or a few fields, found in a single burst, which all begin to decline together. Extended plateaux are often experienced by countries with several producing areas, which are discovered sequentially and so compensate for declines in older areas, such as Alaska and the Gulf of Mexico in the case of the United States. Alternatively, as with Brunei and Malaysia, a national depletion policy may cap production and so lead to an extended plateau rather than a sharp peak.

Peak oil theorists often point to the growing number of countries that are past peak as a warning of inevitable depletion. In fact, it is perhaps an indicator of a growing concentration of production in fewer hands, but it does not tell us much about global peak oil because most production comes from just a few countries. There are fifty countries in the world that produce more than 50,000 bbl/day, but seven of these account for more than 50 percent of the total. There are a few countries with a lot of oil; many with a small amount. If all begin producing at about the same time,

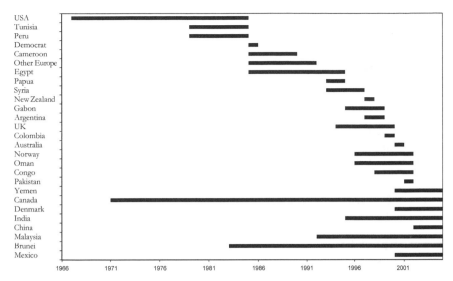

Figure 4.6
Plateau production periods for some major petroleum countries.

then inevitably many will peak early on, but the few big producers will keep global production increasing for a long time. In any case, several new countries have recently, or will soon, throw their hats into the ring as producers, replenishing the ranks of the prepeak: for instance, Mauritania, Uganda, and Cambodia.

Note also that, although some of these past peak countries are significant producers, none, except the United States and perhaps Mexico, is of the first rank. Given Mexico's great remaining potential, it is far from clear that this peak is a final one. Smith (2006)[49] lists "postpeak countries," at first sight an imposing array, but including some utterly negligible hydrocarbon powers: Israel/Palestine, Taiwan, Benin, Jordan, Japan, Spain. In fact, some of the countries he lists (such as Morocco and Suriname) are actively exploring promising basins and have every chance of reaching a new, higher peak. None of the major world reserve holders, among which I would count Saudi Arabia, Russia, Kazakhstan, Iran, Iraq, Abu Dhabi, Qatar (largely for its condensate[50]), Canada (for its oil sands[51]), Nigeria, Libya, Algeria, Mexico, and Venezuela, has entered a phase of inevitable decline. Some are below their historic peaks but largely for economic and political, rather than geological, reasons. Some of the countries shown above have even managed rebounds, with production increasing in 2007 (such as Congo-Brazzaville and Peru), whereas others, such as Oman, have detailed plans to reach a new peak, above the first. This again does not fit the Hubbert model. When a country enters a period of production decline, it often improves investment conditions and opens up new areas. Norway, India, and Colombia are among nations that have followed this policy in recent years, which can also lead to a secondary peak or a long plateau.

Despite the known weaknesses of Hubbert's method, I believe it would be fair to say that there is general agreement that, to predict a supply-side peak (if any) in world oil production, we need some estimate of the world's total endowment of recoverable petroleum. This is not, as most peak oil believers maintain, a fixed quantum. Of course, the amount of oil below ground is fixed.[52] Suggestions have been made by Soviet and some other researchers,[53] and supported by Economists such as Maugeri and Odell, that oil might be produced by "abiotic" or "inorganic" processes at great depth within the earth, perhaps making hydrocarbons vastly abundant and almost a renewable resource. There is strong evidence against this theory, and the vast majority of petroleum geologists (including me) do not subscribe to it.

Yet the amount of this below-ground oil that can be found and recovered depends hugely on prices, markets, investment levels, politics, technology, and, in the short run anyway, serendipity. Can proven reserve numbers, such as those reported by major oil companies, give us a reliable estimate for this recoverable oil?

THE RESERVES CONUNDRUM

In God we trust; all others bring data.

Amory Lovins[54]

Peak oil theorists manage to have their cake and eat it when it comes to oil company reserves. On the one hand, they are very skeptical of "proved" oil reserve disclosures. On the other hand, they gleefully receive news like that of the Shell downgrade as confirmation that they are right, that world oil is running out.

Unfortunately, company reserves, which are usually reported under the SEC guidelines, are highly misleading. Based on rules formulated in 1978, they are incomplete, prone to distortion by accounting conventions, miss out some important categories of hydrocarbons, do not take account of modern technology, and tend to be highly conservative. They also only cover reserves economic to produce at the time the calculation is done; indeed, by definition, reserves have to be commercially viable. They, therefore, do not give any guidance as to how much oil might be available if prices were to rise.

The biggest weakness of relying on SEC reserves, however, is that only a tiny fraction of the world's oil and gas is reported to these standards. The vast majority of reserves are held by NOCs, who, with a few exceptions, are not subject to SEC-compliant audits. In 1972, 92 percent of the production of the top twenty companies (which, in turn, controlled 75 percent of total world production) was reported according to international standards. In 2005, the top twenty share of production had decreased somewhat, to 65 percent, a mere 26 percent of which was under SEC guidelines. The picture for reserves rather than production is even more dramatically skewed toward the state companies, because they generally have much longer reserve lives than the IOCs. Therefore, even a dramatic shake-up in the SEC rules would shed very little light on the key resource holders in the Middle East,[55] Venezuela, and the FSU. Falls in R/P and the reserves replacement ratio[56] amongst IOCs cause great angst for their shareholders and the Western media and give the impression of oil running out, but this is a problem confined to a small, albeit high-profile, subset of global producers.

We can see, therefore, that the stated reserves of companies listed on Western exchanges have almost no utility in determining global reserves. Companies headquartered elsewhere usually provide poorer data, with less scrutiny. National reserves, particularly outside the OECD and held largely by NOCs, are a completely different question. OPEC countries, for example, usually report annually their proven reserves. Are these according to SEC or Society of Petroleum Engineers (SPE) criteria, or some other standard? Can they be relied on as a realistic assessment of global petroleum resources?

It might be expected by an idealist that something so important to the health of the world economy as world oil production and reserves would be subject to stringent reporting requirements. In the real world, this is true for publicly listed western companies but not true for most countries, particularly those in OPEC. This should not be surprising to us. Many key items of economic data from countries outside the OECD are secret or unreliable, such as numbers for the military spending or GDP of China. Even within industrialized nations, key figures such as inflation, unemployment, and balance of payments are subject to frequent revisions and changes of methodology, sometimes for political reasons. Furthermore, reserves, being underground and knowable only within a wide range of uncertainty and by making significant assumptions about the future, are harder to calculate than a number such as government expenditure. Uncertainty about reserves is, therefore, not indicative of some unique conspiracy.

Most of the Geologist persuasion is pessimistic on the world's oil reserves. Conversely, most Economists tend to believe both that world reserves are very large, and that significant additions will occur that will prevent any shortage. There is no intrinsic reason why this should be so; it is perfectly possible to believe simultaneously that the world's oil reserves are very large and that they are fixed. As the following discussion will demonstrate, I remain optimistic on world oil supply, even while being sceptical of some OPEC reserves estimates.

Table 4.1
Estimated oil reserve figures, per country (OPEC countries underlined).

Country	End-2006 oil reserves (billion barrels)		
	BP Statistical Review of World Energy 2007	IHS Energy/ Petroleum Intelligence Weekly[1]	Campbell[2]
Saudi Arabia	264.3	289.0	154
Iran	137.5	134.4	69.2
Iraq	115.0	98.8	63.6
Kuwait	101.5	54.1	51.3
United Arab Emirates	97.8	57.4	41.5
Venezuela	80.0	89.1	33.5
Russia	79.5	128.4	73.0
Kazakhstan	39.8	39.3	36.9
Libya	41.5	26.6	25.9
Nigeria	36.2	36.0	25.6
United States	29.9	79.8	22.9
Canada	17.1	179.6	5.1
China	16.3	25.5	24.8
Qatar	15.2	34.5	5.9
Mexico	12.9	20.4	19.0
Algeria	12.3	13.5	12.3
Brazil	12.2	24.1	2.3
Norway	8.5	11.6	10.5
Angola	9.0	14.4	3.4
Azerbaijan	7.0	13.7	10.6
Sudan	6.4	NA	2.2
India	5.7	NA	5.1
Totals			
Middle East	743		401
Europe and Eurasia	144		147
Africa	117		78
South America	103.5		68
North America	59.9		28
Asia Pacific	40.5		53
World	1208	1459	791

[1]*Petroleum Intelligence Weekly*, vol. XLVI, no. 14, April 2, 2007.
[2]Campbell (2006).

Conventional estimates present the world's proven oil reserves as follows in Table 4.1. I show the BP figures, which are heavily criticized by Geologists for relying on allegedly falsified figures from governments, a consultant view depending on a detailed field-by-field database, and Campbell's estimates (based on some ad hoc adjustment of public figures).

Saudi Arabia's 264 billion bbl of proven oil reserves or Iran's 137.5 billion are, of course, not subject to the same level of public scrutiny as those of ExxonMobil and may not grow in the future in the same way as those of IOCs. The problem, then, is what reserve figures (if any) to trust. Most international agencies and reporters, such as BP in their Statistical Review of World Energy, the IEA, and the Energy Information Administration (EIA) of the United States, take the OPEC figures on trust. BP, no doubt, have much more detailed information in their corporate vaults, at least on some areas, but under confidentiality obligations.

Yet the IHS numbers, based on probably the most comprehensive database of technical petroleum data in existence, show the BP reserves to be conservative, as much as 20 percent too low. IHS is much higher on Canada because of including "oil sands" reserves, recently declared commercial, and for the United States, because of the very conservative definition of proved reserves adopted there. IHS reserve estimates are significantly lower than BP for the UAE, Libya, and Kuwait but a lot greater for Russia and significantly more for Saudi Arabia. Even removing the unconventional oil in Canada and Venezuela yields a global total of 1,287 billion bbl, somewhat higher than BP's estimate. In contrast, Campbell's figures appear far too conservative, amounting to barely half the IHS numbers. He writes off more than half of North America, nearly half the Middle East, and about a third of Africa and South America compared with BP. Part of the difference is caused by his exclusion of anything (oil sands, deepwater, polar, heavy oil, and gas condensate) that does not meet his narrow definition of oil. Another tranche is attributable to his excessive pessimism on the U.S. reserves, because his estimate replicates BP but with the removal of deepwater and polar (Alaskan) oil. He therefore takes at face value these proven reserves, which he argues elsewhere to be conservative, and these reserves, backed up by high-quality technical data, never reappear in his estimates for reserves growth (which he dismisses) or exploration potential. However, the biggest part of the write-off is due to peak oil discounting of OPEC reserves in the leading countries. Is this justified?

Like Campbell, most of the Geologists point, understandably, to suspicious jumps in OPEC reserves during the 1980s and to subsequent long periods of flat reserves (Table 4.2). During the mid-1980s, OPEC was under intense pressure to defend high oil prices, a struggle given up when Saudi Arabia lost patience and sharply increased production in 1986, causing a crash in the oil price and terminating the oil boom. There were sharp disagreements within OPEC at this point about production quotas. A system was suggested in which each country's quota was based on its proven reserves and on population. However, in contrast to repeated peak oil assertions,[57] it is worth noting that this methodology was never adopted by OPEC; quotas were, and continue to be, set by a process of horse trading.

Table 4.2
Allegedly suspicious proven reserves figures from selected OPEC countries.

				Quoted proven oil reserves (billion barrels)				
Year	Saudi Arabia	Iran	Iraq	United Arab Emirates	Kuwait	Qatar	Venezuela	Ecuador[i]
1980	168.0	58.3	30.0	30.4	67.9	3.6	19.9	1.0
1981	167.9	57.0	32.0	32.2	67.7	3.5	24.9	0.9
1982	165.5	56.1	59.0	32.4	67.2	3.4	25.9	0.9
1983	168.8	55.3	_65.0_	32.3	67.0	3.3	28.0	0.9
1984	171.7	58.9	_65.0_	32.5	**92.7**	_4.5_	**54.5**	1.1
1985	171.5	59.0	_65.0_	33.0	92.5	_4.5_	55.5	1.1
1986	169.7	_92.9_	72.0	**97.2**	_94.5_	_4.5_	58.1	1.2
1987	169.6	_92.9_	_100.0_	_98.1_	_94.5_	_4.5_	58.5	1.6
1988	**255.0**	_92.9_	_100.0_	_98.1_	_94.5_	_4.5_	59.0	1.5
1989	260.1	_92.9_	_100.0_	_98.1_	97.1	_4.5_	60.1	1.4
1990	260.3	_92.9_	_100.0_	_98.1_	97.0	3.0	62.6	1.4
1991	260.9	_92.9_	_100.0_	_98.1_	_96.5_	3.0	63.3	1.5
1992	261.2	_92.9_	_100.0_	_98.1_	_96.5_	3.1	64.4	**3.2**
1993	261.4	_92.9_	_100.0_	_98.1_	_96.5_	3.1	64.9	3.7
1994	261.4	94.3	_100.0_	_98.1_	_96.5_	3.5	66.3	3.5
1995	261.5	93.7	_100.0_	_98.1_	_96.5_	_3.7_	72.7	3.4
1996	261.4	92.6	112.0	_97.8_	_96.5_	_3.7_	74.9	3.5
1997	261.5	92.6	_112.5_	_97.8_	_96.5_	_3.7_	76.1	3.7
1998	261.5	93.7	_112.5_	_97.8_	_96.5_	_3.7_	76.8	4.1
1999	262.8	93.1	_112.5_	_97.8_	_96.5_	_3.7_	76.8	4.4
2000	262.8	99.5	_112.5_	_97.8_	_96.5_	13.2	77.7	4.6
2001	262.7	99.1	_115.0_	_97.8_	_96.5_	_15.2_	77.3	4.6
2002	262.8	**130.7**	_115.0_	_97.8_	_96.5_	_15.2_	77.2	_5.1_
2003	262.7	133.3	_115.0_	_97.8_	99.0	_15.2_	_79.7_	_5.1_
2004	264.3	132.7	_115.0_	_97.8_	_101.5_	_15.2_	_79.7_	_5.1_
2005	264.2	_137.5_	_115.0_	_97.8_	_101.5_	_15.2_	_80.0_	4.9
2006	264.3	_137.5_	_115.0_	_97.8_	_101.5_	_15.2_	_80.0_	4.7

[i]Ecuador left OPEC in December 1992, shortly after registering its large increase, which seems odd if the point of increasing reserves was to up its quota. It rejoined in November 2007.

Large jumps are highlighted in **bold**; periods of oddly constant reserves from year to year are underlined.

The result was that, during the period 1984–1988, the major OPEC countries, beginning with Kuwait, allegedly started to game the system by registering sharp annual jumps in reserves, without there being notable new discoveries at the same time, arguably to bolster their cases for higher quotas. For example, Iran's reserves jumped 57 percent in 1986, although no exploration wells at all were drilled between 1984 and 1987. The largest proportionate increase was registered by the UAE, whose reserves went up 195 percent in 1986, whereas the largest absolute rise was the 85.4 billion bbl added by Saudi Arabia in 1988. Since then, there have been some notable subsequent increases, another by Iran in 2002, of 32 percent, and by 12 percent in Iraq in 1996, a time when the national industry was crippled by sanctions and when only one modest gas discovery had been made.

For whatever reason, the other OPEC members, Algeria, Gabon,[58] Indonesia, Libya, and Nigeria, did not record these dubious increases. Perhaps part of the reason for this is that some of them have been serial cheaters on OPEC quotas anyway (Algeria and Nigeria), whereas others have struggled to maintain production at their quota level (Gabon, Indonesia, Libya, and recently Nigeria). Another odd footnote is that Indonesia registered a sharp *decrease* in reserves in 1989, from 9 billion bbl (a level that remained fixed from 1986 to 1988) down to 5.1 billion bbl, in a period when they only produced 1.5 billion bbl, implying write-offs of some previously booked reserves. A non-OPEC country, Mexico, registered a major decline in reserves from 1997 (47.8 billion bbl) to 1998 (28.4 billion bbl), because its state company, Pemex, floated U.S. bonds and, for the first time, recorded its reserves in compliance with SEC rules. This reinforces the point that SEC figures badly understate "true" (expectation, median, or midcase) reserves.

An additional point raising Geologists' suspicions is that many of these countries then proceeded to register identical reserve figures year after year, despite considerable production and, in some cases, a lack of accompanying exploration success. Iraq's reserves were flat at a suspiciously round 100 billion bbl from 1987 to 1995 (perhaps they had other things on their mind), whereas the UAE was stuck on 96.5 billion bbl between 1991 and 1995 and then on 97.8 between 1996 and 2005. The Saudis at least, in the manner of a school pupil making up physics results by adding spurious decimal places, at least put in the effort to vary their reserves slightly around 262 billion bbl to make them seem more plausible. It is, of course, inconceivable that discoveries and revisions in existing fields were exactly offsetting production over these long periods.

The peak oil theorists who challenge the official OPEC reserves usually maintain that the lower numbers, before the revisions, are more reliable and should be taken as a starting point. Without using detailed field-by-field data, treating the various countries differently, or making any allowance for previous conservatism, exploration success, or reserves growth after 1984, the peak oil theorists write off vast quantities of reserves, making the sweeping assumption that the official OPEC figures are EUR (i.e., including all past production), not remaining reserves. So, Saudi Arabia loses 108 billion bbl (104 billion of past production plus 4 billion that disappears for some unclear reason), Iran is stripped of 63 billion and Iraq of 51 billion.[59] Similarly, based on a single source, Khalimov,[60] who amidst the immediate post-Soviet economic chaos stated that Russian reserves were 30 percent overestimated as against Western standards, they downgrade Russia. Globally, 393 billion bbl are removed at a stroke of the keyboard, or more than a decade of production at current rates.

To attack the official numbers, peak oil writers, such as Campbell, Laherrère, and Simmons *et al.*, are forced to posit some great global conspiracy, involving OPEC, the USGS, IHS (although Laherrère uses their database), and major oil companies. British environmental commentator George Monbiot writes, "I have now read 4000 pages of reports on global oil supply, and I know less about it than I did before I started. The only firm conclusion I have reached is that the people sitting on the world's reserves are liars."[61] This kind of conspiracy theorism absolves the peak oil theorists of any need to validate their theories or defend their numbers. It makes the whole enterprise deeply unscientific. The peak oil theorists have not convincingly explained why, let alone how, the oil producers and companies would perpetrate this fraud. If peak oil is imminent, why not make the fact public and benefit from the sudden and immense jump in prices? Of course, this would spur investment in substitutes and conservation, but, according to the conspiracy theory, they will be needed anyway. Past behavior should be a guide: in the 1970s, the U.S. government, OPEC, and the oil companies joined in the fashionable angst about depleting oil along with everyone else. Now, it is difficult to see what Saudi Arabia, the USGS, or ExxonMobil would gain from willfully wrecking the world economy; it is very easy to see what they would lose. With the example of Iraq next door, is Saudi Arabia likely to risk a global oil meltdown?

That said, given the current peak oil fears, it would appear to be in OPEC's interests to be more forthcoming with field data and to release independently audited reports, to avoid catalyzing developments in unconventional oil and conservation that would reduce demand for their product. Indeed, Saudi Arabia has, in the past year or two, released much more data on its total reserves and on field expansion plans. Nearly all major Russian companies now have to meet the listing requirements of Western exchanges, and so the quality of reserves data there has improved greatly.

There may be some merit in looking critically at the public figures, but the IHS figures convincingly demonstrate that the existing reserve estimates were conservative. The increased bookings during the 1980s were arbitrary in timing, but the final numbers are not so unreasonable. The pre-1984 figures were mostly derived by Western companies, who were one-by-one nationalized during the 1970s and early 1980s. These IOCs were naturally taking a fairly conservative view (in line with the SEC philosophy that persists today). In the pre-1973 climate of abundant resources and rapid growth, there was not the same concern with reserve replacement that there is today, nor the same need to prop up share prices by recording increased reserves.

The international companies also had an incentive to report lower reserves for two political reasons. First, during the golden years of Middle Eastern oil discovery in the 1960s, all the producing countries were clamoring for increased output. Prices were kept low and stable by a cartel of the major companies[62] (an arrangement that, contrary to popular prejudice, very definitely does not prevail any more). The major companies relocated their profits to the "downstream" (refining and retail) to keep oil money out of the hands of the producing countries. This skewed arrangement was one of the contributory factors to OPEC's formation and ultimately the 1973 price rise and the nationalization of most of OPEC oil. Because of these low prices, the producing countries could only increase revenues by pumping greater volumes, but the marketing systems of the major companies could not absorb this flood, and, therefore, they persistently restrained the host governments.

Second, when the nationalization wave began, the companies wanted to downplay the "size of the prize" to make their concessions less of a valuable target for the governments and to emphasize how much their technical expertise was needed to maintain production.

The argument that Middle Eastern reserves were persistently *understated* by the Western companies can be supported, for instance, in the case of Iraq. Ninety percent of Iraqi production comes from the Kirkuk Field, which has an EUR of 25 billion bbl, and Rumaila, with EUR of 25 billion, of which 9.3 billion and 4.6 billion bbl, respectively, had been produced by 1981. This yields 36 billion bbl of reserves in 1981, when Iraq's quoted figure was only 32 billion, and this counts no reserves at all for super-giants such as Majnoon (7–20 billion bbl), Zubair (8.2 billion bbl), Nahr Umr (5 billion bbl), and others, all of which were known at the time, although producing little or nothing. Iran's 2002 increase is at least partly justified by the Azadegan discovery in 2000, by booking some of the estimated 16 billion bbl of condensate in South Pars (found in 1992) and by an intensive period of field studies by Western companies during the 1998–2002 period, upgrading the mostly very conservative recovery factors held over from the Shah's era. Countering the charge that the numbers are inflated, I know of one field whose reserves were actually *reduced* by 50 percent based on this reevaluation.

Even after the nationalizations, the OPEC nations had incentives to maintain unrealistically low reserve figures, until Kuwait's actions precipitated the upgrades. It helped them to maintain an impression of world oil scarcity and hence keep prices high. It also reduced the chance of invasion or other unfriendly action being taken against them, by either their jealous neighbours (Iraq against Iran and Kuwait) or the Western world, given threats emanating from the United States in particular.

These revisions were not only confined to OPEC countries. Non-OPEC Canada, with strict regulations and no need to justify quotas, raised its reserve estimates by 22 percent in 1986, at exactly the time of the OPEC revisions, highlighting that changes in reporting standards and technology can lead to justified increases in reserves.

Overall, then, the Geologists' reductions in the reserves they allow each country are excessive and arbitrary. Independent consultants actually suggest *more* reserves, albeit differently distributed, than the official version. This is crucial: we appear to have almost twice as much discovered reserves as Geologists believe.

EXPLORATION POTENTIAL

Formula for success: rise early, work hard, strike oil.

J. Paul Getty[63]

The next key part of the peak oil story, and one stressed especially by Laherrère and Campbell, involves exploration. The argument is that, since the golden age of Middle Eastern exploration from the 1950s to the early 1970s, we have consistently failed to find as much oil as we have produced. In the early years of the twenty-first century, discovery was running at about 11 billion bbl per year,[64] whereas production was 27–29 billion bbl/year, so the world's stock of reserves was not being fully replenished. In fact, the last year in which discovery exceeded production was probably 1979, with 24 billion bbl being produced and about 25 billion being found.[65] Actually, during the post-1979 period, global reserves additions have exceeded production twenty-five years of twenty-seven, but, even if we accept the genuineness of the OPEC revisions in the mid-1980s, the Geologists argue that that most of these reserve additions just relate to fields discovered long before but that were conservatively booked at first, allowing subsequent upward revisions.

Therefore, they backdate all the reserves in a field to when it was first discovered. However, this has to be done with care; many recent, genuine discoveries, particularly in the Middle East, were made by deeper drilling in existing fields, and these are really new finds, not just upward revisions of known reservoirs. For instance, Laherrère ascribes all the gas reserves in the largest conventional oil field in the world, Saudi Arabia's Ghawar, to the oil discovery in the Arab Formation[66] in 1949, at a depth of about 2,000 meters, whereas most of the field's gas is actually nonassociated[67] and was discovered in deeper reservoirs, at depths of 3,000–4,300 meters, between 1971 and 1982.[68] Correct treatment of this issue will gain added significance when (and if) exploration drilling resumes in Iraq in earnest, because many of the large fields have significant deeper potential. Other reserves additions relate to proving up extensions and separate blocks to a structure that, for convenience, may be given one name and regarded as a single field, a major phenomenon in Russia's West Siberian heartland among other basins.

The main objection to this backdating policy, however, is that what is of interest to the industry (as opposed to a geologist) is not when a particular structure was first drilled, but when its hydrocarbons were known with enough confidence to allow development. For instance, published backdated charts of gas discovery show an enormous peak in 1971, when the world's largest gas field,[69] Qatar's North Field, was discovered, partly because the reserves from the Iranian section (South Pars), which was not drilled until 1991, are included, too. But from the industry's point of view, the Iranian reserves were not known and not accessible to development until 1991. Qatari maps even showed the field terminating at the border until South Pars was proved up. Redrawing the discovery curve with some two-thirds of the reserves found in 1971 and the remainder in 1991 would give a more accurate picture of how much gas was becoming available to markets. This is logically consistent with the peak oil theorists' contention that production follows discovery, with a lag; South Pars could not have been developed in, say, 1981, although theoretically the geological structure of which it is part had been found in 1971. Even the Qatari section is still not completely delineated, and gas technology and markets had not advanced enough to make it commercial until the late 1980s.

To give another example, imagine that a new technology that increases oil recovery was invented in 1990 (horizontal drilling, say, or EOR) and applied to Ghawar to add 10 billion bbl of reserves. Why do Geologists then backdate those 10 billion bbl to 1949, the date of field discovery, not to 1990 when the oil first became available? What matters is not when the geological structure was first detected, but when oil was first accessible to the market. This process of "reserves growth" or "reserves creep" is a very well-known and well-authenticated one. Fields discovered many years ago have had more time to go through the process than those found yesterday.

For these reasons, then, backdating makes the discovery peak look unrealistically early. It is like ascribing the whole European discovery of the Americas to Columbus because he landed on one small part, ignoring the thousands of explorers who filled in the map after him[70]; he had no idea of the size of what he had found or even its correct location. In fact, exploration of the whole continent took more than 300 years. Columbus could not have settled California, or Argentina, or even New England, because he had not found them, yet from a Geologist point of view, the whole of the New World became accessible on October 12, 1492.

In a way, the decline in exploration success over the past three decades is inevitable, and there is some truth in what the Geologists say. Usually (but not always), the largest fields in a basin are among the first to be found. We are unlikely to find another province as prolific as that narrow zone centred on the Persian Gulf. Even the vast discoveries of the past thirty years, in the North Sea, the Gulf of Mexico, and the Caspian, do not match up to Ghawar, Burgan (Kuwait), and the North Field. In any geological province, there are a small number of large fields and a much larger number of small fields. This "log normal" distribution is typical for oil fields: there will be just one, or very few, fields in a basin where everything goes right, a large structure with good reservoir qualities. There will be many more where good reservoir is found in a very small structure or where a large prospect is mostly filled with nonreservoir rock.

One area of controversy in exploration, which extends to the peak oil issue, is whether a significant amount of reserves are to be found in small fields. In Saudi Arabia, for instance, Ghawar holds 50 percent of the ultimate recoverable oil, whereas in Norway, the largest field contains 18 percent of the total volumes, the largest seven hold 50 percent of the total, and 80 percent of the reserves are accounted for by 20 percent of the fields (an example of the famous 80:20 rule). Even finding another 1,000 fields of 1 million barrels of oil equivalent (boe[71]) each would not change this statistic very much. However, the scarcity of small fields is an economic phenomenon, not a geological one. The industry has not tried to drill prospects of less than 1 million boe, and, if some were found by accident, their volumes have not been calculated or reported. Seventy-three discoveries in Norway are currently categorized as "development not very likely," hence not qualifying as reserves, and we can expect that most of these are in the smallest size classes. In an environment in which fields of 1 million boe are economic, like the onshore United States, we expect (and find) a large number of discoveries in this category.

Because of this concentration of reserves in a few large fields, exploration in a given end tends to follow a "creaming curve" (because the largest discoveries are, roughly speaking, "creamed off" first, being easier to hit, even if drilling without much geological understanding). The rate of discovery (in terms of reserves found, plotted against time, number of wells, or a similar metric) tends to fall off. Number of wells or a similar measure of effort is better than time, because extended periods with little activity (as in many OPEC countries during the 1980s) show up as false asymptotes.[72] Figure 4.7 shows the creaming curve for Norway, plotted against cumulative number of "wildcat"[73] exploration wells drilled, with an exponential curve fitted.

It can be seen that the curve flattens out as each successive well finds less oil, on average, because the largest prospects are drilled first. Even if the prospects were drilled randomly, we would still expect to see a creaming curve, although less pronounced, because hitting a big field is more likcly than hitting a small one (like the game Battleships). The average

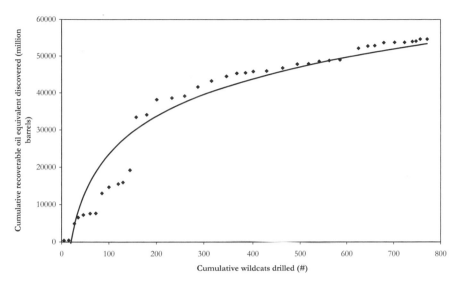

Figure 4.7
Creaming curve for Norway.

success rate may or may not trend downward with time, but the creaming curve mostly develops because the size of new discoveries is falling.

This diminishing trend seems to imply that, because the curve is often used by both by professional explorationists and peak oil scholars, it can be used to find the ultimate volumes to be discovered in the province. The ultimate in this case might appear to be about 54 billion boe.

However, there are some notable jumps. This happens particularly in the early years, when perhaps the geology is not well understood and new areas are being opened up, and so there is the chance for some unexpectedly large finds. Even late in the game, however, around well 600, is a significant increment. This is attributable mainly to two discoveries in a different setting from the early North Sea fields, which make up most of the first part of the curve: Ormen Lange in the deepwater Norwegian Sea, and Kristin in a difficult, high-pressure, high-temperature setting. That is the first weakness of the creaming curve: it is purely an extrapolation of the past and makes no allowance for new plays or the opening up of new areas through regulatory action or technology.

Second, as Figure 4.8 shows, the creaming curve evolves as time goes on. There appeared to be an asymptote, around the seventieth well, and an exploration geologist might have concluded at this point that Norway was already played out, with an ultimate of some 16 billion boe (curve 1) to be reached by drilling 800 or so wells, immediately before finding the 4.3 billion boe Statfjord field. Similarly, after about 150 wells, the 10 billion boe Troll gas field was discovered, after a period when the creaming curve

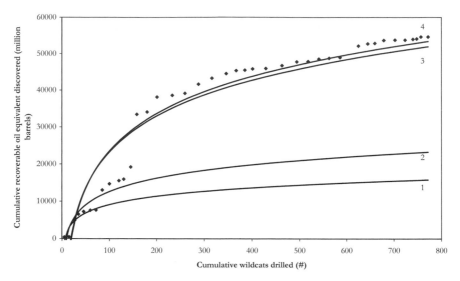

Figure 4.8
Different possible creaming curves for Norway.

seemed to be flattening out at about 23 billion boe (curve 2). Even recently, Kristin and Ormen Lange lifted the curve noticeably (from curve 3 to curve 4), and it would be foolish to be confident these will be the last big discoveries.

Finally, the late flattening of the curve is partly an artifact of reporting. The last few years show very few discoveries, but this is to some extent because data on those wells has not been released and because more appraisal drilling is required to confirm volumes. For instance, of the last ten discoveries in Norway, in the period 2005–2006, only five have had official data released. Shell's Onyx SW discovery, in early 2005, is reported unofficially at about 2 Tcf, but the official number (included here) is only 1 Tcf. The earlier wells also benefit from the reserves growth phenomenon; all kinds of improved oil recovery (IOR) initiatives are included here on these old fields that have been producing now for a long time, whereas the reserve figures for recent discoveries probably include only "plain vanilla" development plans.

Therefore, creaming curves are a poor predictor of the future. There is always the chance of a new play, a new exploration concept, or a technological advance that opens up a new part of a known basin or country, while reserves growth and new developments are continually lifting the end of the curve. Azadegan and Yadavaran are examples of two of the largest fields in Iran, found very recently (2000 and 2004, respectively) and long after the last Iranian discovery of a comparable size (Marun in 1963). Buzzard in the United Kingdom is another big find, made in a very mature area. Buzzard could have been drilled at any time in the past thirty years, but it took some innovative geological thinking to detect it. Fields are not found mechanically in order from largest to smallest; luck and new ideas play a part.

In addition, if the Geologists are removing the OPEC and other reserves that they regard as fraudulent or at least suspicious, then both their back-dated curves and the creaming plots they use to predict future finds will understate actual discovery. This will translate into lower predictions for the yet-to-find (YtF), hence piling conservatism on conservatism.

Despite the general trend to find the larger fields first, there are strong reasons to believe that the fall-off in exploration success, although real, is highly misleading and only weakly indicative of the future. The most promising exploration areas in the world have little activity; what exploration there was has been performed by NOCs, often risk averse and not always highly competent.

Of major resource-holding countries, Iraq had almost no exploration between 1961 and the late 1970s and then virtually none again from the early 1980s to the present. Iran was virtually unexplored from 1979 until very recently, and even now the level of activity is low and not efficiently directed. Saudi Arabia has had a fairly modest campaign. Abu Dhabi has performed some token exploration, usually one well per year onshore and one offshore. In the Middle East, only the peripheral countries, Oman, Yemen, and Syria, have had reasonably intense efforts, and, even here, Oman has been reliant until the past two years or so on its Shell-dominated national company Petroleum Development Oman (PDO) and has not had the risk-taking attitude and fresh ideas that new entrants can bring. Libya has only recently issued a large number of new permits that have not yet had time to bear fruit. Russia has also barely performed any exploration since the end of the Soviet Union, and the legal status of licenses has made exploration of any but the lowest-risk targets highly unappealing. Indonesia's tough fiscal terms, unclear regulatory authority, and political instability have also discouraged many entrants, as has been the case in Venezuela. In Venezuela, Kuwait, and Mexico, dominant or monopoly state companies have had very little or no access to the innovative approaches of the international industry.

Just how effective bringing in the private sector can be has been shown by India, where, for years, the "national champions" Oil and Natural Gas Corporation (ONGC) and Oil India found very little. They were typical state bureaucracies. No one with ability or connections wanted to go to remote Rajasthan. There is a story that, one time the Oil Minister was visiting a well site in Rajasthan and the crew poured diesel on to the drilling mud to make it appear that they had struck oil, about as close as the Minister ever came to a real discovery. Once the new exploration licensing policy was launched in the late 1990s to attract new entrants, there was a wave of success, notably Cairn in Rajasthan and Reliance and others in the eastern offshore. Brazil, whose offshore geology was not considered promising by many,[74] is one shining counterexample in which the NOC Petrobras has, through sensible incentives, become bold and capable. If the startling discoveries made in recent years in the Indian and Brazilian deepwater basins, which did not seem highly prospective, are considered, what more could be achieved in OPEC countries who had tremendous exploration records until the 1970s nationalizations?

Even in countries hospitable to the international oil business, such as the United States and Norway, certain areas, namely the Arctic National Wildlife Refuge (ANWR),[75] the eastern Gulf of Mexico, virtually the entire eastern and western offshore, and many onshore areas in the Rockies and elsewhere in the United States, parts of the Barents Sea and the highly promising Nordland area in the Norwegian Sea, in Norway, have been off-limits for environmental reasons. For instance, as much as 40 billion bbl may be present in those parts of the U.S. offshore not open for drilling.[76]

So, from 1973 or so onward, no one was looking for oil in the most promising parts of the world. The international companies were forced into less favorable areas, although they still did remarkably well. Given this, is it surprising that the discovery rate has dropped off so dramatically?

The discovery rate, in billions of barrels per year, is shown against time in Figure 4.8. A major low in discovery is associated with the Iranian nationalization of 1951–1954, after which the Middle East entered its golden era of discovery. The peak was reached around 1970, with about 55 billion bbl found, shortly after Iraq virtually halted exploration. From this point on, world discoveries fell off sharply and ran at a plateau of about 35 billion bbl/year during the 1970s. During this period, the major OPEC countries all nationalized their industries, and, from 1973 onward, OPEC and the Organization of Arab Petroleum Exporting Countries[77] made efforts to raise prices and reduce production. In this climate, investment in exploration dried up, nor was there much need for it in an environment of depressed demand.

From 1980 onward, with the completion of the nationalizations and the outbreak of the Iran–Iraq war, which put both countries off-limits, discoveries fell sharply. The key countries of the Middle East are still a vastly underexplored region: the drilling density in Saudi Arabia is about 0.05 wells/km^2 of prospective area, whereas the United States in 1970, when output famously began to decline, had reached 3.5 wells/km^2. An additional slump in discoveries occurred when the Soviet Union broke up and its intensive exploration effort virtually ceased. A global low of some 10 billion bbl was reached in a climate of depressed prices, around 1994. However, now that prices have risen, discoveries have rebounded to the

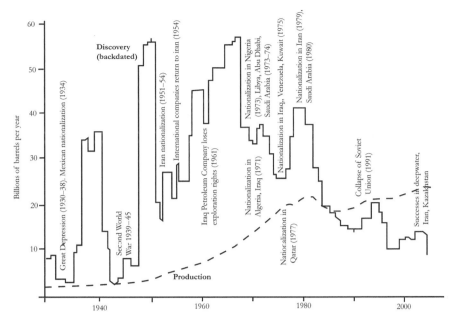

Figure 4.9
Backdated oil discovery and key geopolitical events.

level of the 1980s recently, with the pick up in prices starting after 1998, led particularly by spectacular successes in deepwater (Nigeria, Angola, Gulf of Mexico, and Brazil) and partly also reflecting a limited return to exploration by both IOCs and national/indigenous companies in the FSU outside Russia (e.g., Kashagan in Kazakhstan and Shah Deniz in Azerbaijan) and Iran (Azadegan and Yadavaran). One study suggests that, with thirty-three giant new oil fields and thirty-six new giant gas fields discovered in the period 2000–2006, the "Noughties" could turn out to be the third best discovery decade in history.[78, 79]

Even now, many of the world's most promising areas are off-limits (Figure 4.10).[80]

In some, there is no exploration at all, often for environmental (U.S. offshore, ANWR, and Norway) or political (South China Sea and South Caspian) reasons. In many others, the local NOC (e.g., Pemex in Mexico, Aramco in Saudi Arabia, NIOC in Iran) has to do most or all of the job itself, often with limited funding, technology, expertise, and incentives. In yet another group, exploration can go on but is highly disincentivized by a lack of certainty that discoveries can be developed (e.g., Russia and Iran) and that terms will not be changed retroactively (e.g., Russia and Venezuela) or the fields nationalized (e.g., Bolivia). In most of the OPEC countries, the desire to explore has been weakened by the need to adhere, at

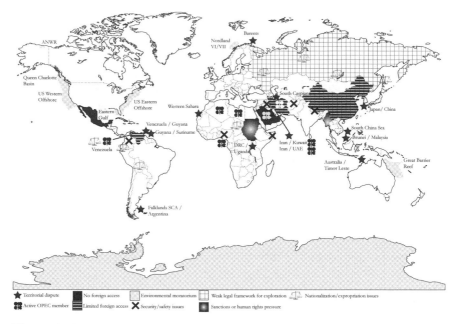

Figure 4.10
Significant global exploration provinces with restricted or no international oil company access.

least notionally, to quotas rather than maximizing production. Even in OPEC countries such as Nigeria, which allow significant foreign participation, the quota issue and funding problems have restrained the pace of activity, at least until the past couple of years. Laherrère states that the first 1,920 exploration wells in the Middle East, up to the year 1980, found 723 billion bbl (377 million bbl per well), but that the following 1,760 discovered just 32 billion (only 18 million bbl per well) and argues, "This ... shows clearly that the belief by some economists that the Middle East has a great potential left is wrong."[81] What he omits to mention, but what this sudden swing from plenty to famine should alert us to, is that the pre-1980 drilling was primarily in the great provinces of Saudi Arabia, Kuwait, Abu Dhabi, Iran, and Iraq, whereas later campaigns concentrated on the second-tier Middle Eastern producers of Oman, Yemen, and Syria, which drilled a considerable number of wells targeted at rather modest potential, hence completely distorting the statistics. Not all Middle Eastern wells are equal.

If the most promising areas of the world had been open for exploration from 1973 onward, would discoveries have continued at the high rate of the 1960s? Exploration was so intense during the 1960s because demand was rising at some 7 percent per year, and it so it appeared that there

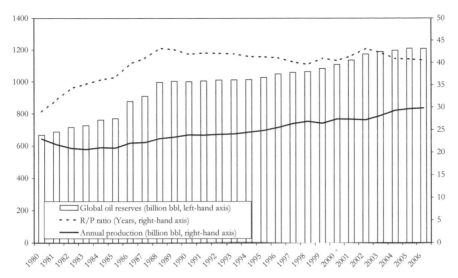

Figure 4.11
Global reserves, production, and R/P ratio, 1980–2005.

would be an imminent need for large new volumes of Middle Eastern oil. When demand actually fell during periods of the 1970s and early 1980s, this rationale evaporated. Figure 4.11 shows the global R/P[82] ratio between 1980 and 2005. Even before OPEC's reserve hikes, the global R/P ratio was 29 in 1980, and, because of falling global production, rose to 35 in 1983, the last year before the sudden jumps in OPEC reserves. Most IOCs have R/P ratios in the range of 11–13; even the FSU, with a large backlog of underdeveloped and undeveloped fields, stands at 28. The high world R/P ratios of this period suggest a world in which *too much* oil had been discovered. It is inefficient to find oil a long time before it is required. The discovered reserves in 1980 (even before the OPEC revisions) could have sustained the actual global level of production at a reasonable depletion rate until about 1995, with no reserve additions or exploration at all! If the Middle East and (former) Soviet Union had continued high levels of exploration and development from 1973 but global production had followed the depressed trend it actually did, then the result would have been to accumulate an enormous stock of undeveloped discoveries. In this case, we would probably even now not have moved seriously on to the North Sea, Alaska, and other remote regions.

This excess of discovered reserves led to low prices and a collapse in exploration. Some 11,000 wildcats were drilled in 1980 but only 2,500 in 2005.[83] With this fall-off of activity, it is hardly surprising that relatively little oil was found. What drilling there was focused mainly on small fields near infrastructure, which could be developed quickly and cheaply. When the oil price situation was transformed in the early 2000s, just as for development, it was hard for the industry to gear up to an intensive new exploration campaign. The prolonged slump had led to a loss of top explorationists, who retired or moved into production, nor were there enough rigs (which were in heavy demand to drill production wells) or seismic vessels. Exploration is an even more prolonged affair than development, particularly in frontier settings where the companies hope for large new finds, because it takes some five to ten years to develop a new play concept, sign up the acreage, conduct initial studies, shoot seismic, and drill wells.

Reserves replacement is now taking place much more by additions in known fields rather than by new exploration. Explorers in the 1960s and 1970s did not know that future reserve additions in their discoveries were going to be backdated to their era. They had the impression of finding less oil than they actually had. Far more oil was found than the world needed at the time, but that only became apparent in hindsight because of future reserves growth and extensions. In 1979, Jimmy Carter said, "Oil wells are running dry all over the world," yet according to the backdated curve, exploration success had outstripped production in that year and in every year before.

Reserves growth continued during the 1980s and 1990s. In the period 1995–2005,[84] exploration discovered 144 billion bbl of oil, whereas 236 billion bbl were produced, at first glance a worrying situation. However, 457 billion bbl were added through field growth[85]; thus, reserves were going up, not down.[86] Small or marginal fields, which were not even economic when discovered, are now entering production because of improved technology and infrastructure and higher prices. If the golden age of exploration was from about 1950 to 1970, so the golden age of commercialization may be today, particularly for gas (and associated NGL[87] streams).

For example, of giant fields entering production recently, the oil fields in the Sakhalin-1 and -2 projects were discovered in the 1970s, Shaybah in Saudi Arabia in 1975, Clair in the United Kingdom in 1977, and the North Field (Qatar), with its enormous condensate volumes, in 1971. The United Kingdom has between 0.5 billion and 3 billion bbl technically recoverable in currently noncommercial fields.[88] When peak oil supporters dismiss reserves growth entirely and ascribe the United Kingdom only 0.8 billion bbl YtF,[89] they make these 0.5–3 billion bbl disappear entirely, as though they will never be developed; history tells us the opposite. Of twenty-three reported oil finds around the world in 2005,[90] only eleven had any reserves data at all given, and in just one case did this refer unambiguously and accurately to the field discovered. Even in this instance, there was a wide range of uncertainty. This gives the impression that much less oil was found in 2005 than, with the benefit of hindsight, we will know in say, 2010.

Inevitably, the proportion of reserves added by revisions and increased recovery will grow over time, because the discovered resource base to which they apply has increased. Because adding reserves through improved recovery is almost always less expensive and less risky than through exploration, companies will prefer this method as long as it can replace their reserves and sustain growing production. Future technologies, such as geochemical "sniffers," electromagnetic surveys, wide-angle seismic to see beneath difficult rock formations such as salt and basalt,[91] and low-cost "finder" wells, are unlikely radically to transform exploration but will make a larger contribution than depletion advocates believe. They will mop up the long tail of small fields in well-known areas and can help in finding oil in frontier areas such as the Arctic or the Falklands, nonconventional traps,[92] deep targets, and those in areas of complex geology. There may be very considerable potential on the ultradeep Gulf of Mexico shelf, beneath basalt in the Green River Basin in Colorado, the Færoes in northwest Europe, the Deccan in India, and the East Siberian Traps, whereas salt overburden is a key issue in many promising areas, particularly the deepwater Gulf of Mexico, West Africa, the northern Caspian, Brazil, and parts of the Middle East. Technology tested in the Rockies of the United States and Canada, and the Colombian Andes could be enormously successful in the Zagros of Iran and Iraq, where even two-dimensional seismic data has hardly been shot.

Surveys of Global Exploration Potential

The most comprehensive analysis of world exploration potential has been made by the USGS. Inevitably, its estimates are highly uncertain—trying to estimate what, by definition, is not known—and have been heavily criticized by peak oil commentators, who see it as highly optimistic, perhaps even politically biased.[93] However, we should remember that the USGS is staffed by professional geologists (*sensu stricto*, as opposed to Geologists). They have examined the geology of each actual or potential petroleum basin around the world rather than, like most of the oil depletion camp, relying on intuition[94] or extrapolations of historic exploration success. Extrapolating past records is highly questionable, because many areas of the world have not been explored at all or have been explored inefficiently, under unfavorable commercial terms or with obsolete technology. By definition, relying on the past misses new basins, such as, in the last few years, Mauritania, Rajasthan, and Uganda. It also inevitably excludes new plays, such as the Euphrates Graben in Syria; by the early 1980s, most observers would probably have considered Syria to have been pretty thoroughly explored, and yet the biggest discoveries were yet to come. Trends that are unlocked by technology, such as deepwater extensions to shallow-water plays, subsalt or deep fields, or smaller or more complex structures that require three-dimensional seismic[95] and so were overlooked before the 1990s, will all not show up on creaming curve methods.

Above all, mere extrapolation, although extolled by Laherrère as the only true way to look at exploration potential, utterly misses the economic and political context. We do not explore in a vacuum. Until recent activity in Kurdistan, no one has looked seriously for oil in Iraq for at least twenty-five years, so to ascribe the country a mere 7 billion bbl of remaining potential[96] on the grounds that not much has been found there recently is completely erroneous. To do as the USGS does and to say that, *geologically speaking*, there are some 43 billion bbl there to be found is far more reasonable; we can then make a judgment as to whether above-ground conditions will be right for this oil to be unearthed.

Another good feature of the USGS reports is that it acknowledges the inherent uncertainty in its work instead of giving point estimates as most peak oilers do. To achieve this, it quotes statistical probabilities, giving low, mid, and high estimates[97] by mathematically combining a wide range of uncertainty on each parameter that determines resources, for example, the area and thickness of key reservoirs, the effectiveness of seal[98] and source rock,[99] and so on. If we add, say the low cases for Saudi Arabia, Iran, Russia, Venezuela, and Nigeria, we will end up with a small number, which represents the extremely unlikely scenario (actually only a 0.0003 percent chance) that exploration in all of these disparate areas is similarly disappointing.

The USGS can be accused of overoptimism in certain areas, particularly in specific cases in which the industry may be in possession of proprietary well or seismic data that downgrades prospectivity. For example, assigning a midcase potential of 850 million bbl to Bahrain seems too high given the tiny extent of its territory, the persistent failure of recent exploration, and the fact that the main remaining play, the Palaeozoic, is regionally almost universally gas bearing. It is always easy to adduce specific examples in which one might feel that an estimate of exploration potential is too high (or too low). On the whole, however, the accusation of excessively high estimates seems incorrect.

The approach of trying to estimate the potential of undrilled areas is naturally fraught with uncertainty. For instance, take Greenland. No commercial oil or gas has ever been discovered there, yet, as discussed in Chapter 5, the country has all the attributes of a major hydrocarbon province. Because of its remoteness, harsh climate, and environmental sensitivity, this vast island has also been only very lightly explored.

Given these facts, what volumetric potential should we assign to Greenland? The USGS says that there is a 30 percent chance that nothing will be found, but there is a 50 percent chance that ultimate volumes will be at least 50 billion bbl of oil. This could place Greenland above Kazakhstan,

Libya, or Nigeria. Furthermore, the USGS has only assessed eastern Greenland; western Greenland has also seen a few wells and is now attracting considerable industry attention.[100] Suriname, for which the USGS has a midcase of 12 billion bbl, is a similar case: a minor producer now[101] but with a geological setting appropriate for major finds, as mentioned in Chapter 5.

Such volumes are considerably greater than that expected by peak oil supporters. For example, Campbell allows only 20 billion bbl of "unforeseen" discoveries in the whole world, a category that would include Greenland, Suriname, and any other countries that are not in his list (those who are not significant producers today).

For all the accusations of USGS overoptimism, it, too, is vulnerable to being conservative, just by the nature of its geologically based approach. Any area that has undergone little exploration tends to get low or zero reserves assigned. For instance, the disputed territory of Western Sahara, currently trying to achieve independence from Morocco as the Saharawi Arab Democratic Republic, lies just north of Mauritania, where there have been at least two substantial oil finds, yet the high estimate for Western Sahara is just 39 million bbl, less than half of Mauritania's smaller field. The USGS's high value for Cambodia is 279 million bbl of oil (its report was published in 2000), and yet the U.S. major Chevron has, during 2005, already discovered 400–500 million bbl and estimates that total reserves could ultimately reach 2 billion bbl.[102] Vietnam, with a high case of 90 million bbl, has found several hundred million barrels during 2006–2007. To take one of the key Middle Eastern provinces, just two discoveries in Iran, Azadegan and Yadavaran, made shortly after completion of the USGS work, contain about two-thirds of all the oil predicted to be found in the country's largest single play.[103]

Furthermore, a number of countries and regions with some potential are not even covered, some with existing discoveries and production, for instance U.K. West of Shetland/Færoes, Ireland, the Murzuq Basin of Libya, the Melut Basin (Sudan), the east coast of India, Chad, Uganda, and Tanzania and others that appear geologically promising, such as the offshore eastern Mediterranean, offshore British Columbia (Canada), Sri Lanka, and Madagascar.

Comparing the most comprehensive peak oiler estimate of future exploration potential, Campbell's figures[104] with the USGS figures are very instructive. Campbell should be commended for presenting this very comprehensive set of figures, which, in contrast to, say, Simmons, make his theory testable. The purpose of the following discussion is not to attack him but instead to show the general pessimism of peak oil YtF estimates.

Some sensible back-calculations have to be made for categories whose YtF Campbell does not specify: heavy oil (less than 17.5 degrees American

Petroleum Institute [API] gravity[105]), deepwater (more than 500 meters), polar oil, and NGLs.[106] With this caveat, it is possible to compare the two sets of estimates. Campbell predicts a global YtF of approximately 180 billion bbl (adding back his implied deepwater and polar oil), much lower than the USGS's 400/690/1211 billion bbl (low/mid/high). The USGS estimates are pushed upward by the large volumes it ascribes to Greenland and Suriname, yet even if we remove these two countries, the USGS totals are well above Campbell, even in the low case. He is below the USGS's low estimate in thirty-four countries, between the low and middle in seventeen cases, and above its midcase in only seven instances,[107] and, on a regional basis, he is below the USGS's low estimate everywhere except Europe (where he is slightly higher than the low case). For the vast majority of countries, there is less than a 5 percent chance of his being correct, if the USGS's probability assessment is right (or, looked at the other way, there is less than a 5 percent chance of the USGS being correct if Campbell's number is right). His global total is less than half of the USGS's low estimate.

It also appears that Campbell is not allowing for any future NGL discoveries compared with the USGS's low estimate of 95 billion bbl. It seems remarkable to forecast *no* future discoveries and, in fact to go beyond this, to imply only a fraction of today's NGLs will be produced in the next fifty years or so in the face of a purported global hydrocarbon supply crisis. In fact, most of the world has barely begun a systematic search for gas and its associated NGLs, while stranded gas, discovered but too remote from markets for immediate development, is abundant.

A third major area of conservatism in Campbell's figures concerns deepwater. His implied YtF for other deepwater areas (outside the "golden triangle" of the U.S. Gulf of Mexico, Brazil, and Angola/Nigeria) is only about 6 billion bbl, which seems ridiculously low when we consider the following: that Mexico has claim to a large part of the Gulf of Mexico, which should be comparably rich to the U.S. side; that already Congo is a major deepwater province, and other West African nations, such as Equatorial Guinea, Mauritania, São Tomé and Príncipe, Ghana, and Côte d'Ivoire are exploring and developing deepwater fields; that major deepwater discoveries have been made in India, Indonesia, Brunei, and Malaysia; and that other areas, such as the northwest European margin, Libya, eastern Canada, Australia, East Africa, the south Caspian, and Suriname are undergoing deepwater exploration.

This conservatism shows up in major revisions, nearly always upward, in Campbell's ultimate recovery estimates by country between 1997 and 2002. Saudi Arabia, Kuwait, and Iran are up by some 5 percent, Iraq boosted by nearly 20 percent, Mexico and Norway increased by 25 percent, and Algeria, and Qatar by about 30 percent. Confirming my point about surprises, Vietnam and Thailand have gone up 100 percent and Bolivia 70 percent. There is one major downgrade, Brazil decreasing by 40 percent, and the FSU is slightly reduced, but the overall trend is sharply upward. What is to say that the next edition won't show similar upward adjustments?

We can compare both USGS and Campbell's estimates with some other studies, in Table 4.3.

For all these areas except Kuwait, Campbell's estimates are not only below those of the USGS's midcase but also much lower than other independent studies, often vastly so. These independent studies are, in most cases, close to the USGS's midcase. A simple sum of the *lowest* other estimates for each of these countries is still some 10 percent *higher* than the USGS's median and more than four times Campbell's figure. This contradicts claims that the USGS is uniquely optimistic or politically biased. In each of the United Kingdom, Indonesia, and China, a single recent discovery has contained more than half Campbell's prognosed remaining, which is statistically very unlikely (in China's case, this discovery contained 80 percent of his prophesied YtF), whereas in Brazil, Campbell appears to foresee about 3 billion bbl of future deepwater discoveries.[108] However Tupi alone, announced in November 2007, holds 5–8 billion bbl while the Carioca-Sugarloaf find of April 2007 is reported at an astonishing 25–40 billion bbl, suggesting that the USGS's total of about 23 billion bbl for the Santos Basin is feasible or even conservative.[109]

As a reality check, in 2005, the USGS compared their own 2000 assessment against real-world results.[110] The 2000 report covered discoveries expected to be made up to 2025, so 27 percent of its timespan had passed (the study used data current up to 1995, and the authors looked at actual discoveries from January 1996 to December 2003). They found that prognosed additions from reserves growth were right on track. However, exploration success was running at about 40 percent of the forecast rate over the period.[111] The USGS, though, chose perhaps the worst time to test its findings, because the 1998 oil price crash all but dried up exploration, and, once the prospect pipeline is emptied, it takes years to refill.

The results of this USGS review make the point that reserves growth (which the peak oil theorists completely discount, as is discussed in the next section) will be more important in the future than exploration. Peak oil supporters make much of the low finding rate and claim that it discredits the USGS numbers. However, the USGS study was never intended as a prediction. It shows what oil and gas is technically out there to be found; how much is actually discovered depends on how hard, how effectively, and where the industry looks. Nevertheless, the discovery (excluding reserves growth) of about 69 billion bbl is still nearly half Campbell's total YtF, in just eight years; the peak oilers lambast the USGS for allegedly

Table 4.3
Comparison of exploration potential estimates for selected countries.

Country	Estimates of future yet-to-find (billion barrels)		
	United States Geological Survey (low/mid/high)	Campbell[1]	Other
All deepwater		29.3	114[2]
China	3.3/11.0/24.6	2.8	44[3]
Iraq	14.2/42.7/83.9	7.1	21[4]
			51[5]
			12–45[6, 7]
			100[8, 9]
Iran	16.3/49.8/100.5	12.2	67
Kuwait	1.2/3.6/7.2	5.7	4
Libya	2.9/7.4/15.3	4.6	17–35[10, 11]
Nigeria	16.1/37.1/60.7	7.9[12]	~28[13]
Norway	3.4/11.6/26.3	1.0	7.3[14]
			9.4[15]
Peru	1.0/3.0/6.4	0.3	3.1[16]
Russia	25.0/71.6/148.1	23.9	95
			43[17]
Saudi Arabia	29.4/82.2/160.9	17.1	136
United Arab Emirates	2.2/7.0/15.5	5.5	10, 17[18]
United Kingdom	2/5.8/12.4	0.8	0.5–1.8–5.8[19]
			2.0–5.1[20]
			5.3[21]
			4.0[22]
			3.9[23]
			2.6–5.6–11.9[24]
			13.4[25]
U.S. Gulf of Mexico deepwater		15.8	40[26]
Total of selected countries	333 (mid)	89	363–544

[1]Campbell (2006). Some deepwater estimates implied by his production figures.
[2]Wood MacKenzie and Fugro Robertson.
[3]Strecker Downs (2000).
[4]Sum of prospects identified by the Iraqi Petroleum Company (Western consortium), multiplied by average success factor.
[5]Iraq, Iran, Saudi Arabia, UAE, Kuwait, and first estimate for Russia from Fraser and Harper (2005).
[6]Iraqi Kurdistan only. It is not clear whether it includes existing discovered reserves and whether Kirkuk is included. This would reduce the figures by some 10 billion bbl, i.e., to 2–35 billion bbl.
[7]Wood MacKenzie, quoted at http://business.timesonline.co.uk/tol/business/industry_sectors/natural_resources/article1555773.ece.

(continued)

Table 4.3. (*continued*)

[8]Western Desert only.

[9]IHS Energy (2007), quoted at *Oil & Gas Journal*, vol. 105, issue 15, April 16, 2007.

[10]The estimate is given in terms of oil in place. An assumed 40% recovery factor is used here to get to reserves. It is not clear whether the estimate also includes gas. Hence the figure of 17 billion bbl of oil assumes 50% of the potential is gas; the 35 billion bbl number assumes that the quoted figures are for oil only.

[11]IHS Energy, in Arab Oil and Gas Directory (2005), Arab Petroleum Research Centre.

[12]Sum of onshore/shallow water potential and estimated deepwater potential from Campbell's production profile, assuming that the 6 billion bbl of deductions in his file relate entirely to deepwater potential (Nigeria having no polar oil, naturally, and insignificant heavy oil reserves as yet).

[13]Total, in Afren (2006).

[14]Norwegian Petroleum Directorate (2005).

[15]Nyland (2006).

[16]Ghazi (2006).

[17]Leonard (2005).

[18]Suwaina *et al.* (2005).

[19]HM Treasury Exploration Steering Group (June 2003), top-down industry survey, minimum-average-maximum technical reserves. The original numbers were in boe, and I have taken 56% to be oil (in line with the U.K. 2005 reserve split).

[20]Webb, M. (November 2005), UK Offshore Operators' Association, assuming 56% to be oil as above.

[21]Department of Trade and Industry (DTI) estimate calculated for PILOT (2003), assuming 56% to be oil as in endnote 128, above. EAG/25.

[22]DTI estimate calculated using Monte Carlo methods (2003), assuming 56% to be oil as in endnote 128, above. EAG/25.

[23]Bottom-up industry estimate quoted by the DTI (2003), assuming 56% to be oil as above. EAG/25.

[24]DTI (2006), http://www.og.dti.gov.uk/information/bb_updates/chapters/Table4_6.htm.

[25]Hannon, J., Hannon Westwood (November 7, 2007), quoted at http://www.upstream online.com/live/article143726.ece. Assuming 56% to be oil as mentioned above. Includes undeveloped discoveries.

[26]http://www.iht.com/articles/2006/11/08/business/oil.php

---

failing to match reality, but their own estimates are at least as far off, in the other direction.

As has been argued, the failure to find the reserves the USGS predicted in 2000 is attributable to a mix of factors: primarily low oil prices and activity levels, and restrictions on exploration in the best areas. Given that the best places to look for oil in the world were, to a large extent, off-limits during 1996–2003, then I would say that the USGS's prediction was largely borne out. Less oil was found than was technically possible, because the new oil is where the USGS says it is: behind borders. Of the 856 billion bbl of YtF oil and NGLs (outside the United States), the USGS study foresaw in 2000 that some 367 billion bbl is located in countries that saw severe or complete restrictions on exploration during the subsequent period; at least another 72 billion in areas where exploration was economically unattractive as a result of the prevailing climate of low prices (frontier basins such as Greenland, Suriname, and the Falklands).

Indeed, of the relatively few giant oil discoveries made by the end of 2004,[112] none were made in closed areas such as Maracaibo (Venezuela), Iraq, most of Arabia, or West Siberia, and few (Azadegan and Yadavaran) in Iran. No significant exploration took place in the important USGS regions of Greenland, Suriname, and the Mexican Gulf of Mexico. However, established provinces such as the North Sea, Brunei, and Bohai Bay (China) saw more giant discoveries in this short period than were forecast to remain in entirety, as did some frontier basins not covered by the USGS: Melut (Sudan) and Murzuq (Libya). Deepwater West Africa and Brazil were also highly successful. Figure 4.12 demonstrates that exploration drilling in the past decade has been concentrated in provinces that are geologically the least promising.[113]

Therefore, for me, the USGS estimates are certainly not disproved by results to date. It is difficult to make a conclusive judgment one way or the other, until significant wildcat drilling, by international companies or competent national oil companies, takes place in the core areas of the Middle East and West Siberia and until some promising frontiers are properly tested. I feel justified in concluding that, in regions where we have other calibration, although the USGS may be somewhat optimistic, most peak oil estimates are wildly pessimistic.

In conclusion, I should make it clear that I think it very unlikely that another Middle East is out there to be found, in one place. However, the

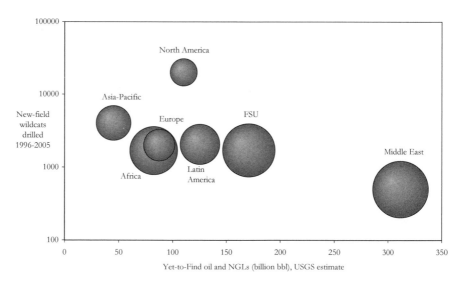

Figure 4.12
Exploration effort and success, 1996–2005 (bubble size represents average reserves per new discovery).

dramatic fall-off in discoveries from the early 1970s onward cannot be interpreted just in terms of running out of oil. There is certainly the potential for new "North Seas" or smaller provinces that add up to a significant contribution to global supply, but this will require returning the level of activity to something like that of the early 1980s. This is why the peak oilers so badly underestimate exploration potential: because they are extrapolating recent discovery rates, achieved in the context of (until 2001 or so) a global oversupply of oil and low activity levels rather than considering what is geologically possible if the oil business has good reasons to explore more. Actually to find the USGS volumes within a reasonable timeframe, will require the industry to restore annual finding rates from some 10 billion bbl to at least 30 billion bbl. This will take a major intensification of activity in the most promising areas, probably with more access to IOCs and the most capable NOCs as well as solving some of the bottlenecks in personnel, rigs, and other resources.

Such a level of exploration will be challenging to achieve: the global rig count peaked at more than 6,000 in 1981, since when it plummeted to about 2,000 in 1986, fell further to barely 1,000 in 1999, and has subsequently limped up to a little more than 2,000.[114] Assuming productivity per rig is the same now as in 1980 (actually, productivity has increased greatly, but the exploration targets today are generally trickier and smaller, and many of these rigs are now drilling for gas rather than oil), we would need to return to 1981 rig levels to boost finding rates from 10 to 30 billion bbl per year. To take Norway, for instance, the 2004 finding rate was about 100 million bbl of oil per year, from eight wildcats. At that rate, it will take about ten years to find Campbell's estimate of Norway's exploration potential but more than a century to unearth the USGS's midcase volumes. However, returning to the activity level of 1997, when thirty-nine wildcats were drilled, would suggest that we might turn up Norway's USGS volumes in a reasonable period of about twenty years.

Not only do we have to put more physical assets to work, we also need to rebuild the human capital. We will need drilling engineers to direct the rigs and geologists to generate prospects for them. The lead time to train even a junior engineer or geologist is at least three to four years or seven to eight years when considering the need for a critical mass of university students choosing the appropriate courses. Giving some reason for optimism, though, the global talent pool has widened enormously in recent years, and there is great opportunity to shift the demographic of the oil industry toward staff from the FSU, the Middle East, India and China, Brazil, and increasingly Africa. The local operating units of the international operating companies in countries such as Nigeria and Angola are now dominated by local staff. To citizens of these countries, a petroleum career does not have the bad reputation (deserved and undeserved) that it has in the West, although this might surprise readers of horror stories about multinationals' activities in West Africa, in particular. Salaries are very good, there is the chance for training and development (often including support for university education, mostly in the West but hopefully, in the future, more in Africa itself), and the strong domestic industry in such places provides an ideal training ground.

The existing mature areas need to realize their full potential. In the North Sea, for instance, a wave of small, mainly AIM[115]-listed, companies are introducing new concepts and establishing new plays or drilling up smaller targets in known fairways. Unfortunately, these companies are mostly too tiny and underfunded to carry out a really intensive campaign, whereas the super-majors are not interested in small prospects but nevertheless tend to sit on fallow acreage rather than allowing it to be recycled. A phase of industry consolidation may, as has happened in the United States, create some "super-independents," who have similar financial strength and risk capacity to the majors but the low cost base and interest in marginal or small fields of the minnows. Although individually these fields may not be large, cumulatively their supply can be important, as in the United States and western Canada.

As for significant new areas, the time has come for a renewed wave of exploration and for the industry to make an attempt to open up some genuinely new basins, probably in untouched deepwater areas, interior Africa, and the Arctic. If politics permit, most significantly, there is the opportunity for a renaissance in exploration in Russia, Mexico, and the main OPEC countries, in which modern technology and concepts would be applied. This would probably best be done by major IOCs, within a reasonable commercial framework. However, Petronas in Malaysia and Petrobras in Brazil have shown that a well-run NOC, with incentives and at least a modicum of foreign competition to keep it under pressure, can do as good a job. Whoever does it, the best place to look for oil is where it has already been found.

RESERVES GROWTH

Reserves growth is exactly about finding oil where it has already been found. This phenomenon is a key point of contention between the Geologists and Economists. It is a long-standing observation that reserves in fields grow with time, and nowadays most increases in companies' reserves are classified as "revisions and additions" rather than new discoveries. Geologists maintain that this is owing to initially conservative booking procedures. They argue that the reserves in a field are generally known pretty accurately on discovery but that the amount booked, particularly when we are talking about proven reserves, is drastically lower. Then, over time, with production experience, the rest of the reserves, that were known about all the time, are returned to the books. Economists, conversely, believe that improvements in technology and possibly more favorable economic conditions (essentially higher oil prices) prompt upward revisions, by making some oil in place, that was always known about, now commercial.

Reserves growth is undoubtedly a real occurrence. There are too many well-supported examples for it to be dismissed. The Geologists have badly erred in dismissing reserves growth, and this, more than exploration success, is the primary reason for the failure of their peak oil predictions since the late 1980s.[116] Inconsistently, they maintain that U.S. bookings are conservative, reflecting only proved reserves rather than the "proved plus probable," which is the best estimate, yet they do not increase their figures for U.S. reserves (Campbell puts U.S. reserves at 23 billion bbl, consistent with removing his "deepwater and polar" oil from BP's 30 billion bbl but far below IHS's 80 billion bbl).

On the other hand, the USGS and the Economists, such as Lynch and Odell, have been content to make global estimates of reserves growth, without really addressing how it will come about. How much is attributable to proving up extensions of existing fields, how much to better reservoir management, and how much to improved or enhanced recovery techniques?

Probably the Geologists are right that the oil in place in the simpler oil fields is generally known with reasonable accuracy once it has been discovered and appraised. Even here, however, many fields undergo substantial upgrades once extensions of the initial area, deeper or secondary reservoirs, and zones with poorer quality are proved up. Gabon's largest field, Rabi, has undergone numerous increases in oil-in-place estimates since the 1980s because, being under a salt layer, it was initially hard to image accurately. In Brunei's biggest field, Seria, new reserves, totaling 100 million bbl, are still being discovered in the northern flank, although the field was originally found in 1929.[117] Iran recently unearthed 2 billion bbl in the well-known Bangestan reservoir of the giant Ab Teymur Field.[118] Still, it is true that downgrades of oil-in-place[119] partly offset upgrades.

Figure 4.13 shows some categories of reserves growth. Categories 4 and 5 (satellite fields, extensions, and deeper pools) result in increases in the known oil-in-place and could be considered as species of exploration; the other types depend on increasing the recovery factor. Reserves may also be upgraded for economic reasons (e.g., higher prices or lower costs extend the productive life of a field, adding reserves in the "tail"), commercial (e.g., gas sales contracts are signed), or contractual ("paper barrels," to do with the split of reserves between company and government, which, in agreement with Geologists, is not true reserves growth but will be aggregated away anyway at a basin or country level).

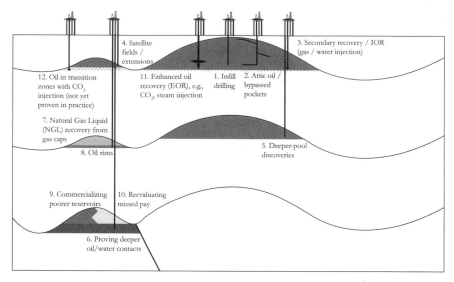

Figure 4.13
Diagrammatic representation of types of reserves growth.

1. Additional wells are drilled to recover oil from pockets of the reservoir that are being drained inefficiently or not at all by existing wells.

2. Oil above the current producing wells, isolated by water encroachment, or in separate reservoir bodies or fault blocks, is targeted.

3. Water or gas are injected to maintain pressure and sweep oil to producing wells.

4. Nearby structures or extensions of the main field are drilled and may be added to its reserves total for reporting purposes or because the hydrocarbon accumulation is continuous.

5. Discoveries are made in deeper reservoirs beneath the first reservoir discovered.

6. Deeper fluid contacts (oil-water, gas-water contacts) are proved, perhaps because of faults or other phenomena that lead to their being deeper than expected.

7. NGLs are recovered from gas caps, leading to increases in liquid reserves (and in total hydrocarbon reserves if the gas was being flared or reinjected).

8. Technology (e.g., horizontal wells) allows commercialization of thin oil rims that were previously noneconomic.

9. Poorer-quality reservoirs are made economic through, for example, improved well designs or stimulation.[120]

10. Reevaluation reveals missed pay (oil/gas-bearing reservoir) that was initially overlooked, perhaps as a result of misleading electric log responses or failed tests.

11. EOR, using for example, steam, CO_2, or chemicals, releases additional oil.

12. CO_2 injection can, in principle, under certain conditions, recover residual oil from beneath the oil-water contact. This is considered technically feasible but has yet to be proved in practice and commercialized.

Reserves changes are a different matter from revisions of oil-in-place estimates. Geologists claim that early booking procedures are conservative. Enough reserves are booked to support the initial development; the rest are left to subsequent phases. This is generally true for proven reserves but not for proven plus probable or "expectation," on which all estimates of future potential should be based. If we are talking about expectation reserves, I disagree with the Geologists' contention that reserves growth is purely a function of conservatism, not of true increases in recovery. This is particularly so in the case of the largest and longest-lived fields, which make the biggest contribution to reserves.

Benchmark recovery factors during the 1970s in the first phase of North Sea development were probably in the range of 40 percent at best, as Shell's Peter Baxendell observed around 1978: "Practical recovery percentages usually vary between 20 and 45 per cent."[121] This was not conservatism; it was the technical limit of what could be done at the time. No reservoir engineer, working on the development plans for the major North Sea fields in the 1970s, predicted that they would reach recovery factors of 60–70 percent, and yet several have or will achieve this. For instance, Forties is targeting ultimate recovery of 65 percent, and more than 65 percent of the oil in Statfjord and Oseberg has been recovered. For 85 percent of Norwegian fields, the initial reserve estimate has been upgraded, by an average of 70 percent, and the oldest fields, those found in the 1970s and 1980s, have experienced the biggest upgrades,[122] exactly as one would expect if technology and our knowledge of these fields were advancing. Backdating misses the fact that the newer fields will experience similar reserves increases, given time.

These fields have also all produced well beyond their original design lives. Fixed costs on the enormous steel and concrete platforms have been reduced, satellite fields have been tied in, helping to cover the operating expenses, and smaller accumulations, not thought to be commercial in the 1970 and 1980s, have been developed with subsea technology, a recent innovation. The great size of these fields and their long lives give ample time and incentive to learn more about how to drain them most efficiently, to try alternative depletion strategies, to pay for specific research and development. As a Shell director puts it, "It took us ten years to learn to 'micromanage' the Brent reservoir." Onshore fields probably present even more possibilities for increasing ultimate recovery with time, because their fixed costs are much lower and the production rate can drop much lower before they become uneconomic. Some companies, such as Apache, have grown into multibillion dollar enterprises almost entirely with reserves growth rather than exploration. They acquire mature producing properties from major companies, for whom they are too small or high cost, and add reserves with reduced costs to postpone abandonment, infill drilling, fine-tuning of secondary recovery, selective appraisal drilling, and EOR initiatives. That this is a viable commercial strategy demonstrates the reality of reserves growth.

Some Geologists might, in contradiction to Economists, maintain that costs do not really matter. The important thing is whether the oil comes out, right, not how much it costs? If prices are going to shoot up uncontrollably, then surely cheap, simple vertical wells will do just as well as horizontal wells? Actually, however, costs are very important, particularly in mature fields, where improved efficiency can keep oil flowing at commercial rates much longer, postpone shutdown, and so reduce decline in the basin as a whole. It is also usually cheaper and less risky to increase recovery in a mature field than to find and develop a new one. And in an environment of limited technical resources (rigs, geologists, and so on), efficient use of these assets is paramount. Because the oil price is set by the marginal barrel, whether the cost for that additional Texas stripper well, whose 10 bbl/day are the final drops that bring supply and demand into balance, is $30/bbl or $60/bbl, is very important.

Finally, in a sign of the validity of reserves growth and the impact of price several North Sea fields, abandoned at times of low prices (and hence at that point having zero reserves, which peak oil supporters would see as confirming their belief that ultimate recovery can be reliably estimated from decline curves) have recently seen plans to reactivate them: for instance, Yme in Norway, with some 50–60 million bbl still to be recovered; Frøy, also in Norway; Ardmore (known as Argyll before its initial decommissioning) in the U.K. North Sea, where the redevelopment will raise the recovery factor from 35 to 50 percent[123]; and Mærsk's Dumbarton (formerly Donan).

Nor is there more than a fraction of truth in the charge that advanced wells and water flooding are super-straws, sucking out the oil faster but not ultimately extracting any more of it. First, faster production is more economically efficient. Second, contrary to the charges of peak oil supporters, higher production rates, if implemented correctly, do not decrease ultimate recovery and may even increase it. Third, producing oil in a dribble in fifty or a hundred years time is of little interest, particularly if we really believe that a decline in global production is imminent. Producing it now helps to delay the peak, hence further invalidating the "Hubbertian" belief that declining output is inevitable beyond 50 percent depletion. Finally, and most importantly, advanced well designs and secondary/tertiary recovery techniques *do* increase reserves by reaching pockets that would otherwise be bypassed, by accessing reservoirs of low permeability that were uncommercial with older methods, by avoiding excessive water production, and by scrubbing out more oil.

Despite some peak oil writers' contentions that the only technologies that ever contributed to oil recovery were the geologists' hammer and the hand lens (and, perhaps, grudgingly, the offshore drilling rig), recent inventions of the 1990s and early 2000s and other advances that we can foresee in the near term have made major contributions to increasing reserves and decreasing costs.

Horizontal wells are the most useful and versatile of these new(ish) technologies, enabling unprecedented targeting of small accumulations, including the latest innovation, "snake" or "dragon" wells with highly undulating paths, and fine control of improved recovery processes. Offshore production systems, such as floating facilities and subsea developments, enable production from smaller and deeper-water fields. Four-dimensional seismic (repeat shooting of three-dimensional surveys to monitor changes in the reservoir), combined with steadily improving reservoir modeling techniques, permits tailored recovery solutions and unorthodox processes. Modern geologists, familiar with computer modeling, were often disparaged by older staff as the "Nintendo generation" and accused of using "black boxes" and not "knowing the rocks," but these new professionals have in fact saved the industry by dramatically increasing productivity and allowing work to go on despite the 1986–1999 decimation. Fine-tuning "brown" (mature) fields has advanced greatly as a result of automation, whereas "managed pressure" drilling enables the industry to add new wells to high-pressure, high-temperature fields, which were originally forecast to have recovery factors of only 10–20 percent.

There are, therefore, undoubtedly many examples of true reserve growth on a massive scale, led by technology. The North Sea and especially Norway have some of the best examples because of the good quality of the documentation and the intense focus on maximizing recovery. Three exemplars are Troll, Valhall/Ekofisk, and Gullfaks. In these fields, the three greatest advances of the 1990s, horizontal wells, three-dimensional seismic, and routine three-dimensional dynamic reservoir modeling, have been crucial in increasing recovery, and an emerging breakthrough of the early 2000s, four-dimensional seismic, has also played a role.

Troll's oil, held in thin rims beneath gas, was not at first thought to be economic. The first phase development planned for a recovery factor of 40 percent; now 70 percent will be achieved, and the field is Norway's largest oil producer, horizontal wells having added 1.5 billion bbl of reserves. Geologists will backdate these oil reserves to 1979, when Troll was discovered, but it was in fact not possible to produce them until 1992 when an oil development was approved.

Valhall and Ekofisk are unusual fields in that their chalk reservoir (the same rock as the White Cliffs of Dover) compacts during production, causing the seabed and platforms standing on it to sink by several meters over the field's life. This puts a premium on specialized reservoir management. Valhall's recovery factor rose from 14 percent when discovered in 1975 to 40 percent in 2003. Ekofisk's ultimate recovery was estimated at about 1,000 million bbl in 1984, about 1,500 in 1987, and 2,260 in 1994, and the Norwegian Petroleum Directorate carried approximately 2,950 million bbl in 2003, now increased to 3,341 million bbl. This increase is more than twice peak oil predictions of all the new oil that exploration will find in Norway.[124]

Gullfaks is a large oil field in the northern North Sea, with 2 billion bbl extracted to date. In 1996, a recovery factor of 46 percent was anticipated[125]; the current recovery factor is 55 percent, and the long-term plan is to raise this to 69 percent, via increased efficiency, and some innovative technologies such as subsea separation of gas, water, and oil.[126]

A U.S. example of reserves growth is the Kern River Field in California, discovered in 1899. In 1942, it was estimated to have only 54 million bbl of reserves remaining. In the next 44 years, it produced 736 million bbl. In 1986, 970 million bbl still remained. The Means Field in Texas, discovered in 1934, was expected to produce 140 million bbl, a recovery factor of about 22 percent. A CO_2 flood was begun in 1982 and increased the EUR factor to 28 percent, which was then increased to 32 percent in 1990, 35 percent in 1995, and 40 percent in 2003.[127]

Can we foresee increased reserves from technological advances in the future? Of course, by definition innovations are unpredictable. Three-dimensional seismic and horizontal wells had long gestation periods, were not immediately accepted by the industry, and took time to reveal their optimal uses. In general, we have not even begun to scratch the surface of what technology can contribute to oil recovery in terms of biotechnology, seismic monitoring, ultra-slim-hole drilling, remediation for contaminated oil and gas, CO_2 separation, nanotechnology, distributed computing, and automation. For instance, 2.1 million bbl/day[128] of oil is lost in produced water, more than the whole output of Algeria; much of this could be recovered by methods such as biotechnology. Ultra-slim-hole drilling could make it possible to drill wells using equipment no larger than an SUV, replacing a conventional rig weighing some thousands of tons.

Ultimately, we might imagine an oil recovery system that acts like the roots of a plant, "sniffing" out oil geochemically or by microseismic and extending itself at nanoscales throughout the pores of a reservoir. This "quaternary recovery" could get at the 30–40 percent of oil in place that even EOR does not touch.

Enhanced Oil Recovery

EOR is probably the key group of technologies for making major gains in oil recovery. The diverse suite of tertiary recovery techniques[129] includes the following: injecting miscible gases such as hydrocarbons, nitrogen, acid gas (a mix of CO_2 and hydrogen sulphide [H_2S]), or CO_2, to strip out remaining oil; modifying the properties of water with polymers to increase its viscosity, or surfactants, effectively soap, to scrub out leftovers; heating the oil with hot water or steam, or burning some of it underground; plus other more esoteric techniques, such as using microbes that "eat" the oil and produce natural surfactants. The relevance of these methods varies. Some EOR approaches, such as steam and "fire floods," are particularly applicable to heavy oil and are discussed in Chapter 6.

The total potential of EOR is very large. What is more, because it operates on currently producing oil fields with developed infrastructure, uses proven technology (albeit with scope for significant improvements), and produces oil identical to that currently in world markets, it is possible to ramp up an EOR effort much faster than developing new frontier regions, going into countries with a hostile investment climate, or bringing tar sands or GtL into play (hence why I treat the subject here, rather than in Chapter 6, on unconventional oil, which is how most writers categorize EOR oil). EOR can therefore make a rapid and major contribution to meeting global oil demand if traditional sources begin to fall short.

Some peak oil supporters suggest that EOR is just another technique for extracting oil faster, for instance: "Usually these measures increase the production rate for a short period of time, but enhance the decline in the long term—they are only intended to extract the oil faster, but not to increase the overall oil recovery."[130] This is incorrect: EOR unquestionably increases recovery from fields. Residual oil, for instance (oil trapped in small pores or adhering to rock grains), will *never* come out of a reservoir, even one with wells drilled into it, even if we wait for a century, unless we take some action to mobilize it.

If Geologists do, reluctantly, concede that EOR can increase reserves, they still usually maintain that it cannot increase or delay peak production but only add reserves in the tail of production. As Bentley opines, "The experience of the USA and Germany has been that enhanced recovery becomes significant only well past the peak."[131] Therefore, they argue that it does not mitigate what they see as the critical problem: the beginning of sharp and irreversible decline in global production. However, this is probably a false argument, for four reasons.

First, in the U.S. experience to which Bentley alludes, large-scale EOR was only researched and implemented *because* of the first oil crisis and the consequent rise in price. This crisis came after the U.S. production peak, an event which was itself essential to make the economic conditions right for EOR implementation. The peak oil theorists are, as they so often do, mistaking economic causality for a law of nature.

Second, tertiary recovery can be implemented much more quickly than most peak oil writers believe, because it operates on known fields with substantial infrastructure already in place. Hubbert made the same mistake with respect to secondary recovery in his seminal 1956 paper: "Because of the slowness of the secondary recovery process, however, it appears unlikely that any improvement that can be made within the next 10 or 15 years can have any significant effect on the date of culmination,"[132] when in fact, it was largely attributable to secondary recovery that the U.S. peak came in 1970, not 1965, which Hubbert prognosed as his most likely case. We also now understand EOR much better than we did in 1973 or 1980, which should greatly shorten the lead time and minimize the number of failed implementations.

Third, the whole world is not going to implement EOR at the same time: what EOR can do is to mitigate declines in mature fields and regions and hence reduce the burden on the newer fields. For example, current EOR production, at some 1.5 million bbl/day,[133] is already virtually replacing a Libya or two Omans.

Fourth, this idea that EOR just prolongs the tail production is based primarily on the U.S. and Canadian experiences (the only place where EOR has really been implemented on a large scale). In these very mature basins, EOR has indeed been used to scrub the last drops out of old fields. This is also due to economic circumstances: the really widespread adoption of EOR in the United States that might have led to a sustained plateau, was halted by the 1986 price crash, which ushered in a period of sharp decline in onshore production. In California, production actually reached its peak in 1985, at about 1.15 million bbl/day, after a decline from 1967 to 1975, because of the widespread adoption of thermal recovery methods for heavy oil. This experience violates three peak oil mantras, showing the following: EOR does add reserves (the level of reserves is not just geologically determined and known at the moment a field is discovered); high prices do stimulate significant additional production; and declines in mature basins are reversible.

Furthermore, with technological advances and a higher-price environment, EOR could be brought in at a much earlier stage of fields' lives. For instance, Cairn's fields in Rajasthan will have hot water injection from the beginning of their lives. Early EOR could actually improve field economics and be more efficient when introduced immediately rather than at the end of conventional production. Such proactive EOR would be analogous to the increased use over the past thirty years of water or gas floods from the start of fields, as in Alaska and the North Sea; before that, secondary recovery was seen as tertiary is today, as a "last resort."

The main reason against the "early EOR" approach has been that EOR schemes are costly, economically unattractive at low prices, and ideally require a good understanding of the reservoir and its fluids. However, advances in reservoir modeling and EOR management, lower costs and higher oil prices, and the desire to sequester CO_2 all make early EOR more feasible today than a decade or two ago. Contrary to some expectations, it also appears that CO_2 floods can add significant recovery to fields that have already undergone another EOR method, miscible hydrocarbon gas injection (for instance, Magnus and Statfjord in the North Sea), or that have been depressurized (such as Brent and, in the future, Statfjord again).[134] EOR can also be an alternative, not a follow-up, to traditional secondary recovery; a major tertiary recovery operator in the United States, Kinder-Morgan, notes that CO_2 injection provides additional recovery of 8–16 percent of oil originally in place when applied after a water flood but up to 40 percent when used *instead* of water flood.[135]

Of the various methods, the most important for the future of light oil production is CO_2 injection. This is an extremely effective process, recovering some 5–10 percent of the original oil *in place* (hence capable of improving a recovery factor of 40 percent to 45–50 percent),[136] and careful management can increase this to even 20 percent.[137] It is at its most efficient with lighter oils and deeper reservoirs, where CO_2 mixes with the oil, but even under immiscible conditions, it can enhance recovery. CO_2 is widely available, from natural and industrial sources, and, of course, burying it would make a great contribution to tackling climate change, as detailed in Chapter 10, the extra oil recovery helping to pay for the sequestration.

After the first field tests in 1960s and large-scale application in the 1980s, CO_2-based EOR fell off in the 1990s as a result of low oil prices. Interest has returned in the last three or four years under the twin pressures of high oil prices and climate change. Weyburn in Saskatchewan is an important current pilot project using anthropogenic CO_2 from a synfuels plant, unique because of the effort that has been put in to understand and optimize the process and disseminate the learnings through the industry. As can be seen from Figure 4.14, tertiary recovery at Weyburn in Saskatchewan will ultimately liberate an additional 130 million bbl or so and has enabled the field to reach a significant secondary production peak, twenty years after the conventional peak, reversing the decline rather than merely stemming it as peak oil theorists generally opined.[138]

Contrary to widespread prejudice, EOR methods are not prohibitively expensive. Many cost $20–25/bbl, or less with favourable conditions, under current circumstances a tolerable price, and some onshore U.S. examples are even cheaper, just $3–6/bbl.[139, 140] With large-scale applications, and advances in technology, there is considerable potential to reduce these costs. For example, linking the power stations of northern Europe with CO_2 pipelines to the North Sea could permit its use ultimately in most of these fields, even the smaller ones. Relatively simple tunings of the process, new materials, and chemicals to modify the recovery process promise additional savings.[141, 142]

Currently, some 4 percent of U.S. oil production, 250,000 bbl/day, comes from CO_2 EOR, most of which occurs in Texas, accounting for

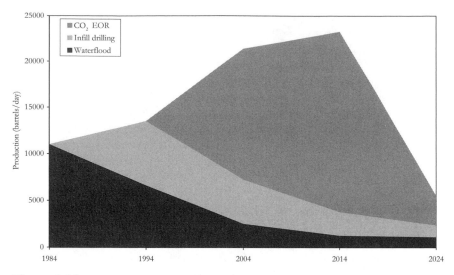

Figure 4.14
Production profile from Weyburn, Saskatchewan, Canada using enhanced oil recovery.

15 percent of that state's output. In January 2006, the Permian Basin in West Texas produced its billionth EOR barrel. Contrary to some reports, this oil comes primarily from carbonate reservoirs (limestones and dolomites), not sandstones, showing that this technique is applicable to carbonates, which is important because of the giant volumes of the world's oil hosted in such rocks in the Middle East. CO_2 injection in the United States sequesters 35 million tons per year of CO_2, about 0.5 percent of national emissions.[143, 144] As shown in Figure 4.15, this involves a substantial amount of existing infrastructure, particularly the pipeline linking natural CO_2 sources in Colorado and New Mexico with fields in West Texas.[145]

The best candidate areas for CO_2-based EOR would seem to be the onshore contiguous United States and Canada, and the North Sea, because of the proximity of large, mature oil fields to big sources of CO_2 in countries with strong and increasing public pressure to tackle climate change. California and the U.S. Gulf Coast have large concentrations of polluters close to big oil resources, whereas Alaska has enormous volumes of oil in the ground but is remote from large industrial CO_2 sources. Norwegian potential from CO_2 EOR alone is estimated at 2–9 billion bbl,[146] while U.K. scope is suggested, with fairly conservative assumptions, as 2 billion bbl.[147] The emissions of the Drax plant on Humberside, the United Kingdom's largest coal power station, at 16 million tons of CO_2 annually,[148] would be sufficient to recover more than 60 million bbl of oil per year. The southern North Sea fields, notably those with chalk reservoirs—

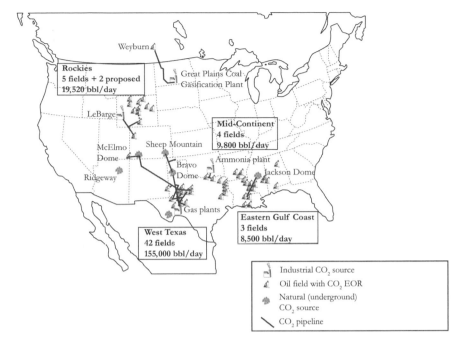

Figure 4.15
CO_2 injection for enhanced oil recovery in the United States.

Ekofisk, Valhall, and the Danish fields—are within reach of Danish and German coal-fired power and, being large with relatively low recovery factors, offer a tempting prize.

The Volga-Urals province in Russia could be another suitable area, because it contains dense concentrations of polluting industries, such as power, steel, and petrochemicals, in a declining oil province. In the Middle East and, increasingly, in West Africa and Indonesia, LNG, petrochemical, power, and GtL plants and refineries produce considerable quantities of CO_2 (in particular, GtL plants produce an almost pure stream), so the UAE, Qatar and Oman, and perhaps later Iran, Kuwait, Saudi Arabia, and Nigeria, are all promising sites for the technology. The UAE is particularly interesting, because CO_2 injection could replace natural gas currently being injected into the country's super-giant oil fields, freeing this up for power generation to feed the explosively growing economy. Because the Middle Eastern fields in particular are predominantly onshore and are so large, economies of scale could make EOR very attractive, quite possibly reversing its high-cost reputation that has been gained in highly depleted U.S. provinces containing many small fields. One CO_2 EOR project has been envisaged by the Japanese company Japan Oil Development Company in Abu Dhabi, where recovery rates of 25–35 percent with gas floods were calculated to increase to 40–50 percent with CO_2.[149] Kuwait's miscible CO_2 potential has been estimated at 10–15 billion bbl.[150]

Declining producers like Oman and Indonesia will find enhanced recovery technology most attractive initially and are indeed already implementing miscible hydrocarbon gas floods, as at Harweel in South Oman, and steam floods, such as Mukhaizna and Qarn Alam in Oman and Duri in Indonesia. With its largest field, Cantarell, beginning to decline, Mexico might also consider CO_2 injection here, because it has numerous industrial sources, and the current nitrogen injection, being immiscible, is probably not as efficient a recovery method as (at least partly) miscible CO_2.

Indonesia's EOR potential would seem, at a rough estimate, to be some 5–10 billion bbl, up to double its current remaining conventional reserves. Indonesia and other areas, notably the remainder of Southeast Asia, and Australia have large volumes of natural, underground CO_2 (notably Natuna D Alpha and Gorgon), which could be used for EOR and possibly supplemented with anthropogenic supplies (for instance, the Bontang LNG Plant in East Kalimantan[151]). Malaysia's EOR potential is estimated at almost 1 billion bbl, mostly in Peninsular Malaysia, close to about 1 Tcf of natural CO_2 fields.[152]

The final key target for this technique will be countries reliant on coal, seeking to meet climate change commitments, the United States, China, and India being the obvious examples.[153] Texas and Alaska have large coal and oil fields in juxtaposition. China possesses a massive concentration of coal-burning industries in the province of Heilongjiang and in and around Beijing, conveniently close to major oil fields, particularly Daqing, the country's largest, while India's biggest oil field, Bombay High, lies offshore the megalopolis of Mumbai.

Total U.S. CO_2 tertiary recovery potential, from the 389 billion bbl of remaining oil in place (of 582 billion originally in place, indicating a recovery factor to date of only 33 percent) is estimated as 47 billion bbl with today's technology (more than Libya's reserves) to 265 billion bbl with advances in technology (about equal to Saudi Arabia). By 2020, CO_2 EOR in the United States could be yielding 3 million bbl/day, or as much as Venezuela, much higher than the Geologists' forecasts for *total* U.S. production by that date. One additional area for CO_2 EOR is to recover large volumes of residual oil, found beneath the oil-water contact in some settings. Potential for this in the United States has been estimated at 20 billion bbl (of 100 billion bbl in place), with further immense scope in the Middle East and FSU in particular.

Because typical recovery factors with secondary recovery are still only in the range of 30–40 percent of original oil in place,[154] improving this to 60–65 percent, a perfectly feasible target, would, if we take the very conservative global ultimate recovery estimates of peak oilers, increase ultimate recovery by some 1.3–2 trillion barrels, that is, double or triple the current stated reserves of the entire Middle East.

In view of the advantages of EOR, particularly using CO_2, why has this technology not yet been taken up more actively? There are a number of contributory factors: perceptions, becoming increasingly inaccurate, that the technique is high cost and risky; the challenges of creating a value chain that satisfies several disparate participants; a lack of a clear legal and health-safety-environment framework for handling CO_2; delays in establishing a cost for carbon; inappropriate fiscal systems that impose high tax rates on all oil fields regardless of profitability; the presence of small companies in mature areas without the technical and financial strength for such projects; a lack of EOR expertise attributable to the 1990s layoffs; and the slow development of CO_2 transportation infrastructure.

The effects of reserves growth from EOR and other activities are easy to underestimate. Annual reserves replacement from 1995 to 2005 (postdating most of the allegedly "suspicious" OPEC upgrades) averaged 250 percent,[155] mostly from reserves growth. With world production running at about 30 billion bbl per year, and ultimate world recovery (if we believe the pessimistic estimates of the Geologists) around 2 trillion bbl, increasing the recovery factor by 1.5 percent per year (in relative terms, e.g., from 40 to 40.6 percent) is sufficient to replace reserves without any exploration success. Applying EOR systematically could add some 8–16 years of global production before decline begins, even at the conservative end of conventional ultimate recovery estimates.

THE FALLACY OF "EASY OIL"

In recent years, it has become a mantra among peak oil believers, the media, and even many industry professionals that "the age of easy oil is over." As William J. Cummings, ExxonMobil's spokesperson in Angola, said, "All the easy oil and gas in the world has pretty much been found. Now comes the harder work in finding and producing oil from more challenging environments and work areas."[156] Mike Watts, the exploration director (nicknamed "Sniffer") of Cairn, responsible for the finds in Rajasthan, India, said similarly, "The easy oil has already been found."[157]

This contention does not stand up to investigation. First, there has *never* been an age of easy oil. If it was so easy to find, why has it taken 150 years to find what we have today? Second, plenty of oil remains that is, if not easy, not particularly difficult to extract. Third, most of the "easy oil" today is politically off-limits, and the international industry has to target the more difficult stuff. Those who talk about easy oil possibly lack a sense of perspective, because one's own problems tend to loom larger than those of others, particularly in the past. Alternatively, and in a more

Machiavellian way, the industry likes the idea of the end of easy oil because it emphasizes the challenges they face. It also appeals to environmentalists because it promises an end to this nasty black stuff. However, although convenient, the idea of easy oil or an end to it is incorrect.

The industry has always operated at the margins of technology. In this, it is like other industries. Are we at the end of "the age of easy microchips"? Was it easy to invent the integrated circuit in 1959? Microchips, being cutting edge, will always be difficult to make. Similarly, the next oil field will always be difficult. Consider some landmarks in petroleum history.

- Colonel Drake's 1859 well, in the then remote township of Titusville, Pennsylvania, which opened up the American petroleum industry, was not easy to drill. Progress was only 1 meter per day (modern drill bits typically penetrate 10 meters per hour). The hole began collapsing, hence Drake's innovation of tubing. The well reached a total depth of 21 meters (compare this with the 6,500 meters of Chevron's widely reported Jack #2).

- William Knox D'Arcy's 1908 discovery at Masjed-e Suleiman in Iran, the first find of oil in the Middle East, was a formidably difficult endeavor. The drilling equipment had to be brought in from Baghdad, then part of the Ottoman Empire, and the Turks refused to allow it to cross the bridge at the border, although it was manifestly strong enough, nor to use any other crossing point. Once the gear finally entered Iran, it was hauled through the foothills of the Zagros Mountains, in negotiation with tribes virtually independent of the central government in Tehran.

At seven in the morning, the temperature was 110° [49°C] in the shade ... and already five of the small band of Europeans, together with a Baghdad mechanic, had been touched by the sun and one of them was dying. For the last six days grasshoppers had swarmed across the country like locusts and devoured every trace of green pasture. The river was full of them and the water stank. Their bodies lay all over the camp and everywhere the men went they trod their way through a squelching mass of dead insects. Every half-hour they skimmed them from the water tanks. Smallpox had broken out at Sekhuan, where they got their food and water. Their dwindling stock of firewood for the boiler was constantly being raided and then the boiler itself collapsed, its tubes corroded by the sulphurous water. Letters from home, always the consolation of the exile, had failed to arrive because the carrier and his camel had died en route—and, to cap it all, some idiot had just dropped a 14-lb. sledgehammer down the well.[158]

A total of £500,000 (up to £25 million, more than $50 million in today's money) was spent, with unsuccessful drilling at several locations, virtually driving D'Arcy and his backers bankrupt until oil was discovered at a depth of 360 meters.

- The development of Middle Eastern oil from the 1940s through to the 1960s was an immense undertaking. Huge sums of money had to be invested in areas that were only just emerging into the twentieth century, remote from the U.S.

and European bases of the operating companies. An entire infrastructure, of roads, air fields, ports, housing, power, and trained labor, had to be built almost from nothing, and the companies contended with nationalizations, strikes, revolutions, coups, political pressure, and undefined borders. While Saudi Arabia was virtually cut off from the West by World War II, an enormous blowout at Dammam in 1940 had to be fought with improvised gear of asbestos shields and water pumps.[159] Some of these firefighters were Exxon men, the professional ancestors of Cummings.

- The development of North Sea oil during the 1970s was the greatest technical challenge the industry had faced. Entirely new technologies, backed up by innovative financing, had to be devised to meet the vast cost of developments in this hostile environment. A series of disasters cost many lives: the sinking of the Sea Gem in 1965, with thirteen deaths,[160] having just discovered the first offshore hydrocarbons in the United Kingdom; the three sailors who died during the evacuation of the Hewett platform during a 1967 blowout[161]; the collapse of the Alexander Kjelland rig in 1980, killing 123[162]; and the fire and explosion on the Piper Alpha platform in 1988, in which 167 people died.[163] Easy oil proponents should try telling a driller who worked in the North Sea in the 1970s that this was easy oil—but keep at a safe distance.

- The Soviet exploitation of the West Siberian oil fields involved the construction of million-strong cities in some of the coldest areas of the planet, such as Novosibirsk (January temperature of $-19°C$).[164] The big Russian gas fields, brought on-stream in the 1970s and 1980s, lie north of the limit of continuous permafrost, in which there are only two months per year when rivers are not frozen (and during those two months, the area floods to a depth of 1.5–2 meters), a treeless region swept continually by gale-force winds. Concrete had to be made with steam to prevent it from freezing.[165]

Another common complaint often made is that the world's key fields are "old." Yes, they are. They are all millions of years old. On a geological timescale, whether they have been producing for one year or a hundred is utterly irrelevant. Only the remaining reserves and the methods of development are important. Simmons says, "No new field whose development program is now underway is projected to have daily production in excess of 250,000 barrels … the world's largest 'old giant fields' still produce on average more than 500,000 barrels per day, in spite of an average age of almost 70 years!"[166] This is a surprising comment in view of new fields such as Kashagan (more than 1 million bbl/day planned plateau), ACG (approximately 900,000 bbl/day), Vankor (665,000 bbl/day), Kurmangazy (600,000 bbl/day), Azadegan (385,000 bbl/day), Yadavaran (300,000 bbl/day), and several others. Even ignoring such new fields with large capacities, a field that has been producing for seventy years with a conservative depletion policy and reasonable reservoir management can continue for decades more without decline; these are not warhorses, which get old and die.

Nor is it true that the *quality* of produced oil is declining significantly, an almost universal mantra in the industry. Yes, heavy oil production in

Canada is rising rapidly, but the average Middle East grade will barely change over the next five years, and major growth is expected in light oil from deepwater (Angola, Brazil, and Nigeria) and the FSU and very light, high-quality condensate, ideal for producing gasoline (Qatar, Iran, Algeria, Australia, Sakhalin, and others).

So, having established that extracting oil was never easy, is it likely to be harder in the future? No, it will be pretty much as easy or difficult as in the past. By definition, we are always pushing the frontiers: as soon as an oil or gas play becomes technologically and economically feasible, someone will be exploiting it. The returns will be marginal until technology has advanced to make that kind of development routine, by which time we will have moved on to a greater challenge. Of course, development goes in phases. The early platforms in the North Sea were phenomenally expensive and challenging to install. Once they were in place, adding new fields was more straightforward, because techniques were known, and supporting infrastructure was in place. As the basin matures, the later fields were smaller and often geologically more challenging (for example, high pressure/high temperature). So there are phases of easy oil, in specific places, for fleeting moments, most of the advantages going to the first movers; once these opportunities are exhausted, we are back to the difficult stuff that is the usual diet of oil companies.

The advocates of the end of easy oil might ask why the IOCs, such as BP, Total, ExxonMobil, Shell, Chevron, and so on, are going to such difficult parts of the world to develop fields, if there is still easy oil left. The issue is that the largest, cheapest fields in the world, in the Middle East, Venezuela, and Russia, are largely off-limits to outsiders. Even where the foreign companies do participate to a limited extent, they are either constrained by OPEC quotas and by dominant government partners (as in Abu Dhabi) or are given the most problematic fields to develop. The world is not short of easy oil, if such a thing exists, but the major foreign companies may be. The super-majors need big fields to keep them going, but such crown jewels are not given away by host nations unless they pose some special challenge.

The idea of easy oil is often linked with that of the end of cheap oil. Yes, the exceptionally cheap oil of the 1986–1998 period has indeed come to an end. As everyone in the oil business knows (or should know—people have disturbingly short memories), the oil price goes up and it comes down. Between 1974 and 1985, the oil price averaged $60/bbl (in real-term 2006 dollars). In the period 2000–2006, it averaged only $41. So are we not still in the era of cheap(er) oil?

SOURCES OF NEW SUPPLY

Examining information about project schedules gives us a view of new supply likely to come on-stream in the next five years or so, as well as potential projects with as yet no definite timeline. Naturally, the "pipeline" becomes somewhat empty after 2010. This is not a reflection of lack of future supply but is merely attributable to the fact that it takes about three to four years to bring a new field on-stream. Few developments that will produce after 2011 have taken final investment decision yet. Conversely, any major development not sanctioned yet is unlikely to come on-stream before 2010 at the earliest, particularly in the current climate of tight markets for oil-field equipment and services.

The total contribution of major projects, with projected output greater than 50,000 bbl/day, to global supply is shown in Table 4.4.[167]

It can be seen that the queue of new fields moving into production is quite strong, at least up to 2010,[168, 169, 170] figures that are broadly consistent with those of Goldman Sachs.[171] These numbers should be compared with world demand growth of 2.8 million bbl/day (3.6 percent) in 2004 and 1.0 million bbl/day (1.25 percent) in 2005. It is clear that the planned production additions are easily capable of meeting even high levels of demand growth, contrary to Geologists' forecasts of peak oil being in 2006 or 2007. Non-OPEC supply growth is even stronger than that from OPEC, again dismissing ideas that a non-OPEC peak might be imminent.

This table also makes the point about project maturation. In 2005, the prediction was for 0.8 million bbl/day of supply additions in 2010. Now we can foresee 3.8 million bbl/day extra production. The world perpetually appears to be short of oil in about five years' time because that is how long it takes to bring new projects to fruition. Nobody drills wells and lays pipes for projects in 2008 that will not produce until 2013. The supply funnel has also become much stronger since 2005: for example, the prediction in 2006 for 2007 supply additions was 1.4 million bbl/day higher than it had been in 2005.

Table 4.4
Summary of new production from major projects, organized by peak year.

New production (thousand barrels/day)	2005	2006	2007	2008	2009	2010	2011	2012+	Other Potential
OPEC	860	1580	1815	1889	2037	1887	739	960	2330
Non-OPEC	816	2166	2316	2442	1785	2267	531	1534	3343
Total (2006 prediction)	1676	3746	4131	4331	3822	4154	1270	2492	5673
Total (2005 prediction)	1676	3258	2351	3315	3305	805	70	1232	5255

Some of the "potential" fields will have to commence development fairly quickly to fill the gap in 2010 and beyond. In practice, too, a number of these projects can be expected to slip.[172] Two of the larger ones, Kashagan and Sakhalin-2, have already been subject to considerable delays, and developments in Iran and particularly Iraq have undergone unending postponements. Mexico is also vulnerable to slippages because of Pemex's weak financial state.

The key question is whether the underlying decline of the current production can be slowed. New projects must not only meet demand growth but replace declines from mature areas. Typical decline rates, their distribution across different types of field, and their sensitivity to oil prices and hence investment levels are not well understood.[173] "Decline" should be defined carefully. Are we talking about the loss in production from a field when no further investment is made (probably high), about the drop off in production from a maturing field despite continued development (lower), or about the decline in an entire basin or country in the absence of major new developments (even lower)? Estimates for the natural decline rates vary widely, with typical estimates being 4–7 percent, implying annual loss of some 3–6 million bbl/day.[174]

However, there is also a case for using lower decline rates. It is fallacious to extrapolate the fall off of a single depleting field or basin to the entire world. As one area becomes mature, capital and resources are redeployed to increase or stabilize production in other areas where returns are higher; drilling rigs are now moving in great numbers from the United States to the Persian Gulf. The result is that specific regions decline faster than purely technical considerations would indicate. Just because a single mature area declines rapidly does not mean that the same will happen across the whole world simultaneously.

To give a specific example, the Saudis, who account for more than 10 percent of global production, have indicated that, with infill drilling and maintenance, they can hold production flat at their main fields without needing new developments and have signed up significant numbers of rigs to do this. This fact reduces the average global decline significantly. The loss of those rigs might accelerate declines in onshore North America, but because Saudi wells are so much more productive, the overall effect will be higher worldwide output.

Holistically, looking at the 2005 figures, total underlying decline is implied to be only about 2.2 percent.[175,176] This suggests that decline rates extrapolated from single fields or basins, particularly those commonly used by peak oil theorists, overestimate the underlying global and non-OPEC declines. Indeed, peak oil believers often propound *total* decline rates around 6 percent annually after peak, which seems to imply that no new projects at all would be being brought online. We might also speculate that the increasing proportion of liquids coming from long-lived gas projects and developments such as tar sands that effectively have no underlying decline might tend to reduce the average decline rate, although the growing maturity of some other areas might increase it.

Putting these numbers together, we can derive two extreme scenarios: for combinations of low demand growth (1 percent) and low decline (2.2 percent); and high demand growth (2 percent) and high decline (6 percent).

In the first case, the known large projects, plus an allowance for smaller ones, adds up to an enormous overbuild of capacity, 13.4 million bbl/day by 2010. In this case, *all* of the new OPEC developments from 2005 to 2010 would be surplus to requirements; they could all have been postponed to 2011 start ups. In such an environment, prices would probably crash, demand might well accelerate, underinvestment in mature fields would increase the decline rate, and many future projects would be canceled. OPEC would probably scale back production to defend prices, so this "buffer" capacity would remain intact, unused, until demand caught up again. Between 2011 and 2018, all of this premature supply would finally be brought into commission. This provides ample time to realize new projects to "fill the hopper" after 2018. Such a scenario may explain OPEC's unwillingness, until recently, to invest in major new capacity additions and risk a repeat of the 1986–1998 period of overcapacity and low prices.

In the second scenario, new capacity additions are not quite able to keep up with demand growth and the underlying decline, until 2010 or so. This would be a period of tight supplies and a continuation of current high prices, which could be exacerbated by any cancellations or delays to the identified project pipeline. The projects in Iraq, Iran, and Mexico appear particularly vulnerable, and those in Kazakhstan, Sakhalin, and Canada also have a mixed history of postponements. Delays, however, will be partly offset by "ramp-up" periods, in which new projects are not yet at maximum. After 2010, some of the 5.7 million bbl/day of potential projects and the 27 billion bbl of reserves with no associated development plan would be brought into service. The period of high prices would not only catalyze these new megaprojects but would also reduce demand and encourage investment in stemming the mature decline rates.

In either case, it is clear that just today's known projects push out the date of peak oil to 2011, even if demand rises quickly and underlying declines are high. This clearly conflicts with a variety of peak oil estimates around 2005–2010, and putting even putting peak oil soon after 2011 assumes that a set of plans that consistently deliver 3–4 million bl/day of capacity additions run for the next four years and then dry up abruptly to almost nothing. No new projects are brought into service, no new discoveries made, no reserves added, no more unconventional oil developed, and even high prices do not stem the decline rate of existing fields. The proportion of minor projects, not tracked here, will increase, as will the contribution of unconventional projects, which have inherently low or zero decline rates. Other independent estimates indicate that that production is likely to increase by as much as 9 million bbl/day from 2006 to 2010, mostly meeting increased demand, with a small increment of spare capacity.[177] This outcome falls somewhere between the two scenarios outlined above, although closer to the lower case.

We can already identify a number of likely contributors to the next wave of developments: an end to the Qatari moratorium, so releasing new North Field condensate volumes and GtL plants; Iranian gas projects in South Pars, such as Phases 6 and 8 (Pars LNG) and Phase 13 (Persian LNG), with their condensate streams, plus North Pars and Kish; development of some recent discoveries and the large backlog of long-undeveloped fields in onshore Iran; NGLs from Shtokmanovskoye in the eastern Barents Sea; East Siberian fields filling the proposed pipeline to China and the Pacific; offshore Cambodian production from recent Chevron discoveries, coming on-stream around 2010; deepwater fields in Southeast Asia, such as Gumusut and Malikai in Malaysia; Jack (2013) in the Gulf of Mexico; deepwater finds in Brazil's Santos Basin; Rosebank-Lochnagar in the United Kingdom; the giant offshore gas and oil finds in India's Krishna-Godavari basin and the rest of Cairn's finds in Rajasthan; new fields in Uganda and Ghana; heavy oil developments following up Mukhaizna in Oman; heavy oil in areas outside Canada and Venezuela, such as Kuwait, Madagascar, and the United Kingdom; condensate from Australian developments such as Gorgon and Crux; a cornucopia of massive projects in Iraq, security and politics permitting; plus discoveries from the recent wave of licensing in Algeria, Libya, and Oman.

Costs for new non-OPEC oil are not prohibitively expensive. Indeed, even with recent cost increases, they are well below recent oil price highs, indicating a strong incentive to continue developing these resources.[178] Many unconventional resources (which we will cover in Chapter 6) have lower costs than oil from significant sources considered conventional— onshore and shallow-water production of light oil, south of the Arctic Circle. The cost of the most marginal oil in the world, U.S. stripper well production, $16–31/bbl, is still well below current prices. There remain, furthermore, enormous resources in the OPEC countries that can be developed cheaply and simply. Redevelopment of Khurais in Saudi Arabia, for instance, will cost some $5 billion to add 1.2 million bbl/day of capacity. Although the absolute cost is large, consider that that level of production will generate some $45 billion of revenues *per year* at current prices, and it is clear that this is very easy oil indeed. Several years of high prices have left oil companies and OPEC nations alike with low debt and healthy cash flow, so there is no capital constraint to investing in new fields.

Industry resource limitations, meaning staff, materials, and equipment, have received much attention recently, with sharp cost increases. This inflation, combined with the early 2007 falls in oil prices, has thrown some spending plans into doubt. Some of the shortages are being addressed. For instance, construction of new rigs is at levels not seen since the late 1970s, with about 100 new units planned to come into service to 2010[179] (compared with a total fleet in late 2006 of some 900). Steel and copper prices will also drop once new mines and plants come online. The resource constraint that will be slowest to address is that of people, because it takes petroleum engineers or geologists at least four years to complete university, followed by several years before they have sufficient experience to make a major contribution. However, the industry can respond in the shorter term by accelerating training and promotions, bringing in consultants and retirees, taking advantage of the large engineering enrolments and experienced petroleum staff from countries such as Russia, Iran, India, and China, working smarter, with more virtual operations and automation, and taking more risk and being more pragmatic in developments (compensated by higher prices). Because oil industry professionals typically spend 33 percent of their time finding data,[180] there are clear gains to be made from better information management, archiving, and search techniques. Therefore, in the medium term, the current constraints on increasing production will relax.

Where are we likely to go in the future that will be more costly? All extremes of deserts, mountains, and jungles have already been reached. Deserts are old hat: oil was found in the Algerian Sahara in the 1950s, and the super-giant Shaybah, in Saudi Arabia's Rub' Al Khali (Empty Quarter), was discovered in 1975. The world's highest oil field is at 4,700 meters altitude in Tibet,[181] and there is not much room to go higher, even if the geology were promising, which it generally is not. Companies operate in the mountainous jungles of Papua New Guinea, where the top has to be sliced off a mountain to make a helicopter landing pad, and they explore in the enormous, trackless malarial swamps of West Papua.

We will continue to push into deeper and deeper water, although the deep ocean floors have only a thin veneer of sediments, so it is difficult to think that we will find large volumes of oil beyond 4,000 meters water depth or so. Already BP/Shell are producing oil at more than 2,000 meters (Na Kika in the Gulf of Mexico) and an exploration well has been drilled at 2,777 meters offshore Brazil, while the latest class of drill ships can reach 12,000 meters below the seabed[182] in 3,660 meters of water.[183] Drilling deeper into the Earth, particularly for oil, is limited by temperature, which will crack hydrocarbon accumulations to CO_2 below about 6,000 meters, except in unusually cool basins (such as the South Caspian or Gulf of Mexico). Drilling ultradeep wells is difficult, as the failure of Inam (Azerbaijan) and Blackbeard (Gulf of Mexico shelf) to reach their objectives has demonstrated, but emerging technologies such as expandable tubulars will lower the costs of such wells.

The obvious next frontier, therefore, is the Arctic. Operations in Alaska (e.g., BP's offshore North Star field), Sakhalin, Newfoundland (the iceberg-resistant Hibernia platform), and Norway (the Snøhvit LNG development) are already testing the waters, or breaking the ice, depending how you look at it, for Arctic operations. They have proven that, although very tough on the workers, and expensive, it is technically and economically feasible to operate onshore and offshore in the Arctic. The only remaining frontier after that would seem to be beneath ice sheets, like Antarctica. I struggle to see how that could possibly be feasible, but no doubt we would find a way if a way were required. No doubt the geologists and engineers in Antarctica will say, "It was simple developing the deepwater and Sakhalin in the early 2000s. That was the age of Easy Oil." However, there is no political will to break the moratorium on exploiting Antarctica's minerals, and, happily, as the rest of this book demonstrates, no need to, either. That is pretty much everything our planet can confront us with, unless we go prospecting for those Soviet "E" category reserves rumored to be on the Moon.

SUMMARY

So, to recap, we have established that the world's total endowment of petroleum is composed of the following elements:

1. Conventional non-OPEC oil.
2. Conventional OPEC oil, which the Geologists believe to be significantly overstated.
3. Future exploration potential (YtF), in which Geologists are rather pessimistic and many other estimates much more bullish.
4. Reserves growth, which the Geologists believe to be small or zero.
5. EOR (which could reasonably be included under reserves growth). Geologists mostly do not believe EOR will make a significant contribution until well after peak oil.
6. Unconventional oil, variously defined, but including some or all of the following: NGL/condensates, deepwater (say, deeper than 500 meters), polar, heavy/extra-heavy oil, tar sands, shale oil, and synthetic oils (from gas, coal, or other feedstocks). Geologists generally maintain that these unconventional oils will make a limited contribution at best, because volumes are limited (deepwater, polar), because costs and logistics are unfavorable, or both.

Table 4.5 (numerically) and Figure 4.16 (graphically) compare some recent prominent estimates of global ultimate recovery. From left to right, we range from one of the most gloomy of the Geologists, Campbell, to one of the most Cornucopian of the Economists, Odell. The range of conventional oil estimates is clearly wide, from 1,972 billion bbl to 3,673

Table 4.5
Comparison of estimates from various sources of global ultimate endowment of oil.

Category		Campbell	Bentley[1]	Shell[2]	IHS/PiW	OECD/IEA[3]	USGS[4]	CERA[5]	Odell[6]
		Ultimate recovery (billion barrels; cumulative production to date included in appropriate categories)							
OPEC conventional		895[7]	1700	1950	1258	1190[8]	2140	1002[9]	1830
Non-OPEC conventional		845			1006[11]	1310[10]		1142	
OPEC YtF		68	300	690	1064[11]	250	732	758	750
Non-OPEC YtF		54				230			
Arctic		46[12]				200[13]		118	
Deepwater		65[14]				120[15]		61	
Reserves growth		0	0	610		300[16]	688	592[17]	450
Total conventional oil		1972	2000	3250	3328[18]	3600	3560	3673	3030
NGLs		128[19]	250	Not given	Included above	Not given	324[20]	[21]	Not given separately
Heavy oil		52[22]	600–1000	Not given	575	Not given	850	444[23]	3000
Total		2152	2850–3250	3250	3903	3600	4734	4117	6030

[1]Bentley (2005).
[2]Williams (2003).
[3]OECD/IEA, Figure 2.19. World ultimately recoverable conventional oil with breakdown of undiscovered oil and addition of EOR potential.
[4]World Petroleum Assessment 2000, in Williams (2003).
[5]Jackson (2006).
[6]Odell (2004).

(continued)

Table 4.5. (continued)

[7] Including Dubai and Sharjah in OPEC, which they are not, for comparability with the USGS figures, which lump the various Emirates of the UAE together. Dubai and Sharjah EUR is fairly small in any case.

[8] Assuming 340 billion bbl of OPEC production to date and split between 700 billion bbl of proven reserves and 150 billion bbl of discovered but unproven.

[9] OPEC Middle East only.

[10] Assuming 660 billion bbl of non-OPEC production to date and split between 400 billion bbl of proven reserves and 250 billion bbl of discovered but unproven.

[11] Includes reserves growth.

[12] Total to 2040. Backcalculated by interpolating between the dates Campbell gives and then assuming continuation of production growth beyond 2030. Assuming that all Alaskan production to date is included in the U.S. historic figure.

[13] YtF only; current Arctic reserves included in non-OPEC conventional.

[14] Total to 2040. Backcalculated by interpolating between the dates Campbell gives and then assuming reasonable extrapolations of given growth or decline rates. Assuming that all deepwater production to date is included in the historic figures for Brazil, the United States, Angola, and Nigeria.

[15] YtF only; current deepwater reserves included in non-OPEC conventional.

[16] EOR only; other reserves growth included in OPEC conventional and non-OPEC conventional.

[17] EOR only; other reserves growth included in OPEC conventional and non-OPEC conventional.

[18] No figures are given for reserves growth or YtF.

[19] Total to 2040. Backcalculated by interpolating between the dates Campbell gives and then assuming a reasonable extrapolation of the given growth rate. Assumes all historic NGL production is included under the relevant country totals.

[20] Of which 7 billion bbl cumulative production, 68 billion bbl remaining reserves, 42 billion bbl reserves growth, and 207 billion bbl YtF.

[21] Not given separately; presumably included in conventional OPEC and conventional non-OPEC oil.

[22] Total to 2040. Backcalculated by interpolating between the dates Campbell gives and then assuming reasonable extrapolations of given growth or decline rates.

[23] Plus 704 billion bbl of shale oil.

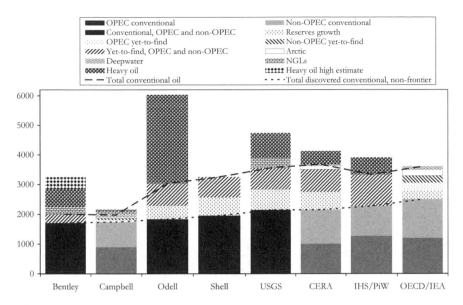

Figure 4.16
Graphical representation of different estimates of world's ultimate oil endowment (billion barrels).

billion bbl, which contradicts the peak oil theorists' common assertion that there is a growing consensus on a global EUR of about 2,000 billion bbl. The table also demonstrates the extreme conservatism of Campbell's YtF figures, with even a fellow depletionist, Bentley, coming in with almost three times as much. The two peak oil advocates, Bentley and Campbell, have at least 1 trillion barrels less than the most conservative (Odell's) conventional oil estimate and are at least as far behind on total (unconventional plus conventional), even taking Bentley's unusually high estimate for heavy oil. The estimates by the USGS, with its host of petroleum geologists, CERA with its access to the uniquely comprehensive IHS database of global oil-field data, and Shell, with its worldwide presence and insight into several OPEC countries, should be especially persuasive.[184] Note that the USGS, Shell, CERA, and Odell all give a prominent role to reserves growth, unlike Campbell and Bentley.

Campbell, and to a lesser extent Bentley, are also pessimistic on the unconventional side. The discrepancy in NGLs is particularly striking given that more than Campbell's estimate has already been discovered (implying that he considers reserves have been heavily overstated or that they will not be developed in his time window). He also hardly sees a role for heavy oil at all, odd given that some 600 billion bbl are recoverable in just two sites, Alberta tar sands and Venezuela's Orinoco Belt, with current technology.

Figure 4.17 presents global EUR figures, plotted by the date of the estimate. The dashed line shows cumulative production to the end of 2006

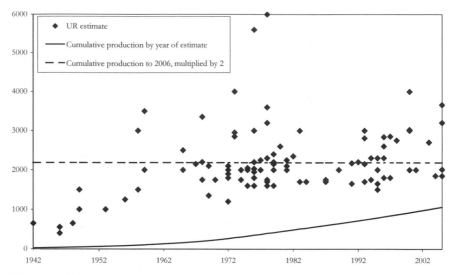

Figure 4.17
Global ultimate recovery estimates by year.

(approximately 1,100 billion bbl), multiplied by two, because the Hubbert theory predicts that at around 50 percent depletion, we should reach peak. Since the project pipeline discussed above shows that, even with high decline rates and high demand growth, we will not reach peak before 2010, I feel justified in rejecting any estimate falling below this line. This means that, of 103 estimates plotted here, sixty-four have already been disproved, and, even of the eleven this century, five already look too low. Not until 1958, two years *after* Hubbert's first paper, was a prediction made that retains any plausibility today. This indicates how pessimistic peak oil theories have persistently been annulled by hard facts.[185]

The Geologists' estimates of known world reserves, reserves growth, and future exploration potential are all too low. Although they have some reasonable suspicions about stated OPEC figures, their approach of simply discounting all reserves additions in the mid-1980s is highly misleading and, in several cases, can be demonstrated to understate likely reserves by a wide margin. Some specific criticisms of the USGS's estimates of YtF volumes can be made but overall they seem reasonable and in some cases even conservative, whereas the Geologists generally badly underestimate future potential across the board. Part of this shortfall seems to be caused by their simplistic extrapolation of recent exploration performance, without considering the economic context of these efforts. In other areas, the smallness of their projections appears inexplicable.

The models used to forecast peak oil are also seriously flawed. Most importantly, they do not allow more intensive investment in production once depletion of the resource base starts to become an issue. Therefore, decline starts much earlier than it would need to in reality. In particular, they do not allow for increases in reserves induced by advances in technology and reservoir management, infrastructure development, higher prices, or other factors but consider them to be entirely determined by geology.

Therefore, limits to production set by the physical quantities of remaining recoverable conventional oil are not currently a problem and will not be until at least 2020. However, two key factors may limit how fast this oil can be brought into production. First, the lack of resources within the industry (rigs, geologists, and so on) to find and develop these hydrocarbons, a problem that is being overcome. Second, the limits that many host governments put on access to prospective areas, either making them completely inaccessible or limiting foreign and/or private sector access, so reducing the availability of modern technology and ideas, and capital.

This is a problem that the industry has faced at least once before, in the early 1970s, when there was a great move into the North Sea and Alaska, while lower-cost oil in the Middle East remained untouched. Let us now consider some of the big beasts of the oil world and whether peak oil arguments applied to them have any validity.

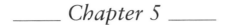

Chapter 5

Dead Dinosaurs?: The Major Oil Nations

Let me tell you something that we Israelis have against Moses. He took us 40 years through the desert in order to bring us to the one spot in the Middle East that has no oil!

Golda Meir, former Prime Minister of Israel[1]

Too much argument about peak oil, on both sides, relies on trendology and qualitative arguments and not enough on hard quantitative evidence. Let us therefore consider the more important oil reserve holding countries in more detail plus a few other cases of interest to consider how reliable the quoted reserves are, what potential there is for additions and future exploration success, and what the key issues are for bringing this potential to fruition. This is not an exhaustive catalog but rather a collection of key highlights, dealing with the Middle East first, then North Africa, the FSU, the Americas, Europe, Asia, and new frontiers.

The following themes emerge from this discussion.

1. Four of the main OPEC states (Kuwait, the UAE, Qatar, and Iran) may, to greater or lesser degrees, be exaggerating their proven reserves, but two of the most maligned, Saudi Arabia and Iraq, appear plausible, even conservative. Total overstatement is at most about 160 billion bbl, 22 percent of the official reserves of these core Gulf countries. Note that peak oil estimates suggest a much more severe downgrade, as much as 335 billion bbl,[2] but adding back reasonable, field-based estimates for recent increases in recovery and new discoveries, heavy underestimation in Iraq, and NGL, suggests that the actual reserves of this group could be *higher* than their official figures, by some 22–50 billion bbl. That is similar to adding a new Kazakhstan to the world.

2. The main OPEC countries are not close to peak production. They are generally producing at conservative depletion rates. Most of them have significant

development plans underway and are in a position to raise production, for the first time, considerably above the levels reached before the 1970s price shocks. OPEC's plans to reach capacity of 38 million bbl/day by 2010[3] are credible. The main threats to this target are not a lack of oil reserves but shortages of personnel and equipment, and project cancellations in view of political issues and OPEC's own concerns on demand security.

3. The main OPEC nations, particularly Iran and Iraq, plus Russia and Mexico, have large remaining exploration potential, contrary to some predictions, plus huge scope for EOR and heavy oil.

4. There is a mixed picture of foreign investment across the major producers. Those, mostly the second-tier OPEC states, that have encouraged greater involvement (Algeria, Angola, Azerbaijan, Kazakhstan, Libya, and Nigeria) have seen production rise sharply. Saudi Arabia, Russia, and Brazil have grown output largely through their own efforts; Iran, Iraq, Kuwait, and Venezuela, with heavy constraints on outside involvement, have stagnated. Further international involvement, or even better domestic organization, could dramatically increase efficiency in several major producers.

5. The mature or maturing OECD countries, such as the United States, Canada, the United Kingdom, and Norway, again contrary to many prognostications, retain significant potential, particularly for exploration, heavy oil, and EOR, which can slow their declines or even reverse the trend.

6. There is an enormous resource base of heavy and extra-heavy oil and tar sands, which has hardly been addressed outside Canada and Venezuela and, even in those places, is still far short of potential.

7. Frontier areas are seeing a new wave of exploration, which has already led to some significant successes, particularly in deepwater. Again contrary to many prognostications, there remains scope for positive surprises in some lightly explored basins, deepwater seems set to make a sustained contribution to global production, and new projects in challenging areas, such as the Arctic and deepwater, are not unfeasibly difficult or expensive.

8. High energy prices, robust demand, environmental concerns, a drive to diversification of supply, and technological advances are all spurring the above developments.

For those, like Golda Meir, perennially sceptical of the potential of new petroleum areas, in September 2006, a (small) oil discovery was made north of the Dead Sea.

SAUDI ARABIA

I pay particular attention to Saudi Arabia in this section because it has been the mainstay of the global business ever since U.S. production started falling in 1970. During this period, it has consistently churned out more than 10 percent of the world's production (currently about 14 percent), except when it was defending prices in the early 1980s. Saudi policies have generally been aimed at a stable oil market and reasonable, not excessive, prices. However, the peak oil theorists, led by Houston investment banker Matthew Simmons,[4] have recently turned their sights on Saudi Arabia and its crown jewel Ghawar, the world's largest known conventional oil field, reasoning that, if they can demonstrate an imminent crash in Saudi production, then this will win the argument about global supply. Small fields in Texas or the North Sea are, they feel, not worth discussing if Saudi production plunges.

Simmons' argument and those of his supporters seems to be primarily along the following lines.

1. We do not know much about Saudi reserves apart from what they choose to tell us, and reported reserves jumped suspiciously in the 1980s.
2. The main fields are old, and technology is accelerating rather than preventing their decline. Technical papers in the public domain indicate increasing problems with the big fields, such as water production.
3. Other discovered Saudi fields are all small, poor quality, or both and will not make a major contribution to production.
4. The Kingdom has been well explored, and nothing more of note will be found.
5. Therefore, Saudi production is about to decline precipitously. Simmons (in 2004) foresaw "a collapse of thirty or forty percent of their production in the imminent future, and imminent means sometime in the next three to five years—but it could even be tomorrow."[5]
6. Saudi production cannot be replaced by any other country.
7. Therefore, we should all be very worried.

This line of argument was created by the ubiquitous Simmons, to be fair to him, one of the few writers on the topic who, like me, has actually been to Saudi Arabia and who has tried to analyze their fields with the scanty public domain data. Most other analysts are content to requote him, uncritically, ignoring the publications of qualified petroleum engineers.

Let us examine these arguments.

Saudi Reserves

Saudi Arabia's stated proven reserves have remained flat at about 260 billion bbl since 1988, a period in which they were producing about 3 billion bbl per year. Peak oil supporters point to this as an impossibility. However, Saudi Arabia, unlike Iran and Iraq, was exploring quite actively and with success during this period. The key was the opening up of the new Hawtah trend, southeast of Riyadh, which contains "Arabian Super-Light" oil of very low sulphur and excellent quality, in reservoirs entirely different from and much older than the Jurassic carbonates of the Saudi super-giants. From the late 1980s to 2003, this play added some 30 billion bbl to Saudi reserves.[6] Success continued thereafter, as Saudi Aramco announced that, in 2006, it discovered 3.6 billion bbl of oil, 6 percent more than it produced.[7]

So, although the year-by-year mathematics of flat reserves despite production may be implausible, the overall total is reasonable. From 1988 to 2006, Saudi quoted proven reserves increased from 255 billion bbl to 264 billion, i.e., 9 billion bbl, while total production was 62.5 billion bbl. Subtracting the Hawtah trend fields leaves 38 billion bbl to be added by other discoveries and improved recovery, revisions, and extensions to other fields, a modest 15 percent increase over the 1988 figure, in a period that saw major advances in three-dimensional seismic, horizontal drilling, and reservoir simulation. IHS puts 2005 Saudi reserves at 289 billion bbl, almost 10 percent *higher* than the official figures, based on a detailed bottom-up field analysis. The peak oilers' alternative—to discount entirely all reserves added after the 1988 revision—requires us to believe that there have been no discoveries whatsoever in the past two decades, nor any improvement in reservoir management. In a country of such hydrocarbon abundance as Saudi Arabia, this seems wildly improbable.

To give an example to illustrate the feasibility of this 15 percent increase, a single reservoir in Ghawar has already produced 23 percent more than its estimated total reserves calculated in 1973 (i.e., before the nationalization and well before the major reserves upgrades in the mid-1980s) and is still yielding more than 2 million bbl/day.[8]

Another line of evidence concerns Aramco's own plans before nationalization and before the reserves upgrades. In 1972, Aramco proposed to raise production from a little more than 6 million bbl/day to 13.4 million bbl/day by 1976 and 20 million bbl/day by 1982[9] (to give an impression of the magnitude of this, total OPEC production from 1982 to 1987 never exceeded 20 million bbl/day). With Aramco's then proven reserve base (168 billion bbl as of 1980), such a production level would have severely depleted the country's reserves, the R/P ratio falling below 10 by the early 1990s, a mere decade after reaching the 20 million bbl/day peak, strongly suggesting that Aramco was confident its reserves were conservatively estimated and could sustain much higher production levels. The timing of the reserve revisions and their subdivision into proved, probable, and possible categories, remains unclear and perhaps somewhat arbitrary, but this simple calculation illustrates that the magnitude of the increase is not so implausible.

Oil Minister Ali Al Naimi recently announced that "Saudi Arabia now has 1.2 trillion barrels of estimated reserve,"[10] but this seems excessive. It is difficult to imagine that even all of Saudi Arabia's oil in place, discovered and undiscovered, would amount to so much. However, in 1979, before the discovery of the Hawtah and other fields, total oil originally in place in Saudi Arabia was estimated as 530 billion bbl,[11] whereas now the figure is 700 billion bbl, of which 99 billion has been produced, and 260 billion bbl is considered to be proven reserves, with an additional 103 billion in the less certain probable and possible categories. Assuming, very conservatively, no additional extensions to known fields, this implies a very good, but not excessive, recovery factor of 51 percent, eventually increasing to 66 percent, a world-class but not unheard-of figure.

The USGS estimates 87 billion bbl yet to be found,[12] and this number could be as high as 200 billion bbl.[13] Applying common global benchmarks for EOR would suggest that Saudi Arabia could recover an additional 40–90 billion bbl, over and above the proven plus probable reserves. Even without EOR or any additional exploration success, Saudi Arabia is at most 30 percent through its total, not 50 percent, the 50 percent being key because this is the "magic number" at which Hubbert enthusiasts believe production must inevitably decline.

After the current wave of major field developments and reactivations (Manifa, Khursaniyah, Abu Hadriya, Khurais, Shaybah expansion, etc.), Saudi Arabia has a second tier of smaller fields—Rimthan in the northeast, the central Juraybiat, offshore Jana, and new reservoirs at Dammam (the kingdom's oldest field) and Wafra in the Neutral Zone—each in the 0.8–2 billion bbl range, plus 50 other fields with lesser volumes, as well as numerous gas developments that yield associated liquids, such as Karan. Shaybah, currently working toward 750,000 bbl/day during 2008, could ultimately reach 1 million bbl/day. Furthermore, Saudi Arabia contains significant heavy oil resources, for example in the Wafra Field, in the Partitioned Neutral Zone between Saudi Arabia and Kuwait, and the giant Manifa field, and Al Naimi has stated that their exploitation could add "tens of billions of barrels of reserves."[14] For instance, the recovery factor at Wafra could be increased from 3 to 40 percent (benchmark recovery factors in western Canada are 60 percent), and trials of steam injection have been promising in producing this heavy crude.[15]

Technology and Technical Problems

Most of the Geologists' arguments about Saudi oil (and I count Simmons as a Geologist, although as an investment banker you might expect him to line up with the Economists) betray a phobia about modern oilfield technology and a lack of understanding of petroleum engineering.

For instance, Simmons states, "It seems unlikely that Aramco would drill these costly [horizontal] wells ... had a great deal of easy oil been left at either Ghawar or Abqaiq that could be tapped by using conventional vertical-well drilling."[16] This demonstrates a confusion of cost with value. When Aramco did begin using horizontal wells, they did so despite the increased cost because the *value* is much higher. When a horizontal well costs 50 percent more than a vertical well but produces 100 percent more, as is often the case, the investment is easy to justify. Nowadays, if reservoir engineers propose a vertical well, they will be asked why it is not horizontal rather than the other way around.

Despite Simmons' contention that "collecting and use of data was superb ... use of 'Best in Class' oilfield technology was even better ... Water injection program was pristine,"[17] Saudi Aramco is far from pushing the technical limits. Individually, they have some very good staff and make full use of the latest technology from service companies such as Schlumberger and Halliburton, but, although one of the more adept NOCs, they are technically much more conservative than IOCs such as BP and Shell or a really able NOC such as the deepwater pioneers Petrobras of Brazil.

I visited Saudi Arabia in 1998, when Aramco was just discovering horizontal wells, touting the benefits on their posters, but the rest of the international industry had woken up to horizontal wells in the early 1990s. So, rather than adopting horizontal wells out of desperation, Aramco was actually slow to use them. The company also still lacks integration between the different technical disciplines: such integration, centered on the use of three-dimensional static (geological) and dynamic (reservoir engineering) models of the reservoir, was one of the key innovations in IOCs during the 1990s. This is pretty much inevitable in a company that remains very much a political rather than commercial animal, has a monopoly in its home country, has a role to play as a job creation agency, and has had a license to print money for the past fifty years. If really pushed, Saudi Aramco can develop its fields much more effectively than is done today.

Critics often point to Yibal in Oman for an example of how technology just accelerates production rather than increasing reserves and how a calamitous collapse in Saudi output will result. However, Yibal is an unusual case and very different from the Saudi fields. First, the drop was not as severe as Simmons portrays it. He states that production fell from 225,000 bbl/day in 1997 to 40,000 by 2005; the actual change was from 220,000 bbl/day to 84,000. Second, the decline is portrayed as being caused by the use of horizontal wells and other advanced technologies; actually, the culprit was poor reservoir management. A high-permeability[18] "thief zone" was not identified and led to premature water breakthrough. The Saudis are well aware of these thief ("super-K") zones and have done a great deal of work to map their occurrence.[19, 20] Third, Yibal has a very different rock type from the nearest Saudi field, Shaybah, whose reservoir formation, albeit with the same name, is of much better quality. Fourth, Yibal is much smaller than the Saudi super-giants. Water breakthrough in a super-K zone in Ghawar would only downgrade a small part of the entire field. Fifth, there are technologies that offer at least a partial solution to such water breakthrough, shutting off or plugging the offending zone, or thickening the injection water with polymers so that it pushes the oil rather than bypassing it.

This paranoia about water shows itself in several other comments on the issue. For instance, "Some oil engineers had written that a water cut of even 2% should send the signal to halt all water injection."[21] If that were true, it would mean shutting down most of the world's production. Another commentator, who claims to have "spent a lifetime in the oil industry" yet believes that Ghawar's main reservoir is sandstone (it is probably the most famous carbonate reservoir in the world, the Arab D), quotes a journalist, Paul Roberts: "At Ghawar, the engineer said, the 'water cut' was 30%." The hairs on the back of my neck stood up. Ghawar's water injections were hardly news, but a 30% water cut, if true, was startling. Most new oilfields produce almost pure oil or oil mixed with natural gas—with little water."[22] This news would only be startling to an industry outsider. A 30 percent water cut (of each one hundred barrels extracted, thirty are water and seventy oil) is nothing surprising. How would Roberts react to the very mature Nimr field in Oman, which has a 96 percent water cut and produces 1.4 million bbl of water per day for only 0.057 million bbl of oil?[23] Yet Nimr manages to cope with this challenge to the extent that it is still Oman's second largest producing field (ironically, in first place is the much-maligned Yibal). The global water cut, incidentally, is about 75 percent.[24] The Ghawar water cut, after increasing during the 1990s, has actually decreased subsequently, whereas oil production has remained steady, except when OPEC quotas intervened.

To take another (nontechnical) commentator, Don Coxe, of the Bank of Montreal, questions why the Saudis would apply water injection to new field developments: "Water flooding on newborn Saudi wells? Isn't water flooding [the] Viagra of ageing wells?"[25] In this, he is at least thirty years out of date. Water injection used to be seen as a method to extract the remaining oil from depleted fields, but, at least since Alaska and the North Sea in the 1970s, many, if not most, new fields have water and/or gas injection installed from the beginning. For instance, Murphy's brand new major deepwater field, Kikeh in Malaysia, will inject 260,000 bbl/day of water to produce 120,000 bbl/day of oil.[26] Water injection accelerates production and boosts ultimate recovery. To take a counterexample, the Valhall field, a 1970s era development in Norway that did not have water injection installed immediately, has probably lost ultimate recovery because parts of the reservoir were allowed to depressurize. It would be poor petroleum engineering practice if the Saudis were *not* water flooding[27] those of their fields that lacked natural pressure support (i.e., most of the onshore ones).

This debate about reservoir pressure highlights another misconception. One writer, discussing Simmons' book, has written:

Simmons in particular has noted that the higher the water pressurization is, the faster high reservoir pressurization will end. When pressure falls to what he terms the "bubble point," gas bubbles to the top of the oil reservoir, accelerating the pressure loss. Eventually, the "dew point" is reached, and the rest of the oil in the reservoir is rendered unrecoverable. This is the natural death that is experienced by oilfields in which recovery is enhanced by water injection.[28]

I am not sure where to begin with the errors in this statement. First, water injection maintains, not decreases, pressure in the reservoir. If done correctly, pressure can be maintained at high levels indefinitely even if water cut rises and oil production falls. Reaching the "bubble point" (an expression used by generations of petroleum engineers, not coined by Simmons as the review implies) is usually a sign of poor reservoir management, although it may be done deliberately in certain circumstances.[29] The "dew point" is a term referring to gas reservoirs, not oil, and is irrelevant to the oil recovery issue. Even if the pressure does go below the bubble point, the remaining oil is just harder to recover, not impossible.

To take another comment on Saudi Arabia that shows how badly the peak oil theorists underestimate the ability of a little ingenuity and technology (helped by higher oil prices) to overcome what they elevate into insuperable problems,

Beneath the seabed off the coast of Saudi Arabia is an oil field called Manifa. It is giant, and its riches are almost untapped. There is, however, a snag. Its oil is heavy with vanadium and hydrogen sulphide, making it virtually unusable. One day the technology may be in place to remove these contaminants, but it will not be for a long time, and when, or if, it becomes possible, it will do no more than slightly reduce the rate at which the world's oil supplies slip away towards depletion.[30]

This paragraph was written in 2000: now Manifa is being developed to start producing in 2011 and reach a plateau of 1 million bbl/day by 2013. Actually, removing vanadium and H_2S has been rather straightforward for several decades.

I could go on with these examples of misapprehension and technophobia, but the point should be clear. Most of the "problems" that Simmons identifies comes from SPE papers. These are written by engineers whose job it is to solve problems in oil fields. Naturally, they write about these problems. Technical papers in which everything goes well and nothing innovative is done are boring to read and do not advance the careers of their authors. Furthermore, most of the issues he identifies—corrosion of pipes by salt water, the installation of electrical submersible pumps, corrosive, toxic H_2S, and scaling (buildup of insoluble minerals in pipes)—are standard oil-field fare, encountered and solved everywhere in the world. Indeed, some of the problems—bacterial souring (generation of H_2S) and scaling—can be attributable to common mistakes in field development. There is no discussion of the *really* advanced technologies that Saudi

Arabia would be introducing if decline were imminent, notably massive EOR programs.

This, of course, brings us to the question of why the Saudis would want to accelerate production using these purported "advanced" technologies. Again, the peak oilers see in this the signature of imminent depletion, a need to produce quickly to stave off decline. However, surprisingly for investment bankers, Simmons and Coxe appear to have forgotten the time value of money. The Saudis save money by only developing fields as and when they are needed and by producing a few fields at relatively high levels rather than many of them very slowly. Still, depletion rates in Ghawar and the other giants are well below those typical in non-OPEC countries.

Exploration Potential

This deals with the existing fields. What about new reserves? Exploration in Saudi Arabia in recent years has focused on natural gas, which either leads us to believe that (as peak oil supporters would like) that they have run out of good oil prospects or, more likely, that they see no immediate need for new oil reserves. Peak oil theorists incline to the view that Saudi Arabia's exploration potential is negligible, for instance, "no major exploration success since the 1960s."[31] I would consider the 14 billion bbl Shaybah Field (found in 1975) and the 30 billion bbl in the Hawtah trend fields (late 1980s to 2003) as major, more than all the reserves of Libya.

The view that Saudi Arabia has enough oil to support its medium-term plans without additional exploration is supported by the structure of the gas exploration contracts let to Shell, Total, Repsol, LUKOil, and other international firms in recent years. These deals give the contractor a modest finder's fee for oil, ensuring that they have very little incentive to look for it; if the Saudis were desperate for new oil, they would reward the discoverer more richly. These contracts focus on the Rub' Al Khali Basin[32] in the south of the country, which is probably the last major frontier in Saudi Arabia. The Red Sea is also largely unexplored but appears much less promising, while a very few wells have been drilled on the Saudi side of the border across from Iraq's Western Desert, without success.

As Figure 5.1 shows, nearly all Saudi exploration drilling has focused on the Eastern Province and the adjoining offshore, with some scattered wells adjacent to Jordan and in the Rub' Al Khali, plus a few along the Red Sea coast. The Arabian Shield (shaded) is composed of Precambrian[33] igneous and metamorphic[34] rocks with no hydrocarbon potential. The Rub' Al Khali, containing a major Infracambrian[35] graben system, and adjacent to Yemen (a reasonably significant oil producer in its own right, although no Saudi Arabia) appears to have potential for reservoirs and source rocks like those of Oman.[36] It is virtually undrilled, especially in

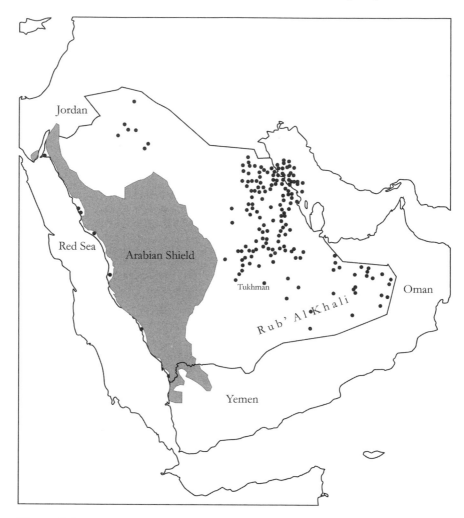

Figure 5.1
Exploration wells in Saudi Arabia.

the southern part, and initial results have been mixed, but LUKOil has already made a discovery at Tukhman.

Excluding surprises in the almost unknown Rub' Al Khali, Saudi Arabia
certainly does not seem to have the remaining exploration potential of
Iran or Iraq, because it has undergone a reasonably thorough and modern
exploration program, and the geological structure of its main fields is
fairly simple. However, there remains potential for additional exploration
in the Eastern Province, for instance in the very shallow-water and interti-
dal areas where seismic is only now being acquired. The concentration of

resources in Ghawar, holding about half the Kingdom's oil, is remarkable and does suggest that, if Saudi Arabia remotely resembles other petroleum provinces, there should be substantially more to discover.[37] Even in under-explored Iran, the largest field, Gachsaran, contains only 16.5 percent of the total; in California, Wilmington accounts for just 9.5 percent of the state's ultimate recovery.

Gas exploration has been very successful over the past decade in deep reservoirs and offshore in the Persian Gulf.[38] If we assume that Saudi gas is similar to the (moderately rich[39]) North Field gas, then the total nonassociated gas reserves would contain some 7 billion bbl of liquid hydrocarbons.

Decline in Saudi Production?

Matthew Simmons argues[40] that the super-giant Saudi fields are aging and depleted and that the next generation will not be capable of making up the decline. An anonymous contributor to Campbell's *Peak Oil* newsletter makes a similar point: "We may also ask why Saudi would prefer to go to such lengths to try to maintain production from its four main ageing fields if it had all these new discoveries ready to yield flush production."[41] The concept of "flush production," or the prolific early output from a new field, dates back to the early years of the twentieth century, before the introduction of modern secondary recovery techniques; the phrase is hardly used now. Nevertheless, the answer to the writer's question is that Saudi Arabia has so far felt that the four main fields were sufficient and were not being overly stretched. Only recently, as discussed above, has it begun development of some of the other fields. It is far cheaper to maintain or expand capacity at an existing field than to develop a new one, so Saudi Arabia's actions were merely the most rational way of maximizing value within the framework of their OPEC quota. Saudi Arabia is behaving *exactly* as one would expect if it had, or at least believed that it had, huge remaining reserves in its key fields. Indeed, Saudi Arabia has screened tertiary recovery methods but specifically concluded that it *does not need them* to meet its current production goals.[42] As discussed below, comparisons with Oman, a relatively minor producer whose output is (perhaps temporarily) in decline, show that, if peak oil were really approaching in Saudi Arabia, activity in drilling, EOR, and so on would be far more intense than it really is. Recent analysis of satellite imagery suggests that drilling on Ghawar is concentrating on new developments, including gas, not on mitigating supposed declines in the mature parts of the field.[43]

Simmons further maintains that Saudi Arabia's production cutbacks in the 1980s were induced by its need to rest its big fields. This is not the case. As shown by its experience when it abandoned a vain attempt to shore up prices and finally increased production in 1986: the oil price fell

50 percent and remained low for the next fifteen years. The world had enough oil. Production was reduced because the *demand* for Saudi oil was not there, not because supply was not. Saudi production went up nearly 50 percent between 1985 and 1986, and, when a rapid increase was required to cover the oil lost as a result of Iraq's invasion of Kuwait, the Saudis delivered within a few weeks, upping output by almost a quarter. Such rapid rises, on demand, are certainly not suggestive of the ageing fields or struggling industry that Simmons portrays. As for the Hawtah trend fields, the main incentive for their exploration and development was not declines in the existing fields; it was that the Arabian Super-Light blend commanded a premium price over the usual Saudi export crudes, and, at a time when the country was limited by OPEC quotas, it made sense to maximize the value rather than the volume of exports. Again, demand limited supply rather than vice versa.

Costs in Saudi Arabia also remain very low by global standards. Accurate estimates are hard to make because of a paucity of data, but they vary from $1.2 to $5.1/bbl,[44] obviously far below the low prices of 1998 let alone recent highs. This implies that even a vast rise in Saudi costs, caused by a need for greatly intensified drilling, new field developments, EOR, or some other techniques to offset depletion, would not affect prices *at all* because global oil prices are set by the marginal barrel.

Could Saudi Arabia Be Replaced?

The final part of the peak oil argument about Saudi Arabia is that its enormous production cannot be replaced. Well, that is true, if the Eastern Province were hit by a meteorite tomorrow, no doubt the global oil industry would find it very hard to recover. However, if Saudi Arabia merely enters a period of rather rapid decline, as the most pessimistic forecasters predict, can we recover?

Let us not exaggerate the importance of Saudi Arabia. Yes, it is key to world oil markets, but it produces less than 14 percent of global oil. If it were declining at a (rapid) 5 percent per year, we would need to develop annually an additional 500,000 bbl/day of capacity (or cut demand). This is only a tenth of the 1978–1980 supply disruptions, and under present industry conditions would be a challenge to replace but far from catastrophic.

IRAN

As I am writing this, I happen to be flying over southern Iran on a clear, almost cloudless day. Beneath me, I can see numerous anticlinal structures, the surface expressions of massive folds. A few of these host large oil and gas fields; the vast majority are so far entirely untested by the drill bit.

Iran's production comes primarily from its "big six" fields, Ahwaz, Agha Jari, Bibi Hakimeh, Gachsaran, Marun, and Rag-e Sefid, which contribute some 60 percent of crude oil output. These fields are old, discovered between 1928 (Gachsaran) and 1963 (Marun). However, Iran has also a huge backlog of undeveloped or underdeveloped discoveries, such as its recent super-giant discoveries Azadegan (1999) and Yadavaran (2004), near the Iraqi border in the southwest province of Khuzestan.

As mentioned in Chapter 4, Iran has been prone to allegedly suspicious revisions of its proven reserves, in the same way as several other OPEC members. Stated reserves jumped sharply from 52 to 93 billion bbl in 1986 and then again to 137.5 billion bbl in 2005. Iran's current commercial reserves (in production or with firm development plans) are independently estimated at only 38 billion bbl. However, there are an additional 75 billion bbl of "technical reserves," that is, proven fields with no current plans for development. This brings the total up to 113 billion bbl. The remaining gap of 24.5 billion bbl, although large in absolute terms, is clearly more modest than the difference between 137.5 and 38 and could represent some more optimistic assumptions on the success of secondary or tertiary recovery initiatives, condensate in as yet undeveloped gas fields, plus some very heavy oil resources that a number of independent observers have not considered to merit the status of reserves. Various other estimates based on real field data (not the extrapolations and rules of thumb of peak oilers) combined with benchmark recovery factors confirm that a figure of about 130–140 billion bbl is reasonable.[45, 46]

Dr. Bakhtiari, a former senior NIOC[47] employee, has brought joy to oil depletionists by saying, "the usually accepted official 132 billion barrels is almost 100 billion barrels over any realistic assay. If the higher figure was for real, its oil industry would not be struggling day in and day out to keep output at between 3.0-3.5 million barrels per day."[48] Dr. Bakhtiari's comments are correct if we are talking only about fields in production. However, Iran's struggles are attributable to a catastrophic lack of investment in new fields, poor management of existing fields, opposition to foreign involvement, and U.S. sanctions. Iran could maintain and even increase production significantly if it could only bring fields such as Azadegan into commission. Very simple measures, such as installing water handling capacity at some major fields and ending rich gas flaring, would lead to significant production gains immediately. In fact, since Dr. Bakhtiari wrote in 2006, Iranian output has increased markedly, to about 4 million bbl/day at the start of 2008.[49]

Iran's exploration drilling peaked in 1975, with twenty-seven wells, and was maintained at this level until 1978, after which the Revolution and Iran–Iraq war brought exploration to a virtual halt. Since 1988, a limited amount of exploration, up to three wells per year, has resumed. The recent, vast discoveries at Azadegan and Yadavaran, with other smaller but still sizeable finds made by international operators, and potential for deeper drilling in many of the big fields confirm Iran's continuing prospectivity. The historic success rate is 69 percent, testament to both the enormous prospectivity of Iran and the limited exploration efforts. Bear in mind, also, that most of these discoveries were made with just surface geology, plus a limited amount of two-dimensional seismic, and that twenty-seven wells annually is hardly a lot for a giant, highly prolific petroleum province like Iran. Modern three-dimensional seismic and structural geology would be invaluable in revealing significant fields in the complex Zagros mountain belt, probably smaller than those known so far but still making a big contribution. For example, one structure defined near the Paris and Karanj fields could hold some 20 billion bbl of oil in place. The deep waters of the South Caspian, partly disputed with Azerbaijan, also appear highly promising although risky, with Iran's sector having potential for some 14 billion bbl. This is not to mention the southern Fars Province and its associated offshore, whose scope for gas and associated liquids is probably unsurpassed anywhere in the world.

IRAQ

Iraq is by far the least developed and explored country for petroleum in the world relative to its potential. Since 1988, war, sanctions, and war again have prevented any serious exploration efforts and hampered attempts to rehabilitate the industry. Iraq's reentry into world markets as a major player depends on a political resolution to the continuing conflict, as discussed in Chapter 8. In fact, exploration has been at a very low level since 1961, when 99.5 percent of the acreage of the multinational consortium Iraq Petroleum Company (IPC) was removed from them, leaving only the producing fields. Even before its various conflicts, Iraq has historically fallen far short of its petroleum potential.

Overall, despite the insinuations of the Geologists, a commonly quoted figure of 100 billion bbl (compared with the official 115 billion bbl) for Iraqi reserves seems a minimum.[50, 51] A figure of as high as 214 billion bbl is plausible[52, 53, 54] plus another 50 or so billion bbl of undiscovered oil and NGLs.

Immediately before the American invasion, of the ninety-eight fields discovered, only twenty-one are known ever to have produced, and, of these, two (Rumaila and Kirkuk) yielded 90 percent of the total. The simplest action, assuming tolerable security conditions, to unlock Iraq's vast potential would therefore be to institute good reservoir management at these two largest producing fields. The Iraqi technicians who run these fields have performed miracles with string and Band-Aids to keep the fields running, but they have been starved of investment and isolated from modern technology for nearly thirty years. Simple measures such as drilling additional wells, patching up facilities and pipelines, installing water handling, and stopping the injection of unwanted heavy fuel oil would lead to a rapid and significant increase in output, probably by some 500,000 bbl/day.

The next step Iraq could take to increase production would be to develop some of its inventory of ninety-six undeveloped or underdeveloped discoveries. These includes world-scale super-giants: East Baghdad, with 36 billion bbl of potential reserves; Majnoon, with some 7–20 billion; West Qurna (the northern extension of Rumaila), with about 10 billion; Zubair, with 8 billion; Nahr Umr, with 5 billion; Jambur, with 3–6 billion; and at least six more fields with more than 1 billion bbl of reserves each. These reserve numbers have not been audited but are generally based on data from the days of IPC,[55] the Iraqi Petroleum Company consortium[56] that operated in Iraq. IPC was, by the standards of its time, a solid technical company, and so these figures can be regarded as fairly reliable although probably conservative if compared with modern recovery rates. Once these fields have been developed, there remain the eighty-four other discoveries, smaller but still sizeable. Within a few years, output of 6.5–7 million bbl/day is quite feasible.[57]

Production on this scale would make Iraq the third largest producer in the world, and its status could be augmented by exploration. As of 1988, when exploration activity virtually ceased, 125 exploration wells had been drilled, discovering some 920 million bbl per well, with a success rate of 78 percent.[58] (In fact, as mentioned above, serious exploration stopped in 1961, with the exception of a brief, but very successful, burst in the 1970s and a few discoveries in the 1980s.) This is a finding rate without parallel in the world. For comparison, drilling in the North Sea in its very successful first phase, from 1960 to 1983, yielded about 42 million boe per wildcat,[59] or only 5 percent of the Iraqi average, with a success rate of little more than 10 percent.

Many of the big fields have been drilled only to very moderate depths of 2,000–3,000 meters; because they are multilayered, like most big Middle Eastern accumulations, there is plenty of low-risk potential for exploring deeper horizons. The Western Desert, a huge area between the Euphrates River to the east and Syria, Jordan, and Saudi Arabia to the west, has barely been explored, although geologically it has significant risks. The Zagros foothills, mostly within Iraqi Kurdistan, are also all but untouched and, as in Iran, have great potential. As the security situation is much better here than the rest of the country, Kurdistan holds the most immediate potential for discoveries and developments. New finds have already been made here by smaller companies, near the village of Tawke in northern Kurdistan. This area looked promising because of local oil seeps; one villager mentioned that "All we knew was that the cows and sheep kept getting stuck in the stuff."[60]

The lead time to rehabilitate and develop the existing fields would be likely to be seven to ten years from the start of serious development. This additional oil could meet more than half of the world's incremental demand if it were possible to begin this development in the period 2008–2010. The addition of future discoveries could raise total production to 10 million bbl/day, on par with Russia and Saudi Arabia today. Because it would probably take three to four years to organize the exploration campaigns, achieving this level would take more than a decade. Iraq's contribution by 2017 could be 40 percent of all the additional oil required by the world.

UNITED ARAB EMIRATES

The production of the UAE is dominated by Abu Dhabi, the largest of the seven Emirates that make up the federation. Contrary to frequent misconceptions, Dubai is neither the capital nor the largest Emirate of the UAE, nor is it especially rich in oil.

The UAE's official reserves are stated as 97.8 billion bbl. Of these, 4 billion are credited to Dubai, a figure that some public sources suggest to be too high; the bulk of the remainder belongs to Abu Dhabi. Industry databases put Abu Dhabi's remaining proven reserves at about 69 billion bbl, including that produced after the 2014–2018 expiry of the licenses for the IOC consortia.[61] Additionally, a number of discoveries, particularly offshore, remain undeveloped and only partially appraised, and the Emirate is also a major producer of condensate from its large gas reserves, the subject of ambitious development plans. The recovery factors implied for the main fields are relatively low: 40–50 percent for Asab, Bab, Bu Hasa, and Upper Zakum. Applying Norwegian best-in-class recovery factors of, say, 60 percent (and recognizing that the reservoirs are probably less favorable but the operating environment is much cheaper) could add on the order of another 15 billion bbl. Nevertheless, chiming with observations by other commentators,[62] this does suggest a degree of overstatement in the official figures, possibly as much as 40 percent. Still, the likely remaining reserves of about 63 billion bbl are still more than 70 percent greater than Campbell's suggestion.

Abu Dhabi performs hardly any exploration. ADCO and ADMA, respectively, the main onshore and offshore operators, each drill a single exploration well per year. To depletion enthusiasts, this is a sign that there is very little remaining potential. Much more plausibly, and as ADCO staff have said to me, there is hardly any point even in drilling that single well: the backlog of undeveloped discoveries is sufficient to increase production to targeted levels and maintain it there indefinitely. The main role of exploration is to keep advancing the geological knowledge of Abu Dhabi and possibly to discover reserves that may be somewhat cheaper to develop than others already known. Surprisingly for its relatively limited territory, Abu Dhabi has not been intensively explored, and there remains a number of unappraised discoveries, as well as unexplored areas, notably the transition zone (between land and open sea) where seismic has never been shot. The potential for stratigraphic traps has been recognized[63] in both the west of the Emirate and the northern part, abutting Dubai, but has not been seriously pursued as yet. Dubai has also been very little explored in recent years and contains a number of undeveloped oil and gas finds. The "Protocol Area" in offshore Sharjah, surrounding the Iranian-occupied island of Abu Musa, is also of interest. Production and future potential in the other Emirates is minor.

In line with underestimates of oil reserves, Campbell's 2010 forecast for Abu Dhabi production of 2.1 million bbl and Simmons' prediction of 2.1 million bbl/day in 2012 are dramatically lower than the Emirate's own, credible plans for 3.3 million bbl/day in 2010 and 3.4 million bbl/day in 2012.

KUWAIT

Kuwait is probably the most controversial among those OPEC nations who sharply increased their stated reserves in the 1980s because of an acrimonious debate in the country over its future oil policy and the leak of a Kuwait Oil Company report in 2006 that seemed to show its reserves were much lower than had been believed.

Kuwait officially states its reserves at 101.5 billion bbl (as of the end of 2005). However, the Kuwait Oil Company report gave a very different picture, suggesting only 23.5 billion bbl proven and an additional 22.3 nonproven. The total is even lower than IHS Energy's figure of 54.1 billion and the Centre for Global Energy Studies' 74.2 billion bbl. Pessimism on Kuwait therefore appears likely partly to temper optimism on Iraq and Iran.

Kuwait's territory is, of course, very small, and exploration has been reasonably thorough. Nevertheless, there have been significant discoveries reported recently of gas and light oil, as much as 10–13 billion bbl, in deeper reservoirs, which greatly exceeds peak oil prognostications. Kuwait also has major potential for redevelopment of its existing fields if it can negotiate satisfactory arrangements with IOCs for its "Project Kuwait" northern fields and for heavy oil production, for which it recently came to agreement with ExxonMobil.

QATAR

Qatar is one of the smaller OPEC oil producers, with output at 1.1 million bbl/day in 2006. However, it has the third largest gas reserves in the world, almost entirely contained in the immense North Field (South Pars in Iran).

Qatari reserves are given as 15 billion bbl. These have undergone one sharp jump, from 3.7 to 13 billion bbl in 2000 (about the time that North Field development got into full swing). A field-by-field analysis based on independent data suggests 5.9 billion bbl of remaining oil reserves, but this apparent overreporting is explained by the enormous volumes of condensate and NGLs that can be extracted from the North Field gas. Adding this suggests some 13.3 billion bbl remaining reserves plus another 45 billion bbl or so of NGL/condensate resources that could be recovered from future phases of North Field development, as yet unsanctioned. The total liquid reserves are therefore credible. Doubts cast on the North Field's potential represent a selective and misleading view of some geological publications. Qatar's decision to halt new developments until 2010 is a sensible response to logistical challenges onshore, not a sign of insufficient gas reserves.

OTHER MIDDLE EAST

The Middle East is sometimes popularly considered as an inexhaustible source of oil. Most production comes from the "Big Five"—Saudi Arabia, Iran, Iraq, the UAE, and Kuwait. Qatar, Oman, Syria, Yemen, and Bahrain are also progressively less significant producers. Is there potential for a new "Saudi Arabia" somewhere in the Middle East?

Most of Middle Eastern production comes from a relatively small area, bounded approximately by an irregular quadrilateral with corners at Kirkuk, Hormuz Island at the entrance to the Persian Gulf, Shaybah (just south of the UAE), and Riyadh. A repeat elsewhere in the Middle East of the massive fields made in the Gulf and the area immediately surrounding it is unlikely. Many areas of the Middle East have been quite sparsely explored, but probably enough has been done to turn up a huge new province if it existed. The one exception may be the Rub' Al Khali of southern Saudi Arabia.

The primary potential in the Middle East lies in drilling up innumerable smaller and deeper structures and nonstructural traps in and around the main fields. There is also some potential in frontier marine areas: Syria's Eastern Mediterranean; Turkey's deepwater Black Sea; and Oman, Yemen, and Iran's Indian Ocean offshore. Onshore through the Middle East, however, there remains huge potential for deep, tight[64] gas and significant scope for other oil discoveries. Three of the success stories of exploration in the 1990s were the opening up of the Arif Graben in Yemen, the Euphrates Graben[65] in Syria, and the deep intrasalt and subsalt formations of Oman; other Middle Eastern countries have the possibility for similar surprises. There is also abundant heavy oil in the Big Five, as well as Oman, Syria, and Bahrain.

Oman presents an example of methods the big producers in the Middle East might turn to as their larger fields enter decline. A crash campaign has been launched to offset recent falls in production. EOR techniques, including steam injection, polymer injection, and miscible gas floods, are being introduced at fields such as Qarn Alam, Marmul, and Harweel.[66] Given the very considerable remaining oil-in-place of Oman, some 50 billion bbl, and the low recovery factor of only 28 percent,[67] EOR could unlock significant new volumes. An enormous heavy oil project has been launched at Mukhaizna, in the south of the country. Most interestingly of all, the near-monopoly position of the NOC PDO[68] is being dismantled. PDO has been forced to relinquish significant tracts of outlying exploration acreage, to give up the rights to several undeveloped gas discoveries (e.g., Khazzan-Makarem was won by BP out of a constellation of industry giants also including British Gas [BG], Shell/Total, and Nexen/Dubai Energy), and to bring in other operators for some of its smaller fields. Even the massive Mukhaizna project is to be managed by a new operator, Occidental (specialists in EOR) rather than PDO. If the Big Five were facing comparable problems to Oman, given the utter reliance of their economy on oil and their generally very responsible and protective attitude toward world oil markets, they would surely be contemplating similar measures.

By 2004, Oman was drilling about 450 wells annually to moderate decline in its production, then at about 800,000 bbl/day. Contrastingly, in the rest of the Middle East, including the Big Five, about 1,000 wells were drilled to keep production at about 20 million bbl/day.[69] In other words, Oman's drilling campaign was more than ten times more intensive, in terms of the production being maintained, than the rest of the Middle East (which still includes some fairly mature production in Syria, Bahrain, and Yemen). This statistic demonstrates what can be achieved with a determined, focused investment campaign and what could, and would, be done in the other states if decline threatened.

Nevertheless, many peak oil theorists, consistent at least in their disbelief in the Middle East, are gloomy on the prospects for the minor countries. For example, considering the future for Omani production, Simmons sees output at 300,000 bbl/day by 2018 and Campbell at approximately 440,000 bbl/day,[70] but analyzing just the country's own existing fields plus identified commercial projects suggests a much higher figure, 618,000 bbl/day, which should be further augmented by future project sanctions, exploration success, and new EOR initiatives. This observation outlines that pessimistic forecasts based on country-level decline curves, extrapolations, and so forth badly undershoot bottom-up predictions based on a knowledge of a country's real projects and plans.

LIBYA

Libya will be an important test case for some other OPEC producers. Isolated from outside technology and investment by sanctions and policy, production fell from its peak of 3.4 million bbl/day in 1970 to a low of

1 million bbl/day by 1987. After that, it slowly recovered to 1.4 million bbl/day in 2002 and has grown strongly since then, reaching 1.8 million bbl/day in 2006. The catalyst for this resurgence has been a great improvement in the investment climate, including the ending of U.S. sanctions in September 2004, bringing in numerous Western companies to operate with modern skills and technology. Libya has also held a number of highly successful licensing rounds for exploration acreage, for which competitors have bid extremely stringent terms to enter. This intense investment in exploration, including opening up all but unexplored areas such as the offshore, has the potential to increase Libya's reserves significantly in the future.

Libya illustrates how harmful the nationalizations of the 1970s were to the global exploration effort and how much they have distorted the finding picture, giving the misleading impression that new oil is drying up. It has been written that "Since then [1970], a less active and more conservative exploration effort has taken place ... Complex and subtle plays ... were rarely pursued prior to the 1990s." With reference to the Libyan Ghadames basin, "in the last 10 years, an estimated 5 billion to 6 billion bbl of recoverable oil equivalent has been discovered ... in the Algerian sector of the Ghadamis [sic] Basin. The key to these discoveries was an understanding of the plays and 3-D seismic. During that same period, there was minimal success in the Libyan sector, although geologic setting and reservoirs are essentially the same."[71] This analysis supports the contention that the failure to find more oil in, among other countries, Libya since the 1960s has been caused mainly by lack of effort and technology, not to unprospective geology. Remaining potential could be as much as 50 billion bbl[72]; 14 billion bbl have been found, primarily by foreign companies, during 1993–2006.

Libyan oil is particularly welcome to world markets, because it is mostly light and low in sulphur, hence more palatable to the current refining setup than heavy, sulphurous Persian Gulf crudes. It has been estimated that flow rates in the older, state-run fields could be doubled by relatively simple measures of upgrading facilities and using improved recovery methods, because recovery factors are very low. Such actions, together with EOR projects and exploration, make the national target of 3 million bbl/day feasible if logistically challenging to achieve by 2015. This would return Libya almost to its 1970 heyday and meet some 20 percent of incremental world demand.

ALGERIA

Algeria is the second largest producer in Africa, after Nigeria, although soon set to lose its silver medal to Angola and perhaps Libya. After nationalization of all French holdings in 1970–1971, it was not possible for IOCs to operate in Algeria until a limited liberalization in 1986. Since then, Algeria has been in the vanguard of those OPEC states opening up their industry to foreign investment and has seen great success from exploration and gas developments. Despite this, the environment of high prices has encouraged the government, in its recent Hydrocarbon Law, to reassert state control over the sector and raise taxes.

Total production was 2 million bbl/day in 2006, of which almost 40 percent was NGLs. Algeria was planning to reach 2 million bbl of crude oil (excluding NGLs) production per day by 2010[73] but may struggle to meet this, partly because of delays in developing some complex projects given the current tight oil service market and partly because of uncertainty over its new Windfall Tax.

Algeria's reserves history is straightforward, with none of the allegedly suspicious jumps of some other OPEC countries. Given striking recent successes, the presence of many undeveloped discoveries, lack of exploration in some frontier basins including the offshore, and EOR potential, Campbell's assignation of only 2.2 billion bbl of additional reserves appears very grudging, besides the USGS's estimated exploration potential of approximately 8 billion bbl of oil and NGLs (and they do not ascribe any oil to the offshore).

SUDAN

The end of Sudan's dreadful civil war between North and South has finally allowed rapid progress on developing some of the country's large oil resources. The genocide in Darfur, for all its horror, is a long way from the known oil fields and has not affected them directly, nor have the operators in the country, dominated by Chinese, Indian, Malaysian, Kuwaiti, and UAE companies, been deterred by Western public opinion. The result is that Sudan has been one of the largest contributors to recent non-OPEC production growth and has even talked of joining OPEC. Oil has been accused of fueling the various civil wars; it certainly appears to have paid for more deadly means of fighting them.

With total production at some 520,000 bbl/day and reserves of 6.3 billion bbl, Sudan has already exceeded peak oil expectations (predicting just 300,000 bbl/day in 2010 and ultimate recovery of 3.5 billion bbl[74]). The USGS has only assessed the coastal zone, while the main fields are well inland, which suggests that its figure for Sudan's future potential is a serious underestimate, too. That said, the prospective acreage is confined in fairly narrow grabens, so it would seem unlikely that Sudan is going to add dramatically to its current reserves and production, short of surprises in some of its frontier areas.

NIGERIA

On January 24, 2006, thirty armed men with AK-47s drew up in speedboats by the offices of the Agip company in the oil city of Port Harcourt, in the Niger Delta. In the ensuing gunfight, nine people were killed, eight of them police, and the gunmen escaped with tens of thousands of dollars from a bank in the facility.[75] In November, the Okono/Okpoho oil field was attacked by gunmen in boats, who took seven workers hostage. During a rescue attempt, one of the hostages, a British man, was shot dead and two others were injured. The 50,000 bbl/day field was closed down as a result.

Such attacks have become increasingly common in Nigeria in recent years. They stem from a variety of causes, including intercommunity rivalries, attempts to extract greater social benefits from the oil companies, protests against real or exaggerated human rights or environmental violations, hostility to the central government, quasi-separatist groups such as Movement for the Emancipation of the Niger Delta, and simple crime. They have closed down large parts of the onshore industry for significant periods: for some time during 2003, 817,000 bbl/day was offline, nearly 40 percent of national output.[76] Furthermore, as much as 300,000 bbl/day of crude is illegally exported out of the country, a practice known as "bunkering."

Nigeria is Africa's largest oil producer, although it is at risk of being overtaken by Angola and perhaps Libya. The unrest has significantly reduced output and investment in the onshore and shallow-water Niger Delta, the heart of the country's oil industry. This area, of marshes crisscrossed by creeks and delta distributaries, contains almost 500 oil fields. Nigeria's onshore fields are generally not that large individually, the largest, Forcados, containing 1.2 billion bbl, but they make up for this in their large numbers and multiplicity of reservoirs. Many smaller, undeveloped discoveries are now being brought into production by indigenous companies and foreign independents, such as Afren and Addax. From 1996 onward, Nigeria, having leased its deepwater to a variety of major companies, was rewarded, as in Angola, by a string of massive oil finds, totaling at least 7 billion bbl, now under development. These fields are not prone to the community disturbances that plague the onshore.

Nigeria has announced additional licensing rounds to keep the momentum going, leasing areas in the deepwater Gulf of Guinea. The "Golden Rectangle," where the maritime borders of Nigeria, Cameroon, and Equatorial Guinea meet, is particularly promising, and another 1–2 billion bbl of oil may be found there in the next three years.[77] Another key focus area is the Nigeria-São Tomé Joint Development Zone (JDZ), where this tiny island nation hopes to become another Kuwait (in per capita income, anyway, if not in other ways). The JDZ could contain as much as 6–12 billion bbl and yield 3 million bbl/day. The first well, in 2006, found oil and gas, although reserve figures have not been released.

With deepwater fields leading the way, Nigeria announced aspirations to reach 3 million bbl/day in 2006 (actual production was around

2.2 million bbl/day, severely hampered by disruptions) and 4 million bbl/day in 2010, although again it seems likely that unrest will prevent these targets being met. Nigeria is also theoretically constrained by OPEC quotas, but, even when disruptions have not intervened, the country has generally shown itself unwilling to offer more than token compliance. One evasion mechanism is to reclassify light oil production as condensate (which is exempt from quotas).

OPEC quotas aside (and presumably in a world of plummeting production, they would be abandoned), Campbell's forecasts, particularly for deepwater, once again look very pessimistic, foreseeing production already in decline by 2020 and all over before 2030. His figures imply some 9 billion bbl of ultimate deepwater reserves in the country, but the known fields alone have some 7 billion bbl, not including several for which no reserves figures have been released, plus 50 percent of the JDZ (which would add 3–6 billion bbl if predictions are realized). It seems inconceivable that the Nigerian deepwater story will reach its end before the young Nigerian geologists of today even reach management positions, let alone retire.

ANGOLA

On December 15, 2006, Dalia started production, the largest deepwater development of the year, joining Girassol among a group of massive offshore projects in Angola. Such fields are set to lead a doubling of production over the next three years, from 1.4 to 2.8 million bbl/day, which would see it overtake Algeria, quite possibly Libya, and even Nigeria, to become Africa's largest producer. It joined OPEC as of January 2007 and could become the third largest producer (after Saudi Arabia and Iran but ahead of Kuwait, Venezuela, Iraq, and the UAE).

A remarkable fifty-five discoveries were made in the northern part of the offshore in just eight years, 1996–2003, and now eight discoveries in the ultradeepwater have followed. Drilling beneath salt layers is now proving fertile; the deepwater Kwanza Basin, farther south, remains promising despite initial disappointments, and onshore exploration is now starting in earnest for the first time, after curtailment by war and land mines, with one discovery already.[78]

This seems like a good place to dispose of another peak oil myth: that deepwater fields decline uniquely fast and are just a "flash in the pan." Campbell more or less allows for Angola's wave of deepwater projects, but, as with Nigeria, he sees it as a temporary phenomenon, forecasting a fall in production to 1.2 million bbl/day by 2020 and zero by 2030, an implied annual decline rate of 8 percent. Such a rapid fall-off seems implausible given that success rates to date have been so high, and there remain substantial unexplored areas. Even if there are no more major finds, given that there have been so many large discoveries to date, there must be a substantial tail of smaller fields. To compare another deepwater province, Shell's Cognac, the first deepwater field in the Gulf of Mexico, started production in 1979, peaked in 1983, but was still going two decades later, illustrating that, contrary to peak oil mantras, deepwater fields can provide sustained flows over a long period. Because Cognac was still producing 15 percent of its peak, seventeen years later, we would expect Angola to be yielding around 400,000 bbl/day by 2030, not zero, even if there are no new discoveries.

RUSSIA

Russia has been the linchpin of non-OPEC oil production growth in recent years, after coming close to collapse in the immediate post-Soviet days. As Thane Gustafson has demonstrated in his remarkable piece of detective work,[79] the Soviet oil industry was already in crisis by the late 1980s as a result of the exhaustion of the larger fields, inefficiency, and damaging production techniques. As a counter to those who hold that improved technology does not increase reserves, the Soviet oil industry is an excellent example. I have myself examined fields where the water injection department was rewarded based on the volume of water they injected, leading to their pumping up the pressure beyond its initial levels, an utterly wasteful procedure leading to excessive water production.

Russian production reached its highest point at 11.5 million bbl/day in 1987 but started to decline even before the dissolution of the Soviet Union, hitting 10.4 million bbl/day in 1990. Thereafter, economic collapse (leading to a slump in demand), a virtual cessation of investment, low oil prices, and the corrupt and chaotic privatization (perhaps "looting" would be a more accurate word) of much of the industry caused production to plummet. At the time of Russia's economic crisis in 1998, production levels were barely half of the peak, at 6.2 million bbl/day, but there then followed a remarkable recovery. This was induced by higher oil prices and to the consolidation of the industry under a number of fairly well-run major companies that brought in Western techniques and technology. Initially LUKOil made the running, but the baton was then taken up by the now defunct Yukos (mostly absorbed by state oil company Rosneft), Surgutneftegaz, TNK (now part of TNK-BP), and Sibneft (bought by national gas giant Gazprom). Companies such as Tatneft and Bashneft, who did not open up to modern methods, virtually stagnated, again illustrating the vital importance of technology in increasing both reserves and production.

This recovery posted production gains of 6–11 percent per year between 2000 and 2004 and took production to a post-Soviet high of 9.9 million bbl/day in October 2007. Contrast this with the peak oil theorists: they quoted "Russian experts" who maintained that 2004 growth would be

2.2 percent (it was 8.7 percent) and saw a peak at just under 8.5 million bbl/day during 2004–2006: "Under no WOCAP scenario could Russian output edge over the 9 million b/d mark,"[80] which suggests a need for rethinking WOCAP rather than writing off Russia. The peak oil gurus are here misled by a single comment from 1993, the previously mentioned Khalimov, into skepticism on Russian reserves. However, the major Russian companies now report to Western standards (albeit usually SPE, rather than the overconservative SEC), and much of the confusion about Soviet reserve standards has dissipated. The long reserve lives of Russian companies, typically around twenty-five years compared with eight to fifteen years for the super-majors, imply great scope to continue growing production. A recent slow-down and even slight reversal in production growth has been due mainly to the consolidation of the industry under two "national champions," and to heavy taxation rendering more marginal developments uneconomic.

Russia's older producing areas, the Volga-Urals and West Siberia, are by now rather mature, yet unconventional oil and EOR initiatives are promising for future growth. Especially in West Siberia, there remains major potential for increasing reserves via better reservoir management, satellite fields, deeper drilling, development of "wet" (hydrocarbon-liquid rich) gas fields, and potentially massive finds in the adjoining offshore.

Several "new" basins are currently being developed in Russia, including Timan-Pechora (onshore Arctic, west of the Urals), which has a number of significant oil fields; the neighboring offshore Barents Sea contains the super-giant Shtokman gas field but is virtually virgin territory. Total resources, discovered and YtF, in the Russian sector of the Barents Sea have been suggested to be as much as a phenomenal 500–600 billion boe,[81, 82] of which about 100 billion bbl is oil.[83] The Russian portion of the Caspian has seen some inviting discoveries, and potential is estimated at 15–22 billion bbl.[84] Other remote areas of Russia's continental shelf have speculative, possibly very large, prospects.[85, 86]

East Siberia is currently the Russian oil industry's new hope for growth. This gigantic area, 90 percent of the size of the contiguous United States, is the most stranded basin in the world; a pipeline from the giant Kovykta gas field to China would equal the distance from Anchorage, Alaska, to Washington, D.C.[87] Only about 5 percent of prospects have been tested, with the discovery of 7 billion bbl of oil and 200 Tcf of gas. The future oil potential is put at as much as 75 billion bbl,[88] although the USGS, considering just a small part of the vast area, estimated a much more conservative median value of some 2.4 billion bbl. The reservoirs are challenging to develop, and above-ground issues include extensive permafrost and marshes, mountains reaching up to 3,000 meters elevation, six months of snow cover per year, temperatures that drop to −68°C, and, above all, the incredible remoteness, wildness, and environmental sensitivity of the region. Lake Baikal, the world's largest body of fresh water, with a unique flora and fauna, is particularly delicate. However, now that agreement has been reached on a pipeline to China and, ultimately, the Pacific, East Siberian oil production should rise significantly, with potential for more than 1 million bbl/day by 2015, even without additional discoveries.

The large island of Sakhalin, in Russia's Far East, was formerly used as a penal colony (and visited by the author Chekhov). Onshore oil production has been going on there since 1922. In the 1970s, the Soviet Union invited a Japanese consortium to explore, lacking technology for offshore exploration in such tough conditions; the sea is frozen for five months of the year, and only the southernmost tip of the island has an ice-free port. The ice gouges the seabed, posing a danger to any pipelines that are not buried, and exerts tremendous forces on fixed structures such as platforms. The Japanese were successful in finding a number of large oil and gas fields, but these were not brought on-stream because of the then-immense cost and technological difficulties. Development is now going ahead under the aegis of ExxonMobil, Shell, BP, and, more recently, Gazprom. Resources, discovered and undiscovered, in the defined projects alone may be as much as 11 billion bbl, especially as the farther offshore areas are expected to be more "oily" (rather than "gassy"). Ultimately, Sakhalin could well rival the North Sea in output.

Different interpretations can be given to the lack of post-Soviet exploration activity. Whereas in the 1980s, more than $10 billion per year (in real terms) was spent from the state budget on exploration, in 2003, the top fifteen Russian companies spent only $3 billion between them. In my opinion, the lack of exploration in West Siberia is not attributable to a lack of prospects. Of course, it is unlikely that any more fields like Samotlor, Russia's largest, will be found in the onshore part of the basin. The Soviet exploration machine was not efficient, but it was very thorough, at least in the straightforward onshore areas. Therefore, deeper drilling, proving up of secondary reservoirs and other kinds of near-field exploration, particularly for stratigraphic traps and structures along the basin margins, will be a primary focus of Russian operators. This is particularly so given that Russian legislation has not historically linked the exploration and production phases, giving no incentive to explore, because discoveries can be taken away and auctioned to the highest bidder.

Another disincentive to exploration is a positive one: Russian companies currently have enough reserves. If the R/P ratios are in the range of 25–30, the most appropriate use of these companies' resources is to bring their undeveloped reserves online. Falling R/P ratios are, up to a point, a reflection of increased efficiency rather than depletion. This point is not appreciated by many commentators, particularly some Russians, for example Erochkine and Erochkine, who mention that "It is undeniable that the exploration activities of Russia's largest oil companies have been inadequate,"[89] and some sections of the Russian political system, which have been putting increasing emphasis on stepping up exploration. Exploration needs to continue at some level to continue filling the hopper for future developments and to open up new areas, such as Sakhalin and East Siberia, by proving up volumes for new export infrastructure. However, in the established areas, such as West Siberia, the companies have had enough to do in the short term with developing satellite fields and fully appraising the existing discoveries, particularly deeper horizons. Only now, with the slowing of post-Soviet production growth, does serious attention seem to be turning back to exploration.

KAZAKHSTAN

In June 1985, the Soviet oil industry experienced its largest ever blow-out, at the Tengiz Field, in Kazakhstan, near the eastern shore of the Caspian Sea. A 200-meter-high fire burned for more than a year and was visible from 140 km away, although the Soviet press took six months even to report the accident. Reportedly, one man and more than 1 million birds died.[90] The field is at the considerable depth of 4,000 meters, under very high pressure, a thick salt layer, difficult to drill through, overlies its complicated carbonate reservoir, and the associated gas contains some 16 percent of deadly H_2S. Each barrel of oil (weighing some 140 kilograms) yields some 19 kilograms of elemental sulphur. This is not toxic, but because it is too expensive to transport it to anywhere it could be used, it has to be stored in giant yellow mountains, the only eminence in the flat coastal plains. From November to March, the temperature is around $-40°C$, with constant winds. In the spring, roads become impassable mud. In the summer, the temperature can exceed $+40°C$.

Developing this field strained the limits of Soviet oil-field technology, despite containing some 25 billion bbl of oil in place. Several other similar giant fields had been discovered in the vicinity, such as Karachaganak, a gas accumulation with 7 billion bbl of condensate[91] (and similarly high H_2S, 3.5–5 percent). Despite this encouragement, the technology was not available to explore the centre of the basin, the North Caspian, and, like other post-Soviet states, production crashed in the early 1990s as investment dried up. But, after the fall of the Soviet Union, a consortium of Western, Russian, and Kazakh companies took over operations at Tengiz and Karachaganak, leading to an almost tenfold increase in output.[92]

However, the greatest success of Kazakhstan's invitations to foreign companies has been the discovery of the super-giant Kashagan Field, the largest find in the world in the past thirty years.[93] In July 2000, a consortium reading like a Who's Who of the international oil business, made up of ENI (until recently the operator), Shell, Total, ExxonMobil, Conoco-Phillips, BG, Statoil, BP,[94] and Inpex (Japan) drilled Kashagan East-1 to a depth of 5,200 meters below sea level. The Caspian is only 3 meters deep at this location, which made ordinary offshore drilling rigs useless, so an artificial island was constructed. The sea freezes every winter, and, because it is so shallow, changes in winds can expose or submerge large areas of land. The level of the Caspian Sea has, for obscure reasons, been rising steadily in recent years and may be as much as 5 meters higher by 2010, which will submerge Tengiz.[95] The area is a center for sturgeon, sustaining the $3 billion caviar industry, and the adjoining wetlands are environmentally sensitive.[96]

The well was extremely expensive because of the region's delicate ecology and tricky subsurface and was also geologically very risky. However, the first well, and several appraisals, demonstrated the presence of a massive oil field. This triumph was followed by several other large finds in the contract area, the first being the much more straightforward Kalamkas (October 2002), with additional discoveries at Kashagan South West (June 2003), Aktote (May 2003), and Kairan (July 2003). More than 40 billion bbl of oil in place have now been found in the contract area, with no dry wells,[97] and the reserves of Kashagan alone are anticipated to be some 13 billion bbl, with recent reports suggesting a 10 percent upgrade.[98]

However, development has proved challenging because of both below-ground and above-ground factors, many of them taking place in the Kazakh capital Astana, thousands of kilometers from Kashagan. The development was always going to be technically and environmentally problematic. Because Kazakhstan is landlocked, exporting the oil requires long and expensive routes, vulnerable to political disruptions. The Kazakhs have reacted badly to repeated delays in Kashagan's development from the initial planned first oil date of 2005, imposing fines and tougher environmental standards, raising taxes, and forcing an entry of the NOC into the consortium. Kashagan is now expected to come on-stream in 2012 and reach 1.5 million bbl/day by about 2019, at a cost of some $30 billion.[99]

The discovery of Kashagan naturally led to tremendous excitement over the future oil potential of Kazakhstan, but subsequent progress has been slow. Still, promising blocks in the remainder of the Caspian are now being licensed. Onshore production, established as far back as 1911,[100] is now benefiting from renewed investment and the completion of a pipeline to China, running through the—for students of Central Asian history—evocatively named Dzhungarian Gate. As China's first direct oil import pipeline and a competitor both for exports through Russia and directly to Europe, this project is of considerable geopolitical importance.

Despite some setbacks, Kazakhstan's state company Kazmunaigaz expects total Kazakh production from known projects (excluding, therefore, any future discoveries) to reach about 2.5–3 million bbl/day between 2013 and 2015, of which about 0.6–1 million bbl/day will come from Tengiz, 1.3 million bbl/day from the Kashagan contract area, some 0.1–

0.2 million bbl/day from Karachaganak, and the remainder from other onshore producers.[101] There is additional potential for extensions of known fields, for instance, part of the Karazhanbas heavy oil field that may lie under the Caspian, and for enhanced recovery. A recent discovery has been made near the Chinese border in the east of the country, at Zaysan, the first in this region.

These figures are well above Campbell's prediction. Although the delays to Kashagan make him appear more bullish in the short term, he has the country reaching a plateau of 2.1 million bbl/day in 2020, which they never exceed. This runs contrary to the country's great potential for more discoveries and expansion of existing fields. Even without additional exploration success, this enormous country, as large as Western Europe, will clearly be one of the major contributors to non-OPEC production over the next decade and more.

AZERBAIJAN

In the early 1990s, the Caspian was hailed as a "new Middle East." Despite great Kazakh success, disappointments in Azerbaijan mean that the region may ultimately only rival the North Sea. Azerbaijan's promise was given early support with the "Contract of the Century," for a BP-led consortium to develop the ACG complex of fields, which had been found by the Soviet Union between 1979 and 1988. Chirag, discovered in 1985, was the deepest offshore well that the Soviet Union ever managed to drill, at some 200 meters (when the Gulf of Mexico had already surpassed 1,000 meters), and only the shallow-water part of Guneshli was put into production (in 1989) before Azerbaijan's independence. BP followed up by discovering the giant Shah Deniz gas field in January 1999, but other explorers had no notable success. The construction of a pipeline ("BTC") from Baku to Tbilisi in Georgia and Ceyhan on Turkey's southern coast, bypassing both Russia and Iran, opens up a secure and economic route for Caspian oil.

ACG will ultimately produce some 6 billion bbl of oil, reaching peak production of some 1 million bbl/day by 2009.[102] With the addition of Shah Deniz, Azerbaijan will greatly exceed its World War II peak production level of about 500,000 bbl/day, another example of a country recovering from and surpassing the reputedly inviolable Hubbert's peak. Despite subsequent exploration disappointments, there is still promise, as discussed in the section on Iran, for the deepwater portions of the South Caspian if borders can be demarcated. Without additional discoveries or significant improved/enhanced recovery, overall production will go into decline after about 2012–2013. Yet with older fields yielding an additional 300,000 bbl/day, once again the peak oil prognosis of 1.1 million bbl/day falls short of likely reality.

VENEZUELA

The Venezuelan oil industry is one of the world's oldest and one of the pioneers of offshore production, in Lake Maracaibo during the 1930s. As a founder member of OPEC, holder of the world's sixth largest reserves, and the eighth-largest producer, Venezuela has a justified place amongst the world's petro-powers, particularly as the largest resource holder in the Western Hemisphere. However, Venezuela is distinguished from the Big Five Middle Eastern OPEC nations (Saudi Arabia, Iran, Iraq, UAE, and Kuwait) by the relatively high cost of extracting its oil, much of which is heavy or extra-heavy. Venezuela has one of the world's two largest accumulation of tar sands (the other being in Canada), concentrated in the Orinoco Belt in the east of the country. Because of this, Venezuela may make a long-lived contribution to world oil supply and has potential greatly to increase production, but it is not in a position to act as a swing producer in the style of Saudi Arabia.

Although PdVSA dominates Venezuela's oil industry, the country is dependent on foreign technology and capital to exploit its heavy oil. Many of these projects involve upgrading extra-heavy crude to high-quality light oil. Despite this reliance, the administration of President Hugo Chávez has drastically increased petroleum taxes and the share of state participation and control. This, and a strike against Chávez followed by mass sackings, have reduced Venezuelan output by some 500,000 barrels per day, although some major new light oil field developments, such as Corocoro and Zumano, totaling about 1 billion bbl of reserves,[103] continue to progress. Venezuelan extra-heavy output from the Orinoco Belt was 700,000 bbl/day in 2003, and there are plans for additional expansions to 800,000 bbl/day by 2011, a number dependent on politics and investment, not geology. Yet Campbell prognoses only 300,000 bbl/day of extra-heavy oil from Venezuela by 2010.

Venezuela also has significant exploration potential, particularly in the virtually unexplored northern offshore. This adjoins Trinidad, which has been very successful in exploration in recent years, particularly in gas but also for oil. Trinidad has drilled a number of deepwater wells; Venezuela's deepest was sunk in 2007, in only 350 meters of water,[104] depths that were surpassed in the Gulf of Mexico more than a quarter of a century ago.

MEXICO

Mexico houses the world's second largest field in terms of production, Cantarell. Cantarell, with 35 billion bbl originally in place, produces about 1.7 million bbl/day, 53 percent of Mexico's total, and is a good example of the potential of EOR because it is currently undergoing the world's largest nitrogen injection scheme, which will raise the recovery factor to about 50 percent[105] or even potentially 55–60 percent.[106] Cantarell is now entering a period of sharp decline, which will result in a drop in Mexico's overall oil production, at least temporarily. Output fell 10 percent in the first half of 2006.

However, Mexico's problems are not caused by a shortage of resources in the ground but by the monopoly position of a single oil company, the state concern Pemex. Pemex is not only one of the least efficient of national oil companies but has also been starved of capital by Mexican tax laws.[107]

For Pemex to achieve its plans of reaching 4 million bbl/day by 2010, $45 billion will be required in the period 2005–2010.[108] This sounds like an enormous sum, but compared with the $100 billion that ExxonMobil plans to spend in the same period[109] for a similar level of production, it is relatively modest. If Pemex were given sufficient financial resources, the successful nitrogen injection project in Cantarell could be extended to other fields, such as Ku-Maloob-Zaap, doubling output to 800,000 bbl/day, and the Offshore Light Crude project.[110] Even Cantarell's slump could be slowed by installing elementary water-separation equipment.[111] These initiatives would reverse Mexican decline, which peak oil believers see as inevitable now that Cantarell's output is falling away.

Additional unexploited resources exist onshore. Chicontepec, a complex of tight (low-permeability) oil fields northeast of Mexico City, is even larger than Cantarell, with oil-in-place of 139 billion bbl, of which 10–13 billion bbl is technically recoverable[112] with some $30 billion of investment over fifteen years[113] (comparable with expenditure on Kashagan, whose reserves are of a similar size).

In contrast to the great success in developing the U.S. side of the Gulf of Mexico, Mexico itself has hardly begun to explore the deepwater, although recent discoveries at Trident and Hammerhead, probably extends across the border. Reserves in the Mexican portion of the Gulf are variously estimated at 30 billion[114] to 131[115] billion boe.[116] Several companies, including Shell, and the Brazilian deepwater specialists Petrobras have offered to assist Mexico in exploring the area, but the current legal structure does not give them the equity or production-sharing participation required for a fair balance of risk and reward. The political climate in Mexico remains strongly opposed to foreign participation. The decline in Mexican output, then, is attributable more to politics than geology.

BRAZIL

On April 21, 2006, President "Lula" da Silva, aboard the P-50 production vessel, proudly announced that Brazil had become a net exporter of oil.[117] Among major consumers, this achievement is almost unique, and what is even more remarkable is that Brazil has achieved self-sufficiency almost entirely through its own efforts. Brazil's state oil company Petrobras[118] has discovered and developed the vast majority of the fields itself, and, in the process, has established itself as a deepwater leader able to take on the super-majors in the Gulf of Mexico and West Africa. Like Statoil Hydro and Petronas, it is a strong counterexample to lumbering state monopolies such as Gazprom and Pemex. This success rests essentially on three pillars: a strong production effort, centered on deepwater, with a dominant but not monopolistic local champion; increasing use of gas; and a determined focus on biofuels. From 2004 to 2007, Brazil commissioned new deepwater fields totalling 1.3 million bbl/day of capacity.

Nearly all of Brazil's oil comes from the Campos Basin off the southeast coast, and 75 percent of the country's reserves are in water depths greater than 400 meters.[119] Being offshore the major demand center of Rio de Janeiro, this basin is ideally situated for development, despite the great water depths and the common occurrence of heavy oil. Discoveries continue at a good pace in this and other basins.[120, 121] It has been speculated that a second oil province, as large as the Campos Basin, could lie beneath the salt in the Santos Basin, southeast of São Paolo, as suggested by Petrobras's successful Tupi well in October 2006, in 2,126 meters of water. Following up a previous find by BG in the same play, 70 km away, Tupi could hold as much as 5–8 billion bbl of light oil[122] and Carioca-Sugar Loaf seems poised to be even larger (25–40 billion bbl), Jupiter is a major gas-condensate find of similar size to Tupi, and Petrobras estimates the whole play might ultimately yield 80 billion bbl. Foreign operators such as BG, Shell, and Devon, combined with Petrobras's own overseas operations, help introduce new technology and keep the Brazilian oil sector competitive. This is an example to oil states that outlaw or heavily restrict foreign investment, such as Mexico and Venezuela, which are consequently struggling to maintain output in the face of much easier conditions than Brazil.

UNITED STATES

On September 5, 2006, Chevron announced a giant discovery in the deepwater Gulf of Mexico, when the Jack #2 well, drilled in about 2,100 meters of water, flowed oil at 6,000 bbl/day. Press reports, misquoting Chevron, indicated the size of the find at between 3 and 15 billion bbl. The truth was, as usual, less dramatic. The 3–15 billion bbl refers to the total potential of the "Lower Tertiary" play in the ultradeepwater Gulf, whose viability has been confirmed by Jack, just a small portion of this. Yet a major new oil play, with an excellent 63 percent success rate to date, in rocks much older than those that have yielded 99 percent of Gulf production to date, further extends the life of the United States as a major producer.

The Gulf of Mexico is one of three main regions to which the United States will have to look for new conventional domestic oil supplies, the others being its offshore regions outside the Gulf, and Alaska. The Gulf of Mexico has habitually been the trailblazer for deepwater exploration and production, and its cycles of boom and bust are a magnification of the rest of the business. In 1947, Kerr McGee drilled the first well out of sight of land ten miles off the Louisiana coast, at Ship Shoal 32, in a mere eighteen feet of water. That field is still producing. The first development in water depths more than 1,000 feet (321 meters) came in 1979, Shell's Cognac field, but in the 1990s, in response to low oil and gas prices, the Gulf of Mexico was dubbed "the Dead Sea," with production and activity levels plunging. Disproving these periodic reports that the Gulf was played out, the late 1990s brought resurgence, with the 1,000 and 2,000 meter water depths being passed, and the discovery of the largest field ever found in the Gulf (BP's Thunder Horse, more than 1 billion boe).

In a sign of the region's continuing potential, the Minerals Management Service estimated in 2000 that 138 billion boe were yet to be found in the Gulf,[123] yet most of America's continental shelves remain off-limits for oil exploitation. Exploration offshore California, Florida (the eastern Gulf of Mexico), and most other coastal states has been forbidden at federal level since 1981. Estimates of the total potential in such off-limits areas are 112 billion boe.[124] No other country in the world has such wide-ranging limits on offshore petroleum production. Even the environmentally exemplary Norwegians have only set aside limited areas and that temporarily.

Alaska has, of course, been a very contentious area for the past few years, mostly revolving around the question of whether to open the ANWR for petroleum exploration. Estimates for its potential are estimated by the USGS to be 6–16 billion bbl.[125] Much argument has focused on whether this amount of oil would make a meaningful contribution to U.S. supply or consumption. Without taking either side, it is worth observing that the mean estimate would increase current proven U.S. reserves by about 35 percent and that, at fairly conservative depletion rates, it could lift American production by about 10 percent. Ultimate recovery from known discoveries in the rest of Alaska is about 15 billion bbl of oil; additional exploration is now getting under way offshore.

The onshore contiguous United States is the most mature petroleum area in the world. Proven reserves are estimated at 29 billion bbl, whereas production in 2005 was 6.8 million bbl/day from some 560,000 wells, a mere 12 bbl/day per well. Yet the United States' remaining oil in the ground, including anticipated future discoveries, totals some 1,100 billion bbl, of which 430 billion bbl is estimated to be technically recoverable.[126] CO_2 injection could unlock as much as 109 billion bbl of light oil in the United States.[127] These resources could support current levels of U.S. production indefinitely. Output has fallen, therefore, not primarily owing to geology or a lack of resources but as a result of political and environmental constraints, because investment has moved to other countries and because oil prices have not been high enough to encourage wider adoption of EOR.

CANADA

Canada's oil industry, to some extent, is reminiscent of the United States'. There is some very mature onshore production with a multitude of small players, EOR, and unconventional gas (the Western Canadian Sedimentary Basin), an offshore/deepwater province (Nova Scotia, Newfoundland, and Labrador), and a frontier Arctic realm.

Canada's distinguishing feature, however, and its main role in the world's future oil supply, is the famous Oil Sands. Despite the maturity of its conventional production, the Oil Sands are expected to help Canada increase production from 3 million bbl/day in 2005 to 3.6–4.6 million bbl/day by 2015.[128, 129] Although light oil output from the Western Canadian Sedimentary Basin is expected to fall and conventional heavy oil and the eastern offshore are plateauing, the Oil Sands will maintain strong growth in Canadian production, vital for supplying its large southern neighbour.

The Oil Sands are found in Alberta and are a vast accumulation of very heavy oils and tar, found at surface or shallow depths. With an effectively infinite resource base, the main constraints on realizing the full potential of the Oil Sands have been cost and logistics. The area is remote, with limited transport infrastructure both in (roads) and out (pipelines), skilled labor, water, and housing are in short supply, the general industry inflation (particularly in steel and natural gas) has hit, and Calgary is experiencing an oil-led boom reminiscent of the Middle East, only colder.

As far as conventional oil and gas goes, there is significant remaining potential offshore eastern Canada, particularly in the deepwater, but exploration has been hampered by high costs, the tough environment, iceberg dangers, bureaucratic obstacles, and the lack of infrastructure to take gas to markets. Several majors (Shell, ExxonMobil, and Chevron) have taken acreage in the Orphan Basin north of Newfoundland and plan to drill in very deep water (2,400 meters). The signature bonuses[130] they paid, totalling $672 million,[131] are a remarkable vote of confidence in this frontier region.

The Queen Charlotte Basin, offshore British Columbia in the far west, has an estimated potential of 10 billion bbl in place (so perhaps 4–6 billion bbl recoverable) but has been under an environmental moratorium since 1972.[132] The Canadian Arctic has substantial potential for oil and, particularly gas, with various discoveries awaiting commercialization. Ironically, increasing melting of the Arctic ice as a result of climate change may make it easier to develop petroleum in the area by opening up seaways (although melting permafrost creates its own problems).

NORWAY

Norway has historically pursued a policy of high taxation and rather measured licensing of its prospective areas. Of its 1.4 million km^2 of continental shelf (almost as much as the entire Gulf of Mexico), 60 percent is theoretically open for exploration, but only 5 percent is currently under license to explorers. This contrasts with the much more rapid pace of development of the United Kingdom, reflecting different needs (rather than, as some have suggested, profligacy on the part of the British). By 2000, some 600 exploration wells had found about 54 billion boe, whereas in a similar prospective area in the United Kingdom, approximately 2,500 wells had discovered only about 42 billion boe, reflecting Norway's much greater total potential and earlier stage of exploitation.

Norway's petroleum basins largely fall into three geographic areas: the North Sea, the Norwegian Sea, and the Barents Sea.

The North Sea is fairly mature but, because of the high rate of petroleum taxation, the historical dominance of a few major companies (particularly the Norwegian ones) and government policies of restricting the number of blocks awarded, it is nothing like as intensely explored as the U.K. sector.

The Norwegian Sea is that part of the Atlantic immediately adjacent to Norway and so north of the North Sea. This "Atlantic Margin" continues from the U.K. West of Shetland province, with several significant fields, up to the dividing line with the Barents Sea in the far north. The Gulf of Mexico has seen more than five times as many exploratory wells and thirty times as many deepwater (more than 600 meters) wells, yet nearly as much oil has been found in the Norwegian Sea as in the Gulf of Mexico. The northern part of the Norwegian Sea, the Nordland sector, lying off the scenic Lofoten Islands, is thought to have high potential, as much as 2 billion bbl,[133] but some key sectors are currently off-limits for exploration because of the islands' tourist industry and fishing interests, somewhat ironic given the environmental damage inflicted by fishing.

The Barents Sea, lying north of mainland Norway and south of the wondrous Arctic archipelago of Svalbard, has proved rather disappointing relative to its perceived potential, but the first oil development is now going ahead at Goliat, followed by a major find, Norsk Hydro's Nucula in February 2007,[134] which could be as large as 550 million boe.[135] It would appear that the western Barents will, at best, be a subsidiary province, but the eastern Barents Sea is a different matter. Overlap between Norwegian and Russian claims has slowed down exploration of this region, estimated to contain 12 billion boe.[136] The "overlapping claims" area, as large as the whole Norwegian sector of the North Sea, more or less coincides with a major geological structure that divides the Barents in two. To the east of this are giant Russian finds, notably the Shtokmanovskoye gas field with some 120 Tcf of gas reserves.[137]

Despite these promising areas, Campbell puts Norway's YtF oil at a mere 1 billion bbl, hardly more than the United Kingdom, although, as we have seen, the Norwegian sector of the North Sea has received barely a quarter of the exploration effort devoted to the U.K. side, not to mention the very significant potential in the Norwegian and Barents Seas.

UNITED KINGDOM

Although the United Kingdom is widely portrayed as entering its petroleum old age, with proven reserves estimated as 4 billion bbl of oil, against nearly 24 billion of production to date, it succeeded in replacing all of 2006 production with new reserves. With the right policies, it may continue in a robust middle age for many years. The U.K. continental shelf still contains scope for big discoveries that confound peak oil believers, such as the Buzzard Field, discovered in May 2001 in the Outer Moray Firth (reserves about 505 million bbl), ConocoPhillips' Shoei gas-condensate discovery in September 2006 in the Central North Sea (100–275 million boe), and Chevron's Lochnagar-Rosebank, West of Shetland, in 2004 (250–530 million boe).

Each is emblematic, in its way, of where new discoveries will be made. Buzzard is a stratigraphic trap, generally considered to be high risk and difficult to map. Shoei lies in a high-pressure, high-temperature play, with challenging drilling conditions. Lochnagar is in the West of Shetland or Atlantic Margin area, so not in the North Sea *sensu stricto*. This area is much less explored than the North Sea because of its even rougher conditions and deeper water, but it holds potential for major discoveries, as Clair, Foinaven, and Schiehallion have proved in the past. Around the tiny islet of Rockall, perhaps soon to be added to the U.K.'s Exclusive Economic Zone, and in the self-governing Danish dependency of the Færoes, is additional potential, much hidden beneath thick layers of basalt that require advanced seismic technology to illuminate.

The U.K. Department for Business estimates YtF potential of 8.3 billion boe, 6.4 billion boe of which is in the North Sea, the remainder being along the Atlantic Margin. This estimate was done from mapped prospects, therefore, known structures with a good chance of being drilled. Making an allowance for new prospect generation and fresh play ideas could lead to significantly higher estimates. Production will also be sustained through life extensions for older fields (often by smaller, lower-cost operators), exploration for smaller fields, the development of fallow discoveries, and EOR initiatives; the total potential from CO_2 EOR could be as much as 2 billion bbl in the U.K. sector.[138]

Campbell forecasts U.K. EUR at 30 billion bbl (past production plus future production from known fields plus new discoveries). The Department for Business study does not give a split between gas and oil, but, if we assume arbitrarily that the current ratio of 55 percent oil applies also to future discoveries, the U.K. EUR would be at least 33 billion bbl, plus 2 billion bbl of EOR, plus other reserve additions from existing fields, undeveloped discoveries, and as-yet unmapped prospects. The 30 billion figure therefore looks extremely conservative because it assumes a mere 800 million bbl of new discoveries. This asks us to believe that two recent finds, Buzzard and Lochnagar, contained the equivalent of all the United Kingdom's remaining oil. Clearly the explorers should stop now!

CHINA

Given the country's massive impact on world energy markets, it is surprising to recall that, as recently as 1992, China was a net exporter of oil. Since then, production has continued to increase, but an explosion in demand has made it the world's third largest importer after the United States and Japan, and the second-largest consumer after the United States. Campbell foresaw a production peak in 2005 at 3.6 million bbl/day, which has already been surpassed, and Chinese plans are for 3.85 million bbl/day in 2010,[139] against his forecast of 2.9 million bbl/day.

China has, in its huge territory, a number of significant oil basins, and exploration continues to be successful. A recent find of a reported 2.8–7 billion bbl in Bohai Bay, offshore Beijing, is one to three times as much as Campbell's 2005 estimate for the YtF of the entire country. The deepwater Pearl River Mouth Basin, offshore Hong Kong, has been the focus of recent efforts. The South China Sea has been estimated to contain some 2 billion bbl of oil, but some Chinese sources put the potential as high as a (rather improbable) 130 billion boe.

Much of the South China Sea is, unfortunately, disputed between the littoral states—China, Taiwan, Indonesia, the Philippines, Vietnam, Malaysia, Cambodia, Thailand, Singapore, and Brunei—all of whom have different views on the correct borders. This dispute revolves around ownership of the Spratly Islands (Nansha in Chinese) and other small islands, reefs, and banks. The Spratlys number more than 200 minute pieces of land, the largest only 1.3 km long and with a highest point of 3.8 meters (implying that global warming may soon render the dispute moot!). The most recent wave of argument was triggered when China objected to the Philippines' granting of an oil exploration area around the aptly-named Mischief Reef. The disputes involving China, the Philippines, and Vietnam appear particularly intractable, and the legal uncertainty has put much of the sea off-limits for exploration. However, recent progress toward agreements between Indonesia and Vietnam and between Brunei and Malaysia is opening up high-potential areas.

INDIA

Like China, India's primary importance in world energy markets is as a large and rapidly growing consumer. However, India is also a reasonably significant oil and gas producer, where exploration has, in recent years, undergone a renaissance.

For many years, India was all but discounted by Western companies, put off by bureaucracy and a perceived lack of prospectivity. No one in the industry in 1999 (except perhaps the far-sighted people at Cairn) would have expected India to make a major contribution to global exploration success. However, efforts from the Indian government to attract investment combined with some spectacular finds have made it a hotspot. The most famous story is probably that of Cairn, who bought out their partner Shell from an exploration block in Rajasthan, in northwest India, for a pittance of $7.5 million and proceeded to discover some 600 million bbl of oil.

An even more significant area than Rajasthan, however, has been the Krishna-Godavari Basin off the east coast, where Reliance, Cairn, and the Gujarat State Petroleum Company have made a series of enormous gas discoveries, along with some notable oil finds. The KG Basin was not even included in the USGS's assessment of future potential, so highlighting that, even if they are overoptimistic in certain areas, this can be counterbalanced by surprises in provinces that have been overlooked. India's aggressive licensing of the remainder of its prospective areas is promising for future discoveries.

NEW FRONTIERS

The usual contention of the Geologists is that there is not another Middle East waiting to be found. Of course, that is unlikely, but we do not know until we have looked. Such pessimism about the world outside of the known oil provinces is not new. A U.S. government report in 1980 stated "the predominant view among geologists is that the chances of discovering enough quickly exploitable oil to offset declines in the known fields are slim. If the Persian Gulf countries and some non-OPEC producers continue to limit production, as we expect, world production of oil probably will begin to decline in the mid 1980's." Although the Persian Gulf countries did limit production and FSU output slumped, world output continued to grow.

Potential non-OPEC sources of new oil include a variety of existing producing countries, plus new exploration frontiers. The recent period of high prices has led to a revitalization of frontier exploration. It is remarkable how thoroughly some areas have been picked over, but it is just as startling how others, with promise for hydrocarbons, have been all but overlooked for a variety of reasons, including remoteness and political problems but also mere unfashionability. As in the 1980s, the success of recent frontiers, such as deepwater India, Rajasthan, Mauritania, Peru, and Uganda, shows that peak oil theorists' assumptions regarding future discoveries are likely to be badly understated, even if much frontier exploration is unsuccessful.

Major highlights are as follows.

West and Southern Africa

Outside the main producers Nigera and Angola, West Africa has significant potential in other countries. Gabon and Cameroon appear to be in decline, barring potential deepwater finds in the former, because exploration to date has been disappointing. However, many of the other states, especially those around the Gulf of Guinea, have significant potential, especially in the deepwater. Campbell lumps all deepwater production outside the Gulf of Mexico, Brazil, Angola, and Nigeria together and estimates a mere 7 billion bbl or so of ultimate recovery. This is far too conservative given recent significant deepwater finds in second-tier African countries.

One of the most significant producers today is Equatorial Guinea, which has come from zero output in 1991 to a significant and still growing 360,000 bbl/day in 2006. Campbell does not cover the country, yet reserves, at 1.8 billion bbl, are a significant fraction, 20 percent, of his "other deepwater" and "minor" categories.

Another notable second-tier producer is Congo (Brazzaville), yielding 260,000 bbl/day in 2006, which has several notable underexplored plays, such as deepwater turbidites[140] and carbonate "rafts," with several recent discoveries, plus the onshore and offshore presalt section, which has yielded the significant onshore Mboundi field. The USGS's estimate of future potential at just 311 million bbl (midcase) seems very low, even lower than Campbell's 500 million (which, moreover, excludes deepwater), since there are a number of known prospects with moderate risk that alone would exceed these estimates if successful.

Mauritania has been another success story, at least initially, with the discovery of significant oil fields at Tiof (with some 500 million bbl in place) and Chinguetti (initially thought to have about 130 million bbl reserves), although Chinguetti's production performance has been disappointing because of complex reservoir. The fact of a petroleum system in this area upgrades perceptions of this whole stretch of African coast. When the sovereignty of Western Sahara (the Saharawi Arab Democratic Republic) is resolved, this offers a chance to extend Mauritanian prospectivity northward, while the oil-prone waters clearly extend south into Guinea-Bissau and Senegal, where an undeveloped heavy oil field, Dome Flore, with 1 billion bbl in place of 10° API crude, has been known since 1960. Côte d'Ivoire is also a notable second-tier producer via its deepwater Baobab Field.[141] Tullow/Kosmos's June 2007 light oil discovery at Mahogany-Hyedua, offshore Ghana, now renamed Jubilee, could be as much as

1 billion boe, exceeding the USGS's high-case estimate of 423 million bbl for the whole country, with just two wells.

In the south of the continent, Namibia has one large offshore gas field, Kudu. South Africa's deepwater basins are virtually untested and have significant potential, with Canadian Natural Resources planning to drill in the Southern Outeniqua Basin in 2008, with estimates of 2 billion bbl in place, and BHP-Billiton targeting the high-profile Cabernet prospect—given its name, with some risk of being dry—although rising rig costs have delayed drilling.

Although the USGS is usually accused by peak oil commentators of being overoptimistic, it should be noted that it does not even cover some of these prospective countries, such as Sierra Leone, Liberia, and Guinea, and gives minimal YtF to others, for instance, Guinea-Bissau, Western Sahara, Mauritania (including nothing to the onshore at all), South Africa, and Congo. Because its estimate was prepared in 2000, before the first finds in Mauritania and deepwater Ghana, it might well be significantly more upbeat now.

East Africa

Both the USGS and Campbell concur in completely dismissing the potential of East Africa by utter silence rather than by saying anything about it. Although certainly not noted as a petroleum province, it contains enough finds to hint at greater promise: gas condensate in central Ethiopia, old and new major gas finds on the Tanzanian coast, a significant gas industry in Mozambique, and massive heavy oil deposits onshore in Madagascar. Recently, there has been a scramble for East Africa, with Shell and Petrobras signing up deepwater acreage in Tanzania with multiple billion-barrel prospects and major companies showing interest also in Kenya and Madagascar. As in West Africa, deepwater appears, with good geological reasons, to be the most promising area. Because the USGS does not even cover the East African countries, any success here will be upside, which can go toward covering their alleged overoptimism elsewhere. Furthermore, political conditions would appear generally more stable than in West Africa, and the benign climate should make developments relatively cheaper than in northern Europe or the Gulf of Mexico.

Interior Africa

This region, which for a long time received very little attention from oil explorers, has gained momentum recently. As we have seen, Sudan (again, not included in the USGS assessment) has been a producer for some time and is set to grow strongly. Similar plays to that in Sudan, namely long, narrow grabens with primarily lacustrine[142] source rocks, may extend into Kenya and have recently yielded success in Uganda, possibly extending under Lake Albert to the Democratic Republic of Congo. Farther south, even Zambia announced the discovery of oil,[143] although exploration seems to be at a very early stage, while, to the north, Chad has now joined the ranks of producing nations.[144]

Chad, remarkably given that the country recently started production and is now at 150,000 bbl/day, with nearly 1 billion bbl of reserves (and some estimates giving 3 billion bbl[145]), is not covered by the USGS, and neither are its neighbors and near-neighbors, Niger, the Central African Republic, and Mali. From 1988 to 1996, Exxon (now ExxonMobil) made eleven oil finds from fourteen wells in Chad, such a high success rate that it indicates there must be additional potential, and the extension of Chad's Doba Basin into the unexplored Central African Republic may have similar promise. Exploration is going on in Mali, in the Taoudeni Basin across from Mauritania where there is one old gas find, and in Niger, where Total and ExxonMobil are active and where, in early 2005, Petronas announced an oil strike in the Agadem concession,[146] with 300 million bbl reserves found to date although 1 billion is thought to be necessary to justify a new export pipeline. China National Petroleum Corporation (CNPC) gave the area an additional vote of confidence by buying out EnCana for $200 million in early 2007,[147] a hefty price for pure exploration acreage. Given how little exploration there has been in this area and how the pipeline from Chad, through Cameroon to the coast, may lower the hurdle to make new fields economic, the Chad basins represents a substantial potential addition of reserves to those calculated by the USGS.

South and Southeast Asia and Australasia

Southeast Asian production is relatively mature, certainly when compared with, say, Africa. The region's rapidly growing, energy-hungry economies and a fairly developed gas market (both pipeline and LNG) have facilitated thorough exploration. However, the area still has new plays to discover. The two most significant are disputed zones and deepwater.

Southeast Asian exploration is plagued by border disputes, mainly because of the rather short independent existence of some of the states and the fragmented archipelagic nature of the region. The most famous dispute, mentioned above, is probably that between virtually every Southeast Asian nation over the Spratly Islands and the surrounding South China Sea. Other important squabbles include that between newly independent Timor-Leste and Australia, which has held back development of the Greater Sunrise gas fields, between Brunei and Malaysia over the intervening deepwater acreage, and between Japan and China over three gas fields.

Deepwater potential is generally thought of as occupying a "golden triangle" between the Gulf of Mexico, Brazil, and the Gulf of Guinea. Peak oilers dismiss the rest of the world's deepwater potential as negligible, yet it is becoming increasingly apparent that these were merely the first areas to attract attention because, in those places, the advance of geological understanding and development led naturally from coast to shelf to abyss. Egypt is a relatively recent example in which the deepwater has proven highly successful although the adjoining onshore had not yielded large finds. Now Southeast Asia is also surrendering its deepwater secrets, with recent large oil finds in Malaysia, mostly offshore Sabah and Sarawak in Borneo. Ten recent discoveries total more than 1.6 billion boe.[148] Vietnam, with water depths up to 2,500 meters, is also attracting the attention of major companies such as Chevron and Petronas.

Deepwater has yielded success in Indonesia, where Unocal (now owned by Chevron) has made several discoveries off the Mahakam Delta,[149] and exploration is beginning in sixteen frontier, mostly deepwater, basins.[150] Another key step in Indonesia has been a final agreement on the long-awaited development of Cepu in Java, which was held up by wrangling between the operator ExxonMobil and the state oil company Pertamina. This project, the main field of which was found in 2001, should come on-stream in 2009 and boost the country's oil output by 20 percent, contrary to peak oil theorists' prognostications of steady decline.[151] This makes a big difference to Indonesia, which, although still a member of OPEC, is now a net importer of oil. Indonesia is also a major EOR player, mainly because of the approximately 260,000 bbl/day produced by the Duri steam flood,[152] where production has hardly declined since the mid-1990s and where operator Chevron sees additional potential with less stringent fiscal terms. Considerable geological prospectivity remains for oil and, particularly, gas in Indonesia, but developments have been hampered by corruption, security problems, tough taxation, and disputes with the regulatory body, local authorities, and Pertamina.

Deepwater exploration is beginning in Pakistan, which is the last major untested Tertiary[153] delta; most of the others, such as the Baram (Brunei), Congo, Ganges-Brahmaputra, Mackenzie (Arctic Canada), Mississippi, Niger, Nile, Ob (West Siberia), Orinoco, Rhine, and Volga, are underlain by massive oil and gas fields. Myanmar (Burma), which has produced oil since 1887, initially under the well-known, now defunct, Burmah Oil Company, has made several offshore gas discoveries recently and has significant deepwater potential. Nearly all Western companies have withdrawn from the pariah state under its repressive military junta and have been replaced by the Indians, Chinese, Thais, and Koreans. Papua New Guinea, a country that, despite its fearsome terrain, has been explored for oil since the 1950s, is now offering deepwater acreage as its onshore production begins to decline.

Deepwater exploration began very early in Australia, with some large gas discoveries off the northwest coast that, however, have taken a long time to commercialize. These, being developed primarily as LNG, often have significant liquids content, leading to the extraction of large amounts of condensate. Australia also produces significant oil, including in deep water, on the northwestern and western coasts, for instance Woodside's Enfield. Several other promising deepwater basins, off the southern and eastern coasts, have seen virtually no exploration, whereas the Great Barrier Reef area is completely off-limits for obvious environmental reasons.

In addition to the main players, some hitherto overlooked Asian countries have also begun to attract attention. The most striking is, perhaps, the previously mentioned Cambodia.[154]

Central and South America

Latin American production is dominated by Mexico, Venezuela, and Brazil, yet most of the countries are oil and gas producers to some degree. Several of them have promise for major new discoveries, generally in the offshore, such as Trinidad, Colombia, and Peru, and for development of heavy oil, such as Ecuador and Peru.

Peru produces some oil of its own, made some significant discoveries in 2005 (promising as much as 1–1.5 billion bbl in two areas), and has some scope for offshore discoveries in the Talara Basin, prolific onshore but not drilled in offshore waters beyond 100 meters depth. The country is also particularly notable for large heavy oil deposits, whose development is now getting under way, and for major gas fields inland, east of the Andes, some of which also contain significant condensate.

The USGS generally gives rather low figures for the offshore potential of these countries. For instance, they do not assess Colombia's offshore at all, yet the country is a significant second-tier producer from its onshore. Cuba is a rather small oil producer, with very complex geology that has frustrated many explorers with its obvious promise combined with tantalizing inaccessibility, some kind of metaphor for the country itself, perhaps. The USGS suggests high-case future discovery of 941 million, yet the North Cuba Basin alone could hold 4.6 billion bbl of oil,[155] and a 100-million-barrel find was reported here in 2004.[156] Suriname and Guyana, like West Africa from which they separated some 100 million years ago, have a known, working, large petroleum system. Trinidad continues to make significant offshore oil and wet (hydrocarbon-liquid-rich) gas finds.

Hardman, the promoter of Mauritania and Uganda, was also active in the Falkland Islands before its acquisition. The Falklands (Las Malvinas) attracted a lot of attention in the late 1990s, when the area was described to me by one explorationist as "'looking exactly like the North Sea." Exploration virtually halted in the teeth of the oil price slump and some inconclusive wells but has since resumed in earnest. Oil was found in 1981 in the adjoining Malvinas Basin, the North Falkland Basin is anticipated to contain very rich source rocks, which may have generated as much as 100 billion bbl of oil,[157] and two of the early Shell wells discovered hydrocarbons, flowing gas, and oil to surface. The South and East Falkland

Basins appear to be even more promising than the North, with thicker sedimentary sections and larger structures[158] and numerous indications of hydrocarbons: gas chimneys[159] and amplitude anomalies[160] on seismic and natural oil seeps detected by satellites. Although recognizing that there is some (10 percent) chance that nothing may be found, the USGS foresees a mid-case of nearly 4 billion bbl and potential for as much as 17 billion.

The Falklands is often written off by peak oil theorists on the grounds that any discoveries would be too remote to develop, but actually distance matters little for oil, which is relatively cheap to ship. The climate, although tough, is not markedly rougher than the North Sea and is certainly less challenging than Sakhalin.

The Falklands' neighbor Argentina is a reasonably significant producer, whose best years were in the late 1990s when it reached almost 900,000 bbl/day. It has declined somewhat since then and in general seems to be fairly mature. However, the industry has also been badly affected by the early twenty-first century economic crisis and subsequent tax rises and price caps, so the impression of irreversible decline may be misleading.

Arctic

The Arctic encompasses a vast area, which (with Antarctica) represents the remotest frontier in the search for petroleum. It is already producing a significant amount of oil and gas, centered on Alaska, the Barents Sea, and Russia's Timan-Pechora and West Siberian basins. Projects such as these, together with Sakhalin (which is seasonally ice bound but south of the Arctic Circle), are laying the groundwork for operations in this region. Ironically, CO_2 emissions from burning oil and gas (and, let us not forget, coal), by warming the Arctic more than the rest of the planet, are melting the ice and making the region much more accessible. Conversely, melting permafrost is affecting pipelines in Alaska and Russia, and the season in which ice roads can be used is becoming very short.

The USGS, in their 2000 assessment, were very bullish on the potential of the Arctic. However, a recent study by the U.K. consultants Wood MacKenzie considerably downgraded expectations, partly because of fundamental geological prospectivity, partly because they shifted the balance much more toward gas than oil, and partly because they expect that developments would be difficult and slow in this harsh environment. They anticipate that 75 percent of future discoveries will be gas (as 85 percent of those to date have been) and that peak production will be 3 million bbl/day of oil. Such an oil contribution, although notable, would only be about that of the United Kingdom at its peak, and so would not transform the world supply picture.

Russia, Alaska, Canada, and Norway's Arctic basins have already been discussed in the relevant sections. This leaves Greenland, which is a key country in the USGS assessment. Peak oil writers usually scathingly dismiss this on the grounds that no commercial oil has been found in Greenland to date. However, because of its remoteness, harsh climate, and environmental sensitivity, there has been almost no exploration. As of the date of the USGS study, six offshore wells and one onshore well had been drilled, all in West Greenland, in a country whose prospective basins cover 350,000 km^2. East Greenland, which, prior to the opening of the North Atlantic in the early Tertiary, was adjacent to Norway and which, onshore, has several large "fossil" oil fields exhumed before the present day, has not seen any drilling.

The USGS 2000 assessment covers only the northeast Greenland basins, not the prospective North Greenland Basin (which Wood MacKenzie also discounts because, being covered by pack ice, they doubt it could be economically developed), nor West Greenland, where the paltry exploration to date has been concentrated. The Greenland Bureau of Minerals and Petroleum has mapped eighteen structures with total unrisked potential of 30–45 billion bbl.[161] These are large, simple dip closures overlying potential source rock kitchens, while there are also deeper faulted structures, possibly analogous to the North Sea. To the north of this area, the Nuusuaq Basin contains widespread oil seeps.

Antarctic

At the risk (indeed, with the intention) of being controversial, I think it is worth addressing the oil and gas potential of the Southern Continent. I personally hope it is never necessary to begin exploiting minerals in Antarctica commercially; there are cheaper and less environmentally sensitive sources of energy. The continent is, in any case, protected until the 2040s by the Madrid Protocol of the Antarctic Treaty. However, in the desperate world portrayed by peak oil theorists, there would probably be strong pressure to open up the Antarctica to energy exploration if the prospects seemed promising. The USGS does not cover Antarctica, and Geologists generally dismiss it, too, or write it off as hopelessly uneconomic.

Opinions on the continent as a whole vary[162] from McDonald, who considers the geological risks prohibitive and potential therefore minimal, to those of Russian institutes, the Japanese Antarctic Survey, and the famous expert Halbouty, who saw scope for 50–200 billion bbl. To produce amidst the offshore pack ice should be feasible given experience from Sakhalin and "Iceberg Alley" in Eastern Canada. Costs would be high but, for a large enough field (1 billion bbl or more), would still probably be below recent years' oil price, and transport costs would not be excessive: Japan is closer to Antarctica than to the Middle East. To extract oil from beneath significant grounded ice sheets does seem technically all but impossible (although I can think of at least one way).

Chapter 6

Scraping the Barrel?
Unconventional Oil Supply

Oil, sweat, dirt, filthy water, all disgusting.

Marcus Aurelius[1]

Just as conventional oil became an important energy source while coal was still king, so we are entering the age of unconventional oil before leaving that of conventional oil. The age of unconventional oil can be said to have begun in 1967, before the first oil shock, when Great Canadian Oil Sands (now Suncor) began mining oil sands in Alberta. The question now is whether unconventional oil will become the major source of liquid hydrocarbons (Odell[2]), a useful contributor to supply growth (CERA), an irrelevance (the Geologists), or an environmental monstrosity (Gore).

Unconventional oil refers to a variety of liquid fuels, typically those of poor quality oil (heavy oil and tar sands) or made synthetically from other sources (shale oil, biofuels, and X-to-liquids [XtL], where X is coal [CtL], gas [GtL], biomass [BtL], or some other feedstock). This kind of oil cannot be produced economically (or, often, produced at all) by standard oil-field methods. Its cost is usually greater and the technology required is more advanced than for conventional sources. Furthermore, generally some kind of additional processing, before conventional refining, is required to yield a usable product, and the end result may still not be a perfect substitute for conventional oil. The key characteristics that make unconventional oil attractive despite these drawbacks are the enormous size of the resource base, and its widespread occurrence outside and, hence independence of, the major OPEC countries.

Five great myths about unconventional oil are propounded particularly by end of oil thinkers. These myths are discussed below.

"Unconventional oil is something unique and special, not comparable to conventional oil." Unconventional oil is a moving target. What was

once unconventional is now conventional as technology advances and familiarity increases. Oil from Ohio, with its high sulphur content, was unconventional until 1888, when a method was found to refine it.[3] Iran's largest field, Gachsaran, found in 1928, was not brought on-stream until 1940 because its oil was too heavy and high in sulphur to be attractive to world markets; now this 31° API, 1.6 percent sulphur crude represents the Middle Eastern average. Today, those oil depletion analysts who label polar and deepwater oil as unconventional oil are mistaken; these are just examples of conventional oil found in unconventional places. Truly unconventional oil will make a growing contribution to supply over the coming years, because, although most of the world's resources are off-limits to international companies and conventional OECD supplies at risk of long term decline, many consuming countries have major stocks of unconventional oil or XtL feedstocks. Furthermore, technological advances and higher prices have made GtL a feasible way for gas-rich countries, notably Qatar, to monetize their vast resources. Finally, biofuel and XtL technologies can have significant environmental advantages.

In the end, consumers do not care about the source of the barrel of oil that finds its way into their gas tank as long as price and quality are acceptable. Whether the oil came from 2,000 meters of water offshore Angola, 70°N in the Barents Sea, Canadian tar sands, Colorado oil shales, Qatari gas, Chinese coal, or European biowaste is irrelevant. Arbitrarily defining some categories of oil as unconventional, as many peak oilers do, leads to proclaiming peak oil events that pass unnoticed by consumers or the market. After all, Kashagan, which the Geologists accept as conventional oil, will take at least ten years from discovery to production; the first Angolan deepwater field, Girassol, came online after only five years. Both produce light, high-quality oil, yet Girassol is considered unconventional oil by Campbell, possibly because deepwater development blossomed after the end of his industry career.

"Unconventional oil relies on unproven or unfeasibly expensive technologies." Of the resources discussed in this chapter, heavy and extraheavy oil, tight oil, biofuels, and tar sands have been in commercial production already for a long time and are experiencing rapid growth. The technology of XtL has been proven at a number of midsize commercial CtL and GtL plants. The main question now is what role GtL plays in optimal gas commercialization strategies, not whether it is feasible. Oil shale is the largest resource component and also the most challenging. Technically, it is known to be possible to produce liquid hydrocarbons from oil shale, and, commercially, a breakthrough appears very close, with advances on several fronts.

During the 1986–1999 period, with oil prices generally in the range of $10–20/bbl, there was little incentive to research or commercialize unconventional technologies. The impetus has returned with the last few years of much higher prices, and, therefore, the efficiency and economics of all kinds of unconventional oil have recently improved considerably and continue to benefit from field experience and research and development. Oil shale is the only one of these technologies that still has significant question marks over its cost.

"Tar sands and heavy oil are found only in significant amounts in Canada and Venezuela." Aleklett and Campbell opine that "heavy oil and bitumen deposits ... are present in large quantities only in western Canada and eastern Venezuela."[4] However, several other countries have huge volumes of bitumen and extra-heavy oil, notably Russia, China, the United States, Saudi Arabia, Kuwait, Iran, and Iraq.[5] Reserves of heavy oil potentially exceed those of light in every region of the world outside Europe and the Middle East, and in the Americas and Asia in particular, bitumen and heavy oil vastly outweigh light oil. The world has about 1.2 trillion bbl of conventional oil reserves,[6] and almost as much, 1.1 trillion bbl, in heavy oil and bitumen recoverable with today's methods; less than half of this, about 450 billion bbl, is in Venezuela and Canada.[7] Worldwide, an additional 4.9 trillion bbl in place of heavy oil and bitumen is known, so if a recovery factor of just 25 percent could be achieved (and modern techniques go up to 60 percent), then the heavy oils would constitute at least double the volumes of the light.

More importantly than this, we have not even begun a serious search for extra-heavy oil and bitumen. Many occurrences are barely reported or have not had their magnitude assessed. Very few have received any kind of engineering or economic study, even a cursory one.

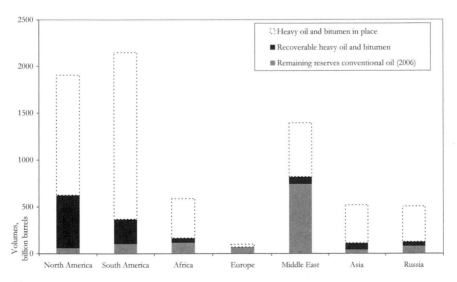

Figure 6.1
Global resources of conventional oil, heavy oil, and bitumen.

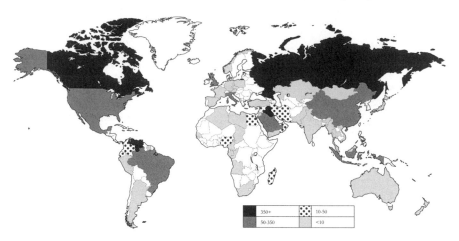

Figure 6.2
World heavy, extra-heavy, and oil sands resources (billions of barrels in place).

"Unconventional oil production cannot be increased quickly enough to offset declining conventional supplies." It is true that, compared with the gigantic resource base, today's production of unconventional oil is small. This is primarily attributable to economic factors: only with improved technology and, particularly, the last five years of high prices has large-scale exploitation of tight oil, tar sands, and extra-heavy oil become attractive. Similarly, the technology for GtL and CtL has been around for nearly ninety years, but it has only recently become worthwhile to make it work in world-scale plants.

Advocates of this myth point to the severe logistical constraints and cost increases that have affected the Canadian oil sands industry. These are real and are due to intense development at a single location. Some of these bottlenecks could be eased by a more coordinated development and improvement of infrastructure (e.g., railways to Fort McMurray). Others will disappear naturally as supply of, for instance, workers and housing, catches up, yet others, for instance, a shortage of steel, have been caused by a global commodities boom, which will run its course. The main solutions, however, to this problem are to continue improving the efficiency of oil sand extraction and to transfer these techniques from the congested West Canadian patch to other unconventional oil areas. Although there are currently political obstacles in Venezuela, several other unconventional oil areas, that have, as yet, received little attention could make major contributions.

Significant declines in conventional oil production would, it is true, be difficult to make up in the short term. However, the same is true of bringing new conventional production online, as was demonstrated during the large production outages of 1973–1974 and 1979–1980. Although unconventional resources require a greater intensity of investment and are in some ways inherently more difficult to develop than conventional oil, they have two advantages. First, their location and approximate magnitude is known: there is no geological risk and no need for a lengthy exploration campaign. Second, the decline rate is essentially zero: once unconventional reserves are producing, they can maintain that plateau rate over several decades, moderating underlying global decline rates.

Heavy oil and tar sands production in Canada has actually succeeded in reversing that nation's production decline. Canadian production peaked in 1979 at 1.8 million bbl/day and fell for three years but has subsequently almost doubled, driven primarily by increases in unconventional oil. Total world production of heavy oil and oil sands, at somewhat more than 3 million bbl/day, is only about 3.5 percent of the total, but, were it a country, it would rank seventh amongst world producers.

"Unconventional oil sources, particularly tar sands and oil shale, result in a small, zero or negative net energy gain." The question of EROEI is dealt with in Chapter 9. It has become a cliché among peak oil theorists and other proponents of industrial collapse that unconventional oil requires almost as much, or perhaps more, energy to produce than the oil itself yields. In fact, even the most energy-intensive processes, such as shale oil production, generate more energy than they consume, and all unconventional oil technologies have considerable room for improvements in efficiency, or technical alternatives.

NATURAL GAS LIQUIDS

NGLs form a major and oft-neglected part of global petroleum liquids supply. They include liquefied petroleum gas (LPG[8]) and condensate (natural gasoline), which can be separated from the methane that constitutes the main component of natural gas. Most gas fields contain some quantity of NGLs; some, like the world's largest field, South Pars/North Field, contain considerably more than average. They are "rich" or "wet" gas.

NGLs can be a like-for-like replacement for oil, particularly because they are light and low in sulphur. Blending them with heavy oils, which are also increasing in the world production mix, gives a medium-grade oil that is acceptable to the majority of global refineries. As world gas production increases, more recovery capacity is installed, and as gas flaring[9] ceases, NGL output will climb sharply. Even if there are insufficient gas markets, NGLs can still be extracted by stripping out the liquid content and reinjecting the dry gas or using it to improve recovery from oil fields. Abu Dhabi is an example of large-scale application of this practice.

Current NGL production is very significant, running at 10.3 million bbl, larger than any single country's oil output. Furthermore, production increased 6 percent from January 2006 to January 2007, whereas conventional supply fell slightly (to avoid exciting peak oilers, this was caused by OPEC cuts). Gas production has been growing steadily at 2–3 percent in recent years, implying that NGL supply, if increasing in step, will make up an increasing fraction of global oil. If peak oil arrives, then gas supply (and associated NGLs) will grow even more quickly because there will be increased demand for gas where it can substitute for oil (mainly power and petrochemicals and to some extent transportation).

Tight Oil

"Tight oil" is ordinary, light crude oil contained in formations of low permeability. Conventional wells produce from such formations at very low, uneconomic rates, if at all, and therefore special methods are needed to access it. This category of unconventional oil has been all but overlooked by most commentators, but recent advances in horizontal drilling and fracturing, in particular, have opened up some tight oil plays, and these methods could be more widely applied. The advantage of tight oil is that, once acceptable flow rates have been achieved, the rest of development follows standard oil-field practice, and the product is identical to that produced from conventional fields.

There is no really systematic account of tight oil, whose definition depends heavily in any case on economic factors. Initial flow rates of several thousand barrels per day are needed in deepwater; onshore, a few tens may be acceptable. Tight oil reservoirs have often been overlooked, but one good example, the Bakken Shale, is now a hot new play in Montana. Key to producing these unconventional reservoirs are a set of synergistic technologies: fracture prediction and imaging; horizontal, underbalanced drilling; and hydraulic fracturing using nondamaging fluids.

The Bakken Shale is a tremendous example of the combination of high prices, new technology, and imagination to add oil reserves that peak oil theorists would never have thought of or would have dismissed. One writer comments:

The recent, highly productive oil field discoveries within the Bakken Formation did not come from venturing out into deep uncharted waters heretofore untapped by man, nor from blazing a trail into pristine environs never open to drilling before. Instead, success came from analysis of geologic data on a decades-old producing area, identification of untapped resources, and application of the new drilling and completion technology necessary to exploit them. In short, it came from using technology to convert unconventional resources into reserves.[10]

Now that the problems of producing this low-permeability reservoir have been solved, production from the Bakken has doubled every year since 2000, and its development has doubled Montana's oil production between 2002 and 2005. The formation is estimated to contain between 271 and 503 billion bbl of high-quality (41° API) oil in place, with recovery factors of 3–18 percent, implying that total reserves could be 8–90 billion bbl, enough to increase U.S. oil reserves by 10–110 percent.

Other tight oil reservoirs are present in the USA, such as the Niobrara Formation of Colorado and Wyoming,[11] and the Barnett Shale,[12] better known for gas, in Texas, and around the world. Many more have probably been overlooked, such as the R'mah Formation of Syria. The Sargelu Formation of the northern Persian Gulf region might contain 25–50 billion bbl of recoverable oil[13]; there are probably additional billions in the Athel of Oman (analogs of which may be found in other Middle Eastern countries) and the Bazhenov and Achimov Formations of West Siberia.

A rather different tight oil reservoir is Chicontepec, described in Chapter 5 under Mexico. This is not a source rock but a complex of tight (low permeability, in this case 0.1–10 mD[14]) sandstones containing enormous in-place resources, some 139 billion bbl, of which some 10–13 billion bbl is technically recoverable. Contrary to frequent descriptions of it as a heavy oil reservoir, the gravities actually range from 18 to 45° API, even the lower figure being at the light end of heavy oils.

Heavy and Extra-Heavy Oil

Heavy oil forms the bridge between light oil and tar sands, and the industry has been able to cut its teeth on heavy oil as a preliminary to moving on to bitumen. Heavy oil is generally considered as having an API gravity of between 10 and 20° (93–100 percent of the density of water) and a viscosity somewhere between olive oil and treacle. Extra-heavy oil has a viscosity similar to treacle, so it will flow naturally to some extent, but is denser than water (API gravity less than 10°).

From a resource point of view, the distinguishing characteristic of heavy/extra-heavy oil (as opposed to tar sands) is that it will flow into wells, but generally special techniques will be required to achieve economic flow rates and recovery factors (dependent on the viscosity), and the crude oil will need extra refining or blending. The main recovery mechanism is injecting superheated steam to reduce the oil's viscosity. Recovery factors from cold production are usually only 5–10 percent of the oil in place; steam floods take this up to 15–20 percent, and newer thermal methods as high as 60 percent. Innovative technologies continue to be introduced, such as generating steam down hole to save energy and trap CO_2 underground.[15]

The largest resources of heavy and extra-heavy oil in the world are found in Venezuela. Most of Venezuela's heavy oil is found in the eastern Orinoco Belt (Faja Petrolifera del Orinoco), which covers 54,000 km^2, almost as large as Ireland or West Virginia, but there are also significant volumes under Lake Maracaibo in the west of the country. Total Orinoco Belt resources are estimated at 1,200 billion bbl, with some 267 billion bbl of this currently recoverable. Venezuelan extra-heavy oil is similar in density to Canada's tar sands but rather deeper and at higher temperatures, which dramatically lowers the viscosity, from more than chocolate to similar to treacle (although less tasty than either), so it is produced via wells rather than by mining as in many Canadian projects.

Four main projects are currently operating in the Orinoco, yielding a total of 700,000 bbl/day, which is upgraded to lighter oils suitable for refining, but these will only recover 3 percent of the reserves, indicating great scope for additional projects. Ultimately, recovery factors could reach 15 or 25 percent, taking Venezuelan reserves to par with Saudi Arabia. However, the unfavorable fiscal terms and unpredictable resource nationalism of Hugo Chávez currently make it difficult to launch more such high-tech and expensive projects.

Numerous other countries outside Venezuela and Canada, including most major petroleum provinces, have significant heavy oil resources. Many of these are currently under development, indicating that the age of unconventional oil, heralded in North America, is now dawning worldwide. New fields are being worked in Italy, Norway, Syria, Egypt, and Oman. In some cases, such as Brazil, the resources are exploited with similar techniques to those used for the lighter oil. In others, notably Canada and California, exploitation requires special thermal methods. In yet others, such as the United Kingdom and Alaska, most developments have not yet been found economic. The inauguration of offshore steam-floods could unlock the U.K.'s heavy oil and increase total reserves by as much as 50 percent. China, with a reported 175 billion bbl of heavy oil in place,[16, 17] and Russia, with some 13 billion bbl technically recoverable,[18] also have the potential to be major players. In the major OPEC states (excluding Venezuela), there has been little or no effort to address very large heavy oil resources; Kuwait, Iran, and Iraq have at least 40 billion bbl of heavy oil in place between them, and Kuwait has recently announced a project with ExxonMobil to produce some 900,000 bbl/day from its heavy oil Lower Fars reservoir.[19]

Peak oil predictions wildly understate the potential for heavy crude, particularly outside Canada and Venezuela, and do not allow for the large and rapid increases in output that would occur if conventional oil were to go into decline. Many heavy oil developments are economic today, and, with advances in technology, the break-even price will fall farther, because there is no real constraint of resource size.

Oil Sands

Oil sands (tar sands) form a truly astonishing resource of liquid hydrocarbons. In these very shallowly buried deposits, usually unconsolidated sandstones, tar (bitumen) is stuck to sand grains. They were probably formed when large amounts of conventional oil were trapped in shallow reservoirs, from which groundwater washed away the low-density components while bacteria consumed the lighter hydrocarbons, leaving the denser compounds, often contaminated with high levels of sulphur and heavy metals such as nickel and vanadium. Some 14 percent of the total rock weight is accounted for by the bitumen.

The best known examples occur in Cretaceous sands in western Canada, primarily in Alberta (with some in Saskatchewan), in three main belts: Athabasca, Peace River and Cold Lake, and one smaller, Wabasca. Of some 1.7–2 trillion barrels in place, 180 billion bbl is estimated to be recoverable. However, with additional exploration, these volumes might increase to more than 2.5 trillion bbl, 300 billion bbl being recoverable with today's technologies.[20] This puts Canada in the same class as Saudi Arabia (with 264 billion bbl) as a reserves holder.

Oil sands are mostly exploited by mining techniques: removing the overburden and then collecting the mixture of bitumen, water, and sand using giant shovels. Mixing with warm water removes the sand, and then the extracted crude oil can be upgraded to a synthetic crude oil similar to a natural medium-light oil. Mining, which recovers about 83–87 percent of bitumen in place,[21] yields about two-thirds of current output, but 80 percent of known Canadian resources are too deep for mining.[22]

Alternative techniques use wells to extract the bitumen. The most important, which can recover more than 60 percent of original oil in place,[23] is steam-assisted gravity drainage (SAGD). A pair of horizontal wells is drilled, one about 5 meters above the other, and steam is injected into the top one, which then heats the bitumen so that it drains into the lower well. More recent refinements use the worthless heavy ends of the oil itself to generate the steam rather than valuable natural gas.[24] Alternatively, the experimental technique of burning the oil in place may be able to increase recovery factors to 80 percent without requiring steam at all.[25] About a quarter of current bitumen production comes from thermal methods (SAGD, cyclic steam, and others), with the remaining 10 percent via cold production.

The total list of announced Canadian oil sands projects currently totals some 1.3 million bbl/day, rising to about 2.7 million bbl/day by 2010. In addition, it is probable that there will be debottlenecking and capacity creep on the existing projects. The growth picture is likely, however, to be altered by delays and cancellations caused by cost increases and logistical constraints in the boom environment. Allowing for this, production from the oil sands is at 1.2 million bbl/day today (from 0.8 million bbl/day in 2003[26]) and is projected to reach 1.8 million bbl/day in 2010 and 2.6–3.5 million bbl/day by 2015, rising to 3.5 million bbl/day in 2017 and 5 million bbl/day by 2030.[27] With most projects taking on the order of four years to come online, the 2015+ figures are likely to rise sharply as new developments are approved. Contrast this to more conservative Geologist figures, which see just 2.5 million bbl/day by 2020, for some reason remaining flat to 2030 despite the vast resource base and purported oil crisis.[28]

Oil sands costs have dropped sharply since the early 1980s, from some $40/bbl (Canadian) in 1985 to around $20/bbl in 2000.[29] Cost reductions continue in the mining operations, but costs appear relatively to have plateaued in the *in situ* projects. With the recent industry cost inflation and intense activity, expenses have jumped up again, but this is a market rather than a geological or technological phenomenon.

The Cretaceous of western Canada is, of course, the oil sands location *par excellence*, but many other countries contain significant oil sand and similar resources.

The Albertan oil sands extend into lesser known deposits in different rocks (the "Carbonate Triangle") and into the neighboring province of Saskatchewan, with anywhere from 160 to 450 billion bbl of additional oil in place.[30, 31, 32] The United States contains 30–58 billion bbl of tar sands, mostly in Utah and Alaska, although of poorer quality than the Canadian example. Russia has gigantic resources, comparable with those of Canada and Venezuela, one estimate putting the total of Russia's extra-heavy oil and bitumen resources at 246–1350 billion bbl.[33, 34] This bitumen occurs mainly in the very shallow Melekess Tar Sands, for which Shell has recently signed an agreement, overlying the huge (conventional) Romashkino Field in the Volga-Urals area, a hub of industry and oil production, and in the Lena-Anabar Basin in East Siberia,[35, 36] very remote from population centers. Other nations with between 20 and 300 billion bbl of bitumen in place include Kazakhstan, Romania, China, Nigeria, and Madagascar. Madagascar, in particular, is pressing ahead with development and, according to major leaseholder Madagascar Oil, plans to reach 500,000 bbl/day by 2017 (i.e., about twice that of all Campbell's non-Canada/Venezuela heavy oil in that year).

Peak oil enthusiasts generally dismiss tar sands as a solution to the problem because of their alleged low net energy yield, high environmental impact, need for natural gas and water, and slow speed of development. The low net energy yield (low EROEI) is neither true nor important, as is discussed in Chapter 9. The last three of these issues remain significant but are being overcome and do not represent insuperable barriers. Technologies such as those outlined above are making a major contribution to improving the economics of tar sand production and reducing their consumption of other resources and can now be exported to other oil sands locations around the world. Enhanced commerciality makes the projects more acceptable to government and corporate stakeholders and quicker to implement. The abundance of other tar sand opportunities around the world can also reduce the congestion in Western Canada. The main objection to oil sands developments will increasingly be their CO_2 emissions; this is problematic, but partial solutions are being developed, as discussed in Chapter 10.

Oil Shale

The process of recovering oil from oil shales essentially involves shrinking time by a factor of millions.

Oil shales is a general term for oil source rocks, deposits rich in organic matter (kerogen), mostly derived from algae. If these source rocks are subjected to sufficient natural heat and pressure over several million years, they will yield oil that, migrating out of the rock, accumulates in reservoirs to form conventional petroleum accumulations. However, in many parts of the world are found oil shales that have not been buried sufficiently to mature the organic matter. The resource base is colossal, at least 3 trillion barrels and probably far more than all the world's conventional and heavy oil.

To produce oil from these rocks, the natural process of maturation has to be stimulated artificially, compressed from a period of millions of years to a few years or months. Attempts have been made for more than a hundred years to extract oil from such rocks, beginning in Scotland in 1850. Sustained, economic production in significant volumes has not yet been achieved, but higher prices and new technologies hold out some hope for the near future.

There are two main processes for extracting oil from oil shales. Mining was tried extensively in Colorado by Exxon, Unocal, Amoco, Occidental, and other companies, who gave up in 1982, and continues in Estonia today, where it still provides 62 percent of primary energy. Mining has historically generated huge volumes of waste, some carcinogenic, required a lot of energy and water, been very expensive, and caused significant environmental degradation, although new techniques offer some improvements.[37]

In situ conversion, being trialled by Shell in its Mahogany Research Project in Colorado, appears more promising and environmentally acceptable.[38] Electrically heating the rock underground for about four years converts the kerogen to oil and gas, which can then be brought to surface by injecting water (turning to steam down hole) to strip out the lighter components. About 65–70 percent of the kerogen in place can be recovered as oil, reportedly as much as ten times more than that obtained by mining and retorting. The product is not a heavy, poor-quality crude, as often reported, but is actually light and low in sulphur. To prevent the oil escaping and possibly contaminating groundwater, refrigeration pipes form a frozen barrier enclosing the heating area. This cryogenic approach sounds exotic but has been commonly used in mining and tunneling

operations, for instance in Boston's "Big Dig" and at the Strategic Petroleum Reserve salt caverns in Louisiana. The process is energy intensive,
but the oil generated contains about 3.5 times the energy input to extract
it, and the byproduct natural gas can be used as a supplementary energy
source. Shell believes that Mahogany can be commercial with oil prices
about $30/bbl.

The U.S. oil shales are the best known and currently thought to be the
largest in the world, being found primarily in the Green River Formation,
covering northwestern Colorado, northeastern Utah, and southwestern
Wyoming. Total resources of U.S. shale oil are estimated at about 1,500
billion (1.5 trillion) barrels,[39] i.e., significantly larger than total world conventional reserves. It is notable that most of the countries with significant
resources are net importers of fossil fuels and so have strong incentives to
develop their indigenous shale oil. Even in the Middle East and North
Africa, oil shale has been bestowed on those countries without conventional oil: Morocco, Israel, Palestine, and Jordan. Jordan's resources are
particularly notable for quality and size. Australia, Brazil, Canada, China,
Germany, and Russia all have huge oil shale deposits, as may Iran, Iraq,
Turkey, and Venezuela, with lesser amounts scattered across many countries. The Brazilian company Petrobras, which has mined commercial oil
shale in Brazil since 1991, is now looking at the Jordanian and Moroccan
deposits.[40]

Total world high-grade shale oil resources are variously estimated at
0.6–15 trillion barrels.[41, 42, 43, 44] No doubt, if they became economically
viable, a systematic search could find many more deposits. Whatever the
total resource, it is virtually infinite for practical purposes if an economic
and environmentally sound development method can be devised.

Despite jibes that "oil shale is the fuel of the future and always will be,"
it actually may be that oil shale is now where oil sands were in the early
1970s, with the first commercial developments on the verge of getting off
the ground. Oil prices will have to remain high, and technological, environmental, and commercial risks are clearly significant until a viable technology proves itself, but, conversely, political and geological risks are low.
Interestingly, in OPEC's heyday in the mid-1970s, they targeted an oil
price below $70/bbl, believing that this was the level at which shale oil
would become competitive, therefore recognizing its phenomenal volumetric potential.[45, 46]

Being used to searching for conventional oil, Geologists generally reject
oil shales as a feasible source of large volumes of liquid hydrocarbons.
This may seem odd given that mapping shale deposits offers the chance
for geologists (in the strict sense) to get away from their workstations and
out in the field, which is where most of them would prefer to be. Oil shale
clearly faces big challenges to commerciality, but it shows a failure of
imagination to dismiss it today because it was unsuccessful in 1982;

technology in many spheres has moved a long way in the intervening quarter century. We could not produce oil in water depths greater than 500 meters in 1982; today the limit is over 2,000 meters, and, to take an example from another industry, hard drive capacity has increased by a factor of some 10,000 over that time.

Gas to Liquids

The phenomenon of GtL technology proves that, even if peak oil is upon us, it is not an energy crisis but a crisis of liquid fuels.

It may not seem like it to hard-pressed homeowners in a North American or European winter, but the world is awash in cheap, abundant gas; North Field/South Pars alone may contain some fifteen times the entire proven gas reserves of the United States. GtL offers a way of powering cars and lorries and potentially, trains, ships, and planes, and incidentally of lubricating the engines, too, even if oil supply declines. When oil prices rise markedly above gas prices, the differential naturally creates an incentive to convert one to the other. Advances in technology have greatly lowered the cost of doing so on a large scale.

The basic principles of GtL have been known for a long time, being discovered in the 1920s. GtL is one subset of a variety of XtL processes, which turn a feedstock, gas, coal, or biomass, into liquid hydrocarbons, usually via a two-stage reaction, the first stage being the classic "Fischer-Tropsch" (F-T) process. Choices of catalysts and operating conditions can tune the reaction to give any of the premium products that are made in a conventional refinery: diesel, home heating oil, gasoline, jet fuel, LPG, petrochemical feedstocks, lubricants, and food-grade waxes, along with drinking-quality water, especially attractive in arid countries reliant on desalination, such as Qatar.

The process, although straightforward in concept, is extremely capital intensive and requires high levels of technical expertise to make it economic, while the products may also require special marketing. There are therefore few major players. Sasol, the South African concern who developed technology to help apartheid-era South Africa survive the boycott, began with CtL but has now adapted to GtL, recently starting up the Oryx plant in Qatar. Shell has long had a large-scale commercial plant operating at Bintulu in Malaysia.

GtL requires large amounts of gas, and some 40 percent of the energy content in the feedstock is lost.[47] In a peak oil scenario, to meet a quarter of world demand growth and production decline of some 4 million bbl/day with GtL alone would imply growing global gas production by about 3.5 percent per year over 2006 levels. The world gas industry has increased production by at least 3 percent every year since 2002, so giving confidence that the increases, although challenging, would be feasible. Just stopping flaring across the world would deliver 15 billion cubic feet per day,[48] enough to produce 1.5 million bbl/day of GtL products. To put it another way, this scale of GtL would require a resource base of some 90 Tcf to be developed annually; average annual reserve additions were 140 Tcf during 2000–2006, again suggesting that this target is realistic.

About 1.6 million bbl/day of GtL projects have been announced recently. If there are few upstream players, similarly there are relatively few countries suitable for the technology. GtL is not economical when there is a good local market for gas. It works best with stranded gas: accumulations that are too small and/or distant to merit a pipeline or LNG plant, hence where the feedstock price is very low. The major client at the moment, however, is countries with large gas resources and major LNG industries who want to diversify their exports and avoid saturating the LNG market. The prime among these is, of course, Qatar, with Shell's gigantic Pearl plant under construction, possibly to be joined by Egypt, Iran, Nigeria, and Australia.

Advances in technology and increases in scale have resulted in major cost reductions. For instance, Sasol estimates that capital costs are down from $34,000/barrel/day of capacity to $20,000/barrel/day,[49] at a very early stage of the industry's development. Shell believes that GtL costs about $25/bbl (coal and biomass feedstocks being substantially more costly).[50, 51] Because GtL plants can also be net generators of power, they could be used to feed electricity into the local grid or, in remote areas, combined with an LNG plant whose compressors require power.

Conversely, general industry cost inflation, logistical issues in Qatar, and the inevitable problems with new technology have pushed costs in the other direction. Learnings from the two Qatari plants will be key for determining the industry's enthusiasm for the second wave of GtL. Alongside these megaprojects, small-scale GtL installations relying on stranded or flared gas could gain in importance given the huge global stock of undeveloped gas fields. West Africa, and perhaps Indonesia and Australia, will probably become the main locations for such smaller-scale operations.

Turning gas into diesel, LPG, and naphtha via F-T is not the only GtL process. One possibility is to convert gas directly to liquid hydrocarbons, which would be much more energy and carbon efficient, but this reaction has to date been difficult to control and has not been commercialized. Other destinations involve turning gas to methanol,[52] dimethyl ether (DME),[53] ammonia, or hydrogen. In the shorter term, DME and methanol are both clean,[54] economic,[55] efficient,[56] transport fuels, requiring limited modification of existing engines, and DME has the added advantage of being nontoxic. Either could, in different ways, be a bridge to the "hydrogen economy."[57, 58]

In the medium term, at least, natural gas is likely to be the main source of hydrogen, which may become a significant vehicle fuel, and can be used to upgrade heavy oil or to convert coal to liquid fuels. New processes can produce hydrogen directly from gas with almost 100 percent efficiency, without generating CO_2, at least on a small scale.[59]

Coal and Biomass to Liquids

If the potential for gas is large, that for coal is enormous. As is shown in Chapter 9, global coal reserves are gigantic and widely distributed, particularly in important energy importers such as the United States, China, and India. Given this, the prospect of converting coal into transport fuels is bound to be an attractive one. Total global potential for liquid hydrocarbon production from coal has been estimated at some 9 trillion barrels,[60] that is, about three to four and a half times the ultimate conventional oil endowment (depending whose estimate you believe). Biomass offers the added incentives of supply security and zero net CO_2 emissions.

Famously, Nazi Germany used coal to manufacture synthetic fuels during World War II, 1939–45, playing a crucial role in sustaining the war economy until the Allies' bombing campaign targeted these plants toward the end of the war.[61] During the later part of the conflict, twenty-seven installations were generating about 80,000 bbl/day, 90 percent of Germany's total petroleum consumption.[62] Currently, one PetroSA and two Sasol plants, all with the same technology, are making liquids from coal in oil-poor South Africa, with a total capacity of 215,000 bbl/day. During the 1980s, when the country was embargoed because of apartheid, these facilities supplied 60 percent of South Africa's oil. The German and South African situations illustrate the feasibility, albeit expensively, of basing a whole economy on CtL. Of course, these were special situations, but so would peak oil be.

Today, some 700,000 bbl/day of CtL plants are in existence or under proposal, mostly in the coal kings of South Africa, Australia, China, and the United States. The products are clean, but CtL is nearly double the cost of GtL, some \$40–50/bbl, and two to three times as carbon intensive,[63] so carbon sequestration (Chapter 10) is required, if a large CtL programme takes shape, to avoid unacceptably high emissions.

BtL (using feedstocks such as wood, straw, and grass) is even more expensive than CtL, costing some \$90/bbl, with potential for reduction to \$70–80. The high cost is attributable to the dispersed nature of the resource and hence lack of economies of scale. However, cofiring a "CBtL" plant with coal and biomass would permit larger plants, as well as partially mitigating CO_2 release. Pure BtL has zero lifecycle net CO_2 emissions.[64] Ingenious CBtL facilities, which coproduce heat, electricity, and synfuels, could reach efficiencies of 63 percent,[65] at which point they would be a viable part of the energy complex for China and perhaps the United States.

Biofuels

With biofuels, we move away from geologically based unconventional oil to a different field of science entirely. Nevertheless, the source of fuel is irrelevant to consumers as long as price and quality (and, ideally, environmental impact) are acceptable.

There are a great variety of techniques for converting biomass to oil substitutes. The two most popular today are to ferment sugar (in corn syrup and sugarcane) to ethanol, the favored biofuel in the United States and Brazil, and to grow biological oils from crops such as soybeans, rapeseed, coconut oil, and jatropha, often in India and Southeast Asia, to make "biodiesel," preferred in the European Union and China. These "first-generation" biofuels rely on food crops.

"Second-generation" techniques, now under development, can use waste (such as paper, sewage, food leftovers, manure, and even tires and waste plastic) and nonfood plant material (such as cotton, neem, hemp, straw, wood, rice husks, chaff, and stalks). These methods include the following: creating other alcohols with better properties than ethanol; using enzymes or gasification to convert woody material into "cellulosic ethanol"; thermal depolymerization (heating to break down long molecules) to treat waste; and F-T conversion (like GtL and CtL, described above), with a variety of feedstocks. Construction on the first commercial cellulosic ethanol plant began in November 2007.[66] Alternatively, nonfood crops can be converted to "biogasoline," a process under development by Shell, with advantages of compatibility with existing distribution networks and engines.

One early-stage technology with the potential to transform the whole oil market is algal biofuels. Certain kinds of algae, grown on substrates of waste or sewage, can reportedly produce 250 times as much oil per square kilometer as soybeans, suggesting that just 28,000 km^2 (0.3 percent of the U.S. land area, about the size of Hawaii or Massachusetts) could fuel the entire country's transport fleet. An additional refinement would be to use CO_2 from industrial sources to enhance the algae's growth. Algae can be grown in desert areas (high insolation) using salt water, so avoiding competition for croplands and water resources, and as a byproduct, they yield a nitrogen/phosphorus-rich fertilizer.[67] The Middle East could transition from extracting oil to growing it.

Costs vary: that of cellulosic ethanol is about \$70/bbl,[68] thermal depolymerization about \$80/bbl,[69] and jatropha only \$20/bbl.[70] These costs are on par with or lower than current oil prices and have potential to fall farther. Ethanol meets more than a quarter of Brazil's gasoline demand; the United States plans, as a component of an admittedly incoherent national energy policy, to reach 3 million bbl/day of ethanol by 2017, most of which will have to be cellulosic; America's solid municipal waste could yield as much as 370,000 bbl/day of oil,[71] and the country disposes of 200,000 bbl/day of waste vegetable oil (similar to the conventional oil production of Brunei).

Many of the drawbacks of biofuels are overstated or can be reduced through improvements in technology and regulation. Although corn ethanol, heavily subsidized, remains controversial, other biofuels, such as sugarcane, have clearly positive net energy yields. The net energy yield of cellulosic ethanol can be as high as 5 (1 joule of input energy yields 5 joules of output). Biofuels have the potential to reduce CO_2 pollution, because they displace fossil fuels (although some greenhouse gases are released by agriculture). The most favorable examples, cellulosic ethanol, and sugarcane, which uses the residue, bagasse, for energy, have 85 percent lower lifecycle emissions than petroleum. Especially useful are biofuels like jatropha, which can be grown on desert lands, use little water,[72] and potentially can sequester carbon in the soil.

Using food crops for biofuels does result in rising prices, so their large-scale adoption will require second-generation feedstocks that do not compete with food. Rising corn prices, caused by a number of factors of which biofuel demand is one, have already led to rioting over the cost of tortillas in Mexico. Yet global biomass production is well above the total required to supply food needs.[73] If tariff barriers imposed by the industrialized world on agricultural products were reduced, this would allow poor farmers in the developing countries to supplement their incomes, thus giving positive rather than negative social impacts. Eliminating subsidies and tariffs on fuels would also make their economics transparent and lead to sensible allocation of resources, for instance, encouraging Brazilian sugarcane ethanol, rather than the "pork barrel" subsidization of corn ethanol currently under way in the United States. Much of biofuels policy revolves less around technology and more on providing sensible incentives that do not distort the market excessively or lead to negative social and environmental impacts.

Kinetics: The Speed of Commercialization

End of oil writers have generally been unable to deny the enormous volumes of unconventional oil resources, and those who have done some serious research (e.g., Hirsch[74]) concede that they can certainly be competitive with conventional oil, at least at recent prices of $50–100/bbl. If, for argument's sake, we then accept a peak in conventional oil supplies, the big challenge becomes how fast unconventional supplies can be brought on-stream.

The great advantage of unconventional projects, particularly tar sands, over conventional oil is that the resource is known; there is no need for an exploration campaign, with its delays and high risk. In addition, the resource base is so enormous that there are ample quantities in politically stable, often net oil importing countries, with attractive investment regimes—heavy oil and tar sands in Canada, the United States, the United Kingdom, and Oman, oil shale in the United States and Australia, and GtL in Qatar—that resource nationalism in Russia or Venezuela will not prevent major growth in unconventional oil. Indeed, a boom in unconventional oil elsewhere could put pressure on holders of large hydrocarbon resources, both unconventional and conventional, to open up to investment. Conversely, the investments required are very large and may be constrained by the availability of skilled people and other resources.

Hirsch's report is a good starting point for investigation, because a large part is devoted to investigating how fast unconventional oil could replace declining conventional supply. I use his date for conventional peak oil of 2016 here purely for illustration, because I have argued earlier that any peak is likely to be much later than this. In 2016, Hirsch assumes a production high of 100 million bbd/day, declining from then on annually at 2 percent (approximately 2 million bbl/day, fairly consistent with the figures of Campbell and Laherrère), plus a (rather high) yearly demand growth of approximately 2.2 million bbl/day.[75] By ten years after peak, unconventional oil would therefore have to replace some 42 million bbl/day of conventional production, i.e., 4.2 million bbl/day of unconventional capacity additions each year. The supply and demand lines are laid out in Figure 6.3.

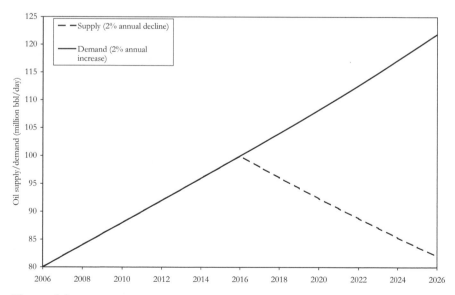

Figure 6.3
Supply-demand deficit to be met with unconventional oil.

Is this pace of capacity additions feasible? It is certainly rapid compared with the current pace of unconventional oil development. Under current conditions, we can foresee additions of about 900–950,000 bbl/day annually compared with the required 3.5–4.2 million bbl/day. How fast could other unconventional oil sources be ramped up given high prices and a sense of urgency?

In its best years (1977, 1979, 1994), the United Kingdom added about 500,000 bbl/day of conventional oil, facing very difficult technical challenges not incomparable with (indeed, perhaps greater than) those facing unconventional oil today. Growth for Canadian oil sands is predicted at 20 percent annually to 2014; Montanan tight oil doubled in three consecutive years. To take the analog of natural gas, as we will see in Chapter 7, North American production rose despite declines in conventional output, as it proved possible to increase unconventional production rapidly by the combination of intense investment and technological advances. Under business-as-usual conditions (i.e., no peak oil), unconventional oil could be contributing 15–22 million bbl/day by 2025,[76, 77, 78] comprising a mix of EOR, extra-heavy oil and oil sands, GtL, CtL, and BtL, and ethanol. This is about half Hirsch's requirement.

This should encourage us that, in a peak oil event, with rising prices and a sense of urgency, unconventional oil could fill the gap. Hirsch's argument contains a fallacy in that it assumes a "standing start," and his "crash program" takes four years to yield any production at all.[79, 80] Actually, we are already well advanced in exploiting EOR, biofuels, heavy oil, and tar sands and have made a start with tight oil and XtL. Total current unconventional production, at about 7 million bbl/day (excluding 10 million bbl/day of NGLs) is already meeting the crash program's seven-year target. There is today a sizeable base of knowledge, skilled people, and capital goods to continue this expansion when needed. Second, Hirsch and most others in the peak oil camp also assume today's technology, for instance, discounting oil shales entirely, whereas, particularly if the peak is some years away, then extrapolating historic improvements suggests that all unconventional oil sources will be cheaper, less cumbersome, and more environmentally benign than they are today. Third, predictions of unconventional oil supply in the past have often been conservative: mid-1990s views were that the oil sands would reach 1 million bbl/day by 2020, but this level was actually achieved in 2004.[81]

Fourth, it is a mistake to think of a sharp dividing line between conventional and unconventional oil: the more expensive conventional sources (e.g., onshore Texas stripper wells and tail-end North Sea fields) have a wide overlap with the cheaper unconventional options. Conceptually, the cost curves can be shown as follows (Figure 6.4). Hirsch and other peak oil advocates argue that there is a sharp cost discontinuity between conventional and unconventional oil (top dashed line), and therefore prices

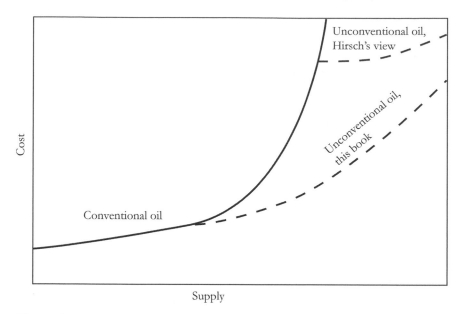

Figure 6.4
Conceptual cost curves for conventional and unconventional oil.

have to rise sharply once conventional oil begins to decline. However, the true situation is more likely to be represented by the bottom dashed line: some unconventional oil is actually cheaper than marginal conventional oil, and the transition from one to the other is therefore a smooth one with only a gentle upward trend of costs.

Another way of thinking about cost is shown in Figure 6.5.[82, 83] This shows the capital cost of various unconventional oil supplies together with the full range of conventional oil costs, in terms of the expenditure required to deliver one barrel per day of production capacity. This metric is meaningful because, as we have observed, most end of oil proponents maintain that the primary issue for unconventional oil is not the volumes in place but how fast they can be extracted or converted. From this chart, it appears that bringing unconventional oil on-stream requires similar effort to moderately expensive conventional oil.

Finally, much of the pessimism about the speed of unconventional ramp-up comes from the U.S. experience of recent years, in which permitting large industrial facilities, such as a refinery, nuclear power station, or LNG terminal (or, for our purposes, a shale oil or CtL plant), takes up to a decade and in some cases is all but impossible. Hirsch extrapolates this to conclude that effective mitigation of declining conventional oil will take up to twenty years. However, in a crisis situation, such barriers could be more easily overcome. In any case, a large portion of the world's

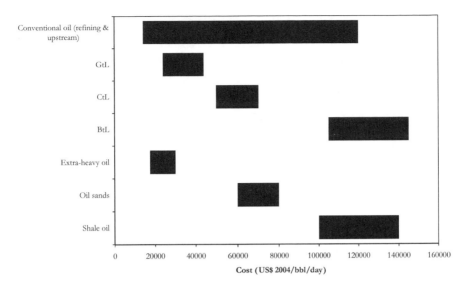

Figure 6.5
Capital cost of unconventional oil options in production rate.

unconventional oil will be developed in countries such as Canada, China, India, Brazil, South Africa, and Qatar, which have in recent years shown their ability to launch enormous new industrial enterprises with dispatch. Hirsch also specifically rules out new or improved technologies, for instance, oil shales,[84] or alternative transport fuels such as DME or methanol.

The unconventional response to peak oil scenarios is shown below. Figure 6.6 assumes the most pessimistic peak oil scenario in which, contradicting the observed project pipeline, 2007 is the peak year, à la Laherrère, Deffeyes, and Bakhtiari. Figure 6.7 follows Hirch's 2016 peak, with conventional supply growing only 1 percent annually up to peak. In both, conventional oil (including Arctic and deepwater) declines at 2 percent annually after the peak year, whereas theoretical demand (the dashed line) grows at 2 percent per year.

Unconventional supply then has to fill the gap. Heavy oil, oil sands,[85] and GtL follow known project plans to 2010 and grow thereafter at 9 percent per year, the lowest forecast for Albertan oil sands growth over the next five years. CtL reaches 0.75 million bbl/day in 2020,[86] of which just China's announced plans would comprise 80 percent, again suggesting some scope for higher output. Oil shales expand relatively quickly from a low base to reach 2 million bbl/day by 2023.[87] Biofuels and other liquids grow at about 14 percent annually (a conservative rate, since some predictions go up to 19.5%[88]) to reach 4 million bbl/day by 2020.[89, 90] NGL

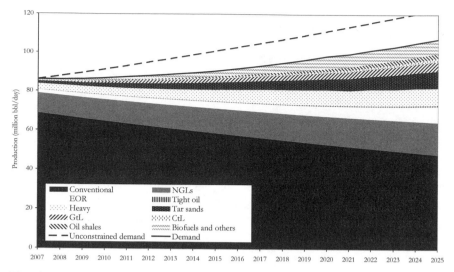

Figure 6.6
Unconventional contribution in peak oil scenario starting in 2007.

production increases 2.7 percent per year, in step with gas output, a very conservative assumption because the 2006–2007 growth rate was actually 6 percent.

In the most pessimistic case, with a 2007 peak, total oil production falls slightly into 2008 and then grows at less than the 2 percent unconstrained demand growth to 2017. From 2018, supply can keep up with 2 percent demand growth, although total output is 9 percent (9 million bbl/day) lower than it would have been in the absence of a peak. Such a situation is consistent with a decade of relatively high prices, tight energy markets, and incentives for efficiency, but not with serious hardship.

By 2025, total unconventional oil production could reach 61 million bbl/day, mostly NGLs and heavy and extra-heavy oil, with significant contributions from oil sands, EOR, and biofuels. Conventional oil, at 48 million bbl/day, is back to the level of 1970 and, with some 600 billion bbl then remaining even under highly conservative peak oil estimates, the comfortable R/P ratio of thirty-five years suggests that it should be possible to stem the decline.

Note that this graph is *not* a forecast: 61 million bbl/day of unconventional oil by 2025 (44 million bbl/day excluding NGLs) is an aggressive target under current conditions, but this discussion is intended to demonstrate that it is feasible in a "postpeak" world. There are even reasons, as outlined above, to believe that some unconventional sources could grow faster under the right conditions, given technological breakthroughs that history suggests will occur but which we cannot yet foresee and given

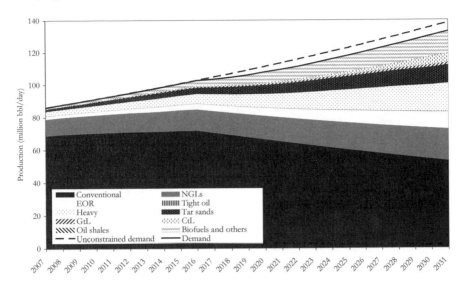

Figure 6.7
Unconventional contribution in peak oil scenario starting in 2016.

geological surprises, for instance, a rapid development of tight oil in Russia or the Middle East. The split between different alternatives is also illustrative: the reality will depend on a complex mix of economics, demand destruction, conservation and efficiency incentives and subsidies, environmental concerns, geographic and political factors, and differential technological advances.

The cumulative production of heavy and extra-heavy oil, tar sands, oil shales, and CtL in these scenarios is trivial compared with the resource base: for instance, the extraction of 50 billion bbl of heavy oil worldwide between 2007 and 2025 would be about 20 percent of just Venezuela's total current estimate for recoverable extra-heavy oil from the Orinoco Belt. A total of 1.8 billion bbl of tight oil, in any case a small contributor, is equal to just 1 percent of the low estimate for oil in place in a single tight play, the Bakken Shale. The GtL production equates to about 160 Tcf of feedstock gas, again a relatively small amount of the world's stranded gas, while the NGLs represent the liquid content of some 2,300 Tcf of gas (some of which can then be fed into GtL plants), or twenty-three years' production at current rates. This gas use is significant but amounts to only 36 percent of today's global proven gas reserves (Chapter 7 covers the size of the gas resource base). These comparisons reiterate that unconventional oil is about patience: there is no problem of volumes.

Combining this scenario with the capital costs of capacity as outlined in Figure 6.7 suggests that reaching these production levels would require

	Coal-to-Liquids		Heavy/extra-heavy oil		Deepwater
	Gas-to-Liquids		Oil (tar) sands		Arctic/polar
	Natural Gas Liquids (NGLs)		Enhanced Oil Recovery (EOR)		Biofuels (ethanol, biodiesel, etc.)
	Tight oil		Oil shale		

Figure 6.8
Key geographic locations for unconventional, enhanced oil recovery, Arctic, and deepwater oil.

some $86 billion annual expenditure on unconventional oil (in 2004 real terms and assuming no cost reductions through technology, economies of scale, etc.). This sounds like a formidable sum, but observed cash flows from major IOCs ($37 billion free cash flow after capital expenditures in 2005[91]), the NOCs, and smaller independents are comfortably enough to finance such capacity creation. There is no reason to fear that capital would not be sufficient to bring this unconventional supply on-stream, as some peak oil theorists suggest, mostly those who are naive about the capital markets.

In Hirsch's slightly less alarmist scenario, with peak oil in 2016, the task of replacing declining conventional oil becomes easier, because the unconventional productive base and related capital stock will be much higher by then and the technologies will be more mature. This situation is shown in Figure 6.7. In this case, even in the year after the conventional peak, total output rises by 1 percent. By 2024, 2 percent annual demand growth can be satisfied again, and production is only about 4 percent lower than it would have been without the conventional oil peak.

Unconventional oil's volumetric potential is, in the long term, practically infinite, especially if we include biofuels. Two realistic scenarios present themselves for the transition from today's conventional to unconventional oil: a seamless process with a gentle substitution of one for the other, or a decade or so of changeover with heavy investment, high prices, and restraint of demand (similar to Peter Tertzakian's "break point" scenario[92]). Given the variety of unconventional options, their relative technological maturity, tolerable costs, and geographic dispersal (Figure 6.8), the Geologists' scenario of a negligible contribution seems implausible.

Chapter 7

Gas Giants

True civilization does not lie in gas.

Charles Baudelaire[1]

The geology of natural gas, and the industry that produces it, is similar to that of oil,[2] and we can therefore learn some lessons about the depletion (or not) of one by studying the other. Gas is a substitute for oil in many applications, potentially in all, and can therefore extend the hydrocarbon age indefinitely even if oil begins to run out. Being much cleaner than oil, in terms of all pollutants including CO_2, gas can play a major role in safeguarding the global environment. Yet Geologists and others are turning the flawed lens of peak oil to examine gas and argue that it is no saviour from oil depletion.

THE PEAK GAS THEORY

2006 was the first year in which world gas reserves exceeded oil in energy content.[3] It would appear, therefore, that gas resources present a partial solution to the purported problem of declining oil resources. Some peak oil writers, realizing that this would discredit their predictions of catastrophe, have applied the same faulty methodologies to take aim at the gas giants of the world, to prophesy that they are approaching a twilight much like that of oil, in other words, to predict that global gas production will peak imminently, shortly after oil. We must therefore consider three questions. What are the prospects for future gas production? And to what extent can gas replace oil? Can this substitution be done with acceptable environmental impact?

Let us sample the flavor of "peak gas" writing. Julian Darley, in *High Noon for Natural Gas*, opines, "The coming shortage of natural gas in the United States and Canada, compounded by global oil peak and decline, will try the energy and economic systems of both countries to their limits. It will plunge first the United States, then Canada, into a carbon chasm, a hydrocarbon hole, from which they will be hard put to emerge unscathed."[4] Richard Heinberg, leading advocate of the Neo-Luddite view, suggests, "it seems more likely that any attempt to shift to natural gas as an intermediate fuel would simply waste time and capital in the enlargement of an infrastructure that will soon be obsolete anyway."[5]

The peak gas theory closely resembles its peak oil sibling and suffers from most of the same weaknesses. The line of argument runs as follows. The United States and Canada are purportedly running short of gas, and this is the precursor to a global shortage. Worldwide gas discoveries peaked about ten years after the oil discovery peak, so peak gas production will also succeed peak oil by about a decade, meaning somewhere around 2020.[6, 7] Gas imports cannot offset regional peak gas events, partly because of safety reasons. There is therefore no point in developing gas aggressively, and gas cannot save us from the consequences of peak oil.

In fact, U.S. and Canadian production has been steady for a decade or more, even increasing at around 5 percent annually during 2007,[8] while prices have dropped sharply. Contrary to doomsayers, it has proved possible to increase output from the abundant unconventional resources. These high-cost sources have been supplemented with imported LNG, substitute fuels such as coal, and "demand destruction" via improved efficiency and the closure or relocation of energy-intensive industries. Nor can the experience in North America, a major gas user since the 1960s, be simplistically applied to the rather early-stage gas business outside the OECD.

The very idea of a 1970 oil "discovery peak" relies on the dubious back-dating method we have met before and is strongly constrained by political and economic rather than geological factors. The pattern of gas use has been so different from that of oil that, even if we accept the peak and lag concepts, the gas peak should come many decades after oil. Peak gas estimates grossly understate global reserves and resources,[9] which are, in fact, very large, and, even if we believe the Hubbert concept, we are nowhere near midpoint depletion. Globalization of gas exports allows markets anywhere in the world to be supplied, and, despite scare stories, LNG's safety record is excellent.

Gas can substitute for oil in nearly all applications (including, with some expense and inconvenience, transport). Given its relatively clean-burning nature and the probability that production can grow strongly for several decades to come, gas would be a major part of the response to a hypothetical decline in oil supplies.

GLOBAL GAS RESOURCES

Because this book is primarily about oil rather than gas, I will not seek exhaustively to enumerate the world's gas resources. Still, it is essential to get a feeling for their magnitude and therefore show that we have more than sufficient to alleviate any tightness in oil supplies. Key observations are as follows:

- Gas is becoming easier to market globally
- Stated gas reserves appear reasonable
- Gas reserves will rise substantially when discovered but hitherto undeveloped fields are commercialized
- There is very substantial remaining exploration potential
- Unconventional gas resources are enormous.

Gas is much harder to transport than oil, and so markets have historically been balkanized.[10] Most gas, some 95 percent,[11] reaches markets through pipelines, for instance, from West Siberia, Norway, and Algeria to the European Union, and from Canada to the United States.

Over longer distances, the preferred delivery system involves chilling the gas to a liquid, transporting it as LNG in special tankers. This is the method of choice for exports to East Asia and is rapidly growing as a supply source for the rest of the world. The siting of LNG import terminals has suffered from many safety concerns, especially in the United States,[12] but these issues are grossly overstated[13]; there have only been three notable LNG accidents over more than half a century, none of them related directly to an import terminal.

With the advance of LNG, and increasingly interconnected pipeline networks, global gas markets are becoming more integrated. This is leading to rising prices, more attractive market options, diversification of supplies, and hence a new wave of exploration and development.

Despite speculation in early 2007, triggered by various visits and comments by the leaders of Algeria, Russia, Qatar, and Iran, there is no gas OPEC (OGEC?), nor is one feasible in the near term or, likely ever.[14] We have, therefore, no repeat of the argument over suspicious increases in proven reserves that we saw for oil. Particularly for major pipeline and LNG projects, reserves have to be certified to satisfy the buyer and international financial institutions; the level of confidence in the data is therefore higher than for oil.[15] There are no suspicious jumps in reserves; some discontinuities can be easily explained by the commercialization of fields in Qatar, Iran, and the FSU. The R/P ratio has actually increased from fifty-eight years in 1980 to sixty-three years in 2006, a strong performance that gives confidence that future gas production can grow strongly and belies the apparent 1970 discovery peak.

Before we are anywhere near worrying about a shortage of gas, we have first to address the enormous backlog of global "stranded gas." Large gas resources have been found around the world, often while searching for oil, that have been too remote for development. Now, the globalization of LNG and pipeline networks and advances in GtL and similar technologies are making such fields economic. Global stranded gas resources are put at some 900–3,500 Tcf,[16] mostly in Russia, Iran, Iraq, Nigeria, Saudi Arabia, and Alaska's North Slope. Of these, some giant fields were found as far back as the 1960s and 1970s. Such a long delay in development hardly suggests an imminent crisis of gas resources.

Figure 7.1 shows the backdated pattern of gas discovery with time.[17] There appears to be a prominent peak in 1970 followed by a subsequent falling-off, giving the frightening impression that we have found little gas subsequently and that therefore decline might be imminent. In fact, this peak reflects Shell's discovery of Qatar's North Field, together with the backdated 1991 find of South Pars, the extension of the North Field into Iran's waters. The Iranians could not have claimed any reserves until 1991, since Qatari maps showed, either because of limitations of geological knowledge or deviousness, that the structure terminated at the border. The field could, technically speaking, have been found at any time between 1948 and, say, 1985, without making any difference to global gas production, as it only started output in 1991. Furthermore, backdating estimates of gas discovery make simple geological errors, such as dating Saudi deep gas finds as contemporary with much earlier shallow oil discoveries in overlying structures. The historical gas discovery peak in 1970 is therefore entirely accidental. Plots of gas finds against number of exploration wells[18] also show no convincing signs of falling discovery. Note in any case that gas discoveries have exceeded production consistently throughout time, with the exception of a few years in the 1990s when energy prices in general were very low.

In any case, the search for gas has barely begun. The great peaks of gas discovery in the 1960s and 1970s were almost entirely achieved when

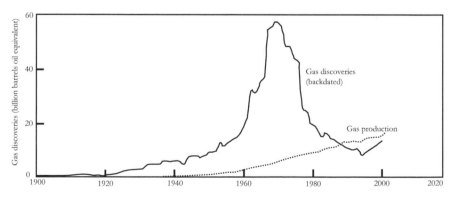

Figure 7.1
Gas discoveries with time (billion barrels of oil equivalent).

searching for oil, particularly in the Middle East. Until recently, basins with "gas risk" in the remoter parts of the world have been shunned. Statistically speaking, we are, I suppose, unlikely to find a field larger than North Field, but we can expect to make numerous discoveries with tens up to several hundreds of Tcf, i.e., of a similar energy content to Kashagan, the largest oil find of the past three decades. North America, Europe, and limited patches of Asia have been quite thoroughly picked over, but, in great swathes of Africa, Eurasia, and the Arctic in particular, there has been no systematic search for gas. Parts of the Middle East, especially Iran and Iraq, retain plenty of potential, as do East Siberia, Central Asia, interior and East Africa, Venezuela, and many countries' deepwater realms. Many of these areas have, for similar political, economic, and environmental reasons to oil, been greatly underexplored.

Most peak oil and peak gas writers (Heinberg, Campbell, Simmons, and Deffeyes[19]), perhaps revealingly, do not specify the world's total endowment of gas. In his book[20] (although not website), Campbell seems to contemplate about 5,800 Tcf remaining, and Laherrère has 6,750 Tcf remaining plus 2,500 Tcf of unconventional gas. Such figures, compared with the 6,405 Tcf (at end-2006) of BP, imply no future exploration or commercialization success and some degree of overstatement of current reserves or gas left in the ground at the end of the "Hydrocarbon Age." Contrastingly, Darley's figure of 12,500 Tcf, if taken at face value,[21] implies a gas peak around 2050 if we trust Hubbert's method, hardly the imminent emergency to which his book is devoted.

The same USGS study that gave estimates for global oil YtF also covered gas. It identified 1,400–5,900 Tcf of reserves growth and 2,700–8,900 Tcf of YtF gas.[22] In addition, various studies suggest 9,000–26,000 Tcf[23] of unconventional gas (excluding hydrates and aquifer gas, not currently commercial[24]). The USGS study did not cover some very successful gas regions of the past decade, such as India's east coast, the offshore Nile Delta, and much of the Arctic. Resources in these regions could be very substantial: the U.K. consultants Wood MacKenzie postulated some 700 Tcf of gas resources in the Arctic, a large part in provinces not covered by the USGS.

These numbers therefore suggest that the USGS midcase for gas is probably pessimistic. The low case certainly seems to have been virtually disproved already, because 70 percent of its postulated reserve additions have already been made, in just a third of the forecast period. A figure for remaining reserves plus reserves growth and YtF for conventional gas of about 12,400 Tcf therefore seems reasonable. Forecasts for ultimate recovery of gas have persistently trended upward since the 1960s, after being relatively stable during the 1970s. There is no sign of the "consensus" on EUR that is alleged for oil (as discussed in Chapter 4), and recent figures cover a wide range from 10,500 to 21,000 Tcf[25] (1.75–3.5 trillion boe).

Because our EUR for conventional oil is upward of 3 trillion barrels, this implies that gas resources are somewhat less, but of the same order of magnitude, as oil. However, including unconventional sources (discussed below) probably tilts the balance the other way. In Chapter 6, we saw that the total world conventional and unconventional endowment of oil is at least 4.7 trillion barrels (excluding oil shales, biofuels, and XtL). The sum of conventional and unconventional gas, excluding aquifer gas and hydrates, is at least 3.3 trillion boe (some 20,000 Tcf) but could easily be up to 7.1 trillion.

It therefore appears that, although world conventional gas resources are (like oil) rather unevenly distributed, the global total is very substantial, enough to keep production growing at a steady annual 2-3 percent until midcentury,[26] even without unconventional gas. Adding unconventional gas (excluding aquifer gas and hydrates) takes the peak out to around 2070. If we reject the symmetry of the "Hubbard's Peak" concept and allow for a longer buildup and faster decline thereafter, the peak could be further delayed. This demonstrates strong potential for gas to replace oil in suitable applications, particularly if oil supplies were to begin to decline.

UNCONVENTIONAL GAS

Just as there is unconventional and conventional oil, the same is true for gas:

- The unconventional resource base is much greater than the conventional but recovery factors are lower.
- Unconventional resources form a continuum from those that are extensions of conventional methods (such as ultradeep, tight, and contaminated gas), through those which are commercial today but require new production methods (such as coal-bed methane), to those that are still not proved to be commercially or even technically viable (aquifer gas and hydrates).
- Unconventional costs are generally higher than conventional, but, in some areas, such as the onshore United States, they may be the same or even lower.
- Geological (exploration) risk is generally much lower than for conventional sources, but technical and economic risks are higher.
- Unconventional production is already under way and much is commercial with today's prices and methods.
- Technology is key to unlocking unconventional plays and continues to advance rapidly.
- There has been little systematic search or cataloging of unconventional sources outside limited areas of North America and Europe.

It is remarkable how, as with unconventional oil, so much of the world's unconventional gas resource base appears to be concentrated in North America: ultradeep gas, tight gas, shale gas, coal-bed methane, sour gas, hydrates, and geopressured aquifers. The coincidence of the remarkable blessings bestowed on this continent with its occupants' voracious appetite for energy surely indicates that more than geology is at work here: the inhabitants have been driven by necessity to exploit unconventional gas sources that, so far, are unnecessary in much of the rest of the world. It is therefore to be expected that unconventional resources will multiply once we begin a systematic search in areas such as Africa and Eurasia.

Current unconventional gas production is about 7 percent of the world total.[27] Virtually all of this comes from the United States, whose unconventional gas output grew at 4–8 percent annually during 2000–2004, showing that unconventional resources can be brought on-stream at relatively high rates.

Unconventional gas resources are so large that they can supply world demand indefinitely. However, as currently in North America, higher costs may make gas uncompetitive against its main competitors for electricity generation: coal, nuclear, and possibly wind. It may then rely on other advantages (superior environmental performance over coal, fewer safety and waste concerns against nuclear, and reliability over wind) to maintain its position.

Unconventional gas can be divided into five categories: extracting more (enhanced gas recovery [EGR]); more difficult locations (ultradeep gas and, I suppose, Arctic and deepwater, although I consider these as conventional); more difficult reservoirs (tight, shale, and coal-seam gas); poorer quality (contaminated gas); and nontraditional sources (geopressured aquifers, hydrates, coal gasification, and biogas).

EGR is a rather new technique, using CO_2 or another gas to flush out remaining hydrocarbon gas, with the additional advantage of sequestering CO_2. The global EGR technical potential could be as much as 1,900 Tcf, that is, more than the entire proven gas reserves of Russia (the world's largest reserve holder).

Ultradeep gas, which is produced from 5,000 meters or more below ground, is expensive and risky but very amenable to technological improvements. Figures for resources of ultradeep gas are very sizeable, perhaps nearly 1,000 Tcf.[28, 29]

Substantial quantities of the world's natural gas is contaminated: instead of consisting only of methane and some heavier hydrocarbons, it also contains quantities of incombustible nitrogen, incombustible, greenhouse-inducing CO_2, and toxic, corrosive H_2S. Contaminated gas is common in Canada, Indonesia, the Caspian, and the Middle East, among other locations, and volumes total at least 330 Tcf,[30] not including multiple tens of Tcf (at least) with high nitrogen content. Contamination has also deterred exploration in promising areas such as Lurestan (Iran) and the Natuna Sea (Indonesia).

Tight gas is gas is found in formations of low permeability, so that gas flows only slowly into wells. In shale gas reservoirs, the gas is adsorbed on the surface of shale (mud) particles rather than stored in pore spaces.

Advanced drilling techniques, such as horizontal wells, and hydraulic fracturing (cracking the rock to allow the gas to flow) have made these reservoirs attractive. The main current locus of tight gas production is in the Rockies of the western United States and Canada; shale gas comes from Texas and, increasingly, from new areas such as the Appalachians, Arkansas, and British Columbia. Global volumes are at least 1,000–2,800 Tcf.[31, 32]

Frequent explosions in coal mines throughout history, such as in China where annual deaths run at more than 5,000, vividly demonstrate the presence of methane in coal. This gas, coal-bed methane, can now be profitably extracted from minable and unminable seams and provides a potentially huge resource. U.S. production, led by the San Juan Basin in New Mexico and the Powder River Basin of Wyoming, has grown rapidly since tax credits were introduced in 1984 to spur the initial developments. Being unrelated to conventional oil and gas source rocks, coal-bed methane is quite differently distributed from conventional petroleum. The Middle East has minimal coal, whereas the United States, Australia, and, significantly, India[33] and China[34] have vast potential, with total global resources of 3,500–9,500 Tcf. CO_2 injection can sequester this greenhouse pollutant and increase gas recovery, a technique that may also apply to gas shales.

A different technique from coal-bed methane extraction is underground coal gasification, pumping oxygen or air into coal seams to convert them to methane and hydrogen. This approach might well enable us to make some use of the vast submarine coal resources, for instance, under the southern North Sea. It could target coal seams that are too thin or deep to mine economically, avoids the surface damage caused by mining, and makes it much easier to sequester the resulting CO_2.

Aquifer gas is found dissolved in saline waters underground. Extracting this gas requires processing large volumes of salty water and has not yet been shown to be economical. An alternate approach might be to drain the water into a shallower, lower-pressure formation, from where the gas would separate into a "gas cap" and could therefore be produced dry. Another method, which I have not seen proposed elsewhere, would be to inject the more soluble CO_2 into these aquifers until they reached saturation, releasing the methane from solution. The aquifer gas resource base in the United States alone has been estimated at 5,000–49,000 Tcf.[35] Estimates for world resources are highly uncertain given the lack of investigation, but a figure of approximately 28,000 Tcf has been adduced.[36] Because of the uncertain technology and high costs, I have not included aquifer gas in my unconventional gas totals above, but it may be a resource for several decades hence.

Under high pressures and at low temperatures, methane and water can form the strange, ice-like "gas hydrates." Hydrates occur naturally on and beneath the ocean floor, including near energy-poor nations, such as Japan, and in permafrost regions on land. They constitute a massive resource of methane, possibly exceeding the carbon content of oil, gas, coal, peat, soils, and biosphere combined. To produce gas from hydrates, it would probably be necessary to inject hot water or some other heat source, reduce the pressure, add an antifreeze agent such as methanol, or inject our problematic panacea, CO_2.[37] Some semisuccessful experiments have occurred in Alaska.[38]

Authoritative estimates put hydrate resources at between 113,000 and 850,000 Tcf.[39] Recovering just 10 percent of the low case would amount to about the same as all the world's conventional gas ultimate recovery. If we can make hydrates commercial and address the climate change issue, the "gas age" can endure for centuries, until our descendants start writing alarmist books about "peak hydrate." Given that there is no certainty of making this resource economic, I do not include it in my unconventional gas totals. However, given that hydrates are so widespread and found at shallow depths, a technical breakthrough could rapidly advance them over the other sources of unconventional gas.

Renewable natural gas is an unusual entry in unconventional gas, being renewable and not geologically derived. However, renewable gas could form an adjunct to fossil fuels. It is derived from landfill gas and "biogas" derived by deliberately digesting waste using bacteria.[40] Worldwide emissions of landfill methane, a potent greenhouse gas, amount to more than the production of fossil-fuel gas from a major producer like Qatar and equal about 2 percent of global output. Examples such as this point up the fallacy, propounded for instance by Heinberg, that fossil fuel infrastructure will rapidly become obsolete; it can actually continue to have great value in facilitating the transition to a renewable energy system.

THE ROLE OF GAS

It seems clear, then, that conventional natural gas reserves have several decades of life remaining and that unconventional gas sources, broadly commercial today, can extend this well past the middle of the twenty-first century. What is the bearing of this on the main subject of this book, the continuing major role of oil in the world economy?

The scope to substitute away from oil will be covered more generally in Chapter 9. Here, it is worth observing that gas, found in similar places and consisting of the same "stuff" as oil, is the easiest substitute, easier than coal, nuclear, or renewables. Gas has proved this by growing its share of world energy consumption by a quarter since 1973; during the same time, oil's share has *fallen* by a quarter.

First, gas is a very useful fuel for extracting more oil: in oil-field power generation (either directly or via electrification) to replace diesel; as injectant (for miscible or immiscible floods or simple pressure maintenance) for improved and enhanced oil recovery; and to provide steam energy and hydrogen for heavy oil production and upgrading.

Second, gas forms a greatly preferable alternative to oil in power generation and heating: cleaner, more efficient, and generally cheaper. Similarly, it beats electricity in applications such as district heating and cooling. Gas is an ideal feedstock for many petrochemicals and for fertilizers. Pipeline grids are now found throughout the developed world and many of the developing countries, giving gas a great incumbent advantage over, for instance, hydrogen from renewables.

Third, gas can even cover the energy system's Achilles heel, transport fuels. It can be used directly (as compressed natural gas [CNG]) in modified car engines, gaining popularity in countries such as India, Pakistan, and Egypt, or converted to electricity to run trains and electric and plug-in hybrid cars. Methane fuel cells are also feasible and probably initially more straightforward than those using hydrogen and are cleaner and more efficient than combustion engines. Furthermore, natural gas can be converted via several alternative routes to liquid fuels (F-T diesel and gasoline; methanol and DME) and used to generate hydrogen, either to upgrade the output from heavy oils and CtL plants or to be used directly in vehicles.

Fourth, gas's climate-changing emissions of CO_2 are much lower than those of oil or coal. It is therefore a much more environmentally robust solution to a possible peak oil event than massive coal development (without carbon sequestration).

We see, therefore, that the world's enormous gas resources can prolong the life of oil supplies significantly and, at the same time, continue their gradual displacement of oil. Gas's market share (24 percent in 2006) is approaching that of coal (28 percent), and oil (36 percent) is not too far distant. We are not running out of oil, but just as oil dethroned coal before Jevons' "peak coal" struck, so gas, the "prince of hydrocarbons," is the new pretender.

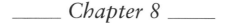

Chapter 8

A Dangerous Neighborhood?
Supply, Investment, and
Geopolitics

It is clear our nation is reliant upon big foreign oil. More and more of our imports come from overseas.

George W. Bush[1]

In the previous chapters, we have discussed oil (and gas) supply mainly in terms of technical potential. Yet, throughout the twentieth century, notably in 1973–1974, 1979–1980, and 1990–1991, and repeatedly during the last decade, the world has been constantly reminded of the leading role of geopolitics in oil. A common contention of Geologists is that a premature peak oil may strike because of a failure or inability of big resource holders to increase production. Militarists believe that oil supplies are threatened by hostile entities of various kinds and need to be secured by force. Mercantilists advocate commercial securing of oil supplies and autarkist policies of energy independence.

BARRIERS TO INVESTMENT

During this century, oil prices have been stubbornly high, which should have caused a wave of investment into promising areas and a consequent sharp increase in supply. This has happened in some countries, such as Kazakhstan and Angola, but not in most of OPEC, while Russian growth slowed during 2005–2007 even as prices continued to rise. Abandoning their geological purity, many peak oil commentators contend that we are on the verge of diminishing oil supplies because, for a variety of reasons, countries with significant remaining potential will fail to increase output.

Of global oil reserves, about 7 percent of reserves have unrestricted access to IOCs, mostly in OECD countries such as the United States,

Canada, the United Kingdom, and Australia.[2] For 25–30 percent, access is partly restricted (primarily in Russia). The remainder, some 65 percent, is totally off-limits to foreign investment.[3] Chapters 4 and 5 have already demonstrated how major exploration provinces, Saudi Arabia, Iran, Iraq, Abu Dhabi, Kuwait, Venezuela, Mexico, and China, are controlled almost entirely by their local national companies, while Libya, Algeria, Russia, Brazil, and others have strong NOC holdings.

Lack of investment and growth in production capacity in these countries represents a complex mix of phenomena. Part of the issue is a rational reluctance by the leading resource holders to create overcapacity and bring prices tumbling down.[4] They frequently point to lack of refining capacity,[5] which is a genuine problem although only a secondary contributor to current high oil prices. Most of OPEC's spare capacity lies in heavy, sour crudes, for which the world's refining setup is currently ill equipped; to produce more of this oil would only boost refiners' margins while depressing the price of heavier oil versus light, sweet crudes such as Brent and West Texas Intermediate.[6] Nor is OPEC likely again to invest in creating and maintaining a large, vastly expensive spare capacity, as it accidentally did during the 1980s, unless a way is found to share the costs with the consumer, to whom the benefits largely accrue.

Other, less rational, factors, however, contribute to holding back production. A cooling of the global investment climate is attributable partly to simple rent-seeking, a desire for host governments to increase their take of high profits. Figure 8.1 shows that twenty-seven countries have increased upstream oil taxation[7] since 1999, against nine who reduced it.[8]

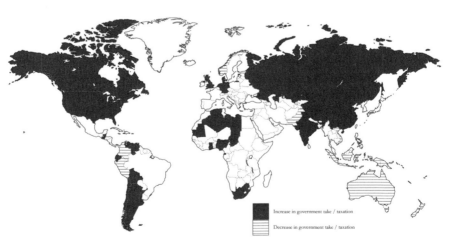

Figure 8.1
Changes in oil industry fiscal terms since 1999.

Yet oil is already probably the most highly taxed business in the world, with effective tax rates ranging from 50 percent in the United Kingdom (30 percent for other industries), to 78 percent in Norway (versus 28 percent for other industries) and approximately 97 percent in Iran. "Production sharing contracts," widely maligned by ill-informed observers such as former U.K. Environment Minister Michael Meacher,[9] usually impose extremely stringent terms on foreign investors: Algerian and Libyan contracts yield about $1 of value per barrel to the contractor when oil is trading at $50–60/bbl. Furthermore, heavy recent cost increases in rigs, steel, and so on mean that the increase in oil company profitability is far less dramatic than the headline oil price jumps would suggest. Excessively tough deals, such as Iran's "buybacks," result in a lack of incentives to good performance and severe misalignments of interest between host country and operator. In the end, being too greedy means that the host country does not sign any deals at all.

Net importers, whose own production is in decline, such as the United Kingdom and United States, are particularly unwise to impose heavy burdens on their domestic upstream. Calls for "windfall taxation," price controls or action against "price gouging" and the oxymoronic "obscene profits" entirely forget the disastrously counterproductive policies of the 1970s that led to physical shortages (U.S. gas lines and the U.K. "Three Day Week") and discouraged U.S. domestic output while encouraging unrestrained consumption. If companies are producing too little oil, taxing them more heavily is not a way of encouraging them to invest more, nor can companies confidently invest money in frontier exploration in countries such as Chad, Mauritania, and Belize, or in high-cost oil sands production in Alberta, if their gains, secured at high risk, are then removed by tax changes. These increases in taxation, therefore, have, from a global perspective, the perverse result of discouraging investment in oil at a time when high prices are signaling a need for more production, thus exacerbating the natural cyclicity of oil prices.[10, 11]

Resource Nationalism and the "Oil Curse"

Another barrier to investment is presented by "resource nationalism," which has received much attention recently. Its last great wave, in 1961–1980, led to state ownership of virtually all OPEC oil. From 1986 to 1999, in a period of low prices and economic stagnation in many oil exporters, there was a limited reopening. In particular, with the fall of communism, the FSU became available to foreign oil companies but with turbulent politics and capricious legal systems.[12] Highlights include the effective nationalization of assets in Russia (the Yukos and Sibneft oil companies, a share in Shell's Sakhalin-2 development, and BP-TNK's Kovykta gas field), Kazakhstan, Venezuela, Ecuador, Bolivia, and elsewhere. From about 2003 onward, resource nationalism, the desire by hydrocarbon-rich[13] countries to assert national and state control over these assets and to use them as a motor for economic and social development, has been resurgent.

These policies are usually popular, being presented as an antidote to colonialism and capitalist exploitation, yet they often stem from a quite different motivation: the desire by an elite to entrench their position and enrich themselves. This phenomenon is well known from many petrostates: Saudi Arabia, Iraq, Iran, Azerbaijan, and Kazakhstan.[14] Putin's desire to destroy Khodorkovsky of Yukos, a potential political rival, is one example; Chávez's use of PdVSA to fund social programs among his political base, the poor of Venezuela, is another. When oil prices are low, the ruling class may, reluctantly, accept some outside participation to keep the country's lifeblood flowing. When prices rise, they can afford to do without foreign help, even at the cost of some inefficiency. "Foreign exploiters" are useful scapegoats for the shortcomings of the leadership.

Resource nationalism usually requires the host nation to have a strong NOC. In most large producing countries outside the OECD (and even some within it, such as Norway), oil production is largely or solely in the hands of one or more NOCs. Some of these, such as Norway's StatoilHydro, Brazil's Petrobras, and Malaysia's Petronas, are highly capable, efficient organizations, equally as good as the IOCs such as ExxonMobil, Shell, and BP.[15] Indeed, in their overseas operations, they compete with, and behave very similarly to, the IOCs. Other NOCs, such as the Abu Dhabi National Oil Company, Saudi Aramco, and Russia's Rosneft, may be fairly good operators within their home territories. However, laggard NOCs, such as Mexico's Pemex, Iran's NIOC, and Indonesia's Pertamina, are plagued by inefficiency, corruption, politicization, overstaffing, risk aversion, competing social goals, support of the government budget, and many other flaws. Their monopolistic domestic positions can degenerate into becoming a stifling block on progress; they have the ability to frustrate foreign involvement but not to participate constructively themselves.

Ultimately, in the context of a privatizing, globalizing world, monopolistic NOCs would appear to be something of an anachronism. Innovations such as inviting outsiders on to the board (as Saudi Aramco has done), selling shares to the public (e.g., Statoil, Petrobras, Rosneft, and Kazmunaigaz), or opening up domestic basins to competition (e.g., Brazil, Indonesia, and India) can radically transform the efficiency of NOCs. In the long term, once the current cycle plays itself out, with prices dropping, alternatives advancing, and oil becoming less of a strategic commodity, the major NOCs of today will face a choice between transmuting into astute, commercially run competitors to the IOCs, being partially or wholly privatized (like, in the past, BP), fading away into growing irrelevance, or, in a few cases, perhaps remaining as dead weights on their country's oil industry, forever preventing it from realizing its potential.

The firebrand oratory of resource nationalism is often associated with hostility to globalization, yet it is a destructive tendency, leading to hostility and xenophobia toward the outside world, cycles of privatization and renationalization, a lack of confidence in property rights and hence to a lack of investment, domestic and foreign, and a weakening of democratic institutions. In the end, possession of a dirty, black liquid is a slippery foundation for nationalism; a constructive nationalism should depend on a wealth of human capital.

Such destructive policies lead us to the topic of the "oil curse." This is the observation, now a commonplace in media discussions, that the possession of oil has a negative impact on most countries. Some such problems include the following: dedemocratization, as mentioned above, or the preservation of autocracies; an inability to diversify the economy; bureaucracy, a heavy state hand and overcentralization; high inflation, an overvalued currency and unemployment; corruption and waste; and military buildups and wars.[16]

In a few countries, particularly Iraq and Nigeria, it is possible to argue that the oil curse has progressed to the extent of severely hampering the oil industry itself. However, although oil has both positive and negative consequences for a country's economy, it is overall a benefit.[17] Saudi Arabia without oil is not Japan, it is Yemen; Morocco is not notably better off than Algeria; Norway is a paragon of wealth, social justice, and environmental protection. Even in the arguably oil-cursed Iran and Iraq, oil money facilitated the emergence of a substantial, well-educated professional class. The worst effects of the oil curse were manifested because of the suddenness of the 1973–1986 oil boom, its irruption into unprepared societies (among both producers and consumers), its equally abrupt termination, and its resonating aftershocks. During the current period of high prices, the income is being spent much more wisely, on the repayment of debt, national development (e.g., Dubai's real estate boom), overseas assets for future generations, and economic diversification.

Ultimately, any reluctance of OPEC to invest and resource nationalist actions will not lead to peak oil. First, as Gately among others has observed, a peak in non-OPEC supplies would make it optimal for OPEC to grow production strongly.[18] OPEC's share of world oil output, at 43 percent, is also too low for a really effective cartel, even if all its members were perfectly aligned, and OPEC is not itself homogeneous. It even includes one net oil importer (Indonesia), and groups together radical anti-Western regimes (Venezuela and Iran), the (rather imperfect) pro-Western democracies of Indonesia and Nigeria, and conservative monarchies and autocracies such as Saudi Arabia and Kuwait. Some of its members, such as Algeria and Nigeria, have relatively limited oil resources, particularly relative to their populations, and seek to grow short-term output (often by cheating on quotas), much more than those like Kuwait, the UAE, and Qatar, with large capital surpluses and limited absorptive capacity.

Even if conventional non-OPEC oil goes into decline, oil prices in the level of recent years ($80–120) are not sustainable in the long term, because they create strong incentives to the development of new frontiers and unconventional production (Chapters 5 and 6), and efficiency and alternative energy sources (Chapter 9). This premature shift to unconventional fuels and alternatives would levy a heavy investment burden and be economically inefficient on a worldwide scale, but eventually the oil exporters would suffer more than the importers, as happened after the past two oil crises. OPEC nations are also well aware that they would ultimately pay the price for a global recession, reducing demand for their main export. This spectre increasingly confronted OPEC during 2008 as the consequences of the credit crisis unfolded.

Most worryingly for oil exporters, if there is a breakthrough such as highly competitive hybrid or electric cars, algal biofuels, solar power, oil shales, acceptable nuclear energy, truly clean CtL with carbon sequestration, or some other area, OPEC might condemn themselves to early extinction. Climate change creates added incentives to move away from oil, just as clean gas displaced somewhat cheaper but dirty coal, and therefore oil will increasingly need an additional competitive edge. Given the enormous sums of money pouring into the alternative energy complex so far this millennium, $100 billion in renewables alone in 2006,[19] oil exporters are playing a very dangerous game by resisting signals to increase output.

Given these competing factors, it seems likely that some OPEC countries, such as Algeria, Angola, and Nigeria, will forge ahead with ambitious expansion plans. Others, such as Venezuela, Kuwait, Iran, and Iraq, will not make major increases in production until they can resolve internal political difficulties. Iraq, if its security problems are ameliorated, will have the most incentive to expand its industry, even at the cost of lower prices, because its starting point is so low relative to its potential. Kurdistan, in particular, given its large undeveloped potential and relative independence of the central government, may be the catalyst to force Iraq into a rapid expansion of output, in turn putting pressure on the other OPEC countries. Saudi Arabia and the UAE, therefore, will have to move forward in a measured way, as both have done by announcing phased expansion programs and developing plans to go to much higher levels when conditions warrant.

Those nations who withhold investment may find, as in the 1973–1985 period, that they have shot themselves in the foot again: their market share is taken away by more aggressive OPEC colleagues and by substitutes. The resulting fall in their income will then make them scramble, as in the late 1990s, to invite foreign investment and achieve production growth.

The same line of reasoning, indeed even more so, is applicable to gas, which makes Russian attempts to bully the European Union over natural gas exports very unwise. Gas, primarily used for power, is much more easily substitutable than oil, having strong competitors in nuclear, coal, and renewables and being available as LNG from a wide and growing variety of suppliers.[20] The Russians need to be careful not to emulate Algeria, which from 1977 until 1983 left the Transmed pipeline to Italy empty and halted LNG exports to the United States in disputes over prices. The results, the only significant example of OPEC-like behavior in gas markets, were as follows: to tarnish Algeria as an unreliable supplier, setting its gas industry back many years; to land the Algerians with an poorly thought-through deal (which would have resulted in negative gas prices when oil fell in 1986![21]); to leave the Algerian LNG business running well below capacity and suffering from undermaintenance until the late 1990s; and to postpone by some two decades the United States' emergence as a major LNG market, which would greatly have benefited Algeria.

ENERGY SECURITY

"Energy security" has been a predominant theme of discussion during the early years of the twenty-first century. A reasonably standard definition of energy security is "Securing adequate energy supplies at reasonable and stable prices in order to sustain economic performance and growth."[22] Fears about energy security have been advanced as reasons to move away from oil.[23] This, however, covers only the security of the importer. Energy exporters have concerns about their energy security, which are, perhaps, in the long term, even greater. From their point of view, "securing adequate energy supplies" should read "securing adequate energy markets."

From the importers' vantage point, there are three areas of concern to energy security. The shortest-term aspect, thrown into relief by our nervous age, concerns the prospect of terrorists or "rogue" regimes taking action against oil installations. Such fears are enhanced by the current tight state of the oil market, in which the loss of a few hundred thousand barrels per day is a serious matter and even rumors of attacks send prices climbing. Yet such fears are greatly exaggerated.

The first threat has been highlighted by a few incidents, of which the most dramatic was the February 24, 2006 attempted suicide attack on the Abqaiq oil processing facility, the world's largest, in eastern Saudi Arabia. Two attackers and two security personnel were killed, but the explosion did not damage the plant, and Saudi production has not been reduced at all by terrorism. Even in the maelstrom of Iraq, oil production has continued only some 15 percent below prewar levels. It has proved remarkably hard for insurgent groups to disrupt production. In Kuwait, which was subject to a prolonged occupation during 1990–1991 and a deliberate "scorched earth" policy, postwar production surpassed prewar levels within two years.

The reason for this lies partly in the nature of oil facilities, as shown by the pattern of attacks in Iraq.[24] Individual wells are isolated and hard to protect, but to do serious damage, explosives have to be planted within the well, a time-consuming exercise and unlikely in the presence of moderate security. The loss of a single well, or even a few, makes little difference to overall output, and they can be capped and redrilled within a few months. Facilities are easier to damage and take longer to repair but are also much easier to guard.[25, 26] Tankers have occasionally been subject to terrorist bombs and piracy, but their defenses could be enhanced, and there are far too many (3,500 plying world sea routes) for a few attacks to have a serious impact on supplies. Pipelines are the most open to attack but can be fixed within a few days or at most weeks.[27]

It appears, then, that oil facilities are harder to damage and quicker to be repaired than is generally appreciated. The main danger of this kind of "oil terrorism" is that output in areas where law and order has completely broken down, such as Iraq and the Niger Delta, will be reduced and long-term investment will be very difficult. The same, to a lesser extent, is true of the loss of confidence, and hence of activity, in countries with high perceived risk levels, such as Yemen and Pakistan. This will have to be met by increased development elsewhere. The main energy impact of terrorism seems to be its psychological effect: the fostering of suspicion and mutual hostility between different societies, making it hard to conduct business and, *in extremis*, culminating in destructive military action. Terrorism, actual or feared, is thus a cost to the world economy but not an urgent threat to energy supplies—as long as it does not encourage counterproductive actions by its victims.

In the medium term, oil consumers are concerned about military threats to oil supplies and the potential of an embargo by a major supplier. This is partly linked to the idea of "chokepoints," which are alleged to control world oil transit. About 43 million bbl of crude oil (half of world supply) and a total of two-thirds of all oil (included refined products) are moved around by tanker. The key chokepoints are shown on Figure 8.2.[28]

A number of these chokepoints are not all they are fabled to be. Some carry relatively little oil (Panama), are bypassed by backup pipelines (Panama, Suez, and Bosphorus), have alternative routes (Suez, Bab Al Mandab, and Straits of Malacca), are physically hard to block (Bab Al Mandab and Hormuz), or are well defended by powerful countries with national interest at stake (Panama, Suez, Straits of Malacca, and Bosphorus).

The Straits of Hormuz is evidently by far the most important chokepoint and the one with fewest alternatives,[29, 30] although even here, there are some bypassing pipelines. The straits, 50 km wide and with rather deep water, are impossible to block physically, and Iran (the most likely

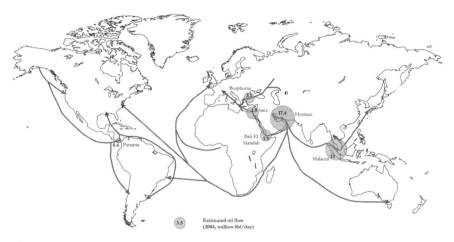

Figure 8.2
World oil chokepoints.

threat) could only close them by military means for a short time given American strength in the area, and the presence of staunchly pro-Western Oman and the UAE on the southern side. For Iran (or another Gulf country, or the United States or China) to try to close Hormuz would be to cut its own lifeline so could only be an act of desperation. The prospect, in the event of a Sino-American confrontation, of the United States blocking the Straits to China-bound tankers is much more threatening (from a Chinese perspective) than a challenge by Iran to the United States but appears, at the moment, far-fetched.

A different scenario involves the takeover of a major producer, most obviously Saudi Arabia, by extremists or perhaps an extended, Iraq-like, period of anarchy. This is conceivable, and as the Iranian Revolution and Iraq War have shown, the oil importers' short-term options might be rather limited. But Saudi Arabia is not Afghanistan. Oil makes up 45 percent of the GDP of the Persian Gulf countries and 80 percent of their exports.[31] It would be suicidal for even extreme rulers of such a country to cut off oil exports, because it is virtually their sole source of support and power. Even revolutionary Iran resumed oil exports as fast as possible, while Chávez's Venezuela has continued to ship oil to the United States without pause, giving only faint nods to increasing exports to China. If such a country attempted to enforce price hikes or selective boycotts, they would soon be frustrated by the disciplines of the market, since oil is a global commodity.

The development of strategic reserves sufficient to cover one hundred days of imports by all IEA members (and more recent accumulation by China) provides a valuable buffer in the case of an interruption or embargo. The actual period of cover would be longer because not all exports worldwide would be cut off simultaneously; at most, one or two countries might be implicated (as with Iraq and Kuwait in 1990–1991). This gives the consumers "staying power," ensuring that a boycott by a major exporter would have to be sustained for a long period, causing them severe economic hardship.

In the long term, and on the largest scale, following Churchill's dictum that "Safety and certainty in oil lie in variety and variety alone,"[32] the energy importers seek to obtain oil from a variety of customers and to use commercial, political, and military means to ensure the reliability of those supplies. Militarists have seen in many actions (the Iraq War,[33] above all, but also in Central Asia[34]) a military competition for oil between the United States, Russia, China, and perhaps other players. Some writers[35] foresee an era of "resource wars" over dwindling oil supplies. Without having any special insight into the motivations of policymakers from these countries, it is worth observing that military control of oil is vastly, disproportionately expensive, and probably impossible.

This impossibility is illustrated by Iraq. The world's most powerful country is unable to maintain order in a nation of some 27 million, of whom only the Arab Sunnis, perhaps 20 percent, were broadly hostile at the outset. Iraq's production of some 2.3 million bbl/day before the invasion was, four years later, hovering around 2 million. If the U.S. invasion of 2003 was a "war for oil," it has been singularly unsuccessful. The major Western oil companies, who according to the "oil war" theory were supposed to reap lucrative oil profits, had, after five years, still not signed a single deal. Halliburton's controversial profits have been made out of the U.S. treasury, not the Iraqis. Despite some recent comments about the Kurdish region's signing of oil contracts,[36] I do not imagine the United States launched the 2003 war so that Norwegian and Turkish companies could get oil blocks.

Immediately before the war, Larry Lindsey, Bush's economic adviser, said, "The successful prosecution of the war would be good for the economy."[37] This view has been rapidly proved fallacious. Quite apart from the appalling human toll, the indirect and direct costs of the war to the United States alone are likely to be in the order of $1–2 trillion,[38] i.e., about four to eight years of the U.S. total oil import bill, at the current (unusually high) prices. Lindsey opined that "the best way to keep oil prices in check is a short, successful war on Iraq," but the instability has helped to boost oil prices from around $25 beforehand to above $100. Even if the Iraqi oil industry enjoys a remarkable resurgence and a substantial part of the profits accrues to Western oil companies, it is easy to demonstrate that the war will never come close to paying for itself.

Similarly, Saddam's wars against Iran and Kuwait devastated his country. The war against Khomeini cost Iraq some $195 billion[39, 40, 41] in indirect and direct expenditure and was, of course, completely unsuccessful in capturing any oil for Iraq; indeed, the country's own output was badly affected. This money, invested in Iraq's own fields, could probably have made the country into the world's top oil producer.

This establishes a general principle: modern resource wars on any significant scale, if such a thing exists, can never pay for themselves.[42] Resources are just not that valuable. This should not surprise us, living in a modern economy in which microchips are worth more than gold and oil is cheaper than Coca-Cola. Despite Militarist claims, the incentives for resource wars are weakening, not increasing, which is not to say that badly informed politicians may not still launch them.

Iraq is, of course, most often adduced as an example of an oil war. Afghanistan is another one, but, save as a base to threaten Iran, it is difficult to see this line of thinking. Nor are other purported oil war theatres, such as Somalia, the Balkans, and Chechnya, of any real energy consequence. Such thinking reminds me of Freud viewing any conceivable object as either an orifice or a phallus—there are not many other possible shapes! Seeing oil behind every geopolitical action, mixing this up with some half-baked ideas about peak oil, as writers like George Monbiot,[43] Michael Ruppert,[44] and a monstrous regiment of bloggers do, together with an unhealthy dose of conspiracy theories about September 11, exaggerates the importance of this resource, fosters misguided cynicism, clouds our understanding of nations' real motivations, and prevents a rational debate on energy geopolitics.[45] By giving the producers excessive notions of their importance and making them suspicious of any outside involvement, however well intentioned, it makes it paradoxically harder to achieve energy security.

An alternative to military control has been advanced in recent years by Mercantilists. The economic philosophy of Mercantilism, popular during the sixteenth to eighteenth centuries, saw international trade as a zero-sum game, disliked imports, and advocated protectionism, state intervention, and the amassing of a large hoard of bullion. Mercantile policies lay behind much European war making and colonialism; their removal, and replacement by Free Trade, helped make Britain the foremost economic power in Europe for half a century.

Mercantilism in its latest reincarnation is the idea that countries can somehow enhance energy security by "owning" oil fields overseas (and other resources) to the exclusion of others, possibly by shipping "their" oil back to the fatherland. This idea has been much trumpeted by Chinese and Indian business leaders in particular, but Western politicians and media are far from immune: "The Chinese-African summit in Beijing [was] the culmination of a masterful campaign by China to lock up a large chunk of Africa's energy and mineral resources."[46]

The Indian state companies (mainly ONGC) and Chinese (PetroChina and its parent CNPC, Sinopec, and CNOOC), as well as other Asian countries,[47] have acquired a number of overseas assets, particularly in Kazakhstan, Sudan, South America, Russia, Syria, and West Africa. CNOOC was also involved in an $18.5 billion bid for the U.S. Unocal, which was scuppered by political pressure. The Indian companies have spent at least $2 billion in these acquisitions and the Chinese $17 billion.

The Mercantilist ideal, however, is utterly misconceived. The common phrase is that various countries are "securing" or "locking up" overseas oil. They have not actually secured anything. History and logic show emphatically that mere commercial ownership of oil fields does not guarantee supply. Much analysis of this phenomenon seems to be based on the belief that Chinese and Indian companies will be able and willing to take their "equity" oil, ship it back to the home country, and sell it at below-market prices.

In the modern era, no significant oil producer would tolerate this except under duress (which gets us back to Militarism). During the 1973 embargo, Western companies, who still dominated Middle Eastern oil, could not protect their home nations, as McFadzean of Shell and Drake of BP made abundantly clear to the then British Prime Minister Edward Heath.[48] The British government's 50 percent stake in BP did not help them in securing oil. International free trade agreements today, including World Trade Organization membership, and, more importantly, the fungible nature of oil, make it impossible to enforce a selective boycott or preferential supply. Even if China or India did somehow manage to "corner" world oil supplies, their export-dependent economies would be devastated by the subsequent depression in their main markets, the United States and European Union.

Nor has the performance of this oil search been particularly impressive in strictly commercial terms. Chinese companies, aided by a willingness to pay large sums and geographical advantage, have built up a significant position in Kazakhstan. Otherwise, they and the Indians have largely been confined to pariah states such as Myanmar, Uzbekistan, and Sudan. Neither has managed to crack Iran, despite the lesser competition and their apparent geopolitical advantage over Western companies; the slow grind of the Iranian oil negotiating process has consumed them, too, apart from a couple of fairly minor exploration deals. Sinopec has joined Western companies in exploring for gas in Saudi Arabia under very stringent terms. The new Asian tigers might do well to learn from the Japanese, who, in the 1960s, set a target for the amount of equity oil they wanted and funded the search generously with government money. The result was to waste billions of dollars in acquiring a rag-tag of fairly insignificant assets. The failure to secure equity oil did not stop Japan from becoming the world's second-largest economy, although it has no domestic oil or gas production to speak of and so is even more import dependent than its Asian rivals.

To be sure, overseas oil assets do have some undoubted merits, as a way to cement relationships and as a (very partial) hedge against a country's own oil import bill. Yet competition amongst companies from the same nation (ONGC, GAIL, and OIL of India, plus private sector players, CNOOC, CNPC, Sinopec, Sinochem, and China International Trust and Investment Corporation) suggests that these overseas acquisitions are more a matter of jockeying for domestic bragging rights, and of protecting companies from controlled, below-market retail prices in their own home bases, than coherent national strategies. In 2004, equity oil[49] constituted only 14 percent of China's total oil imports, a proportion that is planned to rise to 25 percent by 2020, while, of the Chinese companies' 1.3 million bbl/day of overseas equity oil, only a quarter actually came to China. This hardly merits the panic-stricken idea that there will be no oil left for anyone else. Chinese, Indian, and other investment in overseas projects will actually help to enhance, rather than reduce, global oil supplies. In this sense, the angst over the Chinese securing of oil is a reflection of the wider reality: that the West has to get used to sharing its dominance of the planet with someone else.[50]

Energy mercantilism, however, is at most, a new twist on an old idea. Those who see in this competition the heralding of an era of resource wars or a covert recognition by importing countries that peak oil is upon us do not know oil history. There has always been dynamic competition for new oil supplies around the world, from the late nineteenth century tussles of the Rothschilds and Royal Dutch Shell in Baku, the entry into Romania in the early twentieth century, the manoeuvring for Saudi oil in the 1930s and Iranian oil in 1954, and the Japanese arrival in the Middle East in the 1960s, to the early 1990s rush for the FSU. Fears that oil was "running out" may have driven some of these contests, but the unsurprising fact that businesses compete for new and profitable opportunities, and seek to enlist political support where it is available, has no connection with peak oil.

From the exporters' point of view, "energy security," or perhaps, to be more precise, "demand security," is at least as important, perhaps more so, than for the importers.[51] Energy represents about 15 percent of the U.S. total import bill and 2 percent of GDP but 90 percent of Saudi exports and 45 percent of GDP. The Saudis need the United States more than the United States needs them. *In extremis*, the United States can turn to coal and nuclear power; Saudi Arabia has neither of these nor any other realistic way of earning a living. If the United States manages to cut oil demand by just a few percent, it might not import any Saudi oil. During the period of the oil crises, say from 1973 to 1980, real U.S. GDP per head rose by 9 percent.[52] The production cutbacks and low prices that followed led to real Saudi per capita GDP falling by 42 percent,[53] taking them from parity to Switzerland to lying just ahead of Mexico. Who now is "energy insecure"? Swings in price can ravage oil-exporting economies, leaving them with heavy deficits and debt burdens at times of low prices or overvalued currencies and inflation when prices rise.

Energy Security as Interdependence

Understanding the different, but interrelated, motivations of energy importers and exporters makes it obvious that they are mutually dependent. True energy security can be achieved only by a shared understanding of this interdependence.

A common mistake is to confuse energy security with autarky: the Quixotic pursuit of self-sufficiency and energy independence. Churchill's decision in retooling the British navy, from coal to oil, was to trade energy security for increased technological and economic advantage; the result was the continued primacy of the British Navy through World War I. Conversely, Myanmar and North Korea are among the world's most self-sufficient countries. This has not brought them prosperity or security. Those of their energy-poor Asian neighbors who have chosen a path of well-considered mutual reliance on others, such as South Korea, Japan, and Singapore, have flourished. Similarly, Dubai, with modest indigenous energy resources but an openness to trade, has boomed over the past decade, while Iran has stagnated. During the last few years of high oil prices, oil exporting economies such as Saudi Arabia, Russia, and the UAE have grown rapidly, but so have major importers, including India, China, and the United States. Energy is such a fundamental part of a modern country's infrastructure and economy that attempts to build an energy system at odds with commercial reality is highly destructive of competitiveness, in a way that, say, subsidizing opera, or even agriculture, is not.

Energy independence in various guises was touted by Nixon in 1974, by Ford in 1975, by Carter in 1977, by Bush Senior in 1991, by Clinton in 1992, and by Bush Junior in 2003. During this time, U.S. oil imports doubled. Many of the policies introduced, such as price caps, were counterproductive; the others were insufficient in scope and pursued without perseverance. It proved, unsurprisingly, impossible to remove from the global energy system a free-market economy consuming nearly a quarter of the world's supplies. The same would be true of the European Union, China, Japan, or any other major consumer. Even if the United States managed to avoid importing any Middle East oil ("terrorist oil," in some contemptible campaigns[54]), it would still be paying world prices.

Yet this rhetoric has its dangers: the remote possibility that the United States might become serious about energy independence, investing heavily in alternative fuels, opening up its own restricted areas to exploration, and imposing high energy taxes and efficiency measures, discourages oil-exporting countries from heavy investment in new capacity. Writing off the whole Middle East as a nest of terrorists, as many U.S. politicians do, is utterly counterproductive because it prevents sensible energy cooperation. Is it surprising that U.S. investment in Middle Eastern oil is virtually absent, when an attempt to invest in the United States, by a staunch U.S. ally such as Dubai, is rewarded by paranoid, racist caricature from across the political spectrum?

Nor do energy rents all accrue to the producer. Three-quarters of the gasoline price at the pump in the United Kingdom is tax. With gasoline prices around £0.98 per liter in September 2007,[55] the U.K. government's tax take amounted to about $178/bbl compared with oil at $77. The U.K. government earns about $45 billion annually in fuel taxes,[56] virtually pure gain, whereas Libya, which produces about as much as the United Kingdom consumes, receives some $36 billion minus production costs. It appears that the United Kingdom, not Libya, is the petro-state. Fuel taxes are similarly high in the rest of Europe and in Japan, although lower in the United States.

Even the energy exporters are not energy independent. As the supermajor oil company Chevron observes, "There are 193 countries in the world. None of them are energy independent."[57, 58] The smaller ones, at least, rely on military power (mostly that of the United States) to protect them from potentially hostile neighbors and to keep export routes open. All require foreign expertise, technology, and capital to keep their industries running. This is not some neocolonialist hangover; it is a simple recognition of the complexity and size of the global energy business. It is particularly true for small, energy-rich countries such as Qatar—900,000 people holding the world's third largest gas reserves—Kuwait, the UAE, Brunei, Trinidad, and Equatorial Guinea. The miserable state of the oil infrastructure in countries that chose isolation (or had it forced on them)—Iraq, Iran, and Libya—illustrates this dependence, although some, especially Iran, had a large, highly skilled corps of local staff, including senior management levels, immediately before the departure of the IOCs.

Furthermore, no country has access to all forms of energy: Russia and, ironically, the United States, probably come closest. Iran, remarkably for the world's second largest gas reserves owner, is a net importer of natural gas, and of gasoline (40 percent of its needs[59]), Kuwait is desperately short of gas, the UAE imports gas, and Saudi Arabia imports refined products. The Middle East has virtually no coal, biofuels, nuclear power, or hydropower, whereas oil importers such China and India have abundant coal, hydroelectric, and biofuel potential. Even a major shift away from oil would not create energy independence; importers might become equally dependent, at least in the medium term, on Russian coal, Brazilian ethanol, or North African solar power.

The only way forward, therefore, for mutual energy security is a strengthening and deepening of interrelationships. Increasing reciprocal investment, in both oil and nonoil sectors, by oil exporters in the developed world and by oil importers in OPEC and other major producers gives both sides a stake in maintaining supply *and* demand. Oil exporters realize it would be folly to jeopardize the value or security of their vast holdings of Western financial assets by provoking a global crisis. Oil importers need to appreciate the exporters' need for clear and predictable energy and environmental plans. Sensible, proportional, multilateral "police actions," such as expelling Saddam Hussein from Kuwait, or patrolling sea lanes, enhance energy security. Ill-conceived, unilateral, grandiose military adventures, with no clear objective, carried out incompetently, destroy it.

The necessity of this interdependence means that, although geopolitical events and underinvestment will continue to contribute to volatile energy prices, they will not lead to a permanent downturn in oil supply. The interests of producers and consumers are not so divergent as Geologists imagine, nor, even in a postpeak world, would military or mercantile actions be a successful strategy.

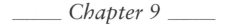

_____ Chapter 9 _____

Keeping the Lights On:
Energy Demand

Oil is often written about by peak oil theorists, Militarists, and so on as though it is some magical ichor that flows in the veins of the gods. Economists have a more sensible view: it is a commodity, useful but not irreplaceable. Many, if not most, peak oil books confuse an "oil crisis" with an "energy crisis" and assume that the end of oil will trigger the end of civilization, as physicist David Goodstein opines, "Civilization as we know it will come to an end sometime in this century unless we can find a way to live without fossil fuels."[1] The key questions for our future energy supply are as follows:

1. Is oil (and gas) supply in danger of imminent decline? As we have seen, the evidence strongly suggests that the answer to this is no.
2. Could declining oil (and gas) be replaced by other energy sources?
3. How much can efficiency cut energy demand?
4. How could we meet the special needs of our transport system for liquid fuels?
5. Can fossil fuels continue to play a large role in our energy system without disastrous environmental effects?

This chapter addresses the second, third, and fourth of these questions; Chapter 10 covers the fifth.

In general, Geologists, unlike their foes the Economists, badly underestimate the elasticity of oil demand: how much oil consumption will decline in response to an increase in price. Much oil use is nonessential and can be sacrificed with only moderate economic pain when prices rise sharply.

In the face of the Iran–Iraq crisis, U.S. oil consumption fell by an astonishing 19 percent between 1978 and 1983 (4 percent annually), yet U.S.

real GDP *rose* by 8 percent (1.5 percent annually) during this period,[2] despite the early-1980s recession. This demonstrates that drastically reduced oil use is compatible with modest economic growth and that savings can be achieved rapidly. The methods by which this was done, substitution and efficiency, are perhaps even more powerful today given technological advances than they were then. For instance, U.S. gasoline demand rose at 1.6 percent per year from 1990 to 2004 but only 0.3 percent in 2005 and 1 percent in 2006, despite robust economic growth. Motorists' average mileage and sales of SUVs, light trucks, and minivans went down. To give a modern, developing-world example, in 2006, Indonesia removed fuel price subsidies. Oil demand dropped 8.5 percent in a single year, yet real GDP growth was a very healthy 5.4 percent.

Drastically underestimating how much and how fast oil demand can be cut in response to increasing prices, without causing economic collapse, leads us into the apocalyptic visions of writers such as Goodstein, who envisage, "a dying civilization, the landscape littered with the rusting hulks of SUVs."[3] Yet oil, although convenient, is not a unique bounty: if we had today a hydrogen- or electricity-based transport system, we would find oil impossibly dirty, noisy, geopolitically insecure, and dangerous, just as we look back condescendingly on the Victorian era of coal-fired, dark, satanic mills belching out smoke. There is no reason for the end of oil to mean the end of civilization; even if, somehow, we cannot keep oil production increasing, we can continue to improve standards of living with a judicious use of the remaining oil combined with the development of substitutes.

A truism often voiced by Geologists is that exponential growth is impossible on a finite planet. Any exponential growth rate, even a low one, will rapidly outstrip the carrying capacity of the planet, yet they present no evidence for their assumption that energy use is growing exponentially. In fact, oil use grew at almost 8 percent annually from 1965 to 1973 but at only 1.2 percent per year from 1973 to 2006. Similarly, after the twentieth-century explosion, population growth is slowing down.[4]

Let us now consider how much oil use can be saved or substituted, when and if the end of oil witching hour arrives.

WORTHY SUBSTITUTES: OTHER ENERGY SOURCES

The most interesting peak oil has already happened. That is not the point at which oil production begins to decrease, as trumpeted by the Geologists. It was the date, in 1973, at which the share of oil in the world energy mix reached its highest ever level, 48 percent. It has declined remorselessly since then and currently stands at 36 percent. It may surprise both the devotees and enemies of oil that it has *never* supplied as much as half our energy. The world has already adjusted to the realization that oil is going to be less significant in the future than it is today. The cushion is thus much more comfortable than peak oil theorists maintain, and the energy mix is far more diversified today than in 1850, when wood still made up 90 percent of energy use, or 1920, when more than 80 percent was supplied by coal.

Up to the first oil crisis, oil strongly increased its market share but has fallen relentlessly from then on, being replaced in particular by nuclear, from 1984 onward by gas, and since 2003 by a modest resurgence of coal. Yet we have not yet realized the Dickensian vision of coal-powered cars nor the futuristic concept of nuclear aeroplanes. How was this substitution of other fuels for oil occurring?

The answer is that, particularly before 1973, oil was widely used in other sectors. In 1978, only 40 percent of oil globally was used in transportation, mostly gasoline and diesel in road vehicles but also including aviation kerosene, ships' bunker fuel, and diesel trains. Now 51 percent is used in transportation and, in the United States, 67 percent.

The biggest declines in oil use came in power and industrial use. Consumption of oil in power generation worldwide has declined from 14 percent in 1978 to 8 percent in 2003 and just 2 percent in the United States. Electricity can be generated by gas, coal, nuclear, and renewables, and hence oil-fired generation has come under most pressure from high oil prices. Global use for power actually shrank in absolute terms from 8.8 million bbl/day in 1978 to 6.3 million bbl/day in 2003. If oil use in the power sector were to drop to U.S. levels globally, 4.4 million bbl/day of demand could be saved, more than Iran's entire output. Similarly, industrial consumption, including oil-fired furnaces, use by the oil industry itself, and so on, also fell overall, and other use, a large part of which is for domestic heating and cooking, dropped in percentage terms although increasing somewhat in absolute terms.

Petrochemicals are clearly a major use of oil and have more than doubled their consumption since 1978, a growth rate twice that of transport fuels. Before the 1960s, the world's chemical business ran largely on coal; now gas is also a major input. In 2004, nonenergy use of oil (petrochemicals, lubricants, asphalt for roads, and so on) was about 11 million bbl/day, and the corresponding figure for gas was 2 million boe/day.[5] Room for additional use of gas and biomaterials in the petrochemical business is therefore very substantial, and high prices are already encouraging substitution of gas for naphtha (light oil) in the fertilizer industry. Other specific demands can be satisfied in other ways: for instance, some 50 percent of asphalt (tarmac) use can be replaced by a material made from crumbled old tires,[6] at lower cost and enhanced safety, while oil-based lubricants can be replaced by bio-lubricants, these two measures totalling some 1.3 million bbl/day.[7]

To replace oil use in the nontransport sector, an alternative source of energy is required. Obvious candidates are natural gas, coal, nuclear, and renewables, with future technologies such as fusion perhaps making their appearance later. However, Geologists, Environmentalists, and Neo-Luddites usually dismiss these sources of energy on various grounds. The arguments have been well rehearsed, and therefore I will not treat them in detail here, but a brief summary is worthwhile.

Resource Constraints on Alternative Fuels

A common argument is that gas, coal, and nuclear (uranium) are not renewable and will run out on a timescale not much longer than that of oil. Substituting them for oil will only cause them to deplete faster.

On the first of these points, we have already seen that the world's conventional gas base is sufficient to sustain growth until midcentury, even allowing for a large swathe of substitution for oil. If we include unconventional sources known to be commercial today, such as shale gas, then gas can take over oil's role and become the leading fuel out to the end of this century, much longer, if gas hydrates are developed.

World reserves of economically recoverable coal are almost 1 trillion tons, about 200 years of consumption at current rates,[8] plus some 2.8–7 trillion tons that would become economic at higher prices.[9, 10] Coal production to date amounts to about 0.2 trillion tons. Note that Hubbert himself used an estimate of 6.3 trillion tons of ultimate coal recovery,[11] and Laherrère's figure of an ultimate recovery of 0.675 trillion tons[12, 13] implies that current reserves are more than twice overstated—yet there is no "coal OPEC" he can blame for this!—and that no new reserves additions will be made. Laherrère makes the mistake of ascribing the slowing in coal production growth to geology, when the real culprit is demand, particularly replacement by gas driven initially by cost, and then by environmental concerns.

Coal is very widely distributed, particularly in major energy consumers such as the United States, Europe, China, and India, so geopolitical problems and barriers to investment are much less serious than for oil. Given that there has been little incentive to explore for coal for many years, it seems likely that huge additions could be made to these resources. For instance, Alaska's coal resources, not reflected in world reserve figures, may be as much as 0.5 trillion tons,[14] or nearly a century of current global production. Coal gasification could access the (no doubt enormous) unminable coal resources under the seabed, for instance the 3 trillion tons discovered beneath the North Sea by Statoil,[15] while improved technology, such as robotic mining, is also likely greatly to increase recoverable coal by allowing access to deeper, lower-quality (e.g., lignite) and thinner seams that are not currently counted as reserves.

Consumption is predicted to grow at about 1.4 percent per year in a business-as-usual case. If we add to this the requirement (in a peak oil scenario) for coal to replace oil entirely in industrial uses, petrochemicals, and power generation (for some reason making no use of our large reserves of clean gas), this would require about another 1.5 billion tons annually, about a quarter of 2006 production. Accepting the (discredited) Hubbert theory, peak coal (when half the global resource base has been produced) would arrive early in the twenty-second century if we allow for only the lower estimate of known, currently noncommercial resources. These figures also make it clear that there are ample coal resources to support a major CtL to replace oil, if required. Goodstein's contention that "we will have to mine coal ... more than ten times faster than we are doing today"[16] seems to rest on oddly questionable mathematics. The correct figure, assuming 60 percent conversion efficiency of coal to oil and requiring coal to replace *all* oil, is about three times, with several decades to get there, given that oil production is not going to cease entirely tomorrow.

Nuclear energy provides a vast, if troublesome, backstop to fossil and renewable energies. Many peak oil supporters and Neo-Luddites argue like Robert Millikan, the 1928 winner of the Nobel Prize for physics, who suggested, "There is no likelihood that man can ever tap the power of the atom. The glib supposition of utilizing atomic energy when our coal has run out is a completely unscientific utopian dream, a childish bug-a-boo."[17] Prophets of doom maintain that we are shortly going to run out of uranium or that the environmental disadvantages of nuclear power prevent its widespread use even in a crisis situation.

Yet Hubbert correctly perceived that global resources of materials for nuclear fission are several orders of magnitude larger than hydrocarbons.[18] Global uranium reserves, 4.7 million tons (about 650 billion boe), represent about 85 years of consumption,[19] which has misled many peak oil theorists and others to think that uranium is also approaching depletion[20] (we appear to be some 25 percent of the way through this highly conservative "ultimate endowment"). However, uranium resources (technically recoverable but either not yet economic or not fully delineated) are up to ten times as much, deposits in coal, black shales, and phosphates in the United States alone are a hundred times greater, and uranium in seawater, known to be technically extractable, amounts to a thousand times current reserves. Hubbert pointed out that a ton of common granite, the main rock from which the continents are made, contains, in the form of uranium and thorium,[21] about thirty times more energy than a ton of oil. Like coal, uranium is widely distributed around the world, including in reliable energy exporters such as Australia and Canada and major importers such as China, India, the European Union, and the United States.

It has been observed that "the amount of uranium exploration is ... equivalent to that which had been put into oil exploration as of the 1900s,"[22] and a mere $95 million was spent globally on uranium exploration in

2002[23] (a single deepwater oil exploration well may easily cost $100 million), so, even more than with coal, there is great potential for major reserves additions. A fall in uranium discovery rates since the early 1990s, ascribed by some to resource depletion,[24] was actually mainly caused by the availability of low-cost uranium from the post–Cold War decommissioning of nuclear weapons.[25] This source is expected to be exhausted relatively soon, at which time increased levels of uranium exploration will be required.

Because the cost of uranium is only about 2–3 percent of the cost of delivered nuclear electricity (completely different from the situation for oil and gas), the exploitation of very low-grade sources can still be economic. The element thorium is also fissionable, and experimental plants were constructed in the 1960s and 1970s but abandoned because of the low cost of uranium. World thorium resources are of similar volumes to uranium. Furthermore, breeder reactors produce more fuel than they consume and can increase the amount of energy extracted from a ton of uranium by a factor of 60. Given these figures, it is technically feasible for nuclear power to supply all of the world's energy indefinitely.

A fallacious continuation of this argument is to say that, because fossil fuels are not, by definition, sustainable forever, we should transition away from them as soon as possible. For instance, Goodstein observes, "And in any case the coal will eventually run out, whereas we're trying to think long-term here."[26] I admire the breadth of his vision, extending over many centuries, but practical people in the energy business would generally think a solution lasting for several decades is good enough, when it assists, or at least does not compromise, our finding the next solution. On the basis of Goodstein's argument, we should dress our children in adult-sized clothes from the day of their birth, because we know they are going to grow out of baby clothes. Adopting suboptimal solutions today merely because they are "sustainable" makes us poorer without any compensating gain.

Energy Intensity of the Energy System

Peak oil commentators contend that the energy intensity of energy production is rising rapidly, so that the whole energy industry is effectively becoming cannibalistic. The point will arrive when it takes more energy to extract oil, gas, coal and uranium than they deliver. As this break-even point is approached, our current energy infrastructure will collapse. This is the concept of EROEI. Simply stated, the idea is that, if it takes more energy to produce a unit of a particular energy type than that unit itself provides, the process is unsustainable because it causes a loss in net energy. So, for instance, if it takes the energy equivalent of one barrel of oil to produce one barrel from a particular field (EROEI of 1), then the activity is pointless because there is no net energy gain.

It is widely claimed that, as we approach peak oil and turn to less convenient sources (heavy oil, tar sands, oil shale), so EROEI will decline toward 1. It is often stated that some liquid fuel sources, such as oil shale and ethanol, have negative EROEI; it takes more energy to produce them than the fuels themselves contain. Even if this is not true, there is a concept that diminishing EROEI will increase the amount of energy used by the oil business and so decrease that available to others (assuming that global oil production is approaching its peak). It is true that the energy used in global oil operations is rising due to the greater share of output coming from mature fields, particularly those producing large amounts of water (which is energy intensive to lift and to treat), and more extraction from tar sands and heavy oil. Shell, for instance, used about 0.14 gigajoules/bbl of oil or natural gas equivalent in 2005, up from about 0.11 gigajoules/boe in 1998.[27]

The EROEI concept is, however, badly flawed for four reasons, in increasing order of importance. First, oil is a premium energy source for transport and petrochemicals, more useful than unadorned coal, nuclear, or renewables. A comparable example is electricity. Generating electricity, usually at a thermal conversion efficiency of less than 50 percent plus transmission losses, has an EROEI of much less than 1 but is still rational and economic because electricity is such a useful form of energy.

Second, there is no clear definition of EROEI. Are we to include just the energy used in the oil field itself, e.g., compressors, pumps, steam generation, and so on? What about energy used in operating the pipelines? Energy in the refining process? What about the energy to produce the steel and smelt the aluminium used in the wells and facilities? The electricity to light the homes of the workers? We could also include the energy to make the cement that builds the steel plant that makes the steel for the wells. And the energy to light the university that trains the geologists. In the end, the energy industry is so inextricably bound up with the rest of the economy that it is impossible to separate out its energy usage.

Third, we are nowhere near hitting the point of negative EROEI. To take the Shell statistics quoted above, because one barrel of oil equivalent contains about 6.1 GJ of energy, this implies an EROEI of about 44, far above 0, so there is no immediate problem: for every joule of energy Shell uses in its upstream unit, it produces oil and gas containing 44 joules. Because of its relatively mature fields and heavy investment in tar sands, Shell is probably inherently a much higher energy user than, say, Saudi Aramco. In other words, typically no more than 2 percent of the energy in the hydrocarbons produced is consumed in its production. In fact, most oil fields manage to power all the on-site equipment purely from the associated natural gas released from the oil, just a small part of the total energy output, and fields in remote regions generally have more associated gas than they can use so have to reinject it.

For unconventional oil, EROEI is lower, but, contrary to the claims of many in the peak oil camp, Shell still calculates a value of 3–3.5 for its *in situ* oil shale process, the most energy intensive of all oil sources. Tar sands are often pilloried as energy intensive: "it takes vast quantities of ... natural gas to turn unusable oil into heavy low-quality oil ... In a sense, this exercise is like turning gold into lead."[28] Yet it requires only 6.7 boe of gas to produce one hundred barrels of oil, suggesting an EROEI of 15, a large net energy gain. For other energy sources, the EROEI is even more favorable. Nuclear with centrifuge enrichment is between 43 and 59,[29] and, for coal, it is about 80.[30] Most energy in the nuclear industry is used to enrich the fuel, not to mine it, and so the EROEI of even very low-grade ores is not much less than that of the high grade ores currently under exploitation.

In any case, there is considerable room for increased energy efficiency in all these processes, as there is in the rest of the economy. The efficiency of LNG plants in Australia has been improved simply by painting the surroundings white rather than black (because this re-radiates less heat and an LNG plant is essentially a large refrigerator). If EROEI in the oil business does start falling significantly, then more efficient extraction techniques will be brought in. For instance, in the tar sands of Canada, SAGD can be fired using the waste residues from the heavy oil, demonstrating that the EROEI must be greater that 1 or the process would not be self-sustaining. Advanced technologies such as laser enrichment can lower even further the energy required to yield uranium fuel.

Fourth, there already is a reliable measure of EROEI, unambiguous, universally accepted, and one, furthermore, that will automatically terminate oil production when (and probably well before) its EROEI drops below 1. It is called *cost*. EROEI might make sense in a communist economy, in which prices are set centrally and do not reflect the realities of supply and demand. However, in a broadly free-market economy, as virtually everywhere is these days (Cuba, Belarus, and North Korea not being major oil producers), the cost to produce oil reflects its energy requirements plus all the other inputs, such as personnel (including some expensive, highly skilled staff), materials, chemicals, land, water, and so on. Therefore, an oil field will become uneconomic as a result of high total costs long before its energy output exceeds input. In some specific cases, particularly agricultural ethanol, subsidies might distort the economics enough to make a negative EROEI investment profitable, but, contrary to popular belief, the oil industry is not highly subsidized.[31] It is a net payer of taxes; in fact, in global terms, it is probably the most heavily taxed business. Therefore, there is no government support for oil over other energy businesses, rather the contrary, because renewables and arguably nuclear do receive significant subsidies. Otherwise, instead of measuring the share price of oil companies in dollars, euros, and pounds, we should start expressing it in ergs, joules, and British thermal units.

Other Consequences of Alternative Energies

Environmentalists argue that gas and coal produce unacceptable CO_2 emissions; nuclear has other environmental and safety flaws that make large-scale adoption undesirable (although some environmentalists, generally reluctantly, accept nuclear as a lesser evil than carbon-based fuels because of climate change).

I address the environmental impact of gas and coal in Chapter 10. The nuclear industry's expansion has been held back by environmental and safety concerns, and, in a business-as-usual scenario, nuclear will struggle to make major gains in market share.[32] However, standardization of nuclear plant designs and development of acceptable solutions for the waste would cut costs and construction times, hence greatly improving the economics of new plants. In countries with less public participation in planning decisions than in the West (such as China) or without a negative history and perception of nuclear power (such as India), nuclear could play a major role. Particularly in a peak oil situation, there would be strong pressure to replace as much energy use as possible with nuclear.

The safety concerns over nuclear power have been greatly exaggerated: the risks of exposure to even severe levels of radiation are comparable with those of air pollution, smoking, or obesity.[33] The Chernobyl disaster, which could not happen in a modern Western reactor, has contributed to a misleading sense of the dangers. Of course, continuing concerns over safety, nuclear contamination, and the disposal of waste may, whether well founded or not, continue to hamper nuclear power. Opponents of nuclear power point to the implicit subsidy it receives for disposal of waste and decommissioning of plants but do not address the penalty it suffers for the very tight safety regulations, drawn-out public planning processes, and interminable redesigns. We demand that nuclear waste disposed underground be secure for 10,000 years or more, when even worst-case scenarios do not result in people's exposure above normal background radiation levels,[34] yet allow cars to emit lung-damaging particulates directly into the air in residential areas. Estimates suggest that nuclear power, with some reasonable cost reductions, could be competitive with coal and natural gas once the price of carbon emissions is factored in.[35]

According to many environmentalists, renewables are the only acceptable solution to our energy needs. Conversely, pessimists, including devotees of the "Olduvai Theory," and Neo-Luddites generally believe that renewable energy cannot be commercialized on a large enough scale to meet energy demand growth. According to them, the only possible outcome is a massive drop in energy use, either catastrophic and probably violent (Militarists) or managed and resulting in a utopian, low-intensity, probably very dull society (Neo-Luddites).

Renewables are, in the long run, capable of meeting most of world energy demand, with a total potential of at least 1,000 million boe/day (compared with current total energy demand of about 200 million boe/day).[36] Advances in technology and economies of scale will lower the price of technologies such as solar in particular, but, with some exceptions (such as wind in high-quality locations, and hydropower), they are not yet widely competitive with fossil-fueled energy or nuclear power, probably even when externalities (such as pollution) are properly taken into account.

Dramatic improvements in the technology and cost of renewables are occurring continually. However, these will be offset, at least to some extent, by diminishing returns as renewables increase their market share; for instance, the best sites for wind and hydropower will be used and more remote or lower-quality locales will have to be developed. The power grid will also have to cope with a larger proportion of intermittent, unreliable sources, in the case of solar, available only half the day. At the moment, intermittent sources such as solar and wind benefit from a "free ride" on fossil-fueled generation; an energy system based primarily on such renewables would need to have a large storage capacity or redundancy, adding substantial costs. Finally, the rapid growth of renewables is already coming up against resource constraints, of materials and people, just as it has in the oil business, a much larger, more mature, and slower-growing industry. If we cannot train geologists fast enough today, will we fare any better with solar panel researchers? It took about fifty years for the near-complete displacement of coal by wood and nearly a century for oil and gas to take over from coal.

The great advantage of renewables, of course, is their environmental acceptability, particularly their very low greenhouse emissions. They should be allowed to compete on a level playing field by recognizing the externalities of their competitors, particularly carbon emissions, and by giving them support when appropriate to help them through early development against established energy sources. Renewables will clearly play a major part in twenty-first century energy, but the logistical and economic challenges to making them the primary source are immense and should not be underestimated. They face tough challenges from fossil fuels with carbon sequestration and possibly from nuclear. Their rise, if it occurs, should be a matter of superior performance (across all metrics), not ideology.

Various writers about the "coming energy crisis" like to rubbish fusion power, which has certainly taken much longer than initially expected to commercialize.[37] As with the red herring of EROEI, they say that fusion power requires more energy input than it yields and often combine this discussion with an examination of crank notions such as perpetual motion and cold fusion to destroy its credibility. Yet it is now reasonably expected that the international ITER consortium will be running an experimental fusion reactor by 2016, producing 500 megawatts of power, ten times as much as it requires to run. By 2035, a 3,000 megawatt prototype power plant is anticipated, comparable in output with a large gas-fired facility.[38] Fusion power produces very little nuclear waste (and none of the long-lived, high-activity material than bedevils fission power), is inherently safe and carbon neutral, is expected to be cost competitive with existing generation methods, and, unlike renewables, provides large volumes of reliable base-load power. It runs off tiny quantities of widely available lithium plus deuterium (heavy hydrogen), which can be extracted from ordinary water.

With all these advantages, it may well be fusion that takes over from hydrocarbons in the second half of the twenty-first century rather than renewables. Such a development would continue the trend, ever since the beginnings of coal power in the seventeenth century, for ever more high-tech and concentrated power sources rather than diffuse renewable energy. However, to forestall objections from energy crisis devotees who accuse me of pinning my hopes on unproved technologies, I should make it clear that, because of the enormous resources of fossil fuels, fission material, and renewables, we do not have to rely on fusion as a savior.

PERSONAL VIRTUE? EFFICIENCY

If peak oil were to arrive, could the world cope by increased efficiency? Alternatively, how much can efficiency reduce energy use and hence cut greenhouse emissions?

The efficiency debate is a fascinating one, with perhaps three identifiable end-member positions.

- peak oil doomsayers do not see a role for efficiency, barely discuss it, or contend that it will be at most a partial solution, insufficient to make up for declining oil supplies.

- Proponents of "negawatts," of whom Amory Lovins is one of the most prominent,[39] see enormous scope for energy savings, aided by modest government action.

- Cornucopians, like Peter Huber,[40] Mark Mills (no relation), and U.S. Vice-President Dick Cheney, maintain that waste is unavoidable and unimportant.

"Negawatt" arguments became popular after the first oil crisis. The contention is that energy use is highly inefficient and that energy-saving measures, although they may have higher capital costs, will overall save money: "Most of the oil now used in the United States (and the world) is being wasted, and can be saved more cheaply than buying it."[41] Efficiency and substitution measures can be applied both to save oil and other forms of energy.

The efficiency argument is superficially appealing. There are a number of serious problems with it, however, in a business-as-usual (nonpeak oil or greenhouse action) case. First, there is a tendency to confuse efficiency (doing things better) with conservation (doing less). Driving a hybrid car is efficient; driving more slowly is conservation; it trades the passengers' time (effectively labor) for energy.

Second, why have reasonably efficient markets not already seized these vast energy savings? This may have to do with inertia, excessive fear of innovation, and poor public policy.[42] However, it is also linked to rational risk aversion against new and untested products; and to the "rebound effect." If we reduce energy use, we lower its cost and hence make it more attractive to consume. If the United States really succeeded in halving its oil use by 2025, as Lovins *et al.* illustrate is technically feasible, and were followed by the rest of the OECD, the removal of 25 million bbl/day of demand would cause world prices to crash, probably to below $10/bbl, making many of their other savings uneconomic and incidentally decimating U.S. domestic oil production, which they rely on for some 7.5 million bbl/day of supply. Oddly enough, their otherwise excellent analysis seems to miss this point entirely (but they do use a very similar argument to suggest that savings in natural gas would cause its price to drop and hence permit its substitution for oil in petrochemicals). In a world of relatively abundant and low-cost fuel supplies, other transport modes might easily appear in the future—for instance, hypersonic intercontinental flight and long-distance, high-speed commuting in robotic automobiles. However, it is fair to say that Lovins acknowledges rebound and suggests a figure of up to 15 percent for transport (of every hundred gallons saved, fifteen are consumed again by more driving, bigger automobiles, etc.).

Even given these weaknesses, however, the energy efficiency argument makes great sense in two scenarios.

Peak oil. As previous chapters have made clear, the world's supply, of conventional and particularly unconventional oil appears to be sufficient for many decades. Yet if this analysis is incorrect or if an oil crisis were to be triggered by a failure of major resource holders to invest or by a war or embargo or similar situation, then the price of oil would increase and remain high.

Effective action against climate change. In a world of meaningfully high CO_2 emission costs, efficiency will be one competing solution, along with fuel substitution and carbon sequestration. Lovins makes a convincing case that it may be one of the most effective measures.

In either of these cases, then, Lovins' oil-saving technologies would come into their own. The nature of the crisis would keep prices high, hence partly obviating the rebound effect, and a sense of urgency would overcome risk aversion and political obstacles.

Concentrating on oil and taking the "State of the Art" scenario by Lovins *et al.*, almost 5 million bbl/day of oil could be saved in the United

States alone by nontransport measures (gas substitution in industry, efficiency, and biosubstitutes). Extrapolating to the rest of the world, allowing for the different demand mix, suggests potential savings of some 24 million bbl/day, or more than a fifth of then demand. There are also large opportunities for saving gas and electricity.

If world oil production were to go into decline, therefore, then we would not be facing an energy crisis. There are ample substitutes and opportunities for efficiency savings. At worst, this would be a crisis of liquid transport fuels.

OILING THE WHEELS: TRANSPORT FUEL DEMAND

One eminent peak oiler, Hirsch, correctly perceives, as most of his sympathizers do not, that, if peak oil occurred, it would not be an energy crisis per se but would present major problems to one specific sector, the current transport system. As we have seen, natural gas and electricity (from gas, coal, nuclear, or renewables) are ready substitutes for oil in nearly all nontransport applications. There is also great scope for efficiency gains in the nontransport sector.

Oil, however, still continues to dominate the transport sector, accounting for some 95 percent of energy use. Oil-based fuels are cheap (unlike hydrogen), have high energy density (unlike natural gas), are easy to transport and relatively clean (unlike coal) and simple to store (unlike electricity and hydrogen), and can be burnt in small, rather simple engines (unlike uranium, which is, of course, used in some submarines and warships).

The average age of the U.S. vehicle stock ranges from seven to nine years, and Hirsch concludes from this that a complete turnover to more efficient vehicles would take on the order of twenty-five to thirty years,[43] hence resulting in a sluggish response to peak oil. He forecasts that efficient vehicles might start entering the fleet five years after the beginning of peak oil and that they could save about 2.5 million bbl/day of U.S. demand fifteen years after the start of the crisis.

Yet he is far too conservative and unimaginative in his responses to this crisis; Lovins' team are far more innovative, as society should be, faced with such a situation. The arrival of peak oil, or even of sustained high prices, as we have seen in the twenty-first century so far, accelerates the turnover of the vehicle fleet in favor of more efficient vehicles. Lovins' team rightly highlights the potential of emerging technologies such as hybrid engines and advanced composite materials. Hybrid engines, already commercially available, combine an electric motor and an internal combustion engine. When the car brakes, the kinetic energy is used to recharge the battery, hence dramatically increasing efficiency.

The full package of transportation measures to 2025 (in their State of the Art scenario) includes lightweight vehicles, hybrid engines, improved aerodynamics, auxiliary power units, improved aircraft and air logistics, and larger, more efficient ships and trains. They choose not to include additional savings from switching automobiles to diesel and electrifying the railroads, nor other technologies that might be developed before 2025. Dieselization of the light vehicle fleet is well under way in Europe, with more than half of new sales being diesel vehicles, and is beginning to take off in the USA. Diesel can deliver 10–40 percent better mileage than gasoline, with further dramatic savings being offered by innovative new diesel engine designs (such as EcoMotors) and diesel-electric hybrids. There are numerous other innovations Lovins' group does not mention,[44] as well as behavioral and infrastructural changes such as increased teleworking, different urban planning, and traffic flow measures.

Total transport savings total 11.5 million bbl/day by 2025, 40 percent of projected oil use. Extrapolating to the world, given that the proportion of oil used in transport is less outside the USA, suggests potential for some 28 million bbl/day of gains.

Because hybrid vehicles and diesel cars are already commercially available, there seems no reason to delay their introduction by five years, as Hirsch does, in response to a supposed crisis. Note also that these technological changes do not include alterations in consumer behavior, such as buying smaller cars or avoiding discretionary travel, because Lovins *et al.* are concerned with achieving their oil savings via efficiency and not by "hair-shirt" style conservation. However, such changes in behavior will undoubtedly occur (and did occur during the last two oil crises) in response to high prices. They result in some loss of personal welfare but relatively modest economic cost, for instance, buying smaller cars and making more use of mass transit systems such as trams and light rail, already the norm in Europe and Japan compared with the United States.

Beyond efficiency, there is great scope for replacement of oil entirely in transport. In Chapters 6 and 7, we have seen the potential for new transport fuels to enter the market: CNG and CtL and GtL, including F-T fuels, methanol, ethanol, butanol, and DME, all of which can also be made from biomass. Fuel cell vehicles, in which the fuel is chemically combined with oxygen without combustion, are more efficient and have dramatically lower emissions; these engines can be run on most of the fuels above or on hydrogen. The respected consultancy CERA's "Break Point" scenario foresees oil losing its dominance of the transport market by 2016, in response to high prices and facilitated by rapid innovation.

In the longer term, the battle for the transport sector may be fought between electricity and hydrogen. These are not primary energy sources; they are energy carriers. Electricity, obviously, has to be generated from other fuels (including solar, wind, etc.). Hydrogen, which does not occur native (chemically uncombined) on Earth in significant quantities, is today mostly made from natural gas, but it can also be generated using coal, nuclear, biological methods, or renewables, by either chemical reactions or the electrolysis (electrical splitting) of water. In the future, breaking down water at very high temperatures, perhaps using nuclear power, may be an attractive way to generate hydrogen.

The next step in the evolution of the hybrid is "plug-in hybrids," whose battery can be recharged from the grid, hence further reducing gasoline or diesel use, and consuming cheap, off-peak, possibly renewable-sourced electricity. This is an additional step toward increasing the intersubstitutability of oil with other energy sources, and could create a "critical mass" of commercial applications to encourage improvements in the cost and performance of vehicle batteries. Hydrogen, environmentally attractive because it produces only water when "burnt" in a fuel cell, remains problematic, however, due to its high cost, difficulty of storage, and need for a completely new distribution infrastructure. Similarly, pure electric cars are still far from competitive with the internal combustion engine on cost and performance grounds. Yet either or both may be the terrain for "early adopters," such as city bus fleets and taxis, which do not need to cover large distances between refueling stops.

Overall, then, even in oil's "home territory" of the transport sector, abundant technologies exist today either to use less fuel or to substitute oil with other plentiful energy forms, at acceptable costs. Proponents of post-peak economic or industrial collapse credit humanity with far too little adaptability.

SYNTHESIS

As we did for unconventional oil, let us consider how the world could react to a peak oil event, beginning tomorrow (Figure 9.1). In that scenario, we assumed that demand, at 86 million bbl/day in 2007, continues to rise at 2 percent per year (the solid line), whereas conventional oil production falls at 2 percent annually, equivalent to Hirsch's assumption,[45] and unconventional oil grows strongly as previously outlined (total oil production, conventional plus unconventional, being the dotted line). Demand, approximated from a chart by Lovins, follows the dashed line, with rather slow adoption of efficiency measures, so no particularly urgent response to the peak oil crisis.

The combination of unconventional supply growth and demand savings therefore eliminates the crisis almost entirely. The maximum gap between theoretical demand and actual supply is only 2 million bbl/day, two years after the start of conventional decline, and, after six years, the deficit is more than eliminated. As a comparison, over the past few years, the world has been very used to interruptions of supply on the order of 1–2.5 million bbl/day, in Iraq, Venezuela, Nigeria, and the Gulf of Mexico, momentarily uncomfortable but not derailing a robust world economy. In fact, this

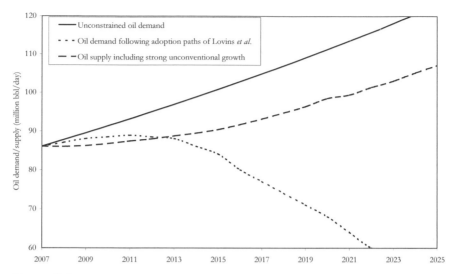

Figure 9.1
Comparison of unconventional growth and efficiency measures.

graph clearly indicates a massive oversupply would develop, starting some six years after the beginning of the crisis, causing oil prices to crash and slowing or even halting both efficiency and unconventional programs (just like the post-1986 experience in the United States).

This conclusion is obviously radically different from that of Hirsch,[46] who foresaw a long, painful adjustment to peak oil. The main differences are twofold:

- First, Hirsch's very conservative view on the potential for demand savings, which seems to ignore the voluminous and very well-documented work of Lovins *et al.*[47] and the rapid efficiency gains made by the industrialized world in 1973–1983.

- Second, his failure to recognize that many of the solutions, both on the demand and supply side, are available *today* and do not require his five-year period of inertia, which puts him disastrously behind in the "oil endgame," indeed in a position from which he can never recover.

Overall, the transition away from conventional oil is likely to happen for economic and environmental reasons, not resource availability. There are many possible paths, involving different combinations of unconventional oil, substitute sources, and efficient technologies. The very multiplicity of possibilities should give us confidence that at least one will prove to be feasible and attractive.

_____ *Chapter 10* _____

Green Oil: Saving the Environment

The use of solar energy has not been opened up since the oil industry does not own the sun.

Ralph Nader[1]

In February 2007, Abu Dhabi, one of the world's most oil-rich states, proved Nader wrong by announcing a $350 million solar plant.[2] But did he have a point? Is our dependence on fossil fuels blocking the way to a renewable future? Can hydrocarbons be part of a sustainable, clean energy system? The answer to this revolves around the local and regional effects of petroleum use and the global danger of climate change.

Oil and other carbon fuels can, and probably will, continue to be the mainstay of our energy system well into the middle of the twenty-first century, because they have a massive installed base, they will continue to be cost competitive with nuclear and renewables for many decades to come and modern technologies are now available, at acceptable cost, greatly to mitigate their environmental impacts.

LOCAL IMPACTS

Quite apart from the climate change issue, oil has a very poor environmental image. Catastrophic impacts include oil leaks from pipelines (BP Alaska, August 2006), tankers (Exxon Valdez in Alaska, 1989), and well blowouts (Santa Barbara, California, 1969, putting most of the U.S. offshore under moratorium[3]). Such leaks damage local ecosystems. Ongoing, cumulative damage includes threats to habitats, for instance in the Amazon, from field developments as a result of ecological fragmentation, air and water pollution, and opening up remote areas to other development such as logging. Finally, oil processing and use creates water and, particularly, air pollution, including unburnt hydrocarbons, ozone, particulates, sulphur dioxide, and nitrogen oxides. These chemicals form smog in urban areas, produce acid rain, which damages the environment over a wide area, may be carcinogenic, and are a major contributor to lung diseases.

However, the environmental impact of the upstream oil industry is much less than popularly imagined and has fallen significantly with time. If Alaska's largest field, Prudhoe Bay, were developed today, its footprint would be barely one-third of its actual size.[4] Much of the misguided debate over ANWR seems to involve a misunderstanding or willful misrepresentation of what a modern oil-field development looks like. Deviated wells can now reach more than 10 km out from the drill-site, and multiple wells can be drilled from a single location. This dramatically reduces the surface footprint of an oil field; modern fields, contrary to popular perception, are not topped by dense forests of derricks. More likely, as at BP's Wytch Farm in Dorset in the southwest of the United Kingdom, a single well pad of modest size is surrounded by trees that make it all but invisible (Figure 10.1).

Figure 10.1
Minimizing the impact of modern oil developments: Wytch Farm Field, Dorset, United Kingdom (Courtesy of BP Photographic Services).

Offshore and transition zone developments, as in the Mississippi Delta and Niger Delta, have been associated with environmental damage. A significant amount of this is caused by the cutting of canals for access, causing flooding and erosion, rather than to the oil development per se, and practices are improving. Underwater structures have often become artificial reefs, attracting marine life. During the 1995 Brent Spar affair, when Shell sought to dispose of an old floating oil facility in the deep waters of the Atlantic (not in the North Sea, a common misconception), Greenpeace released estimates of oil in the structure that were a hundred times the true figure, hence greatly overstating the environmental impact.[5]

Regulation on discharges by the upstream industry have also become much tougher. Drilling in Norway's Barents Sea, in the Arctic, operates under a strict "no discharge" policy, in which no drilling fluids, even rather innocuous ones, can be released into the sea. Statoil's accidental discharge of 1.6 m^3 of hydraulic oil caused a total halt to drilling, yet a single fishing voyage in the same waters probably releases at least as much. Of oil spills worldwide, only 7 percent comes from offshore oil extraction and major tanker spills. Most is natural or the product of land run-off or shipping.[6] All the artificial sources are very amenable to clean-up: a United Nations treaty led to oil pollution from shipping falling about 60 percent during the 1980s. Oil spills have also been found to cause less damage to ecosystems than had been expected, and much of the degradation has been inflicted by misguided clean-up efforts.

Unconventional oil has received particular attention for its environmental impact. To make one barrel of synthetic crude oil from Canadian tar deposits by mining, ten barrels of water and two tons of tar sands are required. However, this oft-quoted "ten barrels of water for one barrel of oil" is somewhat misleading, because 80 percent of the water is recycled, the net therefore being two barrels.[7] The waste sand and water accumulates in giant tailing pits, some up to 15 km^2 in area, from which the oil is skimmed off the top of the water. Birds have to be scared away by regular explosions, because the water is toxic. Currently about 5 percent of the Athabasca River's flow is used in operations, possibly rising to 10 percent in the future. Because the Athabasca River flows north, eventually reaching the Arctic Ocean, whereas the water-scarce areas of Alberta are in the south, the impact on farming is minimal, but wildlife and fishing may suffer from reduced flows, particularly during the summer. However, surface water use can be minimized or even eliminated by recycling water and using nonpotable subsurface water. The oil sands industry has only 7 percent of allocated Albertan water (and uses just one-third of its quota) compared with 45 percent for agriculture.[8]

A variety of techniques may reduce the surface impact, such as accelerated dewatering of the tailings and faster reclamation, but given the nature of mining operations, there is always going to be significant disturbance to the local environment. Oil shale mining appears to have similar issues.

In situ methods, such as SAGD and air injection for oil sands and "Mahogany" for oil shale, because they do not physically remove rock or sand, are much less damaging to the physical environment than mining, require less water, and also produce lower emissions.[9] There is considerable scope for efficiency improvements in all unconventional oil projects, and these advances, yielding cost as well as environmental benefits, will continue incrementally in the future.

As for XtL, apart from greenhouse emissions, the technology is environmentally far superior to alternatives. Firing a facility with biomass can actually consume waste. Large-scale development of CtL, however, would require a corresponding expansion of coal mining, which can lead to severe environmental degradation, and is dangerous and unhealthy for the miners. Underground coal gasification is therefore potentially environmentally more attractive.

Biofuels have environmental concerns related to unsustainable use of soil and water resources, pollution from mechanized farming and fertilizer runoff, the use of genetically modified crops, deforestation (ironically, encouraging climate change), habitat destruction and monoculture, and competition with growing food. However, using cellulose and other waste rather than food crops or growing drought-tolerant crops such as jatropha,[10] would substantially mitigate such worries. Establishing crops on carbon-depleted soils could even result in a net extraction of CO_2 from the atmosphere,[11] and effective carbon management of agriculture is likely to be a key part of the battle against climate change.

In general, without painting the petroleum industry as a hero, it would probably surprise many people how carefully and sincerely most oil and gas professionals take their environmental responsibilities. Awareness, and the time and effort devoted to environmental protection, is greater than in most office jobs, in which these issues are not so immediate. In this regard, with the exception of some cowboys, the IOCs lead the way; the better of the Russian companies are improving, but many incumbent NOCs, insulated from public and shareholder pressure and from modern industry trends, have poor environmental records.

Oddly, the most serious threat to human health, traffic pollution, receives less opprobrium from environmental campaigners. It is easier to blame a faceless oil company than ordinary motorists. Yet particulates, in particular, are associated with high levels of morbidity through lung disease, and about 800,000 deaths annually are linked to urban air pollution.[12] As with the upstream oil industry, emissions from transport have fallen significantly and continue to drop, because a modern car is some twenty times less polluting than a mid-1960s model. Progressive tightening of emission standards and air quality regulations has been accompanied by improvements in engine technology, the installation of catalytic converters, the phasing out of leaded gasoline, and the introduction of cleaner fuels such as ultra-low sulphur diesel. Clean-burning fuels such as CNG, LPG,[13] F-T liquids (synthetic diesel and gasoline[14]), methanol, and DME, offer additional advances, and CNG has already led to notable improvements in urban air quality in India and Pakistan. Air pollution, although still a serious issue, is therefore not an insuperable barrier to the continuing use of fossil fuels in transport.

Modern forms of energy, including kerosene, LPG, natural gas, and electricity, are crucial for improving health in developing countries. Traditional biomass—wood, straw, dung, and so on—contributes to deforestation (and hence CO_2 emissions), is exhausting and time consuming to collect, and, especially when burnt indoors, may be responsible for as many as 1.6 million premature deaths worldwide.[15] Deaths on this scale make it irresponsible, even immoral, to prevent fossil fuel use in developing countries or to insist on their use of expensive alternative sources.

Even the "dirty man" of fossil fuels, coal, has enormous potential for cleaner operation. Flue gas desulphurization, activated carbon filters, and electrostatic precipitation, fitted as standard to newer plants in the West, remove 99.9 percent of particulates, more than 99 percent of sulphur dioxide, approximately 90 percent of mercury, and 90 percent of nitrogen oxides.[16] The appalling coal pollution currently seen in China is attributable to a failure to fit pollution-reducing equipment. The great progress made toward "clean coal" plants shows the power of technological innovations, incentivized by a "cap and trade" system for sulphur dioxide emissions, similar to that being proposed to control CO_2.

GLOBAL CLIMATE CHANGE

The Environmentalist position is summed up by Greenpeace: "Burning more than about one quarter of the current economic reserves of oil, coal and gas, will release sufficient greenhouse gases to create a serious risk of catastrophic climate change."[17]

Climate change is the most serious threat facing us today, more than terrorism or nuclear proliferation. There is broad scientific consensus that the Earth's climate is changing rapidly, on the whole becoming warmer, and that human emissions of CO_2 and other gases, combined with processes such as deforestation, are the primary cause. Overall, the effects of this will be strongly negative on the natural world and on people. The financial costs imposed by climate change greatly exceed the likely costs of its mitigation, the unquantifiable loss of natural biodiversity is a tragedy, and the danger of reaching a "tipping point" of global climate, with swift and irreversible change thereafter, is significant.[18]

Continuing to burn oil, gas, and especially coal in the same way we do now will lead to disastrous increases in the concentration of greenhouse gases in the atmosphere. A massive shift to oil sands, oil shales, and so on, without compensating measures, will significantly increase CO_2 emissions from the energy business. In this, I agree with Greenpeace. Those in the industry, like the American Association of Petroleum Geologists, who maintain that, "Recently published research results do not support the supposition of an anthropogenic cause of global climate change ... The current level of global warming is real and natural,"[19] or, like Michael Economides, dismiss environmentalists as zealots,[20] risk not only further damaging the oil business's public image but also missing important business trends.

Given this, how am I defending the continuing use of oil? In short, I believe in practical solutions. The future evolution of technology, in particular, is highly unpredictable. Now is not the time to attempt to pick winners by government or pressure group fiat; it is the time to set up robust policies and institutions that discourage climate-changing emissions and encourage low- or zero-carbon technologies, whatever they are. The battle against climate change is so wide-reaching and enormous in scope that it would be disastrous to labor under self-imposed restrictions, ruling out some approaches *a priori*. If nuclear ultimately does not flourish because of safety problems or biofuels because of habitat destruction, that is fine, but that should be the outcome, not the starting point. Much of the peak oil argument on the Environmentalist side is bound up with the belief that the two arguments go together: oil is dirty, oil is running out, therefore, however you look at it, it is time to abandon oil in favor of renewables. But wishing that oil will conveniently run out, to save the environment, does not mean that oil *will* run out.

If politics is the art of the possible, too many environmentalists, sadly, practice the art of the impossible. Opposition to natural gas and nuclear power will not, as many fondly imagine, lead to a switch to renewables, which are already growing about as fast as is physically possible.[21] Instead, such campaigns will prolong dependence on coal. Already, Norway maintains its environmental virtue by importing electricity from its Nordic neighbors to satisfy the shortfall of hydropower rather than building "polluting" gas-fired plants, but this imported electricity is generated largely from Danish coal plants!

Changing our energy system will be an enormous, long-running endeavor, requiring unprecedented global cooperation and strong multilateral institutions. It resembles, and is intricately bound up with, the quest for energy security, globalization, and the fight against poverty. Without mutual interdependence and a shared understanding of the needs of producers and consumers, it will be very difficult to reduce CO_2 emissions without alienating one half of the energy marketplace. Without all the positive forces of globalization, we will not be able to muster the consensus to apply efficient, worldwide solutions fairly. Without energy security, without fair and wide-reaching globalization, and in the face of disastrous climate change, the poor of the world will continue to suffer. When major nations and large proportions of the global population remain poor, they will be unable to avoid climate-changing actions such as deforestation and desertification; the slightly richer will not be able to pay for expensive clean technologies and sustainable agriculture. Rapid economic growth in the developing nations is a major threat for the global climate, but it is also the solution, if combined with environmental responsibility. And in that field, the industrialized world, which has so far benefited most from carbon-intensive development, has to set the moral example.

The goal of reducing greenhouse gas emissions has many possible paths. There is no silver bullet; we need a mix of solutions that will vary with place and time. One approach to conceptualizing the solution is to think in terms of "wedges."[22] To keep the atmospheric concentration of CO_2 below 500 parts per million by 2054, considered to be a level beyond which there is a high risk of catastrophic climate change, we need to cut 7 billion tons of carbon emissions from the business-as-usual forecast (current emissions are about 7 billion tons per year, forecast almost to double by 2054[23]).

This target can be divided into seven wedges of 1 billion tons per year each; we can then choose seven wedges from a menu of options (the original authors present a menu of fifteen) to achieve stabilization. Options include improvements in residential energy efficiency, higher vehicle efficiency, zero-emission cars (hydrogen or electricity from carbon-neutral sources[24]), carbon management policies for agriculture, reforestation, increased solar and wind generation, more biofuels in transport, replacing coal generation with gas and nuclear, and capturing landfill gas.[25] Of the full menu of fifteen, only two replace oil, three replace coal, and one substitutes gas for coal, whereas three depend on carbon capture. Such wedges imply a robust future for fossil fuels, gas in particular.

Carbon Sequestration

The primary reason why I am confident oil, gas, and coal can maintain a leading role in energy supply well into the twenty-first century, even in the face of a strong campaign against climate change, is the possibility of capturing CO_2 emissions.

Carbon capture and storage (CCS) involves taking CO_2 from burning fossil fuels and other processes and trapping (sequestering) it safely before it enters the atmosphere. CCS thus follows exactly the same principle as that successfully applied to reduce other pollution from coal burning. It has three components: capture, transport, and storage.

CO_2 capture generally relies on large, point sources. Application to small-scale facilities such as home boilers or to moving targets such as vehicles seems likely to be very difficult and costly (but see[26]!). Vehicular emissions can be tackled by a number of other methods, such as alternative fuels and increased efficiency. Large point sources of CO_2 include power stations (particularly coal), natural gas processing facilities operating with contaminated gas, oil and ethanol refineries, petrochemical and ammonia plants, iron and steel works, GtL and CtL facilities, LNG plants, landfills,[27] and cement works. Even today, large point sources of CO_2 (greater than 100,000 tons of CO_2 per year) amount to three wedges[28] (1 billion tons carbon [C] equivalent each), and this number will have grown significantly by 2050. Diffuse sources, such as transport, can even be tackled by removing CO_2 directly from the air, an approach that, intriguingly, does not appear unfeasibly expensive.[29]

It appears possible to achieve the required carbon reductions for transport largely through increased efficiency. However, an adjunct of the increasing shift of the vehicle fleet towards natural gas, low-carbon synthetic fuels, such as F-T liquids, DME, or methanol, or to a zero-carbon option, such as hydrogen or electricity, would be to move the carbon problem to the large facilities that would generate these fuels, ideal sites for carbon capture. Widespread use of electricity-powered mass transit would fit into this paradigm. Another alternative for tackling transport emissions is to remove CO_2 directly from the atmosphere by biosequestration or technological approaches.

Moving the CO_2 to the storage site is straightforward. As with natural gas, CO_2 can be moved by pipeline or ship. CO_2 tankers resemble LPG tankers and are less costly than LNG ships, while transport by pipeline is well established in the Permian Basin of the southern United States.

There are five main proposals for CO_2 sequestration:

- Inject it into depleted oil and gas reservoirs or coal-seams, possibly enhancing hydrocarbon recovery and hence leading to reduced or even negative costs of capture. Below about 500–1,000 meters below the surface, CO_2 becomes a supercritical liquid with a high density, so it takes up much less space than natural gas and is less likely to leak. This method is in widespread active use today (for EOR).

- Inject it into saline, nonpotable aquifers below ground. This process is successfully under way at BP's In Salah project in Algeria and Statoil's Sleipner in the Norwegian North Sea.

- Inject it as a supercritical, dense fluid into the deep, cold ocean waters. This seems more problematic than the first two options because there is the possibility of leakage, and acidification of the ocean bottom may damage ecosystems.

- Mineralize it, by conversion into solid carbonates that could be stored or injected underground. Reactions with calcium and magnesium silicates, extremely common minerals that make up a large proportion of the earth's crust, may even be energetically favorable, releasing additional energy. For instance, converting CO_2 to silica and calcium carbonate releases about a quarter of the energy that burning the original carbon did.[30] This approach is promising but is in the early research stage.

- Find economic uses for it: in methanol, urea (for fertilizers), propylene and carbonated soft drinks, in building materials, or to enhance biological growth (biosequestration). This may be a niche application but will generally only delay the release of CO_2 to the atmosphere, unless (as with methanol and fertilizer), it is displacing the use of natural gas. Building materials, such as Shell's C-Fix,[31] could partly replace the highly CO_2-intensive process of cement manufacture and represents a kind of mineralization. Enhanced biosequestration, for instance, assisting the growth of plants used to make cellulosic ethanol, oil-producing algae, agriculture using nutrient-enhanced seawater with salt-tolerant crops,[32] or even ordinary biomass that is then buried, is another promising but early-stage route.

Numerous projects are operating or will operate soon to sequester CO_2, with a total sequestration potential of some 10 million tons of carbon per year,[33, 34, 35, 36] (about 1 percent of one wedge). Even so, its contribution to reducing carbon emissions will exceed that of solar electricity, which supplies only about 0.04 percent of all our energy. Two of the highest profile, however, Shell/Statoil Hydro's Haltenbanken and BP's Miller, are currently in jeopardy partly because of delays in establishing a legal framework for carbon capture.[37]

Unfortunately, carbon sequestration faces ill-informed and sometimes ideological opposition from many environmental groups, who should embrace its potential for tackling greenhouse emissions. The three usual arguments are that it is unproven, unfeasibly expensive, and that the CO_2 may leak out. For instance, the Sierra Club said, "We don't have any idea whether or when this [carbon storage] will be possible."[38] Andrew McKillop dismisses

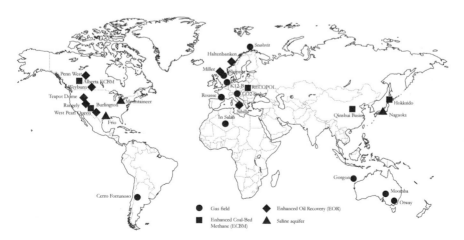

Figure 10.2
Carbon dioxide sequestration projects (active and under development).

something that is happening on an industrial scale today as "exotic techno-logical fantasies,"[39] Greenpeace commented that the Swedish utility Vatten-fall was attempting to deceive ecologists with its carbon capture plans and that "the gas may return to the surface at some point."[40]

Yet the list of projects above shows clearly that injection and long-term storage of large quantities of CO_2 underground is entirely practicable. As the Norwegian environmental group Bellona correctly recognizes, "Capture of CO_2, from power production and industrial activity, to be injected into oil and gas reservoirs for enhanced oil and gas recovery, and not least the technical opportunities of using CO_2 in deep lying coal beds for methane extraction to electricity and hydrogen production, may by Bellona's opinion represent one of the most significant future sources for clean energy."[41] British environmental writer George Monbiot is another supporter.[42]

The technology for carbon capture from power plants is well under-stood, if not yet implemented on a large scale in practice. The Intergovern-mental Panel on Climate Change has found that CCS has the potential to mitigate up to 55 percent of CO_2 emissions to 2100.[43] To sequester all the 7 billion tons of carbon annually required to keep atmospheric concentra-tions below 500 parts per million would cost about $1 trillion, which sounds a lot but is only about 1 percent of then forecast global GDP,[44] very similar to the Stern Review finding that costs to reduce greenhouse emissions to acceptable levels would be about 1 percent of GDP per year.[45] Costs are likely to fall significantly once "learning by doing" and economies of scale come into play. The Intergovernmental Panel on Cli-mate Change found that application of a realistic level of CCS could reduce the costs of meeting CO_2 targets by 30 percent.

Figure 10.3 shows the estimated cost over the twenty-first century of fossil fuel generation with CCS versus other options.[46] From this, it would appear that coal and gas remain better than competitive with nuclear and renewables, even at close to zero emissions. Of these costs, about 1–5¢ per kilowatt hour is the likely cost of the CCS itself; combination with EOR reduces this to 1–2¢.[47] Cofiring Integrated Gasification Combined Cycle (IGCC) coal power plants with more than about 10 percent biomass can create "sequestration plus": actively removing CO_2 from the atmos-phere, so that capture amounts to up to 116 percent of emissions.[48]

The issue of leakage is equally a red herring. Natural gas reservoirs have held their contents for millions of years at least; some giant fields in East Siberia and Oman may have retained gas for half a billion years or more, and CO_2 is significantly less mobile in the subsurface than methane. If suitable storage sites are chosen, there is no reason to doubt that CO_2 can be removed from the atmosphere indefinitely. Furthermore, CO_2 is not plutonium; a small amount of leakage would neither seriously dent the sequestration effect, nor present any safety problems. Studies have found it likely that leaks would be less than 0.001 percent annually. Over long

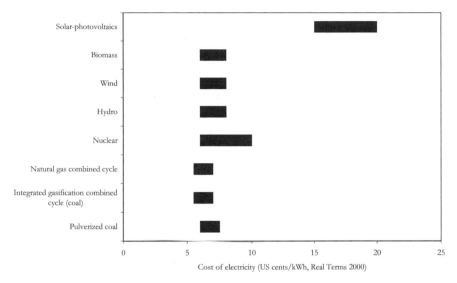

Figure 10.3
Estimated cost of electricity generation from different sources during the twenty-first century (fossil fuels with carbon capture and sequestration).

periods of time, the CO_2 will dissolve in water and become converted to solid minerals, so the security of storage becomes greater, not less, as time goes on. We must be careful that excessively high standards do not make CCS uneconomic, because the current alternative is that CO_2 goes straight into the air. A better approach would be to tighten monitoring standards progressively as the technology approaches maturity.

The underground capacity to store CO_2 is immense. For instance, the Utsira Formation, a saline aquifer beneath the North Sea that is the repository for the Sleipner gas, can hold 160 billion tons of carbon, or a century and a half-worth of one wedge of emission reductions. Such saline aquifers are ubiquitous across the world, underlying half the area of the inhabited continents, their water is not drinkable, and they generally lie well beneath potable water, so there is no issue of contamination (of making large quantities of soda water!). Their location is ideal; all the major oil and gas basins, and all the major industrial regions, with the possible exception of China, are underlain by enormous extents of such formations. The total storage potential of aquifers is highly uncertain (suitable aquifers will have to have reasonable permeability and be isolated from the surface by sealing rocks and geological structuration) but is thought to range from 275 to 2,750 billion tons of carbon.

Oil and gas fields,[49] coal beds,[50] and basalts[51] are all credible sinks; salt caverns, abandoned mines, and oil and gas shales are more speculative and unquantified storage sites. Potential storage capacity is therefore found in the vicinity of all major industrial centers, suggesting at least 65–400 years of sequestration of all "excess" emissions. Ocean storage, although problematic, could have capacity for several trillion (thousand billion) tons of CO_2. Overall, given that CCS will not be applied to all emissions, it would appear that there is at least a century of capacity. By then, the fossil fuel age will surely be drawing to its close.

Just like renewables, CO_2 sequestration is a candidate for support to establish it in its early stages. Key steps are to establish a firm legal, fiscal, and safety framework,[52] establish credibility with the public and environmental organizations, and develop some mega-CCS projects as pathfinders.

As technology advances and the infrastructure develops, we could imagine the development of a network of CO_2 pipelines similar to those that now transport natural gas and oil: CO_2 as both pollutant and commodity. At one end would be the major point sources of CO_2. These inputs could include pure CO_2 streams from advanced coal-fired power generation, hydrogen facilities running on natural gas, and XtL plants (some sequestration plus, using biomass). At the other end would be sequestration sites: aquifers, oil and gas fields (for enhanced recovery), coal beds, and so on.

This system would make CCS much cheaper, because ultimately most sources would lie in easy proximity to a pipeline or sequestration sink. Such a giant network would also get round one of the problems that bedevils individual CO_2 projects: a power plant or refinery may produce emissions continuously for thirty or forty years, but an oil field only needs injection for a much shorter time, say fifteen years, and in its later stages, much of its CO_2 will be recycled from previous injection. Therefore, the ideal is to have a number of fields at different stages of their life, so that a given CO_2 emitter can inject first into one and then into the next. The whole scheme is shown in Figure 10.4.

Carbon Intensity of Unconventional Oil

As we have seen, unconventional oil, particularly oil sands, oil shale, and biofuels, has local environmental impacts that are of concern, although not so serious as to derail unconventional oil as a major energy source. Yet unconventional oil tends to have higher CO_2 emissions than conventional. It would therefore be preferable to use conventional oil as much as possible, a counterargument to Greenpeace's stated belief that we should cease oil exploration. This reasoning is even more applicable for gas; environmentalists should strongly support gas development when it displaces coal (as it generally will). They will need to make up their mind on the worse evil: gas or nuclear. The more conventional oil and gas we can find, the less we need unconventionals, allowing us to delay the

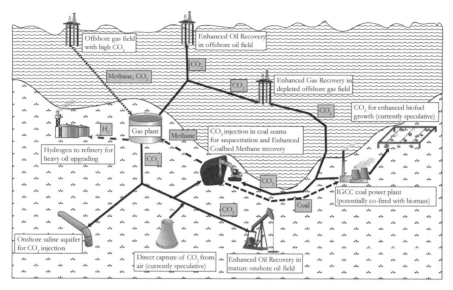

Figure 10.4
Integrated carbon dioxide value chain of the future.

larger-scale introduction of unconventional oil and increased use of coal until CCS is widely available.

Although oil sands are about 15–40 percent more carbon intensive[53] than conventional production, this still implies that the primary focus of a climate change solution has to be at the "wheel rather than the well." New techniques, such as down-hole steam generation and *in situ* combustion, may reduce energy use and emissions significantly, being not only inherently less energy intensive but also automatically sequestering considerable CO_2 underground. Carbon capture, for instance, using highly efficient IGCC power plants running on heavy oil residues, can also be a key enabler for reducing the carbon footprint of the Albertan oil sands. It has been estimated that the cost of making today's oil sands operations carbon-neutral primarily by sequestering large point emissions would be a mere $1/bbl, rising to $3–9 bbl in the future, a significant but not intolerable increase.[54, 55]

Of the other major forms of unconventional oil, GtL suffers from low-energy efficiency of about 60 percent, but CO_2 emissions are about 5–12 percent less than those of traditional liquid fuels on a molecule-to-wheel basis.[56, 57, 58] However, this is significantly higher than using natural gas directly,[59] and CtL produces about double the amount of CO_2 as the same volume of conventional oil. Sequestration of CO_2 is therefore important for large-scale adoption of GtL (reducing emissions by an additional 20 percent over conventional fuels) and essential for CtL. Biomass plants, or to some extent cofiring CtL plants with biomass, can offer "sequestration plus": not just avoiding emissions but actually removing CO_2 from the atmosphere. Ultimately, BtL presents the option of retaining today's transport systems but making them carbon-neutral or even, taking the cycle as a whole, a net sink.

YEAR ZERO: THE NEO-LUDDITES

A significant sect within the peak oil camp, indeed perhaps even the orthodox majority, sees the twin threats of oil depletion and environmental destruction as harbingers of the end of industrial civilization, population crash, famine, pestilence, "war, starvation, economic recession, possibly even the extinction of homo sapiens,"[60] and, in the words of *Ghostbusters*, "Human sacrifice, dogs and cats living together—mass hysteria."[61] They vary from those who are hostile to the free-market system, like Campbell, who seems to blame Norwegian oil for teenage pregnancies, among other things, to anticapitalists with a dash of Marxism, like McKillop, to those I term Neo-Luddites, like Heinberg and Darley, who want to see the whole industrial edifice come crashing down. Some towns, such as the U.K.'s Totnes and Lampeter, have begun planting nut trees to provide food once oil runs out,[62] ironic because, when dealing with this issue, nuts seems already to be abundant.

Some are not even looking for solutions. They set up straw-man policies to demolish them, like reliance on perpetual motion. Lovins has written, "It'd be a little short of disastrous for us to discover a source of clean, cheap, abundant energy because of what we would do with it." This is a kind of "original sin" view of energy, that we cannot be trusted and have to be punished for our misuse of the bounty of hydrocarbons. Because the Neo-Luddites are not looking for solutions, it is hardly surprising that they fail to find them. Unfortunately, some of them have established a certain credibility as experts with the energy-illiterate section of the public.

The Neo-Luddite discourse has four great weakness. The initial premise is false, the rejection of capitalism is wrong, no real alternative is developed, and the utopian end state would be nightmarish.

The first weakness we have already discovered: the belief that oil and energy in general are running out, like Richard Duncan's Olduvai Theory, and that environmental catastrophe is looming inevitably is false. The proponents of a low-energy world are looking into a distorting mirror, mistaking their own wishes for reality, one of the most fundamental mistakes in science. "Just wishing don't make it so"; hating the hubris of capitalism does not mean that oil is going to run out or that the icecaps are going to melt, to destroy it, in some version of a Greek tragedy. It is, in principle, intellectually consistent to be a classical economist and yet believe that oil reserves are overstated or to be a radical anarchist and yet acknowledge how much unconventional oil there is. However, in practice, such combinations rarely exist. For respectable media, such as the *New York Times*[63] and *The Guardian* newspaper in the United Kingdom, to buy into peak oil and end of civilization mantras just discredits the rest of the environmental movement and distracts us fatally from things that might really make a difference.

The second weakness is the attack on free markets and globalization. This is currently fashionable, yet the analyses of peak oil writers are unconvincing. Of course, anyone is entitled to criticize the capitalist system—the worst economic system, apart from all the others. Despite its enormous success in bringing unparalleled prosperity to a majority of the world's population, the wealth has clearly been unevenly distributed, and environmental protection has been patchy. Suggestions for improvement, particularly if they come with realistic implementation, are very welcome. But the Neo-Luddite vision is economically illiterate. They reject mainstream economics without understanding it. They do not acknowledge the vast power of the free-market system to solve problems, especially when externalities are properly priced. Their criticisms of capitalism are polemic rather than analysis. Instead of concentrating on specific areas, such as global trade, in which there is clearly great room for improvement, they want to sweep away the whole system and start again.

For instance, Darley writes, "free-market, hypercompetitive, unregulated,[64] 'pathological' corporations have no responsibility to society or the planet whatsoever.... Permanently reduce the power of corporations. Ideally to nil."[65] Campbell provides a rather economically illiterate analysis of capitalism, not surprisingly, for, as a member of a profession of whom 80 percent of their endeavors are dry holes, he has the nerve to title one chapter, "Economists Never Get It Right." Neo-Luddites argue that mainstream economics makes no allowance for finite, nonrenewable resources when, in fact, Hotelling laid down the basic principles as early as 1930, well before Hubbert. Heinberg thinks that increased labor productivity is solely related to greater energy use, apparently unaware of the decreasing energy intensity of GDP, and argues that a return to muscle power will banish unemployment. This is reminiscent of the fallacy of the person who, seeing a mechanical digger, says, "If it weren't for that machine, ten men with spades could be doing that job," to be met with the rejoinder, "Yes, and if it wasn't for your ten men with spades, a hundred men with spoons could do it."

Third, they present no convincing alternatives, neither a philosophy nor a way to get there. Darley writes that "communism is no better," but it would be more accurate to observe that, on virtually every metric—economic, social, and environmental—it was far worse. Just reading a first-class account of Soviet industry[66] reveals a true energy nightmare, what happens in an economy without rational incentives. Subsistence economies can also perform very poorly on environmental degradation, with over-fishing and desertification. It is impossible to say how the proposed energy system of the Neo-Luddites would perform, because their vision of the economy lacks any real substance. Local actions to reduce pollution and energy use and foster more sustainable communities are admirable, but there is no overarching concept of how these communities would knit together globally. Without such a coherent philosophy, there is no chance of implementing large quantities of renewable energy, carbon capture, efficient technologies. Of all economic systems we know about today, only a dynamic free market, working through cooperative globalization with a strong social conscience, can achieve a sustainable energy future.

Fourth, the Neo-Luddites want to make unimaginable changes in our society and way of life. This would be bad enough, even if they had convincingly demonstrated the onset of peak oil. Their proposed "cure," however, sounds far worse than the disease. Campbell foresees a drop in global population to between 2 and 4 billion by 2150 and advocates the return of "immigrant" communities to their origins because they "live on crime and social security."[67] Presumably this would have to be via forced expulsion; already we are coming dangerously close to Nazism. According to the Olduvai Theory, we are going to return to the Stone Age (but Heinberg, relatively sensibly, observes that plenty of civilizations, including luminaries such as the Romans, Ming Chinese, and the Incas, flourished in the past without using fossil fuels). Heinberg believes that a global population of 2 billion is a maximum and that, by keeping the birth rate to 1.5 per couple, this could be achieved in the course of a century. He does not explain how this is to be enforced. Savinar suggests that humanity can only coexist with nature with even more drastic population cuts, to between 80 and 350 million[68] (taking us back to the levels that pertained before 500 BCE). Ruppert suggests that the world population will have to be reduced by 4 billion if humanity is to survive.[69]

In its milder form, the "oil depletion protocol" or "Rimini protocol," advocated by the Association for the Study of Peak Oil, under the aegis of leading members such as Campbell and Aleklett, proposes that nations will reduce their oil output and use in line with "depletion." This, quite apart from resulting in a multinational command economy that would make us long for the cosy days of Brezhnev, would be a self-fulfilling prophecy, imposing that very oil shortage, which it is designed to mitigate. That, however, would be a paradise compared with any real attempt to achieve low-energy, low-population societies on a large scale. However well intentioned, this would inevitably morph into some totalitarian, bureaucratic, perhaps genocidal nightmare, something like Mao's Great Leap Forward without the optimism, perhaps a Great Leap Backward. The trend of reducing living standards concomitantly with energy use goes against human nature. Maybe some communities in the West might fall in line, although actions today, such as composting and cycling to work seem fairly token compared with the apocalyptic extinction of three-quarters of all people. But is Heinberg proposing to go to war to compel the majority of humankind, now rising from poverty in Asia, to give up their material aspirations? Ruppert wants these decisions to be made by a convention of political, economic, spiritual, and scientific leaders, the elite taking control to solve the problems of the masses.

The salvation of the environment lies not in such irrational and dangerous prescriptions but in well-informed, democratic solutions. We will always face economic and environmental problems. That is part of being a civilization, even part of being a social species. The challenges keep coming, but they are never insurmountable as long as we do not despair.

_____ *Chapter 11* _____

Conclusion

The peak oil argument propounded by Geologists is badly flawed. Unfortunately, their views have attracted many adherents, including politicians, such as former U.K. Environment Minister Michael Meacher, regular columnists in respectable newspapers, such as George Monbiot, and even the Transition Town committee of Lampeter. The idea of the "end of oil," aided by the media's search for sensation, has been absorbed into popular discourse. It has become a common refrain that the oil is "running out," "end of oil" books are reviewed uncritically on Amazon as if the printed word conveyed some seal of scientific approval, and the counterview, representing the mainstream of the energy business and the economics profession, fails to make itself widely heard.

As we have seen, rumors of the death of hydrocarbons are greatly exaggerated. To believe in imminent peak oil requires an unlikely concatenation of overstated reserves, the funnel of major projects drying up, the end of significant reserves growth, very disappointing exploration results across the world, in both well-established and frontier basins, and a failure, despite ideal circumstances, of unconventional oil to deliver what has already been shown to be achievable. In reality, we have more conventional oil than widely reported, unconventional resources are colossal, and there are plentiful energy substitutes. We can use hydrocarbons ever more efficiently and cleanly, and there are realistic ways of avoiding climate disaster. As always in human history, challenges bring forth solutions. As with Jevons' peak coal, the result is a better, not a worse, world.

In contrast to this, peak oil theorists seem to be living in some nightmarish Soviet-style world, in which technology does not advance, efficiency does not increase, demand rises inexorably regardless of price, every forecast is overoptimistic, every expedient we try fails, new frontiers are invariably disappointing, every action we take only accelerates our own doom, and consuming governments and major energy producers conspire, for unexplained reasons, to destroy the world economy. With our finances, way of life, and civilization crashing down around our eyes, we nevertheless proceed on exactly the same course. Although prices are rising, we do not conserve energy. Although oil is running short, we do not open up new areas to exploration. We remain locked in a "low oil price" mind-set in which we do not even apply proven technologies to increase oil recovery, let alone devise innovative new methods. Crash programs to improve recovery or implement unconventional sources are half-hearted, barely exercising the full capability of the existing petroleum industry, let alone mobilizing society and the finest minds of the age, in the style of the Manhattan or Apollo projects. We go down without a fight.

Such misconceptions about energy are in danger of leading us, as in the 1970s, into misguided and even disastrous policies. They encourage Militarist adventures in oil-producing states and the resource nationalist counterreaction. They encourage the use of coal instead of clean gas. They encourage overly expensive energy, penalizing the poorest nations and perpetuating inefficient, authoritarian rule. Yet the opposite policies—refusing to recognize the reality of climate change, the externalities of oil use and the need to balance supply-side measures with action on demand—retain a strong hold in many corridors of power and lead to different but similarly dangerous destinations.

We all need to ensure that the doomsday future does not materialize, that we supply future generations with at least the same abundance of energy as we have had, at reasonable prices, in an economically rational way. And I include in this rationality that our future energy use, whatever form it takes, must have a radically lower impact on the global environment than it does today, particularly in avoiding major climate change. Now is the time to take a holistic view, to look for solutions rather than problems, and to ensure the honorable continuation of the Age of Oil and, in time, its honorable end.

Notes

CHAPTER 1

1. *The Scotsman*, April 19, 2003.

2. Knabb, Richard D.; Rhome, Jamie R.; Brown, Daniel P. Tropical Cyclone Report: Hurricane Katrina: 23–30, 2005. National Hurricane Center.

3. Fagot, Caryl; Winbush, Debra. Hurricane Katrina/Hurricane Rita Evacuation and Production Shut-in Statistics Report as of Wednesday, February 22, 2006. U.S. Government Minerals Management Service.

4. http://www.time.com/time/nation/article/0,8599,1099102,00.html.

5. e.g., Labohm *et al.* (2004); Gray (2002); Kininmonth (2004).

6. e.g. Lomborg (2006); Lomborg (2007).

7. Quoted in *The Observer*, January 14, 2001, http://www.oilendgame.com/pdfs/WtOEg_Quotes.pdf.

8. Dick Cheney, April 30, 2001, http://www.pbs.org/newshour/bb/environment/energy/cheney_4-30.html.

9. Lovins (November/December 1977). The Mother Earth-Plowboy Interview, p. 22.

10. In the style of Bjørn Lomborg but without agreeing with all of his arguments.

11. Durham Mining Museum (1999–2005) http://www.dmm.org.uk/stats/toutput.htm.

12. Indigenous coal, oil, gas, and renewable energy.

13. Skov (2002).

14. Organization for Economic Cooperation and Development, a group of mainly developed countries, including significant oil producers such as Australia, Canada, Denmark, Mexico, Norway, the United Kingdom, and the United States.

CHAPTER 2

1. For example, Zittel and Schinder (2003).

2. To be more accurate, Laherrère is a petroleum engineer.

3. Although others have other backgrounds such as investment banking and law.

4. For example, Zittel and Schindler (2007).

5. For example, Matthew Simmons' *Twilight in the Desert*, an engaging book, but, for an investment banker, oddly short on quantitative data.

6. A basin, so named for its shape, is a depression in the Earth's crust, formed in various ways and filled with sedimentary rocks and is the usual locus for oil and gas accumulations.

7. http://www.gasandoil.com/GOC/news/nte63334.htm.

8. A phrase used by, for example, Zittel and Schindler (2003); Clarke (2007a).

9. Lomborg (2001).

10. For example, Economides and Oligney (2000).

11. Takin (2006).

12. For example, Mitchell *et al.* (2001).

13. I am myself a firm believer in the need for a Middle East peace settlement and in the general futility of military action to solve political problems. However, as I discuss in Chapter 8, I feel many peace activists oversimplify the relationship between oil and war.

14. For example, Croissant and Aras (1999); Kleveman (2003).

15. For example, Klare (2001).

16. Ironically, the government stake was, much later, to be sold by another famous Conservative, Margaret Thatcher, much more of a free marketer. However, national security was enough of a concern for her to force the Kuwaitis to reduce their 21.6 percent holding to 9.9 percent.

17. http://www.sierraclub.org/carlpope/archive/2006_03_07_index.asp.

18. Heavy oil is more dense than light oil, is more viscous (stickier) and hence harder to extract, is worth less, and generally contains more contaminants such as sulphur that are environmentally damaging.

19. Oil shales are petroleum source rocks that have not been "matured" by underground temperature and pressure. Oil can be "cooked" from them artificially, although with present methods at high cost and environmental impact.

20. Heinberg (2005).

21. Darley (2004).

22. Diamond (2006).

23. For example, Schopenhauer (1818/1819).

24. *Monty Python and the Holy Grail*, Scene 3, Line 31.

CHAPTER 3

1. Quoted at http://en.wikibooks.org/wiki/Investing/Stock_market.

2. That part of the oil business concerned with finding and extracting oil from the ground.

3. http://www.financialsense.com/market/puplava/2005/0722.html.

4. *The Economist*, March 1999.

5. PILOT (2006) Exploration Update.

6. I generally quote production figures summing both crude oil and NGLs, because they are widely intersubstitutable and are often not distinguished in official statistics. Many peak oil writers make a point of separating the two.

7. e.g., Cummins and Beasant (2005).

8. Shell itself has generally used the term "recategorization" when perhaps "decategorization" or debooking would be more terminologically exact.

9. Using cost figures from the Department of Energy (1996). Inflated from 1995 to 2007 prices.

10. http://www.earlywarning.com/articles/2005_06_13_china_cars_drive.

11. Verberg (2006).

12. www.ipa.or.id/files/Industry_Cost_Trends_IPA_March_28_2006.pdf.

13. Yergin, D., speech to the Arab Strategy Forum, Dubai, December 4, 2006.

14. Marathon's Garyville plant.

15. Complexity being a measure of how much of the crude oil feedstock a refinery can turn into the more valuable light products, such as gasoline, diesel, and jet fuel.

16. Quoted at http://www.aramcoexpat.com/Articles/Pipeline/Saudi-Aramco-News/Industry-News/795.aspx.

17. Drollas (2006a).

18. http://eh.net/hmit/interest_rate/.

19. http://eh.net/hmit/interest_rate/.

20. http://www.fossil.energy.gov/programs/reserves/spr/index.html.

21. Amuzegar (2001).

22. http://en.wikiquote.org/wiki/George_Best.

CHAPTER 4

1. Quoted at http://www.mkinghubbert.com/tribute/quotes.

2. Campbell (1997) suggests 1,850 billion bbl excluding NGLs and heavy oil. Campbell (2006), spreadsheet downloadable from his website, revised 8/15/2006, indicates 1,900 billion bbl, excluding NGLs, heavy oil, and deepwater/polar oil. Deffeyes (2001) gave a "reasonably generous upper guess" of 2.1 trillion bbl.

3. http://www.mnp.nl/hyde/prod_data/oil/. Includes NGLs.

4. Yergin (1991), p. 567.

5. Quoted at http://www.priweb.org/ed/pgws/history/signal_hill/signal_hill2.html.

6. Noroil, December 1989.

7. Campbell (1997).

8. Quoted at http://www.oilendgame.com/pdfs/WtOEg_Quotes.pdf.

9. Quoted at http://www.bp.com/genericarticle.do?categoryId=9013455&contentId=7026726.

10. World Oil production CAPacity.

11. Samsan Bakhtiari (2004).

12. e.g., Popper (1934).

13. Yergin (1991), p. 567.

14. Not an attempt to replicate Hubbert's original prediction but uses his predicted peak year of 1970, with an EUR of 188.5 billion bbl.

15. http://www.after-oil.co.uk/energy.htm.

16. http://wolf.readinglitho.co.uk/mainpages/reserves.html#.

17. Or, slightly more sophisticatedly but also wrongly, drawn a logistic plot as Laherrère, in particular, among peak oilers, does.

18. Even then, abandoned fields are not infrequently reactivated.

19. Asimov (1994).

20. Laherrère (2003).

21. Heinberg (2005), http://www.apachecorp.com/About_Us/Press_Room/Arrows_Newsletter/Archives/December_2005/Forties_Field_bigger_than_perceived/, December 2005.

22. Lynch (2006b).

23. Laherrère (2001).

24. http://www.upstreamonline.com/live/article142516.ece; http://www.tnk-bp.com/operations/exploration-production/projects/samotlor/.

25. Lyle (2007).

26. The "recovery factor" is a percentage indicating how much of the oil or gas in the ground can be recovered. It is typically between 30 and 65 percent for oil and 60 and 80 percent for gas but depends on factors such as geology, fluid type, development plan, technology, and economics.

27. For instance, Smith (2006), who is otherwise one of the best of the peak oil writers in terms of analytical depth and rigor.

28. Vidal (2005). The Hubbert curve is anyway a logistic curve, superficially similar to a bell curve but with important differences.

29. Rodgers (2005).

30. Nehring (2006).

31. Popper (1934).

32. The injection of gas or water underground to maintain pressure and improve oil recovery, techniques that began to be widely adopted in the 1960s.

33. Hubbert (1956).

34. Tcf is the common industry (non-SI) abbreviation for "trillion cubic feet," the usual measure for large volumes of gas.

35. The part of the oil business concerned with refining oil into products and selling it.

36. Maugeri (2006).

37. http://www.dailywealth.com/archive/2006/oct/2006_oct_31.asp.

38. A reservoir is a porous and permeable subsurface unit of rock, which holds oil, gas, or both in the pore spaces between the rock grains, from where it can be extracted by wells.

39. Kalt (1981), in Taylor and Van Doren (2006).

40. e.g., Associated Press (August 6, 1954), "Statements on Iran Oil Accord."

41. e.g., Bamford, D., *Appreciating Reserves Growth?* http://www.oilvoice.com/ov_features/OV%20Reserves_Growth.doc.

42. Except, possibly, Korpela (2006).

43. "Play" is a somewhat loosely defined term referring to a number of oil/gas fields in the same geographical area with the same key features. For instance, "Northern North Sea Jurassic sandstone reservoirs in tilted fault blocks sourced by Kimmeridge shales" is a play.

44. Campbell (2000), quoted in Lynch (2006b).

45. Reserves/production, i.e., total reserves divided by annual production to give a number that represents, notionally, how many years the reserves would last if production were maintained at a constant rate. This is, of course, not physically possible, but the R/P ratio is a useful benchmark if not taken literally.

46. Hubbert (1956).

47. Hubbert (1971).

48. A graben is a narrow, elongate valley formed by extension of the Earth's crust, as in the Great Rift Valley of East Africa. They are often the locus of major oil and gas accumulations, as in the North Sea, Gulf of Suez (Egypt), Sudan, and Yemen.

49. Smith (2006).

50. Effectively a very light oil, extracted from natural gas, and ideal for refining into gasoline.

51. Very heavy oil, which will not flow naturally and has to be extracted and upgraded using special methods. Found in enormous quantities and at shallow depths in Alberta.

52. Or at least, barely increases over the span of human civilization. Some estimates suggest that about 1 million new barrels of oil are generated within the Earth per year as source rocks mature, an insignificant figure compared with annual extraction of nearly 30 billion bbl. Even if the "abiogenic" theory were correct, there is no reason to believe generation rates to be any higher than this.

53. e.g., Gold (1999), and, for a refutation, Mello and Moldowan (2005).

54. Quoted in Greenwood *et al.* (2007).

55. Apart from Abu Dhabi, which does have significant equity involvement by companies such as ExxonMobil, Total, BP, and Shell.

56. How much of a company's annual production is replaced by new discoveries and revisions, extensions, and increased recovery in existing fields. An reserve replacement ratio of less than 100 percent indicates that a company's reserves are shrinking.

57. e.g., Campbell (1997, 2005); Blanchard (2005).

58. Gabon left in January 1995.

59. Campbell (2006).

60. Peak oil writers laud Khalimov as "the former Soviet deputy oil minister," without mentioning that, as Gustafson (1990) recounts, he oversaw a bungled attempt at enhancing Soviet oil recovery and was fired for attempting to cover up his failure with falsified figures.

61. http://www.monbiot.com/archives/2005/09/27/crying-sheep/#more-952.

62. Yergin (1991); Sampson (1993).

63. Quoted at http://thinkexist.com/quotation/formula_for_success-rise_early-work_hard-strike/209738.html.

64. Harper (2005).

65. Longwell (2002), pp. 100–4.

66. A Formation is a geological unit of rock of a common type, geography, and age. For instance, the Arab Formation, the world's most important oil reservoir, is made up of carbonates (limestone and dolomite) deposited in mostly shallow marine conditions in what is now eastern Saudi Arabia and neighboring countries, during the later Jurassic Period, about 150 million years ago.

67. Found in a separate accumulation from oil, not dissolved in the oil or floating on top of it as a "gas cap."

68. Afifi (2005).

69. And by far the world's largest offshore gas field (indeed, the largest onshore or offshore), despite Russian claims for Shtokmanovskoye in the Barents Sea, often uncritically repeated by the media.

70. Hubbert, independently, used this analogy in his 1956 paper when talking of the progress of petroleum exploration.

71. Converting gas to oil, usually using the energy equivalence of 1 barrel of oil ≈5,700–6,000 cubic feet of gas.

72. Flattening of the curve toward some maximum value.

73. A well drilled to test an entirely new prospect, not an extension of an existing field.

74. e.g., Campbell (2005), p. 151.

75. Arctic National Wildlife Refuge, an area of Alaska in which oil exploration is not currently permitted.

76. U.S. Minerals Management Service, quoted in Hart's E&P, February 2007.

77. Comprising the Arab members of OPEC (Algeria, Kuwait, Iraq, Libya, Qatar, Saudi Arabia, and UAE), plus Bahrain, Egypt, Syria, and (membership currently suspended) Tunisia.

78. Mann (2007).

79. Based partly on Longwell (2002), p. 100–4.

80. I have shown only "active" OPEC members to exclude Iraq and Angola (which are not currently bound by quotas) and Indonesia (which produces well below its quota and, being a net importer, has no incentive to keep prices high). Among countries shown as "No foreign involvement," Saudi Arabia has recently allowed some limited gas (but not oil) exploration by foreign companies. Mexico has had some highly restricted participation in gas by (mostly small) foreign companies under "Multiple Service Contracts." Most Western companies have been obliged, as a result of shareholder, government, and NGO pressure, to withdraw from Sudan and Myanmar in recent years, being replaced by Chinese, Indian, Malaysian, Korean, UAE, Kuwaiti, and other firms. Sanctions are also holding back investment in Iran. Russia has reserved large deposits and the leading role in frontier exploration, for state companies. I could have added Argentina, Brazil, Mauritania, Bangladesh, Indonesia, Turkmenistan, and Kazakhstan to the list, all of which, in different ways, have made things difficult for foreign oil companies in the recent past, or Yemen and Pakistan where (rather exaggerated) security concerns have kept some investors away.

81. Laherrère (2002).

82. The R/P ratio is derived by dividing reserves by annual production, so giving a figure for how many years the reserves would last if production were maintained at that level. It should not be interpreted literally, because production will inevitably fall off as reserves decline below a certain level, but it is a useful comparative benchmark.

83. http://www.peakoil.ie/newsletters/758.

84. i.e., after the OPEC reserves additions of the 1980s that Geologists dismiss.

85. Rushworth *et al.* (2006).

86. The deficit of discoveries against production is also exaggerated by peak oil sympathisers, who often count deepwater, Arctic, heavy, and other unconventional oil in the production total, but not in discoveries.

87. NGLs, light hydrocarbons extracted from natural gas but liquid under room temperature and pressure, and partly a substitute for oil.

88. U.K. Department of Trade and Industry, http://www.og.dti.gov.uk/information/bb_updates/chapters/Table4_5.htm.

89. Campbell (2006).

90. http://www.aapg.org/explorer/2006/01jan/discoveries_list.cfm.

91. A volcanic rock, which makes up the Giant's Causeway in Northern Ireland and most of Iceland.

92. A "trap" is a combination of reservoir rocks and seal, in such a geometric combination that oil and gas can be trapped there for long periods of time (millions of years or more). The simplest trap type is a dome.

93. e.g., Vidal (2005); http://www.peakoil.net/uhdsg/weo2004/TheUppsalaCode.html; Strahan, D., http://www.davidstrahan.com/blog/?p=57#more-57.

94. Campbell (2005), p. 151.

95. Seismic uses sound waves to give a view of the subsurface. Three-dimensional seismic gives a more complete picture and has progressively superseded the older two-dimensional seismic since the early 1990s.

96. Campbell (2006).

97. Technically speaking, P95, P50, and P5. There is a 95 percent chance of finding at least the P95 estimate (low), 50 percent chance of finding more than the P50, and 5 percent chance of exceeding the P5 (high). The USGS uses the equivalent terms F5, F50, and F95.

98. A layer of impermeable rock, such as shale or salt, overlying the reservoir and preventing the oil or gas escaping to surface.

99. A rock, usually black shale or limestone, containing organic material that, when subject to heat and pressure, converts to oil and gas, which have the chance to migrate into reservoir rocks.

100. http://www.upstreamonline.com/live/article142309.ece.

101. 10,000 bbl/day.

102. http://www.rigzone.com/news/article.asp?a_id=37532.

103. The onshore Cretaceous reservoirs in the Zagros-Mesopotamian Cretaceous-Tertiary Total Petroleum System, predicted to have a midcase YtF of 23.755 billion bbl, versus some 16 billion bbl in Azadegan and Yadavaran.

104. Campbell (2006).

105. API gravity is a measure of the density of oil. Confusingly, a low API means a heavy oil, and a high API is a light oil. Water has an API gravity of 10, so any oil with API higher than 10 will float above water. Heavy oil is usually considered to have an API of 10–20°. The benchmark Brent grade is 38.3° API, a light oil. Light oils are generally less viscous, lower in sulphur, and more valuable.

106. I have linearly interpolated Campbell's (2006) production figures up to 2030 (he gives figures for 2005, 2010, 2020, and 2030) and then declined production exponentially after 2030 at the same decline rate as from 2029 to 2030. I have assumed that Campbell's reductions in Congo and Vietnam relate to deepwater, those in Libya and Italy to heavy oil, and those in Russia to polar oil (although some of this could be heavy oil or NGLs). I further assume that Venezuelan YtF is just conventional oil.

107. One of them being the oddity of Hungary, ascribed 4.1 billion bbl, four times Norway and five times the United Kingdom! This may well be a typographical error.

108. Based on Campbell (2006) and Blanchard (2005).

109. Berman (2008).

110. Klett *et al.* (2005); Klett *et al.* (2007).

111. Another estimate is somewhat more positive: Chew (2005).

112. Chew (2005).

113. Birol (2006).

114. Currie (2005).

115. Alternative Investment Market, a section of the market in the United Kingdom where regulatory requirements are less strict, populated mainly by small companies.

116. Along with their initial underestimates of OPEC reserves, the boom in unconventional oil, and the resurgence in FSU production, which are also species of reserves growth, or at least, of translating reserves into production via improved technology and efficient investment.

117. Brunei Shell Petroleum, http://www.bsp.com.bn/main/aboutbsp/about_oil_gas.asp.

118. http://www.gasandoil.com/goc/discover/dix70744.htm.

119. The total oil in a field before the beginning of extraction. Only a percentage of this (the recovery factor, typically 30–65 percent, but less for heavy oil) can be produced to surface. Dissolved gas in the oil is separated out in the surface facilities, causing it to shrink, so oil recovered is slightly less than the volume underground.

120. Fracturing the rock with high pressure or explosives, dissolving it with acid, and other techniques to improve flow in the near vicinity of the well.

121. Baxendell, P., quoted in Arnold (1978).

122. Norwegian Petroleum Directorate, http://www.npd.no/cgi-bin/MsmGo.exe?grab_id=25&EXTRA_ARG=&CFGNAME=MssFindEN%2Ecfg&host_id=42&page_id=7871232&query=yet+to+find&hiword=find+to+yet+.

123. Gould, A., Schlumberger CEO, 35th Annual Offshore Technology Conference, May 4, 2004.

124. Campbell (2006).

125. Rasmussen (2007), p. 99.

126. *Offshore*, October 2006.

127. *The Outlook for Energy—a View to 2020.* ExxonMobil; and *The Lamp* (2005), vol. 87, no. 1, http://www.exxonmobil.com/corporate/Newsroom/Publications/TheLamp_1_2005/html/story3.asp.

128. Aanensen (2007).

129. A synonym for Enhanced Oil Recovery. "Primary recovery" uses only wells; "secondary recovery" involves the injection of gas and/or water to maintain pressure.

130. Zittel and Schindler, *op. cit.*

131. Bentley (2002).

132. Hubbert (1956).

133. Farouq Ali (2003).

134. Thompson *et al.* (2005).

135. Tamayo (2005).

136. Jakobsen *et al.* (2005).

137. Beecy (2005).

138. Isaac (2005).

139. Malaysia (2005).

140. Gielen and Unander (2005).

141. Jakobsen *et al.* (2005).

142. Advanced Resources International (2005).

143. Actually, only about 35 percent of the CO_2 injected is from artificial sources; most is produced from natural underground sources. However, in principle, it could all be anthropogenic, particularly if polluters were required to pay for the safe disposal of their emissions.

144. http://www.bbc.co.uk/climate/policies/usa_policy.shtml.

145. Denbury Resources (2004).

146. Jakobsen *et al.* (2005).

147. Hughes (2006).

148. Hughes (2006).

149. International Energy Agency (2003).

150. Al-Kafeef and Zaid (1994).

151. Lemigas (2006).

152. Malaysia (2005).

153. Moore (2006).

154. Simbeck (2006).

155. Rushworth *et al.* (2006).

156. Quoted at http://en.wikipedia.org/wiki/Peak_oil.

157. http://news.bbc.co.uk/2/hi/business/4713186.stm.

158. Longhurst (1959).

159. Brown (1999).

160. http://www.dukeswoodoilmuseum.co.uk/the_tragedies.htm.

161. Orrell (2000).

162. http://heritage.scotsman.com/diagrams.cfm?cid=7&id=603202006.

163. http://news.bbc.co.uk/onthisday/hi/dates/stories/july/6/newsid_3017000/3017294.stm.

164. Hill and Gaddy (2003).

165. Gustafson (1990).

166. Simmons (2002).

167. Based mostly on Skrebowski, C. (2005).

168. http://petrochemical.ihs.com/news-05Q2/cera-global-oil-production-capacity.jsp.

169. Wood MacKenzie, quoted at http://www.rigzone.com/news/article.asp?a_id=42236.

170. *Petroleum Intelligence Weekly*, vol. XLV, no.48, November 27, 2006.

171. Goldman Sachs, Europe: *Energy: Oil Services*, August 7, 2007, foreseeing an additional 16 million bbl/day of new oil production from their "top 170" projects by 2014.

172. Overestimates attributable to slippage of projects may be at least partly compensated by underreporting of new field developments.

173. Gould, A., Schlumberger CEO, 35th Annual Offshore Technology Conference, May 4, 2004.

174. Rodgers (2005).

175. 1.7 million bbl from major new fields, 1 million bbl from smaller fields (37 percent of world supply comes from fields yielding less than 50,000 bbl/day). This assumes that new smaller fields made a pro rata contribution to supply with the new larger fields. World production increased by 0.9 million bbl/day from 2004 to 2005, implying total underlying decline of 1.8 million bbl/day. The same methodology suggests non-OPEC underlying decline of 3.4–5 percent, which is consistent with IEA figures of 4–5 percent (*Oil & Gas Journal*, March 18 2008). Actually, smaller fields probably made an even greater contribution than purely pro rata, which would reduce underlying declines still further. CERA's research suggests a somewhat higher total (OPEC & non-OPEC) decline of 4.5 percent, but still significantly lower than many peak oil forecasts (Jackson and Eastwood (2008)).

176. Estimated from data in Simmons (2002).

177. UBS (2007).

178. Drollas (2006b).

179. World Oil, December 2006, p. 75.

180. Dylan Powell (2004).

181. http://www.gasandoil.com/goc/discover/dix93997.htm.

182. Directional wells, i.e., 12,000 meters of well-bore length, not 12,000 meters straight down.

183. Kliewer (2006a), p. 42.

184. The peak oil camp have not managed to generate similar multidisciplinary estimates from major research organizations or corporations, which no doubt some of them would adduce as evidence of a conspiracy.

185. From data compiled in Al-Husseini (2006).

CHAPTER 5

1. Quoted in numerous locations, e.g., http://www.jewishworldreview.com/kathleen/parker093002.asp.

2. Campbell (2006).

3. Henriques *et al.* (2006).

4. Simmons (2005).

5. http://www.fromthewilderness.com/free/ww3/031704_two_planets.html.

6. Jeans, P. J. "New Developments in Middle East Exploration and Production," http://www.pj-exploration.com/aapg.htm.

7. http://www.gasandoil.com/goc/discover/dix71383.htm.

8. Busby (2005).

9. Maugeri (2006).

10. http://www.arabnews.com/?page=6&section=0&article=44011&d=29&m=4&y=2004.

11. Simmons (2005).

12. Takin (2005).

13. Saudi Aramco, in Drollas (2006b).

14. World Oil, August 2006.

15. http://www.globalinsight.com/SDA/SDADetail6310.htm.

16. Simmons (2005), p. 91.

17. Simmons, M.R. "The Saudi Arabian Oil Miracle."

18. Permeability is a measure of how easily fluid will flow through a rock. High-permeability reservoirs produce oil and gas at a higher rate and hence are cheaper to develop than those of low permeability. However, a mixture of high and low permeability complicates reservoir development.

19. Cantrell and Hagerty (2003).

20. Cantrell *et al.* (2004).

21. http://mysite.verizon.net/vze495hz/id65.html.

22. http://home.entouch.net/dmd/ghawar.htm. The original quotation is from Roberts (2005), p. 1. Roberts makes the initial error about the sandstone in Ghawar, perhaps more forgivable in a journalist.

23. Al-Wardy, A. http://gcceu-conference.epu.ntua.gr/LinkClick.aspx?link= documents%2F07.Al-Wardi.pdf&tabid=76&mid=451.

24. Wojtanowicz (2003).

25. Coxe (2005).

26. *Offshore*, October 2006.

27. Or maintaining pressure with gas injection, depending on the reservoir characteristics and production strategy.

28. http://searchingforthetruth.typepad.com/searching_for_the_truth/2005/05/the_ questionabl.html.

29. Usually to recover extra gas, and some oil, as in the Brent and Statfjord fields in the North Sea.

30. Fleming (2000).

31. http://home.entouch.net/dmd/ghawar.htm.

32. The "Empty Quarter."

33. The time before the emergence of hard-shelled fossil life, earlier than 542 million years before present.

34. Rocks crystallized from molten lava or magma, or altered by great heat and pressure, and (except in very rare circumstances) nonprospective for hydrocarbons.

35. Around the end of the Precambrian.

36. Dyer and Husseini (1991).

37. Lynch (2006a).

38. *American Association of Petroleum Geologists Explorer*, vol. 28, no. 1, January 2007.

39. "Rich" gas contains a high content of valuable liquid hydrocarbons, such as condensate ("natural gasoline") and LPG.

40. Simmons (2005).

41. Anon., *Association for the Study of Peak Oil and Gas Newsletter*, no. 39, March 2004.

42. Fageeha (2006).

43. *Oil and Gas Journal*, December 10, 2007.

44. Lynch (2006a).

45. Bordenave (2002).

46. Saidi (1996).

47. National Iranian Oil Company. National oil companies always have unimaginative names compared with Shell, Total, Venture, Endeavour, Golden Dynasty, Nighthawk, Merlin, and other such companies that have to market themselves. Even boring British Petroleum tried to become Beyond Petroleum a few years ago.

48. http://www.moneyweek.com/file/18243/why-we-must-take-peak-oil-seriously.html.

49. World Oil (February 2008), p. 35.

50. Centre for Global Energy Studies, end 2002.

51. Takin (2005), *op. cit.*

52. Winsloe (1999).

53. Ghadban *et al.*, Middle East Economic Survey (MEES), 20th March 1995.

54. Arab Oil & Gas Directory, 2001.

55. Not, admittedly, in the case of some of the more recent discoveries, such as Majnoon, found in 1975 by Braspetro, the forerunner of Petrobras, Brazil's national oil company.

56. 23.7 percent Shell, 23.7 percent BP (then Anglo-Persian), Compagnie Française des Pétroles (now Total), 23.7 percent between five American companies including Exxon (then Standard Oil of New Jersey) and Mobil (then Standard Oil of New York), 5 percent Gulbenkian (now Partex).

57. Takin (2005), *op. cit.*

58. Indicating the generally poor data quality for Iraq, there is doubt even on the number of wells drilled. The Centre for Global Energy Studies quotes 514 prospects, of which 114 have been drilled, yielding seventy-three discoveries, a success rate somewhat lower, but still very good, at 64 percent. Of the 400 undrilled prospects, 239 are considered to have a "high degree of certainty."

59. Attanasi and Root (1988).

60. *Time Europe*, October 10, 2006.

61. Even if they are not extended, the reserves will obviously continue to be produced, by either new participants or the Abu Dhabi national oil company ADNOC.

62. Takin (2006), *op. cit.*

63. e.g., Loutfi and Abul Hamd (1987).

64. Low-permeability, hence requiring many wells to extract.

65. A graben, from the German for "grave," is an elongate geological feature, where the Earth's crust has been extended, leading to sinking of a central valley and elevation of the flanks. It may be several kilometers wide and tens or hundreds of kilometers long. The Great Rift Valley of East Africa consists of a long chain of such structures. They are very promising sites for oil and gas formation and accumulation, as in the northern North Sea, Egypt's Gulf of Suez, and other places.

66. Luker, T., address to the Society of Petroleum Engineers, Dubai, April 3 2008.

67. http://www.pdo.co.om/PDO/NewsandLibrary/Speeches/Oil+and+Gas+West+Asia+Conference+and+Exhibition+2002.htm.

68. The Government of Oman owns 60 percent of PDO, Shell has a 34 percent shareholding, Total 4 percent, and Partex 2 percent.

69. Takin (2005), *op. cit.*

70. Linear interpolation from Campbell's 2010 and 2020 figures. Campbell is probably not including the Mukhaizna field in Oman in his figures, because it is

heavy oil (15° API) and he has a separate category for oil <17.5° API. If he is excluding it, some 14,000 bbl/day should be added back to his figures.

71. Rusk, in Downey *et al.* (2001).

72. IHS Energy, in Arab Oil and Gas Directory (2005), Arab Petroleum Research Centre. Assuming a very good but not leading-edge recovery factor of 57 percent.

73. http://www.signonsandiego.com/news/business/20061209-0145-energy-algeria.html.

74. Campbell (2006).

75. http://news.bbc.co.uk/2/hi/africa/4646068.stm.

76. Energy Information Administration, http://www.eia.doe.gov/emeu/cabs/World_Energy_Hotspots/Nigeria.html.

77. Busby (2005).

78. http://www.ob-data.com/pressreleases/roc070807.txt.

79. Gustafson (1990).

80. Samsam Bakhtiari (2004). Also repeated in Busby (2005).

81. http://www.environmenttimes.net/article.cfm?pageID=61.

82. Kliewer (2006b).

83. http://www.offshore-environment.com/russianoil.html.

84. http://www.offshore-environment.com/russianoil.html.

85. http://www.gasandoil.com/GOC/company/cnr44172.htm.

86. First Break (September 2005), http://www.firstbreak.nl/content.php?section=3&id=1858&issue=113&TAB=2&lang=&PHPSESSID=bc29ed9c89bd484f2e130ec443ffd80f.

87. Which puts into perspective the United States' difficulties over deciding on a gas pipeline from Alaska's North Slope to the contiguous United States.

88. Ferguson (2005).

89. Erochkine and Erochkine (2006).

90. *St. Petersburg Times*, October 23, 2001.

91. *Pravda*, May 13, 2004.

92. e.g., Elliott *et al.* (1998).

93. If Brazil's recent Carioca-Sugar Loaf is not ultimately found to be bigger.

94. BG, BP, and Statoil (now Statoil Hydro) have subsequently sold their shares.

95. Thus justifying its name ("Sea" in Kazakh, related to Genghis, the "Oceanic" or universal Khan).

96. Zempolich (2002).

97. http://www.agipkco.com/en/what_we_doing/what_we_doing_en.htm.

98. *Oil and Gas Middle East*, p. 13, January 2007.

99. *Financial Times*, November 26, 2006.

100. Ulmishek (2001).

101. Lower estimates from Busby (2005). Higher estimates from Lee (2006).

102. Busby (2005).

103. http://www.rigzone.com/news/article.asp?a_id=39102.

104. *Oil & Gas Journal*, vol. 105, issue 1, January 1, 2007, http://www.ogj.com/articles/article_display.cfm?article_id=280966.

105. http://home.entouch.net/dmd/cantarell.htm.

106. Kuo (2001).

107. Suarez Coppel and Yepez (2006).

108. Busby (2005).

109. http://www.forbes.com/business/2006/05/10/oil-company-expenditures-cx_0511oxford.html.

110. "Pemex poised to offset declining reserves," *Offshore*, September 2006.

111. Luhnow (2007).

112. Mondragon (2001).

113. Busby (2005).

114. "Pemex poised to offset declining reserves," *Offshore*, September 2006.

115. Mondragon (2001).

116. A substantial portion of which may be natural gas.

117. The United Kingdom is the other major counterexample, achieving the fabled "energy independence" in 1981, a prospect that had provoked the former Prime Minister Harold Wilson to comment that he looked forward to joining OPEC. However, the United Kingdom is shortly to lose this status, and other countries, such as the United States and China, have seen, like Wilkins Micawber, expenditure exceed income some time ago.

118. 52.5 percent of the shares are held by the Brazilian state, which has managerial control.

119. http://news.bbc.co.uk/2/hi/business/4563896.stm.

120. http://www.noticiaspetrobras.com.br/interna.asp?idioma=ing&id_noticia=2498&nome=Economia&id_editoria=22.

121. http://www.rigzone.com/news/article.asp?a_id=39551.

122. http://www.upstreamonline.com/live/article143799.ece.

123. http://www.aapg.org/explorer/2003/09sep/gulf.cfm.

124. Hofmeister, J., http://www.newsobserver.com/126/story/501206.html.

125. Attanasi (2005).

126. http://www.fe.doe.gov/programs/oilgas/eor/index.html.

127. Hughes (2006).

128. Busby (2005).

129. Canadian Association of Petroleum Producers, in *Petroleum Intelligence Weekly*, vol. XLV, no. 42.

130. Fees paid to obtain exploration rights.

131. *Offshore*, November 2006, p. 16.

132. Locke *et al.* (2006).

133. Terje Overvik, Statoil Vice President for Norway E&P, quoted in *Upstream*, vol. 11, week 41, October 13, 2006.

134. http://www.signonsandiego.com/news/business/20070228-1029-norway-arcticoilfind.html.

135. *Offshore*, April 2007.

136. http://www.rigzone.com/news/article.asp?a_id=25997.

137. http://www.eubusiness.com/Energy/060324142729.0nrvketg.

138. Hughes (2006).

139. http://www.rigzone.com/news/article.asp?a_id=43697.

140. Rocks formed by submarine flows of sand and other material, one of the key reservoirs in deepwater basins.

141. *Offshore*, October 2006.

142. Formed in lakes, unlike most source rocks, which are marine.

143. http://news.bbc.co.uk/2/hi/business/6076636.stm.

144. And promptly begun to squander its wealth on corruption and arms and to extort money from the companies who took the risk to develop the oil in the first place, despite elaborate financial procedures put in place by the World Bank.

145. Grynberg (2005).

146. http://www.gasandoil.com/goc/discover/dix50439.htm.

147. *Oil & Gas Journal*, vol. 105, issue 3, January 15, 2007.

148. Busby (2005).

149. *Oil & Gas Journal*, vol. 105, issue 3, January 15, 2007.

150. http://www.tgsnopec.com/newsroom/newsroom_details.asp?id=310.

151. e.g., Blanchard (2005).

152. http://www.chevron.com/news/speeches/2002/26feb2002_robertson.asp.

153. i.e., formed during the Tertiary sub-era, 65–1.8 million years ago.

154. http://www.gulfnews.com/business/Oil_and_Gas/10079756.html.

155. http://www.arabnews.com/?page=6&section=0&article=89745&d=8&m=12&y=2006&pix=business.jpg&category=Business.

156. Busby (2005).

157. *Offshore*, November 2006, p. 60.

158. *Offshore*, November 2006, p. 60.

159. Distortion of seismic images caused by gas leaking from a trap, found over many fields worldwide with imperfect seals.

160. Unusually high or low reflectivity of seismic waves induced by the presence of oil and gas.

161. EnCana Corp., "Farmin Opportunity in Offshore West Greenland."

162. *American Association of Petroleum Geologists Explorer*, http://www.aapg.org/explorer/2006/10oct/antarctica.cfm.

CHAPTER 6

1. http://classics.mit.edu/Antoninus/meditations.8.eight.html.

2. Odell (2004).

3. Yergin (1991), *op. cit.*, p. 53.

4. Aleklett and Campbell.

5. Meyer and Attanasi (2003).

6. With, as I have argued, plenty more to be added through future exploration and reserves growth.

7. Partly based on Schlumberger, www.heavyoilinfo.com.

8. A mixture of propane and butane, familiar as bottled gas used for home cooking, camping, etc. Not to be confused with LNG, which consists almost entirely of methane.

9. Burnt, in the absence of productive uses for it.

10. Grape (2006).

11. "EOG to pursue North Park basin Niobrara oil," *Oil & Gas Journal*, Vol.106, Issue 12, March 24, 2008; Finn and Johnson (2005).

12. "EOG makes Barnett shale oil discovery," *Oil & Gas Journal*, Vol.106, Issue 12, March 24, 2008.

13. Goff (2005).

14. Alcazar-Cancino *et al.* (2004).

15. *World Oil*, January 2007, p. 19.

16. Jiayu and Jianyi (1999).

17. Gao *et al.* (2006).

18. http://www.rigzone.com/analysis/heavyoil/insight.asp?i_id=193.

19. http://www.arabianbusiness.com/502422-kuwait-in-deal-to-boost-output-by-900000-bpd?ln=en.

20. Nasr and Ayodele (2005).

21. Oxenford and Sit (2004).

22. Saxton (2006).

23. Snyder (2000).

24. Kerr *et al.* (2002).

25. http://www.petrobank.com/hea-overview.html.

26. http://www.utilisenergy.com/oilsands.html.

27. Busby (2005).

28. Campbell (2006).

29. Alberta Chamber of Resources (2004).

30. CHOPS—Cold Heavy Oil Production with Sand in the Canadian Heavy Oil Industry.

31. Stanton (2004).

32. Oilsands Quest Inc., company presentation, March 2007.

33. http://rigzone.com/analysis/heavyoil/insight.asp?i_id=193.

34. World Energy Council, http://www.worldenergy.org/wec-geis/publications/reports/ser/bitumen/bitumen.asp.

35. http://www.rigzone.com/analysis/heavyoil/insight.asp?i_id=193.

36. Meyer and Freeman (2006).

37. http://www.oiltechinc.com/profile.html.

38. Other *in situ* oil shale extraction methods are under investigation. See, for instance, Shurtleff and Doyle (2008).

39. Dyni (2005).

40. Millan and McMahon (2007).

41. Wood MacKenzie, quoted at http://www.rigzone.com/news/article.asp?a_id=41484.

42. World Energy Council Survey of Energy Resources (2001). http://www.worldenergy.org/wec-geis/publications/reports/ser/shale/shale.asp.

43. Dyni (2005).

44. USGS Professional Paper 820, quoted by Pitman, W., http://www.ldeo.columbia.edu/edu/dees/U4735/lectures/12.html.

45. Of course, they overlooked the much more serious immediate competition: new conventional oil (North Sea, Mexico, Alaska, and the Soviet Union), efficiency and fuel substitution, and demand destruction via recession.

46. Maugeri (2006).

47. Davis (2004).

48. Global Gas Flaring Reduction, http://web.worldbank.org/WBSITE/EXTERNAL/TOPICS/EXTOGMC/EXTGGFR/0,,contentMDK:21023030~menuPK:2856589~pagePK:64168445~piPK:64168309~theSitePK:578069,00.html.

49. Davies (2004).

50. Fabricius (2006).

51. Institute Français du Pétrole (2006a).

52. Puri (2006).

53. Larson and Tingjin (2003).

54. Larson and Tingjin (2003).

55. Larson and Tingjin (2003).

56. McCandless, J. (2001).

57. e.g., Task Force on Energy Strategies and Technologies (2003).

58. Williams (2004).

59. Kojima (1999).

60. Farrell and Brandt (2006).

61. Longmate (1983).

62. http://www.eia.doe.gov/oiaf/servicerpt/erd/fossil.html.

63. Gielen and Unander (2005).

64. Excluding some, potentially significant, emissions from the agricultural process, such as nitrogen oxides from fertilizers and CO_2 from fossil-fueled machinery.

65. Bohn and Benham (1999).

66. *Oil & Gas Journal*, November 6, 2007.

67. Briggs (2004).

68. Rocky Mountain Institute, http://www.rmi.org/sitepages/pid1157.php.

69. *Discover*, vol. 25, no. 7, July 2004.

70. Jatropha Partners (2007).

71. http://www.changingworldtech.com/.

72. http://www.seawaterfoundation.org/.

73. Binder (2007).

74. Binder (2007).

75. 2 percent per year, so averaging 2.2 million bbl/day of extra demand added each year in the first ten years after peak oil. This growth rate is somewhat higher than the 1.6–1.7 percent average seen over the last two decades and assumed in the IEA's central forecast.

76. Simbeck (2006).

77. Quoted at http://www.rigzone.com/news/article.asp?a_id=41484.

78. Lynch (2005).

79. Hirsch (2006).

80. Hirsch *et al.* (2005).

81. http://cnews.canoe.ca/CNEWS/Canada/2007/03/02/3686893-cp.html.

82. Conventional oil costs shown include a range from Saudi Arabia ($5 billion for 1.2 million bbl/day, i.e., $4167/bbl/day) to an onshore U.S. stripper well ($1 million for 10 bbl/day, i.e., $100 000/bbl/day), plus $10–20,000 bbl/day for refining costs.

83. After Cochener (2006). Conventional costs are the author's own.

84. He acknowledges their potential but excludes them from his chosen supply options.

85. Canadian Energy Research Institute (2004).

86. Gray (2005).

87. Johansen et al. (2004), their growth rate is actually faster than I use here, reaching 2 million bbl/day in 2020 as opposed to 2023.

88. *World Biofuels* (Freedonia Institute), quoted in *Oil & Gas Journal* (April 2, 2008).

89. Frost and Sullivan research, quoted at http://www.oilbarrel.com/feature/arti cle.html?body=1&key=oilbarrel_features_en:1171222526&feed=oilbarrel_en. Conversion from tons to barrels assuming biodiesel density of 0.88 g/cm^{-3} but reducing by 5 percent to allow for lower energy density versus petrodiesel (http://www.biodiesel.co.uk/press_release/submission_for_biofuels_4.htm).

90. Watts (2007). His forecast is even more aggressive than this up to around 2010, the critical phase for mitigating a 2007 peak oil event, although with slower growth thereafter.

91. Energy Business Reports.

92. Tertzakian (2006).

CHAPTER 7

1. http://quotationsbook.com/quote/36366/.

2. Much more similar, at least, than say oil and iron or even oil and coal.

3. Cambridge Energy Research Associates, *CERAWeek*, February 2007.

4. Darley (2004).

5. Heinberg (2005).

6. e.g., Campbell (2002); Darley (2004), p. 122.

7. Campbell (2005), *op. cit.*

8. LeBlanc (2007).

9. Heinberg, for instance, puts global reserves at 300–1400 Tcf. Even the upper number is barely one-fifth of official figures, and there is no reason to believe these to be significantly overstated.

10. Chandra (2006).

11. Cornot-Gandolphe *et al.* (2003).

12. D'Andrea (1977).

13. Hightower *et al.* (2004).

14. Of course, several large gas exporters are members of the Gas Exporting Countries Forum, and there may be cooperation between them on some issues. However, it is highly unlikely that it would be able to influence prices by controlling production, as OPEC seeks to do, and it is even more unlikely that such an attempt would benefit its members.

15. There are certainly inconsistencies in the data, caused by differences in definition: gas before or after stripping out valuable liquid hydrocarbons such as LPG; gross or net of reinjection, fuel, and flare. Laherrère makes much of these, but overall they are matters of a few percent and do not affect the overall picture. There is no reason to believe that public reserves estimates are systematically and materially too high or low.

16. Clements.

17. Based partly on Longwell (2002), pp. 100–4.

18. Laherrère (2004a).

19. Deffeyes (2001).

20. Campbell (2005).

21. I make this caution because his total is suspiciously close to Laherrère's figure for ultimate recovery, therefore including gas already produced.

22. Conventional estimates from *U.S. Geological Survey World Petroleum Assessment 2000*, USGS. Unconventional from various sources cited below.

23. Assuming enhanced gas recovery applied to conventional gas only; total technical potential. Using enhanced gas recovery on unconventional sources could boost the total further; however, not all conventional and unconventional accumulations will be suitable for enhanced gas recovery. There may be some double-counting for that ultradeep gas, which is already commercial and appears in the conventional or tight gas totals. Contaminated gas amounts to 80 Tcf with more than 20 percent CO_2 and 250 Tcf with more than 15 percent H_2S. There may be some double-counting with the conventional and ultradeep categories for those contaminated fields that are already producing. However, no estimate is given for nitrogen-contaminated gas resources, which are also very substantial. See Préel and Lepoutre (2006); Gerling; and Institute Français du Pétrole (2006b).

24. Institute Français du Pétrole (2006b) and Pratt (2004).

25. Gerling and Rempel (2005).

26. Victor and Hayes (2006).

27. Institute Français du Pétrole (2006b).

28. Dyman *et al.* (2003).

29. Lawson (2005).

30. Préel and Lepoutre (2006).

31. http://www.naturalgas.org/overview/unconvent_ng_resource.asp.

32. http://www.centreforenergy.com/generator.asp?xml=/silos/ong/ShaleGas/shaleGasOverview04XML.asp&template=1,2,4.

33. Busby (2005).

34. Busby (2005).

35. http://www.naturalgas.org/overview/unconvent_ng_resource.asp.

36. Bundesanstalt für Geowissenschaften und Rohstoffe (BGR) (2005).

37. I wanted to claim the credit for thinking of this independently, but I discover that it has already been proposed: Hyndman and Dallimore (2001).

38. Fischer (2004).

39. Pratt.

40. Van der Drift *et al.* (2005).

CHAPTER 8

1. *New York Times*, October 30, 2004.

2. Although this statistic excludes most unconventional oil, which, via Canada, would boost the open reserves enormously.

3. Giusti (2006).

4. For example, Mabro (2006).

5. For example, "OPEC Leader Says Market Lacks Refining Capacity," *Moscow Times*, September 10, 2007.

6. Brent and West Texas intermediate are light, sweet (low-sulphur) crudes used as two of the world's three key price markers (the third is the somewhat heavier, sour Dubai grade).

7. Using "taxation" in the broad sense to refer to all the means—royalties, cost/profit oil, fees, export tariffs, and so on—by which governments extract value from their oil sectors, in addition to corporate taxes *sensu stricto*.

8. Partly based on Kellas (2006) and Agalliu (2006). Fiscal changes in Canada and South Africa are prospective as of October 2007.

9. http://commentisfree.guardian.co.uk/michael_meacher/2007/03/the_recent_cabinet_agreement_i.html, March 22, 2007.

10. Currie (2006).

11. "Barking louder, biting less," *The Economist*, March 8, 2007.

12. For example, Freeland (2000); Hoffman (2003); Midgley and Hutchins (2004).

13. And other resources as well, such as metals, http://www.fin24.co.za/articles/default/display_article.aspx?ArticleId=1518-25_2132680, http://uk.reuters.com/article/oilRpt/idUKL0690388720070619.

14. Karl (1997).

15. Baker Institute (2007).

16. For example, Karl (1997); Amuzegar (2001).

17. Mabro (2006).

18. Gately (2004).

19. Greenwood *et al.* (2007).

20. Yergin (2007).

21. Hayes (2004).

22. Asia Pacific Energy Research Centre (2003).

23. For example, Lovins *et al.* (2004), p. 8.

24. From reports at http://www.iags.org/iraqpipelinewatch.htm.

25. http://www.saudi-us-relations.org/articles/2006/ioi/060228-rodhan-abqaiq.html.

26. http://www.saudi-us-relations.org/articles/2006/ioi/060224-daly-saudi-target.html.

27. For example, Clawson and Henderson (2005).

28. Mostly based on International Energy Authority, World Energy Outlook 2005, and Energy Information Administration (November 2005), *World Oil Transit Chokepoints*.

29. Kumins (2005).

30. Brito and Myers Jaffe, in Sokolski and Clawson (2005).

31. Maugeri (2006).

32. Quoted by, for example, Yergin, D., June 20, 2002, address to the Committee on International Relations.

33. http://commentisfree.guardian.co.uk/michael_meacher/2007/03/the_recent_cabinet_agreement_i.html, March 22, 2007.

34. Kleveman (2003).

35. For example, Klare (2001).

36. http://business.timesonline.co.uk/tol/business/industry_sectors/natural_resources/article1555773.ece.

37. Quoted in Bilmes and Stiglitz (2006).

38. Bilmes and Stiglitz (2006).

39. Direct military spending only, not including war damage and the human cost of deaths and injuries.

40. Hiro (1991).

41. Rajaee (1993), p. 48.

42. Of course, this does not rule out small-scale guerrilla actions, coups, etc., in the developing world over local resources, where the costs are far smaller.

43. For example, *The Guardian*, November 5, 2002.

44. Ruppert (2004).

45. Clarke (2007b) provides a far more nuanced account.

46. http://www.lewrockwell.com/margolis/margolis72.html.

47. I ignore Malaysia here, because it is a net energy exporter and its motives for foreign expansion are different.

48. Sampson (1993), p. 332.

49. Excluding, of course, China's own domestic production.

50. A nervousness revealed also by the early-2008 controversy over "Sovereign Wealth Funds," in which the United States and several European countries displayed an odd hostility to the idea of reinvestment of oil revenues in their home markets by oil exporters.

51. For example, *Oil & Gas Journal* newsletter, vol. 104, issue 15, April 17, 2006.

52. http://eh.net/hmit/gdp/.

53. http://www.eia.doe.gov/emeu/cabs/carbonemiss/chapter5.html.

54. Debunked at http://www.breakthechain.org/exclusives/foreignoil.html.

55. http://www.theaa.com/motoring_advice/fuel/index.html.

56. Ignoring the U.K. government's substantial tax take from North Sea production.

57. Grammatically incorrect and tautologous (should read "None is energy independent"), but the idea is right.

58. Advertisement in *Offshore*, April 2007.

59. *JP Morgan Oil and Gas Monthly*, March 8, 2007.

CHAPTER 9

1. Goodstein (2004).

2. "What Was the GDP Then?," http://eh.net/hmit/gdp/gdp_answer.php?CHK nominalGDP=on&CHKrealGDP=on&CHKGDPdeflator=on&CHKpopulation= on&CHKnominalGDP_percap=on&CHKrealGDP_percap=on&year1=1977& year2=1990.

3. Goodstein (2004).

4. e.g., http://www.census.gov/ipc/www/idb/worldpopinfo.html; "How to deal with a falling population," *The Economist,* July 26, 2007.

5. International Energy Agency (2006).

6. Lovins *et al.* (2004).

7. Based on 2025 figure for the United States given by Lovins *et al.* (2004), reduced back to 2005 to allow for demand growth to 2025, scaled up to match

world consumption and reduced in proportion 50:67 to allow for lower transport demand in the rest of the world compared with the United States.

8. Coal Industry Advisory Board (2003). I use Imperial tons here, not US tons, an imperial ton being very close to the metric tonne.

9. McKee (2003).

10. Jaccard (2005).

11. Hubbert (1949).

12. Assuming 1.5 tons of coal per 1 ton of oil equivalent.

13. Laherrère (2004b).

14. Mayer (2006).

15. Nieuwsblad (Belgium), December 20, 2005, http://www.nieuwsblad.be/Article/Detail.aspx?ArticleID=G5RLQB1J; http://www.planetark.com/dailynewsstory.cfm/newsid/34152/story.htm.

16. Goodstein (2004), p. 34.

17. Quoted in *World Oil*, August 2007.

18. Hubbert (1971).

19. http://www.worldenergy.org/wec-geis/publications/default/tech_papers/17th_congress/3_2_12.asp, http://www.iaea.org/NewsCenter/News/2006/uranium_resources.html.

20. For example, http://www.theoildrum.com/node/2379.

21. Hubbert (1956).

22. http://www.americanenergyindependence.com/uranium.html.

23. http://www.worldenergy.org/wec-geis/publications/reports/ser04/fuels.asp?fuel=Uranium.

24. For example, http://www.theoildrum.com/node/2379.

25. For example, http://www.world-nuclear.org/sym/2001/macdonald.htm, http://www.uic.com.au/nip75.htm.

26. Goodstein (2004).

27. The Shell Sustainability Report 2005, assuming 7.29 bbl/ton of oil equivalent.

28. Quoted in *Financial Times*, February 18, 2007, http://www.ft.com/cms/s/11ba213e-bf7e-11db-9ac2-000b5df10621.html.

29. http://www.world-nuclear.org/info/inf11.htm.

30. Farrell and Brandt (2006).

31. There are, of course, major externalities to the oil business, notably pollution and security (the cost, primarily to the United States, to maintain armed forces in the Middle East and elsewhere to protect oil supplies), but these are only tangentially relevant to the EROEI question.

32. Jaccard (2005).

33. Smith (2007).

34. Peterson *et al.* (2006).

35. Ansolabehere *et al.* (2003).

36. Jaccard (2005).

37. e.g., Heinberg, (2005), p. 178.

38. Llewelyn Smith (2007).

39. e.g., Lovins *et al.* (2004).

40. Huber and Mills (2005).

41. Lovins *et al.* (2004), p. 1.

42. Cambridge Energy Research Associates (2007).

43. Hirsch *et al.* (2005).

44. Like "SkySails" for ships, which reduce oil consumption by 10–35 percent, http://www.skysails.info/index.php?id=66&L=1.

45. Obviously, we are decoupling supply and demand here, although as we have seen, there is no such thing as "unconstrained demand"; demand always responds to price and, *ceteris paribus*, would be higher were the price lower. The difference between demand in the absence of a peak oil event and demand in its occurrence should be taken as a measure of economic pain, demand destruction, and reduced growth, combined with more painless efficiency measures.

46. Hirsch *et al.* (2005); Hirsch (2006).

47. Lovins *et al.* (2004).

CHAPTER 10

1. Quoted at http://www.news society.info/2007/11/04/pctrolcum-frcc-by-2023/.

2. *Arabian Business*, http://www.arabianbusiness.com/index.php?option=com_content&view=article&id=8167:abu-dhabi-to-build-350m-solar-power-plant&Itemid=1, 18th February 2007.

3. Yergin (1991), *op. cit.*, p. 569.

4. *Oil and Gas Middle East*, p. 25, January 2007.

5. Schoon (1995).

6. http://seawifs.gsfc.nasa.gov/OCEAN_PLANET/HTML/peril_oil_pollution.html.

7. Isaacs and du Plessis (2005).

8. Harding and Cattaneo (2007).

9. Long Lake project fact sheet (Fall/Winter 2005), http://www.nexeninc.com/Newsroom/landing.asp.

10. Tilman (2006).

11. Williams (2007).

12. World Health Organization (2002).

13. Davies (2004).

14. Five Winds International (2004).

15. Jaccard (2005).

16. Ansolabehere *et al.* (2007).

17. Hamilton (1998).

18. For example, Stern (2006).

19. http://dpa.aapg.org/gac/papers/climate_change.cfm.

20. Economides and Oligney, *op. cit.*, pp. 147–9.

21. Wind and solar, at least.

22. Pacala and Socolow (2004).

23. One ton of carbon (C) being equivalent to about 3.7 tons of carbon dioxide (CO_2). Emissions may be quoted in either unit.

24. Hotinski (2007).

25. Wright (2005).

26. http://www.greencarcongress.com/2007/07/welsh-greenbox-.html.

27. Which produce both carbon dioxide and methane. Methane is an even more potent greenhouse gas than carbon dioxide and can, of course, be burnt to provide energy or injected into oil fields for improved and enhanced recovery.

28. Audus (2006) and Metz *et al.* (2005).

29. Lackner, in Mabro (2006), p. 271.

30. Groeneveld (2006).

31. Sweeney and Barry (2006).

32. http://www.seawaterfoundation.org/.

33. http://www.upstreamonline.com/live/article129657.ece.

34. http://www.upstreamonline.com/hardcopy/alternatives/article127861.ece.

35. http://www.co2crc.com.au/dls/media/08/OtwayLaunch_Nirranda.pdf.

36. McDonald (2004).

37. Based on http://www.co2captureandstorage.info/docs/IEAGHGccsworld-map.pdf, http://recopol.nitg.tno.nl/index.shtml, www.upstreamonline.com/live/article144549.ece, http://www.ccap.org/domestic/Domestic%20Dialogue%20July%202007%20Presentations/Rachel%20Miller%20-%20decarbonized%20fuels.pdf, and http://pangea.stanford.edu/research/bensonlab/presentations/Carbon%20Diox ide%20Capture%20and%20Storage%20-%20Research%20Pathways%20Progress %20and%20Potential.pdf.

38. http://news.yahoo.com/s/afp/20070318/ts_alt_afp/ usclimateenvironmentenergycoal.

39. McKillop and Newman (2005), p. 141.

40. http://news.bbc.co.uk/2/hi/europe/4642837.stm, http://www.planetark.com/ dailynewsstory.cfm/newsid/30899/story.htm.

41. Jakobsen *et al.* (2005).

42. For example, "A Fondness for Fossil Fuels," http://www.monbiot.com/ archives/2006/04/25/my-new-fondness-for-fossil-fuels/.

43. Fageeha (2006).

44. From the IPCC's IS92A scenario, converting from US$1990 U.S dollars to 2007 U.S. dollars.

45. Stern (2006).

46. From data in Jaccard (2005).

47. Metz *et al.* (2005), p. 9.

48. http://www.rigzone.com/news/article.asp?a_id=44228.

49. Oldenburg (2003).

50. de Coninck (2006).

51. McGrail *et al.* (2005)

52. For example,, Coddington (2004).

53. Cupcic (2003).

54. Raynolds (2006).

55. http://www.prnewswire.com/cgi-bin/stories.pl?ACCT=ind_focus.story& STORY=/www/story/02-22-2007/0004533136&EDATE=THU+Feb+22+2007,+07: 00+PM.

56. Davies (2004).

57. Five Winds International (2004).

58. And with opportunities for additional gains if engines are tuned to run on GtL fuels.

59. Converting stranded gas to LNG and bringing it to markets, where it could be used as CNG in vehicles, probably consumes somewhat more than 10 percent of the gas's energy content. Conversely, turning such gas to hydrogen or electricity for transport is currently considerably less efficient than GtL.

60. Colin Campbell, quoted at http://www.fromthewilderness.com/free/ww3/102302_campbell.html.

61. Spoken by Dr. Peter Venkman (Bill Murray).

62. http://environment.guardian.co.uk/energy/story/0,,2051912,00.html.

63. Semple (2006).

64. If he tried working for a corporation, he would discover the true amount of regulation they face—a great deal—and the strenuous efforts they usually make to comply with (not to evade) regulation.

65. Darley (2004).

66. Gustafson (1990).

67. Campbell (2005), *op. cit.* Oddly enough, he himself lives in France.

68. Savinar (2004).

69. Address to the Commonwealth Club, San Francisco, California, August 31, 2004.

Bibliography

Aanensen, G. (April 2007) "Monitoring offers oil-in-water control." *Harts E&P*, p. 97.

Abdul Baqi, M. M. and Saleri, N. G. (February 24, 2004) *Fifty-Year Crude Oil Supply Scenarios: Saudi Aramco's Perspective*. Center for Strategic and International Studies, Washington, D.C.

Adams, N. (2003) *Terrorism and Oil*. PennWell.

Adelman, M. A. (Spring 2004) "The real oil problem." *Regulation*, pp. 16–21.

Adelman, M. A. and Watkins, G. C. (2008) "Reserve prices and mineral resource theory." *The Energy Journal*, Special Issue.

Advanced Resources International (March 2005) *Basin Oriented Strategies for CO_2 Enhanced Oil Recovery, Illinois*. U.S. Department of Energy.

Afifi, A. M. (2005) *Ghawar: the Anatomy of the World's Largest Oil Field*. Adapted from American Association of Petroleum Geologists Distinguished Lecture, 2004.

Afren (July 6, 2006) *An Emerging African Oil Company*. OilBarrel Conference, London.

Agalliu, I. (March 7, 2006) *A Look at Regulatory and Fiscal Terms in a High Price Environment: Have the Sharks Begun to Circle?* IHS.

Alberta Chamber of Resources (January 30, 2004) "Oil Sands Technology Roadmap."

Alcazar-Cancino, L. O., Rodriguez-Dominguez, J. M. and Robles-Vega, L. (2004) *Exploitation of the Chicontepec Turbiditic Plays, Central Mexico*. American Association of Petroleum Geologists Annual Meeting 2004, Columbus, Ohio.

Aleklett, K. and Campbell, C. J. *The Peak and Decline of World Oil and Gas Production*. Uppsala University, Uppsala, Sweden, http://www.peakoil.net/Publications/OilpeakMineralsEnergy.doc.

Al-Husseini, M. (2006) "The debate over Hubbert's Peak: a review." *GeoArabia*, vol. 11, no. 2.

Al-Kafeef, S. and Zaid, A. (October 16–19, 1994) *Screening of Kuwait Oil Reservoirs for Application of Different Enhanced Oil Recovery Techniques.* 6th Abu Dhabi International Petroleum Exhibition and Conference, Abu Dhabi.

Amuzegar, J. (2001) *Managing the Oil Wealth: OPECs Windfalls and Pitfalls.* I.B. Tauris.

Ansolabehere, S., Deutch, J., Driscoll, M., Gray, P. E., Holdren, J. P., Joskow, P. L., Lester, R. K., Moniz, E. J., Todreas, N. E. and Beckjord, E. S. (2003) *The Future of Nuclear Power.* Massachusetts Institute of Technology.

Ansolabehere, S., Beer, J., Deutch, J., Ellermann, A. D., Friedmann, S. J., Herzog, H., Jacoby, H. D., Joskow, P. L., Mcrae, G., Lester, R., Moniz, E. J., Steinfeld, E. and Katzer, J. (2007) *The Future of Coal.* Massachusetts Institute of Technology.

Arnold, G. (1978) *Britain's Oil.* Hamish Hamilton.

Asia Pacific Energy Research Centre (2003) *Energy Security Initiative: Some Aspects of Oil Security.* APEC no. 203-RE-01.3.

Asimov, I. (1994) *Foundation.* Collins.

Attanasi, E. D. and Root, D. H. (1988) "Forecasting petroleum discoveries in sparsely drilled areas." *Mathematical Geology,* vol. 20, no. 7.

Attanasi, E. D. (2005) *Economics of 1998 U.S. Geological Survey's 1002 Area Regional Assessment: An Economic Update.* United States Geological Survey Open File Report 2005–1359.

Audus, H. (October 17, 2006) *An Update on CCS: Recent Developments.* 2nd International Energy Agency Workshop on Legal Aspects of Storing CO_2, Paris, France.

Baker Institute (March 2007) *The Changing Role of National Oil Companies in International Energy Markets.* Baker Institute Policy Report, no. 35.

Beecy, D. J. (April 17–20, 2005) *Opportunities for Increasing Revenues from State and Federal Lands: Pursuing the "Stranded Oil" Prize.* Eastern Lands and Resources Council and Western States Land Commissions Association Joint Spring Conference, Washington, D.C.

Bentley, R. W. (2002) "Global oil & gas depletion: an overview." *Energy Policy* vol. 30, pp. 189–205.

Bentley, R. W. (May 2005) *Global Oil Depletion: Methodologies and Results.* IWOOD-IV, Lisbon.

Berman, A. (February 2008) "Three super-giant fields discovered offshore Brazil." *World Oil,* pp. 23–24.

Bilmes, L. and Stiglitz, J. (February 2006) *The Economic Costs of the Iraq War: An Appraisal Three Years after the Beginning of the Conflict.* Working Paper 12054, National Bureau of Economic Research.

Binder, T. P. (July 18, 2007) *Potential Biomass Energy Supply in 2030 to 2050 Time Frame.* Working Document of the National Petroleum Council Global Oil and Gas Study.

Birol, F. (January 10, 2006). *Oil Market Outlook and Policy Implications.* Prepared Testimony to the United States Senate Committee on Energy and Natural Resources.

Blanchard, R. D. (2005) *The Future of Global Oil Production.* McFarland & Company.

Bohn, S. and Benham, C. (March 8–11, 1999) *Coal-to-Liquids via Fischer-Tropsch Synthesis*. 24th International Technical Conference on Coal Utilization and Fuel Systems, Clearwater, Florida.

Bordenave, M. L. (March 10–13, 2002). *The Middle Cretaceous to Early Miocene Petroleum System in the Zagros Domain of Iran, and its Prospect Evaluation*. American Association of Petroleum Geologists Annual Meeting, Houston, Texas.

Briggs, M. (August 2004) *Widescale Biodiesel Production from Algae*. University of New Hampshire, http://www.unh.edu/p2/biodiesel/article_alge.html.

Brito, D. and Myers Jaffe, A. (October 2005) "Reducing vulnerability of the Strait of Hormuz," *Getting Ready for a Nuclear-Ready Iran* (edited by Sokolski, H. and Clawson, P.). Strategic Studies Institute.

Brown, A. C. (1999) *Oil, God and Gold: the Story of Aramco and the Saudi Kings*. Marc Jaffe.

Bundesanstalt für Geowissenschaften und Rohstoffe (BGR) (2005) *Reserves, Resources and Availability of Energy Resources 2005*.

Busby, R. L., ed. (2005) *International Petroleum Encyclopedia 2005*. PennWell.

Cambridge Energy Research Associates (February 28, 2007) *Meeting the Power Conservation Investment Challenge*.

Campbell, C. J. (1997) *The Coming Oil Crisis*. Multi-Science Publishing.

Campbell, C. J. (2002) *Peak Oil: an Outlook on Crude Oil Depletion*. http://www.mbendi.co.za/indy/oilg/p0070.htm.

Campbell, C. J. (October 2005) *Oil Crisis*. Multi-Science Publishing.

Campbell, C. J. (2006) http://www.hubbertpeak.com/campbell/ProductionDepletion 2005.xls.

Canadian Energy Research Institute (March 3, 2004) *Oil Sands Supply Outlook*.

Cantrell, D. and Hagerty, R. M. (2003) "Reservoir rock classification, Arab-D reservoir, Ghawar Field, Saudi Arabia." *GeoArabia*, vol. 8, no. 3, pp. 435–62.

Cantrell, D., Swart, P. and Hagerty, R. (2004) "Genesis and characterization of dolomite, Arab-D reservoir, Ghawar field, Saudi Arabia." *GeoArabia*, vol. 9, no. 2, pp. 11–36.

Chandra, V. (2006) *Fundamentals of Natural Gas: An International Perspective*. Pennwell.

Chew, K. (June 28, 2005) *World Oil and Gas Resource and Production Outlook*. OAPEC-IFP Joint Seminar, Paris, France. IHS Energy.

Chew, K. and Stark, P. H. (November 13–17, 2006) *Perspective on Oil Resource Estimates*. IHS Energy, American Association of Petroleum Geologists Hedberg Research Conference, Colorado Springs, USA.

Clarke, D. (February 1, 2007a) *The Battle for Barrels: Peak Oil Myths and World Oil Futures*. Profile Books.

Clarke, D. (2007b) *Empires of Oil*. Profile Books.

Clawson, P. and Henderson, S. (November 2005) *Reducing Vulnerability to Middle East Energy Shocks*. The Washington Institute for Near East Policy, Policy Focus no. 49

Clements, C. L. *The Economics and Opportunities of Stranded Gas*. IHS Energy.

Coal Industry Advisory Board (December 10, 2003) *World Coal Demand Supply Prospects*.

Cochener, J. (March 27, 2006) *The Outlook for Unconventional Liquids in AEO2006*. Energy Information Administration.

Coddington, K. (December 7–8, 2004) *Legal, Regulatory and Policy Issues Impacting CO_2 EOR*. Second Annual EOR Carbon Management Workshop, Midland, Texas.

Cornot-Gandolphe, S., Appert, O., Dickel, R., Chabrelie, M-F. and Rojey, A. (June 1–5, 2003) *The Challenges of Further Cost Reductions for New Supply Options (Pipeline, LNG, GTL)*. 22nd World Gas Conference, Tokyo, Japan.

Coxe, D. G. M. (March 30, 2005) *Big Footprints on the Sands of Time and Little Footprints of Fear*. Harris Nesbitt.

Croissant, M. P. and Aras, B., eds. (1999) *Oil and Geopolitics in the Caspian Sea Region*. Praeger.

Cummins, I. and Beasant, J. (2005) *Shell Shock*. Mainstream Publishing.

Cupcic, F. (May 26–27, 2003) *Extra Heavy Oil and Bitumen*. Total.

Currie, J. R. (2005) *The Sustainability of Higher Energy Prices—the Revenge of the Old Economy*. Goldman Sachs.

Currie, J. (May 2006) *Reassessing Long-Term Commodity Prices*. Goldman Sachs.

D'Andrea, L. (1977) *Liquified Natural Gas Imports—Are They Worth the Risk?* Society of Petroleum Engineers Paper 6338.

Darley, J. (2004) *High Noon for Natural Gas*. Chelsea Green Publishing.

Davis, P. (2004) *Sasol Overview*. Howard Weil Energy Conference, Houston, Texas.

de Coninck, H. (April 20, 2006) *The IPCC Special Report on Carbon dioxide Capture and Storage*. Workshop on CDM and CCS, Government of Japan, Paris, France.

Deffeyes (2001) *Hubbert's Peak*. Princeton University Press.

Denbury Resources Inc. (December 7, 2004) *Impact of CO_2 Flooding in the State of Mississippi*. 2nd Annual Enhanced Oil Recovery Carbon Management Workshop, Midland, Texas.

Department of Energy (1996) *Oil Production Capacity Expansion Costs For the Persian Gulf*. DOE/EIA-TR/0606.

Diamond (2006) *Collapse: How Societies Choose to Fail or Survive*. Penguin Books.

Drollas, L. P. (2006a) *The Oil Market—Key Questions*. Centre for Global Energy Studies.

Drollas, L. P. (2006b) *We Have Plenty of Oil—We Just Need to Invest More*. Centre for Global Energy Studies.

Dyer, R. A. and Husseini, M. (1991) *The Western Rub' Al-Khali Infracambrian Graben System*. Society of Petroleum Engineers Paper 21396.

Dylan Powell, W. (January 2004) "results management captures key information on quality and context of data interpretations." *The American Oil and Gas Reporter*.

Dyman, T. S., Wyman, R. E., Kuuskraa, V. A., Lewan, M. D. and Cook, T. A. (2003) "Deep natural gas resources." *Natural Resources Research*, vol. 12, no. 1, pp. 41–56.

Dyni, J. R. (2005) *Geology and Resources of Some World Oil-Shale Deposits.* United States Geological Survey publication 2005–5294.

Economides, M. and Oligney, R. (2000) *The Color of Oil.* Round Oak Publishing Company.

Elliott, S., Hsu, H. H., O'Hearn, T., Sylvester, I. F. and Vercesi, R. (Autumn 1998) *The Giant Karachaganak Field, Unlocking Its Potential.* Schlumberger Oil Field Review.

Energy Business Reports. *Performance Profiles of Major Energy Producers for 2005.*

Erochkine, P. and Erochkine, V. (2006) *Russia's Oil Industry: Current Problems and Future Trends.* Centre for Global Studies.

Fabricius, N. (September 12, 2006) *Opportunities and Challenges from XtL.* Shell Global Solutions, Asia Pacific Refining, Bangkok.

Fageeha, O. (September 2006) *Carbon Management: a Saudi Aramco Perspective.* EU-OPEC Round Table on CCS, Riyadh, Saudi Arabia.

Farouq Ali, S. M. (2003) *The Unfulfilled Promise of Enhanced Oil Recovery.* University of Calgary.

Farrell, A. E. and Brandt, A. R. (October 30, 2006) *Risks of the Oil Transition.* Environmental Research Letters 1.

Ferguson, A. (September 27, 2005) *Energy Supplies in Eurasia and Implications for US Energy Security.* Testimony before the United States Senate Committee on Foreign Relations, Subcommittee on International Economic Policy, Export and Trade Promotion.

Finn, T. M. and Johnson, R. C. (2005) *Niobrara Total Petroleum System in the Southwestern Wyoming Province.* United States Geological Survey Digital Data Series DDS-69-D.

Fischer, P. A. (August 2004) "Unconventional natural gas will have to pinch hit for conventional natural gas." *World Oil.*

Five Winds International (August 2004) *Gas to Liquids Life Cycle Assessment Synthesis Report.* Prepared for ConocoPhillips, Sasol Chevron, Shell International Gas.

Fleming, D. (November 2000) "The real problem with oil: it's going to run out." *Prospect,* Issue 57.

Fraser, A. and Harper, F. (March 2005) *Our Exploration Future: the Middle East and Russia.* APPEX, BP.

Freeland, C. (2000) *Sale of the Century.* Little, Brown.

Gao, Y., Yang, S., Zhou, Y., Jia, L., Sun, H., Zhang, Y., Castanier, L. M. and Kovscek, A. R. (September 24–27, 2006) *Interpretation of Heat Distribution, Remaining Oil Saturation, and Steamflood Potential of Block Wa38, Liaohe Field.* Society of Petroleum Engineers Paper 102500.

Gately, D. (April 2004) "OPEC's incentives for faster output growth." *The Energy Journal,* 25(2), pp. 75–96.

Gerling, J. P. *Non-Conventional Hydrocarbons—Where, What, How Much.* Bundesanstalt für Geowissenschaften und Rohstoffe (BGR).

Gerling, J. P. and Rempel, H. (May 26–27, 2005) *The World's Endowment with Natural Gas.* Bundesanstalt für Geowissenschaften und Rohstoffe (BGR).

Ghazi, T. (April 11, 2006) *Stochastic Play Assessment of the Offshore Basins of Peru*. American Association of Petroleum Geologists Convention, Houston, Texas.

Gielen, D. and Unander, F. (March 2005) *Alternative Fuels: An Energy Technology Perspective*. Office of Energy Technology and R&D, International Energy Agency.

Giusti, L. (September 6, 2006). Presentation to the World Affairs Council of Houston, Texas.

Goff, J. (March 12–15, 2005) *Origin and Potential of Unconventional Jurassic Oil Reservoirs on the Northern Arabian Plate*. Society of Petroleum Engineers Paper 93505.

Gold, T. (1999) *The Deep, Hot Biosphere*. Copernicus Books.

Goodstein, D. (2004) *Out of Gas*. W. W. Norton & Company.

Grape, S. G. (November 2006) *Technology-Based Oil and Natural Gas Plays: Shale Shock! Could There Be Billions in the Bakken?* Energy Information Administration.

Gray, V. (August 2002) *The Greenhouse Delusion: A Critique of Climate Change 2001*. Multi-Science Publishing.

Gray, D. (October 20–21, 2005) *Producing Liquid Fuels from Coal*. Mitretek Systems, presented at the National Research Council Board on Energy and Environmental Systems Workshop, Washington D.C.

Greenwood, C., Hohler, A., Liebreich, Sonntag-O'Brien, V. and Usher, E. (2007) *Global Trends in Sustainable Energy Investment 2007*. United Nations Environment Programme and New Energy Finance.

Groeneveld, M. (September 14, 2006) *Shell CO_2 Mineralisation*. Shell.

Grynberg, J. J. (2005) *Exploration Potential in the Northern Portion of the Central African Republic*. http://www.searchanddiscovery.net/documents/abstracts/2005intl_paris/grynberg.htm.

Gustafson, T. (1990) *Crisis Amid Plenty: the Politics of Soviet Energy Under Brezhnev and Gorbachev*. Princeton University Press.

Hamilton, K. (August 1998) *The Oil Industry and Climate Change*. Greenpeace International.

Harding, J. and Cattaneo, C. (February 3, 2007) "Mixing oil and water." Calgary, *Financial Post*.

Harper, F. (March 2005) *The Future of Global Hydrocarbon Exploration*. APPEX, BP.

Hayes, M. M. (May 2004) *Algerian Gas to Europe: The Transmed Pipeline and Early Spanish Gas Import Projects*. Working Paper no. 27, James A. Baker III Institute for Public Policy.

Heinberg, R. (2005) *The Party's Over*. New Society Publishers.

Henriques, D., Gilbert, J., Boyd, D. and Lee, C. (March 28, 2006) *Energy: Oil Services*. Goldman Sachs.

Hightower, M., Gritzo, L., Luketa-Hanlin, A., Covan, J., Tieszen, S., Wellman, G., Irwin, M., Kaneshige, M., Melof, B., Morrow, C. and Ragland, D. (December 2004) *Guidance on Risk Analysis and Safety Implications of a Large Liquefied Natural Gas (LNG) Spill Over Water*. Sandia National Laboratories, SAND2004–6258.

Hill, F. and Gaddy, C. (2003) *The Siberian Curse: How Communist Planners Left Russia Out in the Cold.* Brookings Institution Press.

Hiro, D. (1991) *The Longest War: The Iran-Iraq Military Conflict.* Routledge.

Hirsch, R. L., Bezdek, R. and Wendling, R. (February 2005) *Peaking of World Oil Production: Impacts, Mitigation, & Risk Management.* U.S. Department of Energy.

Hirsch, R. L. (October 23, 2006) *Peaking of World Oil Production.* Atlantic Council Workshop on Transatlantic Energy Issues, Washington, D.C.

Hoffman, D. E. (2003) *The Oligarchs: Wealth and Power in the New Russia.* Perseus Books.

Holditch, S. A. (2006) *Tight Gas Sands.* Society of Petroleum Engineers Paper 103356.

Hotinski, R. (January 2007) *Stabilization Wedges: A Concept & Game.* Carbon Mitigation Initiative. Princeton University.

Howell, D. and Nakhle, C. (2007) *Out of the Energy Labyrinth.* I.B. Tauris.

Hubbert, M. K. (February 4, 1949) "Energy from fossil fuels." *Science*, vol. 109, no. 2823.

Hubbert, M. K. (May 7–9, 1956) *Nuclear Energy and the Fossil Fuels.* Drilling and Petroleum Practice, American Petroleum Institute.

Hubbert, M. K. (1971) "The energy resources of the earth." Energy and Power, *Scientific American*, pp. 31–40.

Huber, P. W. and Mills, M. P. (2005) *The Bottomless Well.* Perseus Books.

Hughes, P. (2005) *UK Gas—the Opportunities Ahead.* BG Group.

Hughes, D. S. (2006) *CO_2 EOR and Storage in the North Sea—UK Perspective.* Society of Petroleum Engineers Bergen Seminar, Bergen, Norway.

Hyndman, R. D. and Dallimore, S. R. (2001) Natural Gas Hydrate Studies in Canada. *Recorder*, vol. 26, pp. 11–20, Canadian Society of Exploration Geophysicists.

Institute Français du Pétrole (2006a) *GTL: Prospects for Development.*

Institute Français du Pétrole (2006b) *Gas Reserves, Discoveries and Production.*

International Energy Agency (2003) *The Utilisation of CO_2.* Working Party on Fossil Fuels.

International Energy Agency (2006). *Key World Energy Statistics.*

Isaacs, E. (June 15, 2005) *Enhanced Oil Recovery for Conventional Resources.* Economics Society of Calgary.

Isaacs, E. and du Plessis, D. (2005) *Energy Development and Future Outlook for Standing Senate Committee on Energy, the Environment and Natural Resources.* Alberta Energy Research Institute.

Jaccard, M. (2005) *Sustainable Fossil Fuels: The Unusual Suspects in the Quest for Clean and Enduring Energy.* Cambridge University Press.

Jackson, P. M. (2006) *Why the "Peak Oil" Theory Falls Down.* Cambridge Energy Research Associates.

Jackson, P. and Eastwood, K. (2008) *The Future of World Oil Supply—Filling the Missing Link.* CERAWeek 2008.

Jakobsen, V. E., Hauge, F., Holm, M. and Kristiansen, B. (August 2005) *CO_2 for EOR on the Norwegian Shelf.* Bellona.

Jatropha Partners (February 1, 2007) *Feedstock for Biodiesel.*

Jiayu, N. and Jianyi, H. (1999) "Formation and distribution of heavy oil and tar sands in China." *Marine and Petroleum Geology*, vol. 16, no. 1, pp. 85–95.

Johnson, H. R., Crawford, P. M. and Bunger, J. W. (March 2004) *Strategic Significance of America's Oil Shale Resource*. Office of Deputy Assistant Secretary for Petroleum Reserves.

Karl, T. L. (1997) *The Paradox of Plenty*. University of California Press.

Kellas, G. (April 2006) *The Terms, They Are a-Changin'*. Wood MacKenzie.

Kerr, R., Birdgeneau, J., Batt, B., Yang, P., Nieuwenberg, G., Rettger, P., Arnold, J. and Bronicki, Y. (2002) *The Long Lake Project—The First Field Integration of SAGD and Upgrading*. Society of Petroleum Engineers/Petroleum Society of CIM/CHOA 79072.

Kininmonth, W. (September 10, 2004) *Climate Change: A Natural Hazard*. Multi-Science Publishing.

Klare, M. T. (2001) *Resource Wars: The New Landscape of Global Conflict*. Henry Holt and Company.

Klett, T. R., Gautier, D. L. and Ahlbrandt, T. S. (August 2005) "An Evaluation of the U.S. Geological Survey World Petroleum Assessment 2000." *American Association of Petroleum Geologists Bulletin*, vol. 89, no. 8, pp. 1033–42.

Klett, T. R., Gautier, D. L. and Ahlbrandt, T. S. (2007) *An Evaluation of the USGS World Petroleum Assessment 2000—Supporting Data*. Open File Report 2007–1021, United States Geological Survey.

Kleveman, L. (2003) *The New Great Game: Blood and Oil in Central Asia*. Atlantic Books.

Kliewer, G. (October 2006a) "New design drillship pushes operations depths to meet future needs." *Offshore*.

Kliewer, G. (October 2006b) "Barents Sea sets Arctic development pace." *Offshore*, p. 36.

Kojima, M. (January 1999) *Commercialization of Marginal Gas Fields*. Energy Issues, World Bank, no. 16.

Korpela, S. A. (November 10, 2006) "Oil depletion in the world." *Current Science*, vol. 91, no 9.

Kumins, L. (April 13, 2005) *Iraq Oil: Reserves, Production and Potential Revenues*. CRS Report for Congress RS21626.

Kuo, J. C., Elliot, D., Luna-Melo, J. and De Léon Pérez, J. B. (March 12, 2001) "World's largest N2-generation plant." *Oil & Gas Journal*.

Laherrère, J. (September 28–29, 2001) *Forecasting Future Production from Past Discovery*. OPEC seminar, Vienna, Austria.

Laherrère, J. (May 23, 2002) *Modelling Future Liquids Production from Extrapolation of the Past and from Ultimates*. International Workshop on Oil Depletion, Uppsala, Sweden.

Laherrère, J. (December 10, 2003) *How to Estimate Future Oil Supply and Demand?* International Conference on Oil Demand, Production and Costs, Copenhagen, Denmark.

Laherrère, J. (May 25, 2004a). *Future of Natural Gas Supply*. ASPO Berlin.

Laherrère, J. (June 22–24, 2004b). *Natural Gas Future Supply*. IIASA-IEW.

Labohm, H., Rozendaal, S. and Thoenes, D. (2004) *Man-Made Global Warming: Unravelling a Dogma*. Multi-Science Publishing.

Lane, D., ed. (1999) *The Political Economy of Russian Oil*. Rowman & Littlefield Publishers.

Larson, E. D. and Tingjin, R. (December 2003) "Synthetic fuel production by indirect coal liquefaction." *Energy for Sustainable Development*, vol. VII, no. 4.

Lawson, W. F. (April 21, 2005) *R&D: Catalyst for the Next Stage of Seismic Industry Growth*. Sercel Land Acquisition Forum, Houston, Texas.

LeBlanc, R. (November 27, 2007) *Global Gas: Pressures, Risks, and Opportunities*. PFC Energy Seminar, Bahrain.

Lee, J. (June 2006) *Can Kazakhstan Export its Future Production?* Centre for Global Energy Studies.

Lemigas (June 13, 2006) CO_2 *Sequestration Potential for EOR in Indonesia*. Jakarta, Indonesia.

Leonard, R. (May 2005) *The Reality of Russia*. MOL.

Llewelyn Smith, C. (2007) *The Path to Fusion Power*. UKAEA Fusion Power.

Locke, W., Sheppard, C., Goulding, S., Shrimpton, M. and Whitford, J. (April 15, 2006) *Economic Overview of Oil and Gas Resources Found in the Queen Charlotte Basin*. Natural Resources Canada, http://www2.nrcan.gc.ca/es/erb/CMFiles/Economic_Overview_of_Oil_and_Gas_Resources_Found_in_the_Queen_Charlotte_Basin212MBJ-21032007-4947.pdf.

Lomborg, B. (2001) *The Sceptical Environmentalist*. Cambridge University Press.

Lomborg, B. (November 2, 2006) "Stern Review: the dodgy numbers behind the latest warming scare." *Wall Street Journal*.

Lomborg, B. (September 25, 2007) *Cool It: The Skeptical Environmentalist's Guide to Global Warming*. Cyan-Marshall Cavendish.

Longhurst, H. (1959) *Adventure in Oil: the Story of British Petroleum*. Sidgwick and Jackson.

Longmate, N. (1983). *The Bombers: Royal Air Force Air Offensive Against Germany, 1939–1945*. Hutchinson.

Longwell, H. (2002) *World Energy*, vol. 5, no. 3. ExxonMobil.

Loutfi, G. and Abul Hamd, M. (1987) *Cenomanian Stratigraphic Traps in Western Abu Dhabi, U.A.E.* Society of Petroleum Engineers Paper 15684.

Lovins, A. B., Datta, E. K., Bustnes, O-E., Koomey, J. G. and Glasgow, N.J. (2004) *Winning the Oil Endgame*. EarthScan.

Luhnow, D. (April 5, 2007) "Dying giant: Mexico tries to save a big, fading oil field." *Wall Street Journal*.

Lyle, D. (April 2007) "High Potential Tames Bear's Risk." *Harts E&P*, p. 23.

Lynch, M. C. (April 12, 2005) *Unconventional Oil: Filling in the Gap or Flooding the Market?* Department of Energy, National Energy Modeling System.

Lynch, M. (2006a) *Crop Circles in the Desert: the Strange Controversy over Saudi Oil Production*. International Research Centre for Energy and Economic Development, Occasional Papers no. 40.

Lynch, M. C. (October 27, 2006b) *The New Pessimism about Petroleum Resources: Debunking the Hubbert Model (and Hubbert Modelers)*. http://www.gasresources.net/Lynch(Hubbert-Deffeyes).htm.

Mabro, R., ed. (2006) *Oil in the 21st Century*. Oxford University Press.

Malaysia (October 4–7, 2005) *EOR in Malaysia*. 4th Petroleum Project Management Seminar, Hua Hin, Thailand.

Mann, P. (2007) *Emerging Trends from 69 Giant Oil and Gas Fields Discovered from 2000–2006*. American Association of Petroleum Geologists Annual Convention and Exhibition, Long Beach, California.

Maugeri, L. (2006) *The Age of Oil: The Mythology, History and Future of the World's Most Controversial Resource*. Praeger.

Mayer, A. J. (2006) *Rethinking US Coal Reserves and Resources*. Live Free.

McCandless, J. (2001) *DME as an Automotive Fuel*. Powertrain Technologies.

McDonald, D. (December 7, 2004) *Bringing the Power Plant of the Future Home to Texas*. Clean Coal Foundation of Texas.

McGrail, B., Schaef, H., Reidel, S. and Dooley, J. J. (2005) *Carbon Sequestration in Flood Basalts: An Overlooked Sequestration Option*. The Joint Global Change Research Institute.

McKee, B. N. (2003) *Fossil Fuels for Economic Development and Security*. Cleaner Fossil Fuels Systems Committee, World Energy Council.

McKillop, A. with Newman, S. (2005) *The Final Energy Crisis*. Pluto Press.

Mello, M. R. and Moldowan, J. M. (2005) *Petroleum: To Be or Not to Be Abiogenic*. American Association of Petroleum Geologists Research Conference, Calgary, Canada.

Metz, B., Davidson, O., de Coninck, H., Loos, M. and Meyer, L. (2005) *Carbon Dioxide Capture and Storage*. Intergovernmental Panel on Climate Change.

Meyer, R. F. and Attanasi, E. D. (August 2003) *Heavy Oil and Natural Bitumen— Strategic Petroleum Resources*. United States Geological Survey Fact Sheet FS-070–03, http://www.centreforenergy.com/viewLargeImage.asp?ImagePath=/images/GlobalOccurancesOfOilAndBitumen.jpg.

Meyer, R. F. and Freeman, P. A. (2006) *Siberian Platform: Geology and Natural Bitumen Resources*. United States Geological Survey Open-File Report 2006–1316.

Midgley, D. and Hutchins, C. (2004) *Abramovich: The Billionaire from Nowhere*. HarperCollins.

Millan, R. and McMahon, C. (August 20, 2007) *Morocco Reaches for the Unconventionals*. Wood MacKenzie.

Mitchell, J., Morita, K., Selley, N. and Stern, J. (2001) *The New Economy of Oil*. The Royal Institute of International Affairs.

Mondragon, M. Y. (November 2001). "Mexico's northern region launches massive development." *World Oil*.

Moore, M. E. (February 23, 2006) *Next Generation CO_2-EOR in the US and Globally*. IEA European Seminar and Dialogue.

Nasr, T. N. and Ayodele, O. R. (December 5–6, 2005) *Thermal Techniques for the Recovery of Heavy Oil and Bitumen*. Society of Petroleum Engineers Paper 97488.

Nehring, R. (April 3, 2006a) "Hubbert's Unreliability. 1. Two basins show Hubbert's method underestimates future oil production." *Oil & Gas Journal*, vol. 104, issue 13.

Nehring, R. (April 17, 2006b) "Hubbert's Unreliability. 2. How Hubbert method fails to predict oil production in the Permian Basin." *Oil & Gas Journal*, vol. 104, issue 15.

Nehring, R. (April 24, 2006c) "Hubbert's unreliability. 3. Post-Hubbert challenge is to find new methods to predict production, EUR." *Oil & Gas Journal*, vol. 104, issue 16.

Norwegian Petroleum Directorate. (2005) *The Petroleum Resources on the Norwegian Continental Shelf.*

Nyland, B. (March 29, 2006) *Resource Outlook.* Norwegian Petroleum Directorate.

Odell, P. R. (May 21, 2003) *The Global Energy Outlook for the 21st Century.* Address to the Annual Luncheon of The Netherlands Oil and Gas Exploration and Production Association, Wassenaar, Netherlands.

Odell, P. R. (2004) *Why Carbon Fuels Will Dominate The 21st Century's Global Energy Economy.* Multi-Science Publishing.

Oldenburg, C. M. (May 12–14, 2003) *Carbon Sequestration in Natural Gas Reservoirs: Enhanced Gas Recovery and Natural Gas Storage.* Proceedings, TOUGH Symposium, Lawrence Berkeley National Laboratory, Berkeley, California.

Orrell, R. (2000) *Blowout.* Seafarer Books.

Oxenford, J. and Sit, S. (2004) *Bitumen Recovery and Cleanup.* Oil Sands Technology Roadmap.

Pacala, S. and Socolow, R. (2004) "Stabilization wedges: Solving the climate problem for the next 50 years with current technologies." *Science*, vol. 305, pp. 968–72.

Paik, K-W. (1995) *Gas and Oil in Northeast Asia.* The Royal Institute of International Affairs.

Peterson, P. F., Kastenberg, W. E. and Corradini, M. (Summer 2006) "Nuclear waste and the distant future." *Issues in Science and Technology.*

Popper, K. R. (2002) *The Logic of Scientific Discovery.* Routledge (originally published in 1934).

Pratt, R. G. (Winter 2004) *Gas Hydrates—an Introduction.* Queen's University, Kingston, Canada.

Préel, X. and Lepoutre, M. (November 14–15, 2006) *Research and Development.* Total.

Puri, R. (December 12–15, 2006) *UCG Syngas: Product Options and Technologies.* Workshop on Underground Coal Gasification, Kolkata, India.

Rajaee, F., ed. (1993) *Iran-Iraq War: The Politics of Aggression.* University Press of Florida.

Rasmussen, Å. (March 2007) "Optimizing field production using multiphase and wet gas metering." *World Oil.*

Raynolds, M. (September 26, 2006) *Presentation to the Oil Sands Multi-Stakeholder Committee.* The Pembina Institute.

Roberts, P. (April 4, 2005) *The End of Oil: The Decline of the Petroleum Economy and the Rise of a New Energy Order.* Bloomsbury Publishing.

Rodgers, M. R. (2005) *Recent Trends in Exploration Results and the Implication for Future Non OPEC Petroleum Liquids Supply.* PFC Energy, prepared for the National Academy of Sciences.

Rogner, H. (1997) *An Assessment of World Hydrocarbon Resources.* Institute for Integrated Energy Systems, University of Victoria.

Ruppert, M. C. (October 1, 2004) *Crossing the Rubicon: The Decline of the American Empire at the End of the Age of Oil.* New Society Publishers.

Rushworth, S., Stark, P. and Chakhmakhchev, A. (2006) *The Challenge of a New Global Competitive Environment*. Marathon.

Rusk, D. C. (2001) "Libya: Petroleum potential of the underexplored basin centers—a twenty-first-century challenge," in *Petroleum Provinces of the Twenty-First Century* (edited by Downey, M. W., Threet, J. C. and Morgan, W. A.), American Association of Petroleum Geologists Memoir 74, pp. 429–54.

Saidi, A. M. (1996) *Twenty Years of Gas Injection History into Well-Fractured Haft Kel Field (Iran)*. Society of Petroleum Engineers Paper 35309.

Sampson, A. (1993) *The Seven Sisters*. Coronet Books.

Samsam Bakhtiari, A. M. (April 26, 2004) "World oil production capacity model suggests output peak by 2006–07." *Oil & Gas Journal*.

Savinar, M. (January 2004) *The Oil Age is Over*. Savinar Publishing.

Saxton, J. (June 2006) *Canadian Oil Sands: a New Force in the World Oil Market*. Joint Economic Committee United States Congress.

Schoon, N. (September 6, 1995) "Greenpeace's Brent Spar apology." *The Independent*.

Schopenhauer, A. (1819–1819) *Die Welt als Wille und Vorstellung*. Konemann (Koneman edition February 1998).

Semple, Jr., R. B. (February 28, 2006) "The end of oil." *New York Times*.

Shah, S. (2004) *Crude: The Story of Oil*. Seven Stories Press.

Shurtleff, K. and Doyle, D. (March 2008) "Single well, single gas phase technique is key to unique method of extracting oil vapors from oil shale." *World Oil*, pp. 118–27.

Shwadran, B. (1977) *Middle East Oil: Issues and Problems*. Schenkman Publishing.

Simbeck, D. (March 27, 2006) *Emerging Unconventional Liquid Petroleum Options*. EIA Energy Outlook and Modeling Conference, Washington, D.C.

Simmons, M. R. (2002) *The World's Giant Oilfields*. Hubbert Center Newsletter no. 2002/1.

Simmons, M. (2005) *Twilight in the Desert: The Coming Saudi Oil Shock and the World Economy*. John Wiley & Sons.

Skov, A. M. (2002) *World Energy Beyond 2050*. Society of Petroleum Engineers Paper 77506.

Skrebowski, C. (October 2005) "Prices set firm, despite massive new capacity." *Petroleum Review*.

Smith, J. T. (April 3, 2007) "Are passive smoking, air pollution and obesity a greater mortality risk than major radiation incidents?" *BMC Public Health* vol. 7, p. 49.

Smith, M. R. (2006) *Resource Depletion: Modeling and Forecasting Oil Production*. Oak Ridge National Laboratory.

Snyder, R. E. (2000) "Optimizing deepwater rig use; new records—report on ultra-deep water rig utilization and various new drilling records from around the world. Brief article, industry overview, statistical data included." *World Oil*.

Spector, K., Speaker, S. and Choi, S. (September 15, 2005) *Energy Markets Grow Up: How the Changing Balance of Participation Influences Oil Price*. JPMorgan.

Spector, K. (January 8, 2007) *Energy Markets Grow Up Part II: Who Trades Energy Now and How Much Does It Matter?* JPMorgan.

Stanton, M. S. (July 2004) "Origin of the Lower Cretaceous Heavy Oils ("Tar Sands") of Alberta." *Wired*, pp. 102–4.

Strecker Downs, E. (2000). *China's Quest for Energy Security*. RAND MR-1244-AF.

Stern, N. (October 30, 2006) *Stern Review on the Economics of Climate Change*. http://www.hm-treasury.gov.uk/independent_reviews/stern_review_economics_climate_change/stern_review_report.cfm.

Suarez Coppel, J. J. and Yepez, A. (June 5, 2006) "Mexico adopts new tax structure for oil, gas exploration, production." *Oil & Gas Journal*.

Suwaina, O., Al Menhali, S. and Al Mehsin, K. (June 2005) *Yet to find hydrocarbon potential, Abu Dhabi, UAE*. OAPEC-IPF Joint Seminar, Paris, France.

Sweeney, G. and Barry, J. (2006) *Greener & Faster: CO_2 Management*. Shell Renewables & Hydrogen.

Takin, M. (2005) *Future of Oil and Gas Exports from MENA*. Centre for Global Energy Studies.

Takin, M. (2006) *Middle East Oil Production Potential: Myth or Reality?* Centre for Global Energy Studies.

Tamayo, R. L. (June 2005) *Geologic Carbon Dioxide Sequestration for the Mexican Oil Industry: An Action Plan*. Master of Science thesis, Massachusetts Institute of Technology.

Task Force on Energy Strategies and Technologies (December 2003) "Transforming coal for sustainability: a strategy for China." *Energy for Sustainable Development*, vol. VII, no. 4.

Taylor, J. and Van Doren, P. (January 12, 2006) *Economic Amnesia: The Case against Oil Price Controls and Windfall Profit Taxes*. Policy Analysis no. 561.

Tertzakian, P. (2006) *A Thousand Barrels a Second*. McGraw-Hill.

Thompson, M. A., Balbinski, E. F., Cidoncha, J. G., Wikramaratna, R. S., Element, D. J., Paterson, G. A. and Goodfield, M. G. (April 2005) *UKCS CO_2 Injection Potential Update*. Department of Trade and Industry, United Kingdom.

Tilman, D., Hill, J. and Lehman, C. (December 8, 2006). "Carbon-negative biofuels from low-input high-diversity grassland biomass." *Science*, vol. 314, no. 5805, pp. 1598–1600.

Tsui, K. K. (November 11, 2005) *More Oil, Less Democracy?: Theory and Evidence from Crude Oil Discoveries*. Job Market Paper, University of Chicago.

UBS (February 13, 2007) *Emerging Energy Players Round Table*.

Ulmishek, G. F. (2001) *Petroleum Geology and Resources of the North Caspian Basin, Kazakhstan and Russia*. United States Geological Survey Bulletin 2201-B.

van der Drift, A., Rabou, L. P. L. M. and Boerrigter, H. (October 17–21, 2005) *Heat from Biomass via Synthetic Natural Gas*. 14th European Biomass Conference and Exhibition, Paris, France.

Verberg, G. H. (2006) *European Security of Supply and Geopolitics*. European Forum Gas, Berlin, Germany.

Verma, M. K. and Ulmishek, G. F. (2003) "Reserve growth in oil fields of West Siberian Basin, Russia." *Natural Resources Research*, vol. 12, no. 2, pp. 105–19.

Verma, M. K. (October 2007) *The Reality of Reserve Growth*. GEO ExPro, pp. 34–35.

Victor, D. G. and Hayes, M. H. (December 3, 2006) *Geopolitics of Natural Gas*. Program on Energy and Sustainable Development, Stanford University.

Vidal, J. (April 21, 2005) "The end of oil is closer than you think." *The Guardian*.

Watts, L. (November 27, 2007) *Overview of the Global Energy Sector: Critical Shifts*. PFC Energy, Client Seminar, Bahrain.

Williams, B. (July 14, 2003) "Debate over peak-oil issue boiling over, with major implications for industry, society." *Oil & Gas Journal*, vol. 101, issue 27.

Williams, R. H. (November 2004) *Toward Polygeneration of Fluid Fuels and Electricity via Gasification of Coal and Biomass*. Princeton Environmental Institute.

Williams, R. H. (January 3, 2007) *Toward Optimal Use of Biomass in Addressing Climate Change, Oil Supply Insecurity, and Biodiversity Concerns*. Princeton Environmental Institute.

Williamson, J. W. (1928) *In a Persian Oil Field*. Ernest Benn Limited.

Winsloe, R. (November 1999) *The Background to Iraqi Oil and Gas*. IHS Energy.

Wojtanowicz, A. K. (2003) *Downhole Water Separation*. Los Angeles Society of Petroleum Engineers Forum, Los Angeles, California, http://laspe.org/petrotech/petrooct03.html.

World Health Organization (2002) *The World Health Report 2002*.

Wright, I. (September 15, 2005) *CO_2 Reductions in Oil and Gas: BP Program*. BP, IFP Colloque.

Yergin, D. (1991) *The Prize: Epic Quest for Oil, Money and Power*. Simon & Schuster.

Yergin, D. (January 23, 2007) *Energy Independence*. Cambridge Energy Research Associates, http://www.cera.com/aspx/cda/public1/news/articles/newsArticle Details.aspx?CID=8560.

Zempolich, W. G. (February 27, 2002) *The Caspian Kashagan Oil Field as a Multi-Disciplinary Risk Reduction Model*. Northern California Geological Society.

Zittel, W. and Schindler, J. (2003) *Future World Oil Supply*. International Summer School on the Politics and Economics of Renewable Energy at the University of Salzburg, Salzburg, Austria.

Zittel, W. and Schinder, J. (October 2007) *Crude Oil: The Supply Outlook*. Energy Watch Group, EWG Series no. 3/2007.

Data Sources

American Petroleum Institute, www.api.org

BP Statistical Review of World Energy 2007, www.bp.com

IHS Energy, www.ihs.com

International Energy Agency, www.iea.org

Middle East Economic Digest, www.meed.com

Middle East Economic Survey, www.mees.com

Oil & Gas Journal, www.ogj.com

Oljedirektoratet (Norwegian Petroleum Directorate), www.npd.no

OPEC Statistical Bulletin, www.opec.org

Petroleum Intelligence Weekly, www.energyintel.com

U.K. Department for Business—Oil and Gas, www.og.dti.gov.uk
Upstream, www.upstreamonline.com
U.S. Energy Information Administration, www.doe.gov
U.S. Geological Survey, www.usgs.gov
Wood MacKenzie, www.woodmacresearch.com
World Energy Council, www.worldenergy.org
World Oil, www.worldoil.com

Index

economic problems of, 25; electrical submersible pumps in, 114; EOR in, 89, 111, 117; exploration in, 60, 63–66, 68, 70, 99, 109–11, 115–17; and geopolitics, 197, 201, 203; heavy oil in, 114, 155; horizontal wells in, 111–12; investment conditions in, 65n80, 190, 192–94; natural gas in, 58, 117, 182, 200; oil booms and, 31, 202; oil reserves of, 52–56, 60, 107, 109–11, 160–61; OPEC quotas and, 22, 44, 53, 118; as petro-state, 192; possible production decline in, 7, 117–18; production peak in, 48–49, 96; scaling in, 114; spare capacity of, 24–25, 28; "super-K" zones, 112; technology in, 111–15; terrorism in, 29, 195, 197; water production in, 112–14; YtF estimates for, 72, 74. *See also* Arabian Shield; Arabian Super-Light; Eastern Province; Middle East; Al Naimi, Ali; OAPEC; OPEC; Partitioned Neutral Zone; Persian Gulf; Red Sea; Riyadh; Rub' Al Khali; Saudi Aramco; Yamani, Sheikh Zaki; names of individual fields
Saudi Aramco, 65, 110–12, 192, 211. *See also* NOCs; Saudi Arabia
Scaling, 114
Schiehallion Field (UK), 142
Schlumberger, 112
Schopenhauer, Arthur, 20
Scientific method, 34
Sea Gem, 93. *See also* North Sea
Seal: and CCS, 231; for hydrocarbons, 70, 69n92, 150n159
SEC (Securities and Exchange Commission), xvii, 6, 23, 50–51, 55, 57, 131. *See also* reserves; Shell reserves crisis
Secondary recovery, 42, 62, 82, 84n129, 86–87, 90, 117, 119. *See also* EOR
Seismic, 68, 116, 123, 142, 150n159, 150n160, 247n95; amplitude anomalies on, 150; four-dimensional, 83; microseismic, 84;

three-dimensional, 13, 70, 83–84, 110, 120, 126; two-dimensional, 69, 120; wide angle, 69
Senegal, exploration potential of, 145. *See also* Dome Flore Field
Seria Field (Brunei), 79
"Seven Sisters," 44. *See also* IOCs
Shah Deniz Field (Azerbaijan), 65, 135
Al Shaheen Field (Qatar), 37
Sharjah, 102n7; and Protocol Area, 123. *See also* Abu Dhabi; Dubai; UAE
Shaybah Field (Saudi Arabia), 68, 99, 111–12, 115, 124
Shell, 35, 51n55, 81, 94, 112, 119n47, 192, 200–201; Bintulu GtL plant, 165; and biogasoline, 168; in Brazil, 138; and Brent Spar, 223; in Canada, 140; and CCS, 229; in deepwater, 99, 130, 137, 139; interest in East Africa, 146; EROEI of, 211–12; exploration in Falklands, 149; and GtL, 165–66; and Hubbert, M. King, 35; in India, 144; in IPC consortium, 121n56; in Kashagan consortium, 133; in Norway, 62; and oil shales, 163–64, 212; in Oman, 63, 125, 125n68; in Qatar, 166, 182; reserves crisis at, 1, 23–24, 24n8, 50; in Russia, 28, 132, 162, 191; in Saudi Arabia, 115; share buybacks by, 26; discoveries in Syria, 48; ultimate recovery estimate of, 101, 103. *See also* IOCs
Ship Shoal 32 Field (Gulf of Mexico), 139. *See also* Kerr McGee; offshore oil
Shoei discovery (UK), 142. *See also* ConocoPhillips; high-pressure, high-temperature fields; North Sea
Shtokmanovskoye Field (Russia), 59n69, 98, 131, 141. *See also* Arctic
Sibneft, 130, 191
Sierra Club, 18, 229. *See also* Environmentalists
Sierra Leone, 146
Silicates, in CCS, 228

About the Author

ROBIN M. MILLS is an oil industry professional with a background in both geology and economics. Currently, he is Petroleum Economics Manager for the Emirates National Oil Company in Dubai. Previously, he worked for Shell. Mills, who speaks Farsi and Arabic, is a member of the International Association for Energy Economics and Association of International Petroleum Negotiators. He holds a Master's Degree in Geological Sciences from Cambridge University.